MW01154671

Unity 2020 By Example

Third Edition

A project-based guide to building 2D, 3D, augmented reality, and virtual reality games from scratch

Robert Wells

BIRMINGHAM—MUMBAI

Unity 2020 By Example
Third Edition

Copyright © 2020 Packt Publishing

All rights reserved. No part of this book may be reproduced, stored in a retrieval system, or transmitted in any form or by any means, without the prior written permission of the publisher, except in the case of brief quotations embedded in critical articles or reviews.

Every effort has been made in the preparation of this book to ensure the accuracy of the information presented. However, the information contained in this book is sold without warranty, either express or implied. Neither the author, nor Packt Publishing or its dealers and distributors, will be held liable for any damages caused or alleged to have been caused directly or indirectly by this book.

Packt Publishing has endeavored to provide trademark information about all of the companies and products mentioned in this book by the appropriate use of capitals. However, Packt Publishing cannot guarantee the accuracy of this information.

Commissioning Editor: Pavan Ramchandani

Acquisition Editor: Pratik Tandel

Senior Editor: Hayden Edwards

Content Development Editors: Akhil Nair, Aamir Ahmed

Technical Editor: Deepesh Patel

Copy Editor: Safis Editing

Project Coordinator: Kinjal Bari

Proofreader: Safis Editing

Indexer: Tejal Daruwale Soni

Production Designer: Alishon Mendonsa

First published: March 2016

Second edition: June 2018

Third edition: September 2020

Production reference: 1280920

Published by Packt Publishing Ltd.

Livery Place

35 Livery Street

Birmingham

B3 2PB, UK.

ISBN 978-1-80020-338-9

www.packt.com

Packt.com

Subscribe to our online digital library for full access to over 7,000 books and videos, as well as industry leading tools to help you plan your personal development and advance your career. For more information, please visit our website.

Why subscribe?

- Spend less time learning and more time coding with practical eBooks and Videos from over 4,000 industry professionals

- Improve your learning with Skill Plans built especially for you

- Get a free eBook or video every month

- Fully searchable for easy access to vital information

- Copy and paste, print, and bookmark content

Did you know that Packt offers eBook versions of every book published, with PDF and ePub files available? You can upgrade to the eBook version at packt.com and as a print book customer, you are entitled to a discount on the eBook copy. Get in touch with us at customercare@packtpub.com for more details.

At www.packt.com, you can also read a collection of free technical articles, sign up for a range of free newsletters, and receive exclusive discounts and offers on Packt books and eBooks.

Contributors

About the author

Robert Wells is an author and games developer with 10 years of industry experience who is passionate about education. He is currently an engineering manager at Hopster, where he has led development on award-winning educational games. He founded *that games guy*, a studio devoted to releasing free assets on the Unity Asset Store to help other developers learn, and has written several tutorials on AI and game engine development on his website.

About the reviewers

Sitki Emre SOLAK is an expert game developer who has worked professionally in the industry since 2009, while using Unity3D as his main development tool since 2011. He is running his own game development studio named DreamHarvesters, based in Turkey. Besides software engineering and game development being his main expertise, he also has experience with content creation and game design.

Sungkuk Park is a game engineer based in Berlin. He has participated in multiple game jams around the world and creates indie games to polish his skills. He is currently interested in the technical arts area—mainly CG, animation, gameplay, and VFX. He spends most of his spare time learning new skills, including drawing, animation, and VFX, which might come in handy once he pursues his next path: a games director for the next gaming generation!

Packt is searching for authors like you

If you're interested in becoming an author for Packt, please visit `authors.packtpub.com` and apply today. We have worked with thousands of developers and tech professionals, just like you, to help them share their insight with the global tech community. You can make a general application, apply for a specific hot topic that we are recruiting an author for, or submit your own idea.

Table of Contents

3
Creating a Space Shooter

4
Continuing the Space Shooter Game

5

Creating a 2D Adventure Game

6

Continuing the 2D Adventure

7

Completing the 2D Adventure

14

Completing the AR Game with the Universal Render Pipeline

Other Books You May Enjoy

Index

Preface

Video games are a cultural phenomenon that have captivated, entertained, and moved billions of people worldwide over the past 60 years. As an industry and movement, video games are an exciting place to be, both for the developer and the artist. In these roles, your vision, ideas, and work can influence wide audiences, shaping and changing generation after generation in an unprecedented way. There has been a general movement toward democratizing game development recently, making the development process simpler, smoother, and more accessible to a wider audience, including developers working from home with minimal budgets. Instrumental in this movement is the Unity engine, which forms the main subject of this book. The Unity engine is a computer program that works with your existing asset pipeline (such as 3D modeling software) and is intended for compiling video games that work seamlessly across multiple platforms and devices, including Windows, Mac, Linux, Android, and iOS. Using Unity, developers import ready-made assets (such as music, textures, and 3D models) and assemble them into a coherent whole, forming a game world that works by a unified logic. The latest version is free for most people to download and use, and it works well with many other programs, including free software such as GIMP and Blender. This book focuses on the Unity engine and how it can be used in a practical context for making playable and fun games. No prior knowledge of Unity is expected, although some knowledge of programming and scripting, such as JavaScript, ActionScript, C, C++, Java, or ideally C#, would be beneficial.

Who this book is for

You don't need to have any previous experience with Unity to enjoy *Unity 2020 by Example*, although ideally, you will have basic knowledge of C#.

What this book covers

Chapter 1, Exploring the Fundamentals of Unity, begins our journey into Unity by creating a first-person collection game. This is a great starting point if you are totally new to Unity and are ready to create your first game.

Chapter 2, Creating a Collection Game, continues from the previous chapter and completes the first project. It assumes that you have completed the first chapter and brings closure to our project, leading neatly to the next chapter.

Chapter 3, Creating a Space Shooter, marks the beginning of our second project, focusing on the creation of a space shooter game. Here, we will create a project in which the player must shoot the oncoming enemies.

Chapter 4, Continuing the Space Shooter, completes the space shooter project by adding final touches to it, including projectile spawning and object pooling.

Chapter 5, Creating a 2D Adventure Game, enters the world of 2D and UI functionality. Here, we'll explore Unity's wide range of 2D features by making a side-view platformer game that relies on 2D physics.

Chapter 6, Continuing the 2D Adventure, continues the 2D adventure game project that was started in the previous chapter, linking together with the overarching game logic and adding additional levels using Sprite Shaping.

Chapter 7, Completing the 2D Adventure, completes the project started in *Chapter 5, Creating a 2D Adventure Game*, with the addition of a quest system and an NPC. This is a great place to see how multiple parts and facets of a game come together to form a whole.

Chapter 8, Creating Artificial Intelligence, focuses on artificial intelligence and creating enemies that can patrol, chase, and attack the player's character at relevant times, while cleverly navigating their way around the level.

Chapter 9, Continuing with Intelligent Enemies, brings closure to the AI project started in the previous chapter. Here, we'll see how to use finite-state machines to achieve powerful intelligence functionality that'll help us in a variety of scenarios.

Chapter 10, Evolving AI Using ML-Agents, approaches AI from a different angle. Whereas previous chapters have relied on hardcoding NPC behavior, in this chapter, we will evolve the required behavior using ML-Agents.

Chapter 11, Entering Virtual Reality, explores how to create a first-person shooter in VR where the player must tackle waves of oncoming enemies. In this chapter, we will lay the foundations for creating a VR game.

Chapter 12, Completing the VR Game, completes the VR project by adding gameplay elements and core functionality, and by creating a build.

Chapter 13, Creating an Augmented Reality Game Using AR Foundation, continues the exploration of Extended Reality, but this time by creating an Augmented Reality game. In this chapter, you'll also be introduced to the Universal Render Pipeline.

Chapter 14, Completing the AR game with the Universal Render Pipeline, completes the project started in the previous chapter. You'll learn how to detect surfaces in the real world and use that data to spawn AR objects.

To get the most out of this book

This book contains almost everything you need to follow along. Each chapter considers practical, real-world projects for learning Unity and includes companion files that can be downloaded and used. Apart from this book, the only thing you need is a copy of the latest version of Unity. At the time of writing, this is Unity 2020.1. This software is available for free as a personal edition, and it can be downloaded from the Unity website at `https://unity3d.com/get-unity/download`.

In addition to Unity, if you want to create props, character models, and other 3D assets, you'll also need 3D modeling and animation software, such as 3DS Max, Maya, or Blender; you'll also need image editing software, such as Photoshop or GIMP. Blender can be downloaded and used for free from `http://www.blender.org/`. Also, GIMP can be downloaded and used for free from `https://www.gimp.org/`.

If you are using the digital version of this book, we advise you to type the code yourself or access the code via the GitHub repository (link available in the next section). Doing so will help you avoid any potential errors related to the copying and pasting of code.

Download the example code files

You can download the example code files for this book from your account at `www.packt.com`. If you purchased this book elsewhere, you can visit `www.packtpub.com/support` and register to have the files emailed directly to you.

You can download the code files by following these steps:

1. Log in or register at `www.packt.com`.
2. Select the **Support** tab.
3. Click on **Code Downloads**.
4. Enter the name of the book in the **Search** box and follow the onscreen instructions.

...e is downloaded, please make sure that you unzip or extract the folder using
...sion of:

- ...R/7-Zip for Windows
- ...zipeg/iZip/UnRarX for Mac
- 7-Zip/PeaZip for Linux

The code bundle for the book is also hosted on GitHub at `https://github.com/PacktPublishing/Unity-2020-By-Example-Third-Edition`. In case there's an update to the code, it will be updated on the existing GitHub repository.

We also have other code bundles from our rich catalog of books and videos available at `https://github.com/PacktPublishing/`. Check them out!

Download the color images

We also provide a PDF file that has color images of the screenshots/diagrams used in this book. You can download it here: `https://static.packt-cdn.com/downloads/9781800203389_ColorImages.pdf`.

Conventions used

There are a number of text conventions used throughout this book.

`Code in text`: Indicates code words in text, database table names, folder names, filenames, file extensions, pathnames, dummy URLs, user input, and Twitter handles. Here is an example: "Rename it `Turtle`."

A block of code is set as follows:

```
public class ObjectPool : MonoBehaviour
{
    ...
    public void DeSpawn(Transform ObjectToDespawn)
    {
        ObjectToDespawn.gameObject.SetActive(false);
        ObjectToDespawn.SetParent(transform);
        ObjectToDespawn.position = Vector3.zero;
    }
```

Bold: Indicates a new term, an important word, or words that you see onscreen. For example, words in menus or dialog boxes appear in the text like this. Here is an example: "Select the **Android** tab."

Tips or important notes
Appear like this.

Get in touch

Feedback from our readers is always welcome.

General feedback: If you have questions about any aspect of this book, mention the book title in the subject of your message and email us at customercare@packtpub.com.

Errata: Although we have taken every care to ensure the accuracy of our content, mistakes do happen. If you have found a mistake in this book, we would be grateful if you would report this to us. Please visit www.packtpub.com/support/errata, selecting your book, clicking on the Errata Submission Form link, and entering the details.

Piracy: If you come across any illegal copies of our works in any form on the Internet, we would be grateful if you would provide us with the location address or website name. Please contact us at copyright@packt.com with a link to the material.

If you are interested in becoming an author: If there is a topic that you have expertise in and you are interested in either writing or contributing to a book, please visit authors.packtpub.com.

Reviews

Please leave a review. Once you have read and used this book, why not leave a review on the site that you purchased it from? Potential readers can then see and use your unbiased opinion to make purchase decisions, we at Packt can understand what you think about our products, and our authors can see your feedback on their book. Thank you!

For more information about Packt, please visit packt.com.

1
Exploring the Fundamentals of Unity

Unity is a game engine that works with your existing asset pipeline (such as 3D modeling software) and can be used to compile video games that work seamlessly across multiple platforms and devices, including Windows, Mac, Linux, Android, and iOS. Using Unity, developers import ready-made assets (such as music, textures, and 3D models), and assemble them into a coherent whole, forming a game world that works according to a unified logic. This book focuses on developing games in Unity 2020 — taking you step by step through how to create increasingly complex projects.

This chapter starts the first project on our list, which will be a fun collection game. By the end of the next chapter, you'll have pieced together a simple but complete game. As part of the process, you'll become familiar with the fundamentals of developing in Unity, including the following:

- New features in Unity 2020
- Creating new projects using Unity Hub
- How to navigate the Unity editor
- Unity project structure
- Importing assets using the Package Manager
- Using the Unity editor to create a level
- Creating optimized lighting effects
- How to playtest the game

Using the information in this chapter, you will gain an understanding of how to create new projects from scratch, navigate the Unity editor, and import assets, information that will be invaluable for years to come as you develop your own projects in Unity.

Remember, it doesn't matter if you've never used Unity before. We'll go through everything that is required step by step, starting with the new features found in Unity 2020.

Technical requirements

This book is about Unity and developing games in that engine. The basics of programming as a subject is, however, beyond the scope of this book. So, I'll assume that you already have a working knowledge of coding generally but have not coded in Unity before.

You can download the example code files for this book from GitHub at `https://github.com/PacktPublishing/Unity-2020-By-Example`.

Once downloaded, you can find the `CollectionGame` project in the `Chapter01/End` folder.

Exploring new features in Unity 2020

Before we start our first project, let's take a moment to look at the new features introduced since the previous edition of this book. We'll cover all of these, and much more!

Starting with **Unity Hub**, while not technically part of Unity 2020 (it is a separate application), it makes it easy to manage multiple Unity projects and versions. I will guide you through creating a new project using Unity Hub in this chapter. Once an empty project has been created, we will import assets using the new **Package Manager** — an easy way to manage a project's assets (more on this shortly).

In the world of 2D, a new tool called **Sprite Shape** will help us create more dynamic and flexible environments from within the Unity editor. Whether 2D or 3D, **Artificial Intelligence** (**AI**) is an ever-evolving field, and not to be left behind, Unity has introduced a new **machine learning** toolkit called **ml-agents**. This is an exciting new way to create intelligent **agents** (any dynamic non-playable character) in a game. Rather than defining exactly how an agent should act in every situation, we can provide the tools for the agent to learn how best to achieve their goals, whatever they may be.

It's an exciting time for **Augmented Reality (AR)**, with the inclusion of **ARFoundation** in Unity, an AR toolkit, which we will use to blend reality and gaming. Lastly, we'll take a look at state of the art and investigate how we can optimize our games by using **DOTs**, a **multi-threaded data-oriented technology stack**. Don't worry if that sounds scary; it will all become clear as we progress through the book.

Now that we have an understanding of the some of the new topics covered in this book, let's design the first game we will implement in Unity 2020.

Introducing the first game

In the first game we will create, the player will control a character in the first person to explore an environment, collecting coins before a time limit runs out. If the timer runs out, the game is over. On the other hand, if all coins are collected before the timer expires, the player wins. The controls will use the industry-standard *WASD* keyboard setup, where *W* moves forward, *A* and *S* move left and right, and *D* walks backward. Head movement is controlled using the mouse, and coins are collected by **colliding** with them.

The benefit of developing this type of game is that it will demonstrate all the core Unity features, and we won't need to rely on any external software to make assets, such as **textures**, **meshes**, and **materials**.

See *Figure 1.1*, which features the coin collection game in action in the **Unity Editor**:

Figure 1.1 – The completed coin collection game

> **Important note**
>
> The completed `CollectionGame` project, as discussed in this chapter and the next, can be found in the book companion files in the `Chapter02/End` folder.

Now that we have an idea of the type of game we'll be making, in the next section, we can start development by creating the initial project structure.

Getting started with Unity

Every time you want to make a new Unity game, including coin collection games, you'll need to create a new **project**. Generally speaking, Unity uses the term *project* to mean a game. There are two main ways to make a new project, and it really doesn't matter which one you choose because both end up in the same place. If you're already in the Unity interface, looking at an existing scene or level, you can select **File | New Project...** from the application menu, as shown in *Figure 1.2*:

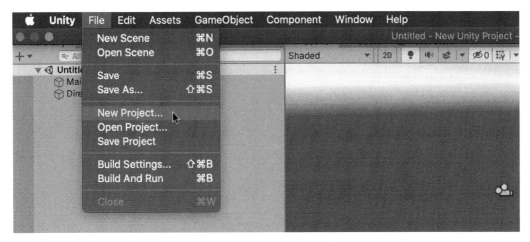

Figure 1.2 – Creating a new project via the main menu

After selecting the **New Project** option, Unity leads you to the project creation wizard.

Alternatively, you can create a new project using **Unity Hub**, as shown in *Figure 1.3*. Unity Hub is a standalone application that you can use not only to manage your projects, but your Unity installations as well. So, if you want to have multiple different versions of Unity installed (for example, 2019 and 2020), Unity Hub makes this easy. With Unity Hub open, you can access the new project wizard by choosing the **NEW** button:

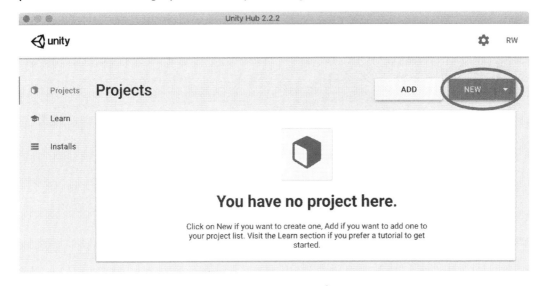

Figure 1.3 – Unity Hub

On reaching the project creation wizard, Unity can generate a new project for you on the basis of a few settings:

1. Fill in the name of your project (such as `CollectionGame`).

2. Select a folder on your computer to contain the project files that will be generated automatically.

3. Unity provides several project templates, as outlined here:

   2D: A standard project setup for working in a 2D space. 2D-specific settings are configured for texture importing, the scene view, and the lighting and camera settings in the sample scene.

   3D: A project configured to use Unity's built-in render pipeline.

   3D With Extras: The same as 3D, but includes a new **post-processing stack** and additional sample content to show off the new processing stack.

   High Definition RP: A project configured for high-end platforms. It uses a **Scriptable Render Pipeline (SRP)** called **High Definition Render Pipeline (HDRP)**, which provides additional rendering control by allowing you to configure render settings using C# scripts.

   Universal RP: This uses the **Universal Render Pipeline (URP)**. This pipeline is similar to HDRP but suitable for a broader range of devices, including mobile. The URP will be explored in more detail in a later chapter.

   Throughout the book, we'll create a number of 2D, 3D, and URP projects. For this project, choose the 3D option from the template section to create a 3D game.

4. Finally, click on the **CREATE** button to complete the project generation process, as shown in *Figure 1.4*

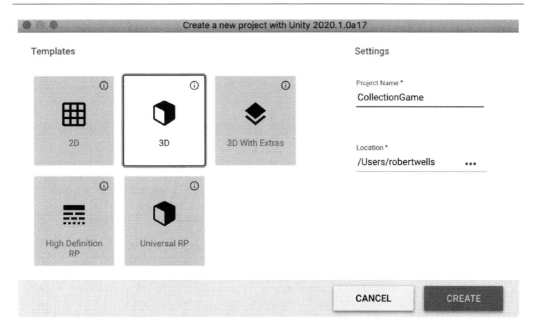

Figure 1.4 – Creating a new project

Once you've clicked on **CREATE**, after some initial setup, the Unity editor will open. If this is your first time viewing the editor, it may seem daunting, but don't worry, I will guide you through how it all works, and you'll be creating games in no time. We'll start by taking a look at the **Project** panel and how we can import assets into the project, which we'll use to make our game.

Introducing the Project panel

You now have a new project. This represents the starting point for any game development in Unity. The newly created project contains an example **scene**, but nothing else: no meshes, textures, or any other **assets**. You can confirm this by checking the **Project** panel area at the bottom of the editor interface. This panel displays the complete contents of the project folder, which corresponds to an actual folder on your local drive created earlier by the new project wizard, as shown in *Figure 1.5*:

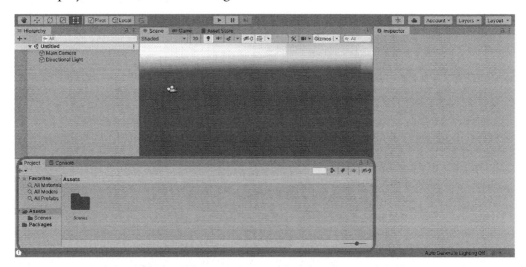

Figure 1.5 – The Unity Project panel docked at the bottom of the interface

This panel will soon be populated with more items, all of which we can use to build a game.

If your interface looks different from *Figure 1.5*, in terms of its layout and arrangement, then you can reset the UI layout to its defaults. To do this, click on the **Layout** drop-down menu from the top-right corner of the editor interface, and choose **Default**:

Figure 1.6 – Switching to the default interface layout

> **Tip**
>
> The sample scene can safely be deleted. You will be shown how to create a new scene shortly.

As well as a sample scene, Unity also includes a `Packages` folder, just below the `Assets` folder, as shown in *Figure 1.5*. A **package** is a collection of assets that can be used in your game. A new project already contains several packages, but they can be safely ignored for now, as we won't be using them for this project. We will instead install a new package shortly.

> **Important note**
>
> If you navigate to the `Packages` folder in a file browser, you may reasonably expect to see the installed packages. Instead, however, you'll be greeted with a **JSON** file that lists the packages included in your project. The packages are actually stored with Unity. This way, you don't need to re-download packages that are used in other projects. They can be downloaded once and shared between all of your projects as required.

You can view the contents of your project folder directly, via either Windows Explorer or Mac Finder, by right-clicking the mouse in the **Project** panel from the Unity Editor to reveal a context menu, and from there, choose the **Show in Explorer** (Windows) or **Reveal in Finder** (Mac) option:

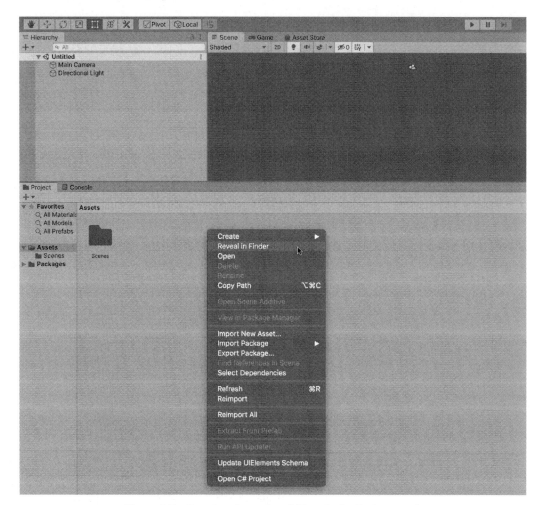

Figure 1.7 – Opening the project folder via the Project panel

Clicking on **Reveal in Finder** displays the folder contents in the default system file browser. This view is useful to inspect files, count them, or back them up. However, don't change the folder contents manually this way via Explorer or Finder. Specifically, don't move, rename, or delete files from here; doing so can corrupt your Unity project irretrievably. Instead, delete and move files where needed within the project window in the Unity Editor. This way, Unity updates its metadata as appropriate, ensuring that your project continues to work correctly.

The common folders and files that are generated with a Unity project include:

- `Assets`: This is the folder where all your game's resources are stored, including scripts, textures, and audio files.
- `Library`: Unity processes and converts the files in the `Assets` folder so they are ready to be compiled in your game. The processed files are stored here.
- `obj`: This folder stores temporary files generated by `MonoDevelop` when a project is built.
- `Temp`: This folder also stores temporary files, but these files are generated by Unity during the build process.
- `Packages`: As mentioned previously, this folder contains a JSON file with a list of packages added to the project. More on packages shortly.
- `ProjectSettings`: This folder stores project-level settings, including physics, layers, tags, and time settings.
- `UserSettings`: This folder stores settings related to your editor; for example, if you apply a custom layout to the Unity editor, that will be saved here.
- `Assembly-CSharp.csproj`: This is a project file generated by `MonoDevelop`.
- `CollectionGame.sln`: This is a solution file that stores the structure of the `CollectionGame` project in Visual Studio (the IDE used to create the C# scripts).

> **Important note**
> Viewing the project folder in the OS file browser will display additional files and folders not visible in the **Project** panel, such as `Library` and `ProjectSettings`, and maybe a `Temp` folder. Together, these are known as the project metadata. They contain additional settings and preferences that Unity needs in order to work correctly. These folders and their files should not be edited or changed.

With a solid understanding of how to view assets using the Project panel, we'll next import external assets that will help us create our game.

Importing assets

Assets are the ingredients or building blocks for games—the building blocks from which they're made. There are many different types of assets, including:

- Meshes (or **3D models**), such as characters, props, trees, houses, and more.

- Textures, which are image files such as **JPEGs** and **PNGs** (these determine how the surface of a mesh should look)

- Music and sound effects to enhance the realism and atmosphere of your game

- Scenes, which are 3D spaces or worlds where meshes, textures, sounds, and music live, exist, and work together holistically as part of a single system

Games cannot exist without assets—they would otherwise look completely empty and lifeless. For this reason, we'll need assets to make the coin collection game we're working toward. After all, we'll need an environment to walk around and coins to collect!

Unity, however, is a **game engine** and not primarily an asset creation program, like Blender or Photoshop (though it can create assets). This means that assets, such as characters and props, are typically made first by artists in external, third-party software. From here, they are exported and transferred ready-made to Unity, and Unity is only responsible for bringing these assets to life in a coherent game. Third-party asset creation programs include Blender (which is free), Maya or 3DS Max to make 3D models, Photoshop or GIMP (which is also free) to create textures, and Audacity (which again is free) to generate audio. There are plenty of other options, too. The details of these programs are beyond the scope of this book. In any case, Unity assumes that you already have assets ready to import to build a game. For the coin collection game, we'll use assets created by Unity. So, let's import these into our project.

To do this, you first need to download the **Standard Asset** package from the **Unity Asset Store**. The standard asset package contains a number of useful objects that will help us create a game. However, we'll go into the contents of this package in more detail shortly. For now, follow these steps:

1. Navigate to `https://assetstore.unity.com` and search for **Standard Assets**.

2. Once on the **Standard Assets** page, click on **Add to My Assets,** as shown in
    Figure 1.8:

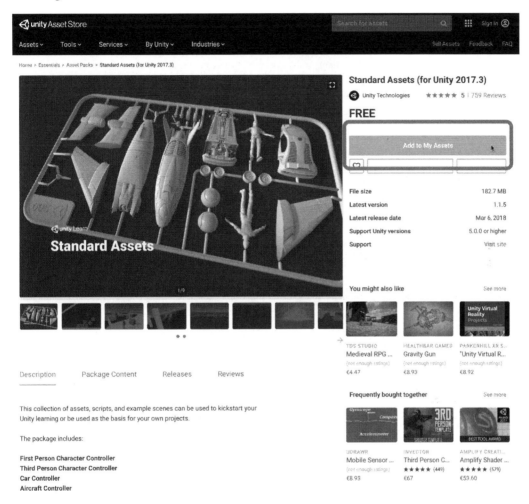

Figure 1.8 – Standard Assets page on the Unity Asset Store

The Unity Asset Store is a great place to find assets made by other developers, from 3D models to complete projects. Some are free, but many can be downloaded for a small fee.

> **Important note**
>
> If you have difficulty in finding the **Standard Asset** package or it doesn't work with your version of Unity, please follow the instructions in the *Entering the world* section in *Chapter 8, Creating Artificial Intelligence*, where we write our own.

3. Once the package has been added to your assets, you can find it in the **Package Manager**. Head back into Unity and select **Window | Package Manager** from the application menu:

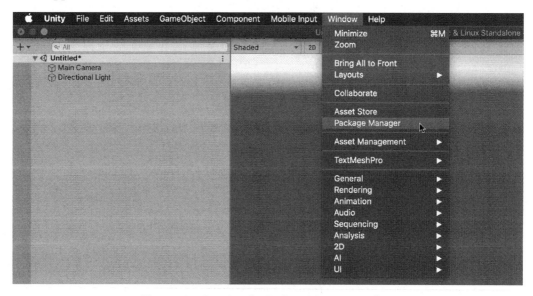

Figure 1.9 – Opening the Package Manager window

4. The **Package Manager** is a relatively new feature of Unity. It is used to add packages to, and remove packages from, the current project. Remember, a package is simply a collection of assets. We want to add the **Standard Assets** package, so select that and click on **Import**:

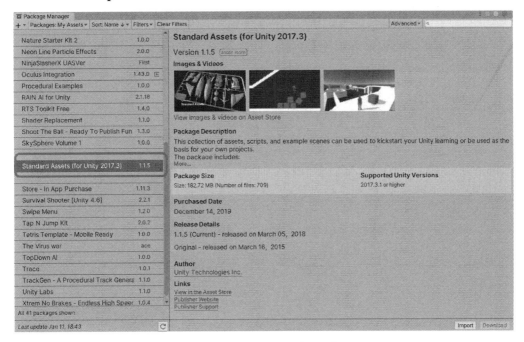

Figure 1.10 – Importing assets via the Package Manager

Important note

Your list of packages will most likely differ from mine. Unity contains many built-in packages, and any package added from the Unity Asset Store will also appear here.

Each time you import a package, you will be presented with an Import dialog. Here, you can specify which assets you want to add to your project. Leave all settings at their defaults, and click on **Import**:

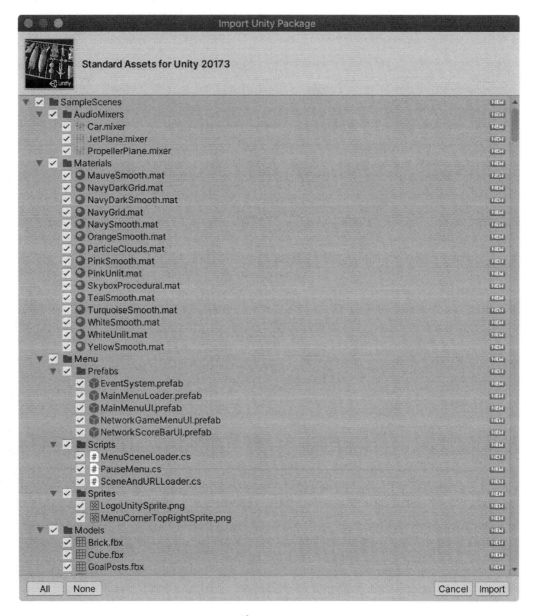

Figure 1.11 – Choosing assets to import

> **Important note**
> Make sure you don't modify the folder structure of imported assets. Unity will only be able to determine whether an asset has changed if the project structure remains the same. For example, if you import a package that places a material in the `Assets/Materials` folder and you move that asset when you come to update the package, Unity will think the material is missing and re-add it to the project—resulting in two versions of the asset.

By default, Unity decompresses all files from the package into the current project, ready for use. These files are copies of the originals. So, any changes made to them will not affect or invalidate the originals, which Unity maintains internally in a `.meta` file. Every asset (including folders) has a corresponding meta file, which contains information on the import settings of the asset and should not be deleted or renamed unless you are also deleting or renaming the associated asset.

The files include models, sounds, textures, and more, and are listed in the Unity Editors project window:

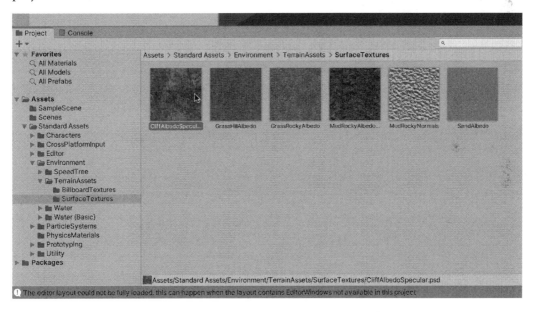

Figure 1.12 – Browsing imported assets from the Project panel

The imported assets don't yet exist in our game scene or level. They don't appear in the game, and they won't do anything when the level begins! Rather, they're only added to the **Project** panel, which behaves like a library or repository of assets, from which we can pick and choose to build up a game when needed. To get more information about each asset, you can select the asset by clicking on it with the mouse, and asset-specific details will be shown on the right-hand side of the Unity Editor in the **Inspector** panel. **Inspector** is a property sheet editor that appears on the right-hand side of the interface. It is context-sensitive and always changes to display properties for the selected object, as shown in *Figure 1.13*:

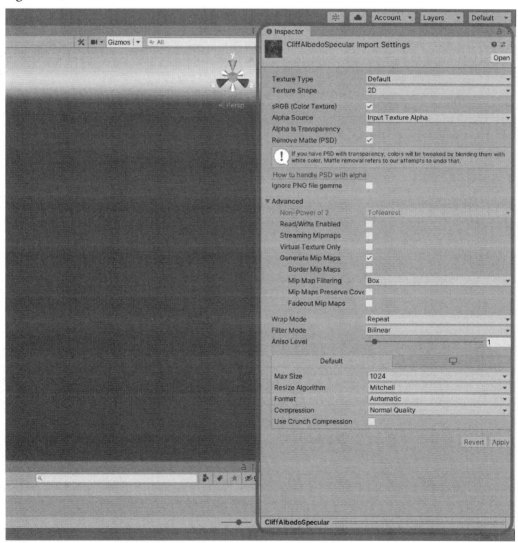

Figure 1.13 – The Inspector window displays all the properties for the currently selected object

We've now created a Unity project and imported a large library of assets, in the form of a package, using the Package Manager. The package includes architectural meshes for walls, floors, ceilings, and stairs. This means that we're now ready to build our first level using these assets!

Starting a level

This section covers many fundamental topics that will be useful not only for the remainder of this book, but for your career as a Unity developer:

- In **Creating a Scene**, you'll be introduced to the space that will contain our level. I'll show you how to create a new scene and explain what is included in a scene by default.

- Once we've created a new scene, we can start customizing the space by adding and positioning objects. In **Adding a Floor Mesh**, we add a floor object to the scene, which our character (which we'll add later) will be able to traverse.

- With the first objects added, we'll take a moment to look at how we can customize their size and position in **Transforming Objects**.

- Before we add additional objects to the scene, it is essential to be able to navigate around the scene view so you can place objects exactly where you want them. This is covered in **Navigating the Scene**.

- Once we can navigate the scene, we will continue to add new features in **Adding Level Features**, including houses and a bridge. The houses will be positioned using a Unity feature called **Vertex Snapping**.

- At this point, the level will look flat with minimal shadows and lighting. We'll improve this by enabling lighting and adding a sky to the game in **Adding Lighting and a Skybox**.

There's a lot to cover! So, let's jump right in and create the first scene of our game.

Creating a scene

A scene refers to a 3D space, the space-time of the game world—the place where things exist. Since all games happen in space and time, we'll need a scene for the coin collection game. In our game, a scene represents a **level**. The words *scene* and *level* can be used interchangeably here. In other games, you may find that a scene contains multiple levels, but in this book, we will limit each scene to one level.

To create a new scene, perform the following steps:

1. Select **File | New Scene** from the application menu.

2. Alternatively, press *Ctrl + N* on the keyboard.

When you do this, a new and empty scene is created. You can see a visualization or preview of the scene via the **Scene** tab, which occupies the largest part of the Unity interface:

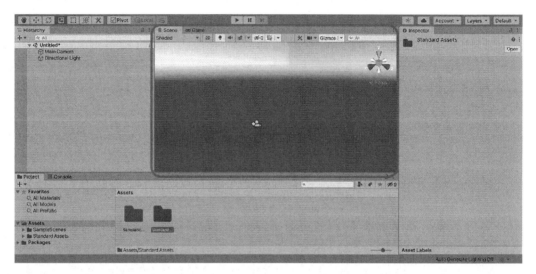

Figure 1.14 – The Scene tab displays a preview of a 3D world

Important note

As shown in *Figure 1.14*, other tabs besides the scene are visible and available in Unity. These include a **Game** and a **Console** window; in some cases, there could be more as well. For now, we can ignore all the tabs except scene. The scene tab is designed for quick and easy previewing of a level during its construction.

Each new scene begins empty; well, almost empty. By default, each new scene begins with two objects; specifically, a **light** to illuminate any other objects that are added, and a **camera** to display and render the contents of the scene from a specific vantage point. You can view a complete list of all the objects existing in the scene using the **Hierarchy** panel, which is docked to the left-hand side of the Unity interface, as shown in *Figure 1.15*. This panel displays the name of every GameObject in the scene. In Unity, the word GameObject refers to a single, independent, and unique object that lives within the scene, whether visible or not. When a GameObject is first created, it only has a **Transform** component, which includes position, scale, and rotation fields (more on the **Transform** component in the *Transforming objects* section). To extend the functionality of GameObjects, you add components. **Component-based architecture** is one of the core tenants of Unity; as such, we'll be taking advantage of existing components and creating entirely new components in every project in this book. GameObjects and components are discussed further in the section entitled *Improving the scene*:

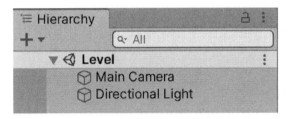

Figure 1.15 – The Hierarchy panel

> **Tip**
> You can also select objects in the scene by clicking on their name in the **Hierarchy** panel.

With the scene created, we can start building the environment by adding a traversable floor mesh.

Adding a floor mesh

Next, let's add a floor to the scene. After all, the player needs something to stand on! We could build a floor mesh from scratch using third-party modeling software, such as Maya, 3DS Max, or Blender. However, the Standard Asset package, which was imported earlier, conveniently contains floor meshes that we can use. These meshes are part of the `Prototyping` package.

To access them via the **Project** panel, follow these steps:

1. Open the `Standard Assets` folder by double-clicking it and then accessing the `Prototyping/Prefabs` folder.

2. From here, you can select objects and preview them in the **Inspector** window:

Figure 1.16 – The Standard Assets/Prototyping folder contains many meshes for quick scene building

> **Tip**
> You could also quickly add a floor to the scene by choosing **GameObject | 3D Object | Plane** from the application menu. However, this just adds a dull, gray floor, which isn't very interesting. Of course, you could change its appearance. As we'll see later, Unity lets you do this. However, for this tutorial, we'll use a specifically modeled floor mesh via the Standard Assets package from the **Project** panel.

The mesh named `FloorPrototype64x01x64` (as shown in *Figure 1.16*) is suitable as a floor. To add this mesh to the scene, drag and drop the object from the **Project** panel to the scene view. Notice how the scene view changes to display the newly added mesh within the 3D space, and the mesh name also appears as a listing in the hierarchy panel:

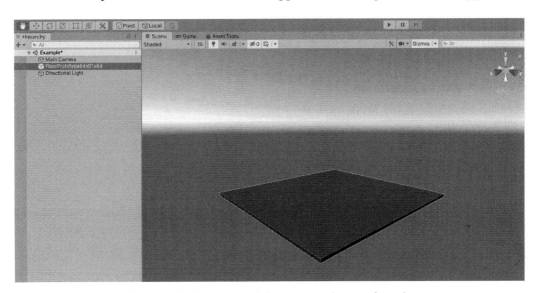

Figure 1.17 – Dragging and dropping mesh assets from the
Project panel to the Scene view will add them to the scene

The floor mesh asset from the project window has now been instantiated as a GameObject in the scene. This GameObject is a copy or clone of the mesh asset. The **instance** of the floor in the scene still depends on the floor asset in the **Project** panel. However, the asset does not depend on the instance. Deleting the floor in the scene will not delete the asset; but, if you remove the asset, you will invalidate the GameObject. You can also create additional floors in the scene by dragging and dropping the floor asset from the **Project** panel to the scene view.

Each time, a new instance of the floor is created in the scene as a separate and unique GameObject, although all the added instances will still depend on the single floor asset in the **Project** panel:

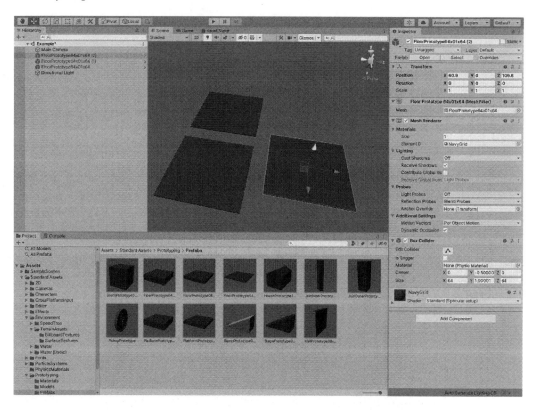

Figure 1.18 – Adding multiple instances of the floor mesh to the scene

We don't actually need the duplicate floor pieces. So, let's delete them. Just click on the duplicates in the scene view and then press *Delete* on the keyboard to remove them. Remember, you can also select and delete objects by clicking on their name in the hierarchy panel and pressing *Delete*. Either way, this leaves us with a single floor piece and a solid start to building our scene. One remaining problem, though, concerns the floor and its name. By looking carefully in the hierarchy panel, we can see that the floor name is `FloorPrototype64x01x64`. This name is long, obtuse, and unwieldy. We should change it to something more manageable and meaningful. This is not technically essential but is good practice in terms of keeping our work clean and organized. There are many ways to rename an object. One way is to first select it and then enter a new name in the name field in the Inspector window. I've renamed it to `WorldFloor`:

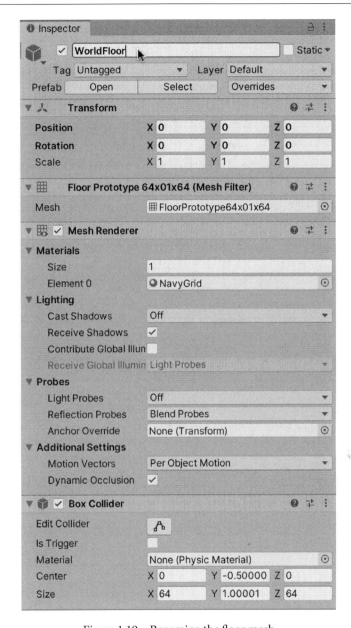

Figure 1.19 – Renaming the floor mesh

As you can see from *Figure 1.19*, there are a number of other variables you can change on the object. Just below the name field, you'll notice a **Transform** heading. It is here where you can change the **Scale**, **Rotation**, and **Position** of an object, which we will often want to, as when we add an object to the scene, it may not always have the correct size or be in the right place. We'll look at the **Transform** component in the next section.

Transforming objects

A scene with a floor mesh has been established, but this alone is not very interesting. We should add more varied objects, such as buildings, stairs, columns, and perhaps even more floor pieces. Otherwise, there would be no world for the player to explore. Before building on what we have got, however, let's make sure that the existing floor piece is centered at the world **origin**. Every point and location within a scene are uniquely identified by a **coordinate**, measured as an (X, Y, Z) offset from the world center (origin).

The current position for the selected object is always visible in the Inspector panel. In fact, the **Position**, **Rotation**, and **Scale** of an object are grouped together under a category (**component**) called **Transform**:

- **Position** indicates how far an object should be moved in three axes from the world center.

- **Rotation** indicates how much an object should be turned or rotated around its central axes.

- **Scale** indicates how much an object should be shrunk or expanded to smaller or larger sizes. A default scale of 1 means that an object should appear at normal size, 2 means twice the size, 0.5 means half the size, and so on.

Together, the position, rotation and scale of an object constitute its transformation.

To change the position of the selected object, you can simply type new values in the **X**, **Y**, and **Z** fields for position. To move an object to the world center, simply enter (0, 0, 0), as shown in *Figure 1.20*:

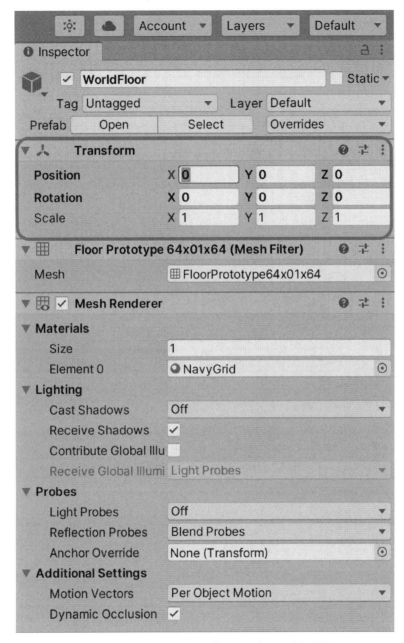

Figure 1.20 – Centering an object to the world origin

This will move the objects **pivot** point to the world origin. The pivot point is the designated position around which the object will rotate and scale. For the floor mesh, the pivot point is set to the center of the mesh, so when it is positioned at the world center, it will be this point that resides at the location (0, 0, 0).

Setting the position of an object, as we've done here, by typing numerical values, is acceptable and appropriate for the specifying of exact positions. However, it's often more intuitive to move objects using the mouse. To do this, let's add a second floor piece and position it away from the first. Drag and drop a floor piece from the **Project** panel to the scene to create a second floor GameObject. Then, click on the new floor piece to select it and switch to the Move Tool. To do this, press *W* on the keyboard or click on the Move Tool icon from the toolbar at the top of the editor interface. The move tool allows you to reposition objects in the scene:

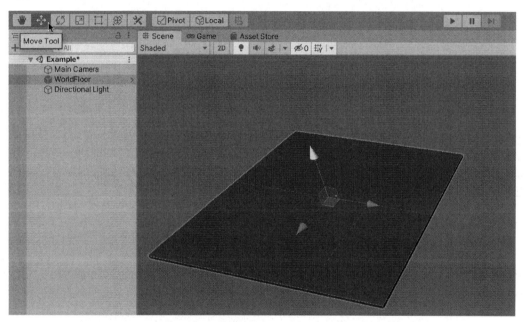

Figure 1.21 – Accessing the move tool

When the translate tool is active and an object is selected, a **gizmo** appears centered on the object. The translate gizmo appears in the scene view as three colored perpendicular axes: red, green, and blue, corresponding to *X*, *Y*, and *Z*, respectively.

To move an object, hover your cursor over one of the three axes (or planes between axes), and then click and hold the mouse while moving it to slide the object in that direction. You can repeat this process to ensure that your objects are positioned where you need them to be. Use the translate tool to move the second floor piece away from the first, as shown in *Figure 1.22*:

Figure 1.22 – Translate an object using the translate gizmo

You can also rotate and scale objects using the mouse, as with translate. Press *E* to access the rotate tool or *R* to access the scale tool, or you can activate these tools using their respective toolbar icons from the top of the editor. Other available tools are the rect tool and the combined tool, which allow you to move, rotate, or scale an object using one tool. When these tools are activated, a gizmo appears centered on the object, and you can click and drag the mouse over each specific axis to rotate or scale objects as needed:

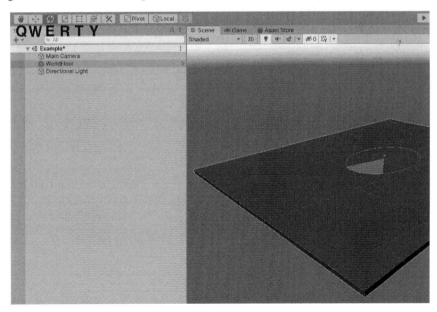

Figure 1.23 – Accessing the tools

Being able to translate, rotate, and scale objects quickly through mouse and keyboard combinations is very important when working in Unity. For this reason, make using the keyboard shortcuts a habit, as opposed to accessing the tools continually from the toolbar.

Navigating the scene

In addition to moving, rotating, and scaling objects, you'll frequently need to move around yourself in the scene view in order to see the world from different positions, angles, and perspectives. This means that you'll frequently need to reposition the scene preview camera in the world. You'll want to zoom in and zoom out of the world to get a better view of objects and change your viewing angle to see how objects align and fit together properly. To do this, you'll need to make extensive use of both the keyboard and mouse together.

To zoom closer or further from the object you're looking at, simply scroll the mouse wheel up or down—up zooms in and down zooms out.

To pan the scene view left or right, or up or down, hold down the middle mouse button while moving the mouse in the appropriate direction. Alternatively, you can access the **hand tool** from the application toolbar or by pressing Q on the keyboard, and then clicking and dragging in the scene view while the tool is active. Pan does not zoom in or out, but slides the scene camera left and right, or up and down.

Sometimes, while building levels, you'll lose sight entirely of the object that you need. In this case, you'll often want to shift the viewport camera to focus on that specific object. To do this automatically, select the object by clicking on its name in the hierarchy panel, and then press the F key on the keyboard. Alternatively, you can double-click its name in the hierarchy panel.

After framing an object, you'll often want to rotate around it in order to quickly and easily view it from all important angles. To achieve this, hold down the *Alt* key on the keyboard while clicking and dragging the mouse to rotate the view.

Lastly, it's helpful to navigate a level in the scene view using first-person controls, that is, controls that mimic how first-person games are played. This helps you experience the scene at a more personal and immersive level. To do this, hold down the right mouse button and use the *WASD* keys on the keyboard to control forward, backward, and strafing movements. Movement of the mouse controls head orientation. You can also hold down the *Shift* key while moving to increase movement speed.

The great thing about learning the versatile transformation and navigation controls is that, on understanding them, you can move and orient practically any object in any way, and you can view the world from almost any position and angle. Being able to do this is critically important in building quality levels quickly. All of these controls, along with some others that we'll soon see, will be used frequently throughout this book to create scenes and other content in Unity. With these controls in mind, we'll continue to build the environment by adding additional level features, including houses and a bridge to connect the two floor meshes.

Adding level features

Now that we've seen how to transform objects and navigate the scene viewport successfully, let's proceed to complete our first level for the coin collection game:

1. Separate the two floor meshes, leaving a gap between them that we'll fix shortly by creating a bridge, which will allow the player to move between the spaces like islands. Use the translate tool (*W*) to move the objects around:

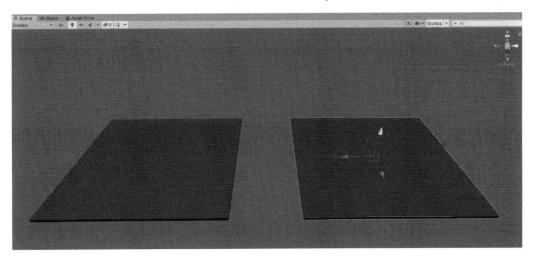

Figure 1.24 – Separating the floor meshes into islands

> **Tip**
>
> If you want to create more floor objects, you can use the method that we've seen already by dragging and dropping the mesh asset in the **Project** panel in the scene viewport. Alternatively, you can duplicate the selected object in the viewport by pressing *Ctrl* + *D* on the keyboard. Both methods produce the same result.

2. Then add some props and obstacles to the scene. Drag and drop the house prefab onto the floor. The house object (HousePrototype16x16x24) is found in the Assets/Standard Assets/Prototyping/Prefabs folder:

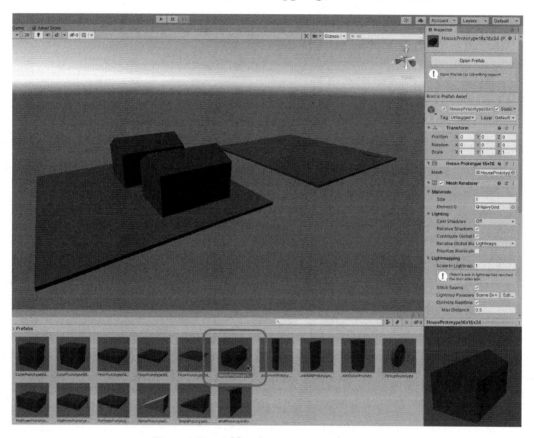

Figure 1.25 – Adding house props to the scene

On dragging and dropping the house in the scene, it may align to the floor nicely with the bottom against the floor, or it may not. If it does, that's splendid and great luck! However, we shouldn't rely on luck every time because we're professional game developers! Thankfully, we can make any two mesh objects align easily in Unity using vertex snapping. This feature works by forcing two objects into positional alignment within the scene by overlapping their vertices at a specific and common point.

For example, consider *Figure 1.26*. Here, a house object hovers awkwardly above the floor and we naturally want it to align level with the floor and perhaps over to the floor corner. To achieve this, perform the following steps:

1. Select the house object (click on it or select it from the **Hierarchy** panel). The object to be selected is the one that *should move* to align and not the destination (which is the floor), which should remain in place:

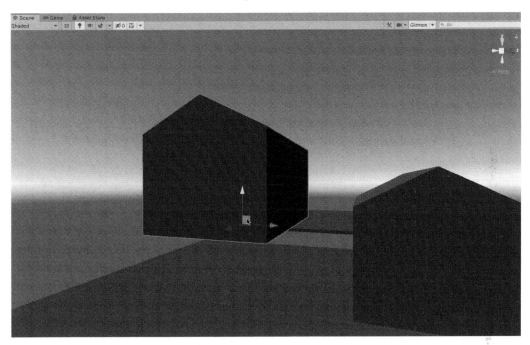

Figure 1.26 – Misaligned objects can be snapped into place with Vertex Snapping

2. Next, activate the translate tool (*W*) and hold down the *V* key for vertex snapping.

3. With *V* held down, move the cursor around and see how the gizmo cursor sticks to the nearest vertex of the selected mesh. Unity is asking you to pick a source vertex for the snapping.

4. Move the cursor to the bottom corner of the house, and then click and drag from that corner to the floor mesh corner. The house will then snap align to the floor, precisely at the vertices.

5. When aligned this way, release the *V* key. It should look similar to *Figure 1.27*:

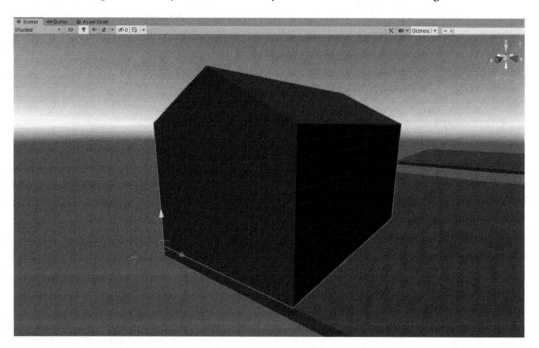

Figure 1.27 – Align two meshes by vertices

6. Now you can assemble a complete scene using the mesh assets included in the `Prototyping` folder. Drag and drop props in the scene, and using translate, rotate, and scale, you can reposition, realign, and rotate these objects; using vertex snapping, you can align them wherever you need. Give this some practice.

See *Figure 1.28* for the scene arrangement that I made using only these tools and assets:

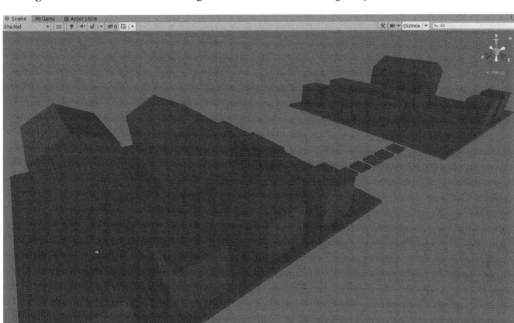

Figure 1.28 – Building a complete level

You'll notice in *Figure 1.28* that everything looks relatively flat, with no highlights, shadows, or light or dark areas. This is because scene lighting is not properly configured for best results, even though we already have a light in the scene, which was created initially by default. We'll fix this now.

Adding lighting and a skybox

The basic level has been created in terms of architectural models and layout; this was achieved using only a few mesh assets and some basic tools. Nevertheless, these tools are powerful and offer us a number of options to create a great variety of game worlds. One important ingredient is missing for us, however. This ingredient is lighting.

Let's start setting the scene for the coin collection game by enabling the sky, if it's not already enabled. To do this, perform the following steps:

1. Click on the **Extras** drop-down menu from the top toolbar in the scene viewport.

2. From the context menu, select **Skybox** to enable skybox viewing. A **Skybox** is a large cube that surrounds the whole scene. Each interior side has a continuous texture (image) applied to simulate the appearance of a surrounding sky. For this reason, clicking the **Skybox** option displays a default sky in the scene viewport:

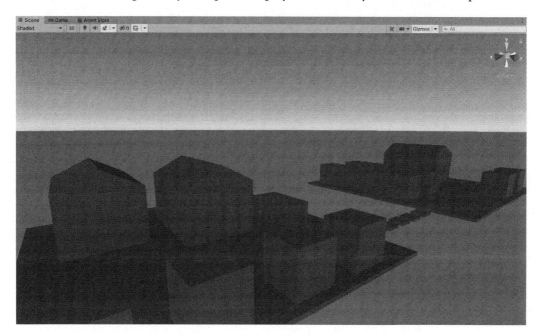

Figure 1.29 – Enabling the sky

3. Although the skybox is enabled and the scene looks better than before, it's still not illuminated properly—the objects lack shadows and highlights. To fix this, be sure that lighting is enabled for the scene by toggling on the lighting icon at the top of the scene view, as shown in *Figure 1.30*. This setting changes the visibility of lighting in the scene view but not in the final game:

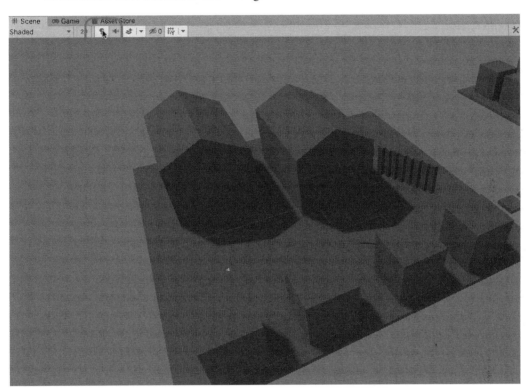

Figure 1.30 – Enabling scene lighting in the Scene viewport

Enabling the lighting display for the viewport will result in some differences to the scene appearance and, again, the scene should look better than before. You can confirm that scene lighting is taking effect by selecting **Directional Light** from the **Hierarchy** panel and rotating it. All objects in the scene are illuminated based on the rotation of the directional light, so by rotating the light object, you are, in effect, changing the time of day. Moving the object, in contrast, will not affect the scene lighting. A directional light represents a large and very distant light source, existing far beyond the bounds of our game. No matter where you position the lighting object in the scene, the other objects will stay illuminated in the same way. Instead of moving the light object, you can change the **Intensity** field on the **Light** component to alter the mood of the scene. This changes how the scene is rendered, as seen in *Figure 1.31*:

Figure 1.31 – Rotating the scene directional light changes the time of day

Undo any rotations to the directional light by pressing *Ctrl + Z* on the keyboard. To prepare for final and optimal lighting, all non-movable objects in the scene should be marked as **Static**. This signifies to Unity that the objects will never move, no matter what happens during gameplay. By marking non-movable objects ahead of time, you can help Unity optimize the way it renders and lights a scene.

To mark objects as static, perform the following steps:

1. Select all non-movable objects (which includes practically the entire level so far). By holding down the *Shift* key while selecting objects, you can select multiple objects together, allowing you to adjust their properties as a batch through the **Inspector** panel.

2. Enable the **Static** checkbox via the **Inspector** panel. The **Static** checkbox is shown in *Figure 1.32*:

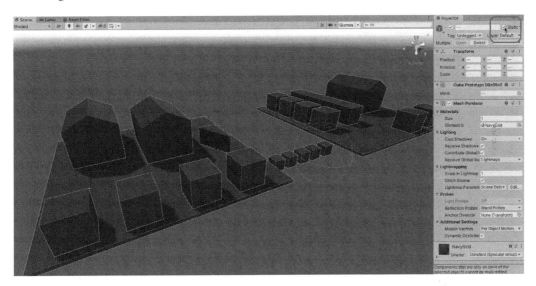

Figure 1.32 – Enabling the Static option for multiple non-movable objects
improves lighting and performance

When you enable the **Static** checkbox for geometry, Unity autocalculates scene lighting in the background—effects such as shadows, indirect illumination, and more. It generates a batch of data called the **GI Cache**, featuring **light propagation paths**, which instructs Unity how light rays should bounce and move around the scene to achieve greater realism.

If your objects are not casting shadows, they may have the **Cast Shadows** option disabled. To fix this, perform the following steps:

1. Select all meshes in the scene.

2. Then, from the **Inspector** panel, click on the **Cast Shadows** context menu from the **Mesh Renderer** component, and choose the **On** option.

When you do this, all mesh objects should cast shadows, as shown in *Figure 1.33*:

Figure 1.33 – Enabling cast shadows from the Mesh Renderer component

Voilà! The meshes now cast shadows. Splendid work! In reaching this point, you've created a new project, populated a scene with meshes, and successfully illuminated them with directional lighting. That's excellent. However, it'd be even better if we could explore our environment in the first person. We'll see how to do precisely that next.

Testing the game

The environment created thus far for the coin collection game has been assembled using only the mesh assets included with the **Standard Assets** package. My environment, as shown in *Figure 1.28*, features two main floor islands with houses, and a stepping-stone bridge that connects the islands. Your version may be slightly different, and that's fine.

Now, the level, as it stands, contains nothing playable. It's currently a static, non-interactive, 3D environment made using the editor tools. In this chapter, we'll correct this by allowing the player to wander around and explore the world in first-person, controlled using the standard *WASD* keys on the keyboard. Once the character has been added to the scene, we can then perform our first playtest of the game using the **Game** panel. Lastly, we will deal with any warning messages shown when we play the game.

Adding a playable character

For the playable character, we will use a ready-made asset, which contains everything necessary to create a quick and functional first-person character:

1. Open the `Standard Assets/Characters/FirstPersonCharacter/ Prefabs` folder.

2. Then, drag and drop the **FPSController** asset from the **Project** panel in the scene. You will then have a scene that looks similar to the one in *Figure 1.34*:

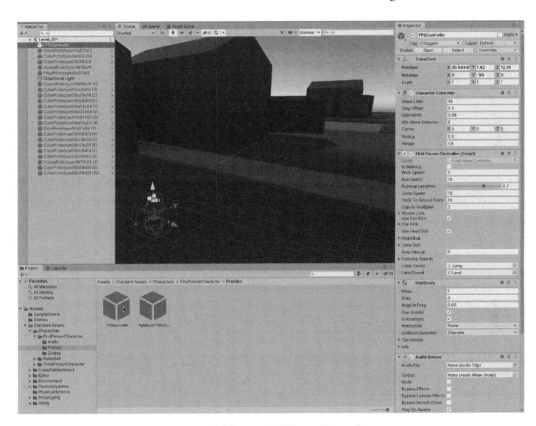

Figure 1.34 – Adding an FPSController to the scene

3. After adding the first-person controller, click on the Play button in the Unity toolbar to playtest the game:

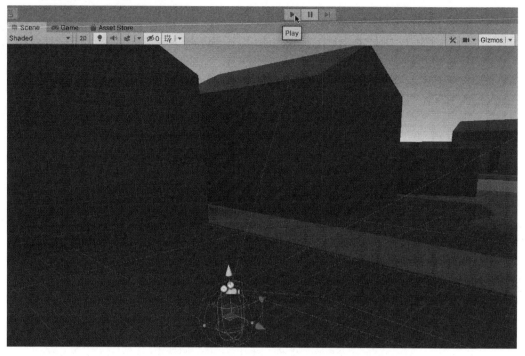

Figure 1.35 – Unity scenes can be playtested by clicking on the play button from the toolbar

On clicking Play, Unity typically switches from the **Scene** tab to the **Game** tab, which will be explored in the next section.

Using the game panel

As we've seen, the scene tab is a *director's-eye view* of the active scene; it's where a scene is edited, crafted, and designed. In contrast, the **Game** tab is where the active scene is played and tested from the perspective of the gamer. From this view, the scene is displayed through the main game camera. While play mode is active, you can playtest your game using the default game controls, provided that the game tab is *in focus*.

The first-person controller uses the *WASD* keys on the keyboard and mouse movements control head orientation:

Figure 1.36 – Playtesting levels in the Game tab

> **Important note**
>
> You can switch back to the scene tab while in play mode. You can even edit the scene and change, move, and delete objects there too! However, any scene changes made during play will automatically revert to their original settings when you exit play mode. This behavior is intentional. It lets you edit properties during gameplay to observe their effects and debug any issues without permanently changing the scene. This rule, however, doesn't apply to changes made to assets in the Project panel, including prefabs. Changes to these objects are *not* reverted when you exit play mode.

Congratulations! You should now be able to walk around your level. When finished, you can easily stop playing by clicking on the play button again or by pressing *Ctrl + P* on the keyboard. Doing this will return you to the scene tab.

> **Tip**
> Unity also features a *Toggle-Pause* button to suspend and resume gameplay.

You may notice that, on playing the level, you receive an information message in the **Console** window. In the next section, we'll go through the types of messages you may receive, what is causing this specific message, and how we can resolve it.

Understanding console messages

The console window is where any errors, warnings, or information messages are displayed. Sometimes, a message appears just once, or sometimes it appears multiple times, as in *Figure 1.37*:

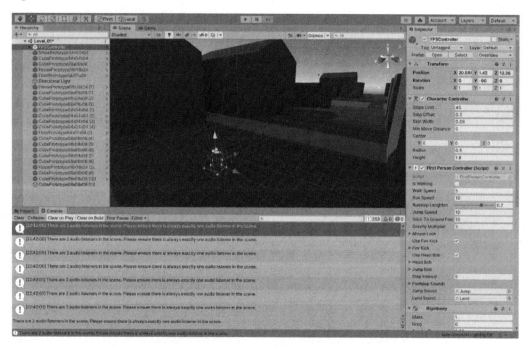

Figure 1.37 -The console outputs information, warnings, and errors

By default, this window appears at the bottom of the Unity Editor, docked beside the **Project** panel. This window is also accessible manually from the application menu, **Window | General | Console**.

Information messages are typically Unity's way of making best practice recommendations or suggestions based on how your project is currently working. Warnings are slightly more serious and represent problems either in your code or scene, which (if not corrected) could result in unexpected behavior and suboptimal performance. Finally, errors describe areas in your scene or code that require careful and immediate attention. Sometimes, errors will prevent your game from working altogether, and sometimes errors happen at runtime and can result in game crashes or freezes. Errors are printed in red, warnings in yellow, and information messages appear as a default gray.

The console window, therefore, is useful because it helps us debug and address issues with our games. *Figure 1.37* has identified an issue concerning duplicated **audio listeners**. An audio listener is a component attached to an object, which represents an *ear point*. It enables the ability to hear sound within the scene from the position of the audio listener. Every camera, by default, has an audio listener component attached. Unity doesn't support multiple active audio listeners in the same scene, which means that you can only hear audio from one place at any one time. We are receiving this message because our scene now contains two cameras, one that was added automatically when the scene was created, and another one that is included in the first-person controller. To confirm this, select the first-person controller object in the hierarchy panel and click on the triangle icon beside its name to reveal more objects underneath, which are part of the first-person controller:

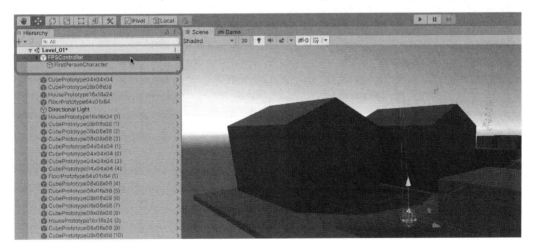

Figure 1.38 – Finding the camera on a first-person controller

Select the **FirstPersonCharacter** object, which is underneath the FPSController object (as shown in *Figure 1.38*). The FirstPersonCharacter object is a **child** of the FPSController, which is the **parent**. This is because FPSController contains or encloses the FirstPersonCharacter object in the **Hierarchy** panel. Child objects **inherit** the transformations of their parents. This means that as parent objects move and rotate, all transformations will cascade downward to all children. From the **Inspector** panel, you can see that the object has an Audio Listener component:

Figure 1.39 – The FirstPersonController object contains an Audio Listener component

We could remove the audio listener component from `FPSController`, but this would prevent the player hearing sound from a first-person perspective. So, instead, we'll delete the original camera created by default in the scene. To do this, select the original camera object in the hierarchy and press *Delete* on the keyboard. This removes the audio listener warning in the console during gameplay. Now, if you play the game, the message should no longer appear.

We've come a long way, we've added a first-person character to the game, playtested using the **Game** panel, and made changes in response to a message shown in the **Console** panel. Great work! This iteration of playtesting and reacting to messages in the Console window will become second nature as we progress through the book, and understanding and debugging these messages is a big part of developing in Unity.

Now that we have covered the basics, we can work on improving our scene by adding water around our islands and starting on the collectible coins (an important part of a collectible coin game!).

Improving the scene

The collection game is making excellent progress. We now have something playable insofar as we can run around and explore the environment in the first person. However, the environment could benefit from additional polish. Right now, for example, the floor meshes appear suspended in mid-air with nothing beneath them to offer support. It's also possible to walk over the edge and fall into an infinite drop. And there's a distinct lack of coins in our collectible coin game. We'll fix both of these issues in this chapter, starting with adding a water plane to support the islands.

Adding a water plane

To add water, we can use another ready-made Unity asset included in the **Project** panel:

1. Open the `Standard Assets/Environment/Water/Water/Prefabs` folder.

2. Drag and drop the `WaterProDaytime` asset from the **Project** panel into the scene. This appears as a circular object, which is initially smaller than needed:

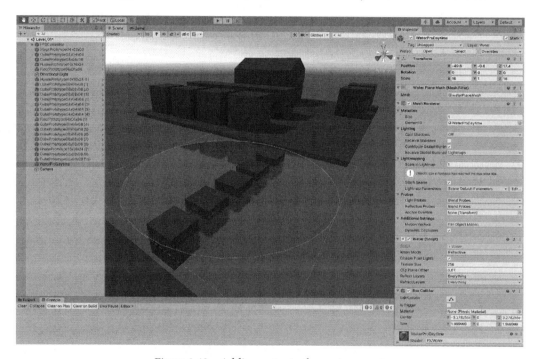

Figure 1.40 – Adding water to the environment

3. After adding the water prefab, position it below the floor and use the scale tool to increase its planar size (`X, Z`) to fill the environment outward into the distant horizon. This creates the appearance that the floor meshes are smaller islands within an expansive world of water:

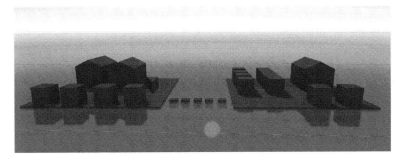

Figure 1.41 – Scaling and sizing water for the environment

Now, let's take another test run in the game tab. Press Play on the toolbar and you should see the water in the level. Unfortunately, you can't walk on the water, nor can you swim or dive beneath it. If you try walking on it, you'll simply fall through it, descending into infinity as though the water had never been there. Right now, the water is an entirely cosmetic feature.

The water is a substanceless, ethereal object through which the player can pass easily. Unity doesn't recognize it as a solid or even a semi-solid object. As we'll see in more detail later, you can make an object solid very quickly by attaching a **Box Collider** component to it. Colliders and physics are covered in more depth from *Chapter 3, Creating a Space Shooter*, onward. For now, however, we can add solidity to the water by first selecting the **Water** object from the **Hierarchy** panel (or in the scene view) and then by choosing **Component | Physics | Box Collider** from the application menu:

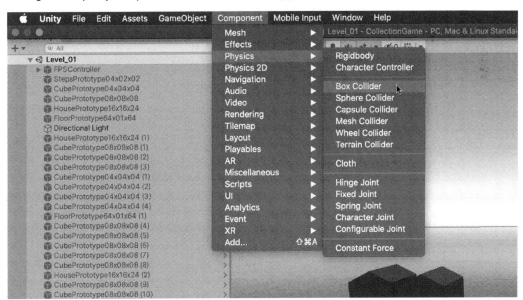

Figure 1.42 – Attaching a Box Collider to a Water object

Attaching a component to the selected object changes the object itself; it changes how it behaves. Essentially, components add behavior and functionality to objects, making them behave in different ways.

When a **Box Collider** is added to the water, a surrounding green cage or mesh appears. This approximates the volume and shape of the water object and represents its physical volume, namely, the volume of the object that Unity recognizes as solid. You can see this approximation in *Figure 1.43*:

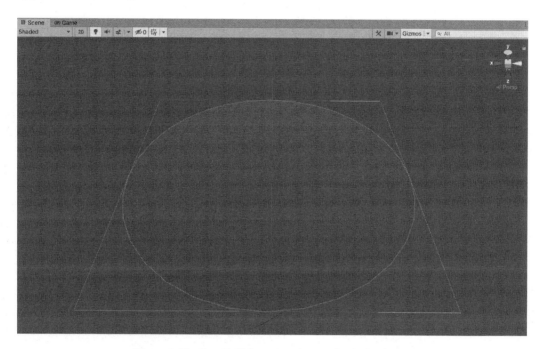

Figure 1.43 – Box Collider approximate physical volume

If you play the game now, your character will walk on water as opposed to falling through. True, the character should be able to swim properly, but walking might be better than falling. To achieve full swimming behavior would require significantly more work and is not covered here. If you want to remove the Box Collider functionality and return the water back to its original state, select the **Water** object, click on the cog icon on the **Box Collider** component, and then choose **Remove Component** from the context menu, as shown in *Figure 1.44*:

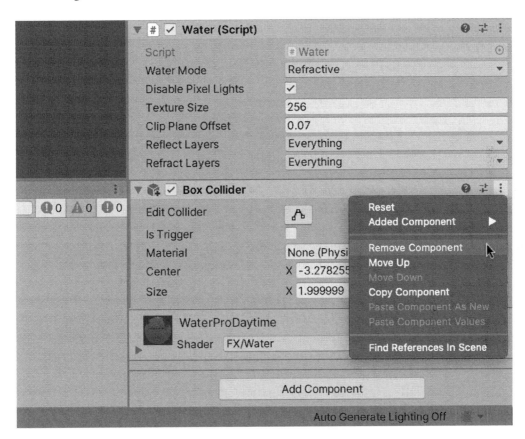

Figure 1.44 – Removing a component from a GameObject

With the water set up precisely as we want it, we'll move back on land and start creating the coins for our game.

Adding a coin

At this point, our game has an environment and a method of navigation. But we're missing a core feature of our collection game – there are no coins for the player to collect! So far, we haven't had to write a single line of code. However, in order to implement collectible coins, we'll need to do just that. We'll write the C# scripts in the next chapter, but we can get started here by creating the coin object itself. To do this, we'll use a **Cylinder** primitive that's scaled to form a coin-looking shape:

1. Create a cylinder by selecting **GameObject | 3D Object | Cylinder** from the application menu:

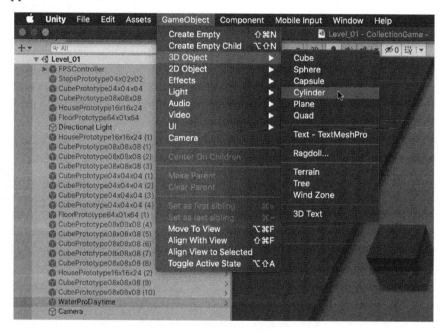

Figure 1.45 – Creating a cylinder

Initially, the cylinder looks nothing like a coin. However, this is easily changed by scaling non-uniformly on the *Z* axis to make the cylinder thinner. Switch to the scale tool (*R*) and then scale the cylinder inward so that it looks similar to *Figure 1.46*:

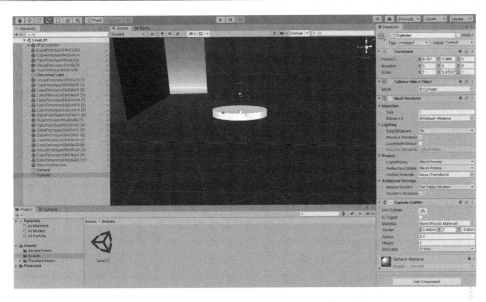

Figure 1.46 – Scaling the cylinder to make a collectible coin

2. By default, the cylinder is created with a **Capsule Collider** as opposed to a **Box Collider**. As you scale the object, the collider will also change size. However, sometimes it may not have the dimensions we would like. You can change the size of the **Capsule Collider** component by adjusting the **radius** field from the **Inspector** panel when the coin is selected. Alternatively, you could remove the **Capsule Collider** altogether and add a **Box Collider** instead. Either way is fine; generally, choose the simpler shape where possible. The colliders will be used in a script in the next chapter to detect when the player collides with a coin:

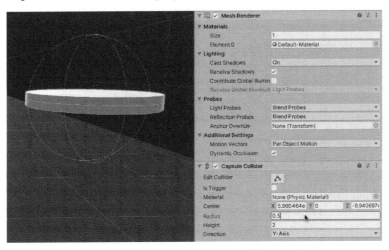

Figure 1.47 – Adjusting the Capsule Collider for the coin

We now have the basic shape and structure for a coin. We will improve it in the next chapter by making it collectible and assigning a material to make it look shiny. However, by using only a basic Unity primitive and scale tool, we were able to generate a shape that resembles a coin.

Saving the scene

Overall, the scene is looking good and is worth saving to disk so that we don't lose it. To save the scene, perform either of the following steps:

- Choose **File | Save Scene** from the application menu.

- Alternatively, press *Ctrl + S* on the keyboard or else.

If you're saving the scene for the first time, Unity displays a pop-up save dialog, prompting you to name the scene (I called it Level_01 and saved it in the Scenes folder). After saving the scene, it becomes an asset of the project and appears in the **Project** panel. This means that the scene is now a genuine and integral part of the project and not just a temporary work in progress as it was before. Notice also that saving a scene is conceptually *different* from saving a project. For example, the application menu has entries for **Save Scene** and **Save Project**. Remember, a project is a collection of files and folders, including assets and scenes. A scene, by contrast, is one asset within the project and represents a complete 3D map that may be populated by other assets, such as meshes, textures, and sounds. Thus, saving a project saves the configuration between files and assets, including scenes. Saving a scene, in contrast, just retains the level changes within that specified scene:

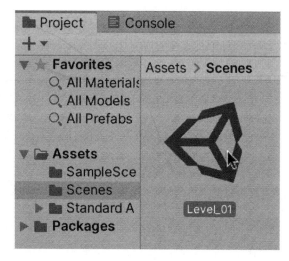

Figure 1.48 – Saved scenes are added as assets within your project

> **Tip**
>
> You can see in *Figure 1.48* that I've saved my scene in the Scenes folder.
> If you want to save it somewhere else, folders can be created in your project
> by right-clicking on any empty area in the **Project** panel and choosing **New
> Folder** from the context menu, or else choose **Assets | Create | Folder** from the
> application menu. You can easily move and rearrange assets among folders by
> simply dragging and dropping them. And that's it! The scene is saved to a file
> at the location you specified. As we progress through the book, make sure you
> regularly save your scenes to ensure that you do not lose any progress.

Summary

Congratulations! On reaching this point, you have laid the foundations for a coin
collection game that will be complete and functional by the end of the next chapter. Here,
we've seen how to create a Unity project from scratch and populate it with assets, such
as meshes, textures, and scenes. In addition, we've seen how to create a scene for our
game and use a range of assets to populate it with useful functionality. This knowledge is
fundamental to becoming a Unity developer. By mastering these topics, you lay a solid
foundation on which you will build the rest of the projects in this book and your own
games.

In the next chapter, we'll resume work from where we ended here by making a coin that is
collectible and establishing a set of rules and logic for the game, making it possible to win
and lose.

Test your knowledge

Q1. To manage Unity projects and installations, you can use…

    A. Unity Editor

    B. Unity Hub

    C. Package Manager

    D. Project Panel

Q2. Once you've added an asset using the Unity Asset Store, you can import it into your
project using…

    A. the Unity Asset Store itself

    B. the project creation wizard

C. Unity Hub

D. Package Manager

Q3. Assets are imported directly into the…

A. Object Inspector

B. Hierarchy

C. scene

D. **Project** panel

Q4. You can quickly create first-person controls using…

A. camera objects

B. capsules

C. first-person controllers

D. Box Colliders

Q5. The Prototyping package is most useful for...

A. building levels

B. prototyping code

C. animating objects

D. creating camera effects

Q6. When pressed in the scene tab, the *F* key will...

A. center the view on the selected object

B. remove the selected object

C. hide the selected object

D. freeze the selected object

Q7. You can access the Snapping Feature by pressing...

A. the *C* key

B. the *V* key

C. the *D* key

D. the *E* key

Further reading

Refer to the following links for more information:

- `https://docs.unity3d.com/Manual/GettingStartedInstallingHub.html`

- `https://learn.unity.com`

- `https://docs.unity3d.com/Manual/upm-ui.html`

- `https://docs.unity3d.com/Manual/CreatingScenes.html`

- `https://docs.unity3d.com/Manual/GameObjects.html`

- `https://www.packtpub.com/gb/game-development/unity-by-example-build-20-mini-projects-in-unity-video`

2
Creating a Collection Game

In this chapter, we will complete the collection game that we started in the previous chapter. As a reminder, in this game, the player wanders an environment in first-person, searching for and collecting coins before a global timer expires. So far, the project features a complete environment, a first-person controller, and a simple coin object. The coin has been shaped, and a **Material** has been applied, so it looks the part, but cannot yet be collected (something we will rectify shortly).

This chapter completes the project by making the coin object collectable and adding a timer system to determine whether the total game time has expired. In essence, this chapter is about defining a system of logic and rules governing the game, including the win and lose conditions. To achieve this, we'll need to code in C#.

In this chapter, we'll customize the Material (specifying how an object should be rendered) for the coin object to make it look more realistic. Once our coins look the part, we'll write scripts in C# for coin collection, counting, and spawning. As part of this process, we'll create custom **Tags** (which we'll use to identify the coin objects in the scene), and convert the coins to **prefabs** (which will enable us to spawn them during gameplay). We'll also write a timer to add a sense of urgency to the game.

Overall, this chapter will demonstrate the following topics:

- Creating Materials
- Coding with C#
- Working with prefabs
- Unity Tags
- Using particle systems
- Building and compiling games to be run as standalone

Technical requirements

This book is about Unity and developing games in that engine. The basics of programming as a subject is, however, beyond the scope of this book. So, I'll assume that you already have a working knowledge of coding generally but have not coded in Unity before.

You can download the example code files for this book from GitHub at `https://github.com/PacktPublishing/Unity-2020-By-Example`.

Once downloaded, the project so far can be found in the book's companion files in the `Chapter04/Start folder` you can find the completed `CollectionGame` project in the `Chapter02/End` folder.

Working with Materials

The previous chapter closed by creating a coin object from a non-uniformly scaled cylinder primitive, as shown in *Figure 2.1*:

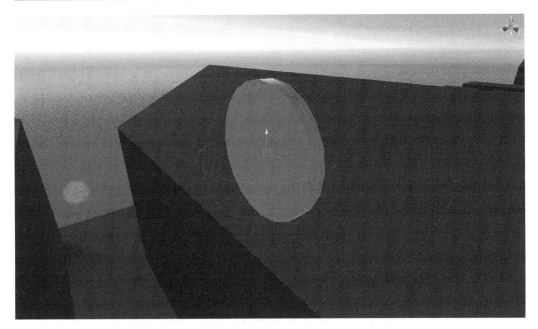

Figure 2.1 – The coin object so far

The coin object, as a concept, represents a basic or fundamental unit in our game logic because the player character should be actively searching the level looking for coins to collect before a timer runs out. The coin has a functional purpose in this game and is not just an aesthetic prop. Therefore, the coin object, as it stands, is lacking in two essential respects. Firstly, it looks dull and gray—it doesn't stand out and grab the player's attention. Secondly, the coin cannot be collected yet. The player can walk into the coin, but nothing appropriate happens in response.

In this section, we'll focus on improving the coin appearance using a Material. A Material defines an **algorithm** (or **instruction set**) specifying how the coin should be **rendered**. A Material doesn't just say what the coin should look like in terms of color; it defines how shiny or smooth a surface is, as opposed to being rough and diffuse. This is important to recognize and is why the terms **texture** and Material refer to different things. A texture is an image file loaded in memory, which can be wrapped around a 3D object via its **UV mapping**. In contrast, a Material defines how one or more textures can be combined and applied to an object to shape its appearance. So now we know the difference, let's create a Material to make the coin objects look more realistic.

Creating a coin Material

To create a new Material asset in Unity, do the following:

1. Right-click on an empty area in the **Project** panel.

2. From the context menu, choose **Create | Material**. You can also choose **Assets | Create | Material** from the application menu:

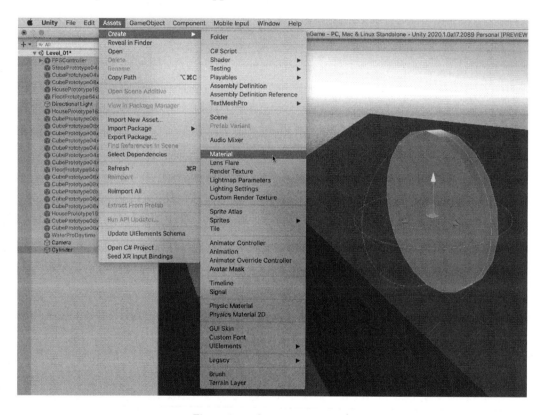

Figure 2.2 – Creating a Material

> **Important note**
>
> A Material is sometimes called a **Shader**. If needed, you can create custom Materials using a Shader language or you can use a Unity add-on, such as **Shader Forge**.

After creating a new Material, do the following:

1. Assign it an appropriate name from the **Project** panel. As I'm aiming for a gold look, I've named the Material GoldCoin.

2. Create a folder to store the Material (if not already present) by right-clicking in the **Assets** folder and selecting **Create | Folder**. Name the folder Materials.

3. Move the Material to the newly created Materials folder.

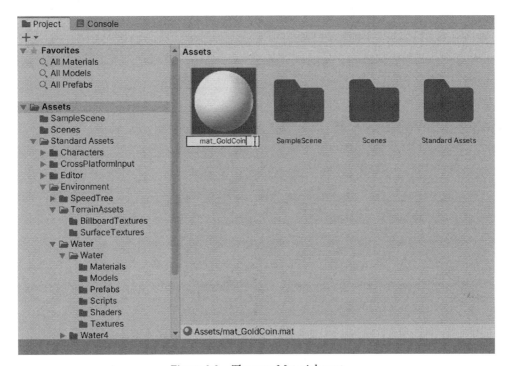

Figure 2.3 – The new Material asset

We now have a generic Material that we can edit to suit our purposes; now, let's edit the Material.

Editing the Material

To edit the Material, first, select the Material asset in the **Project** panel to display its properties in the **Inspector**. Several properties will be listed in the **Inspector**, as well as a preview. The preview shows you how the Material would look, based on its current settings, applied to a 3D object. As you change the Material's settings from the **Inspector**, the **Preview** panel updates automatically to reflect your changes, offering instant feedback on how the Material would look:

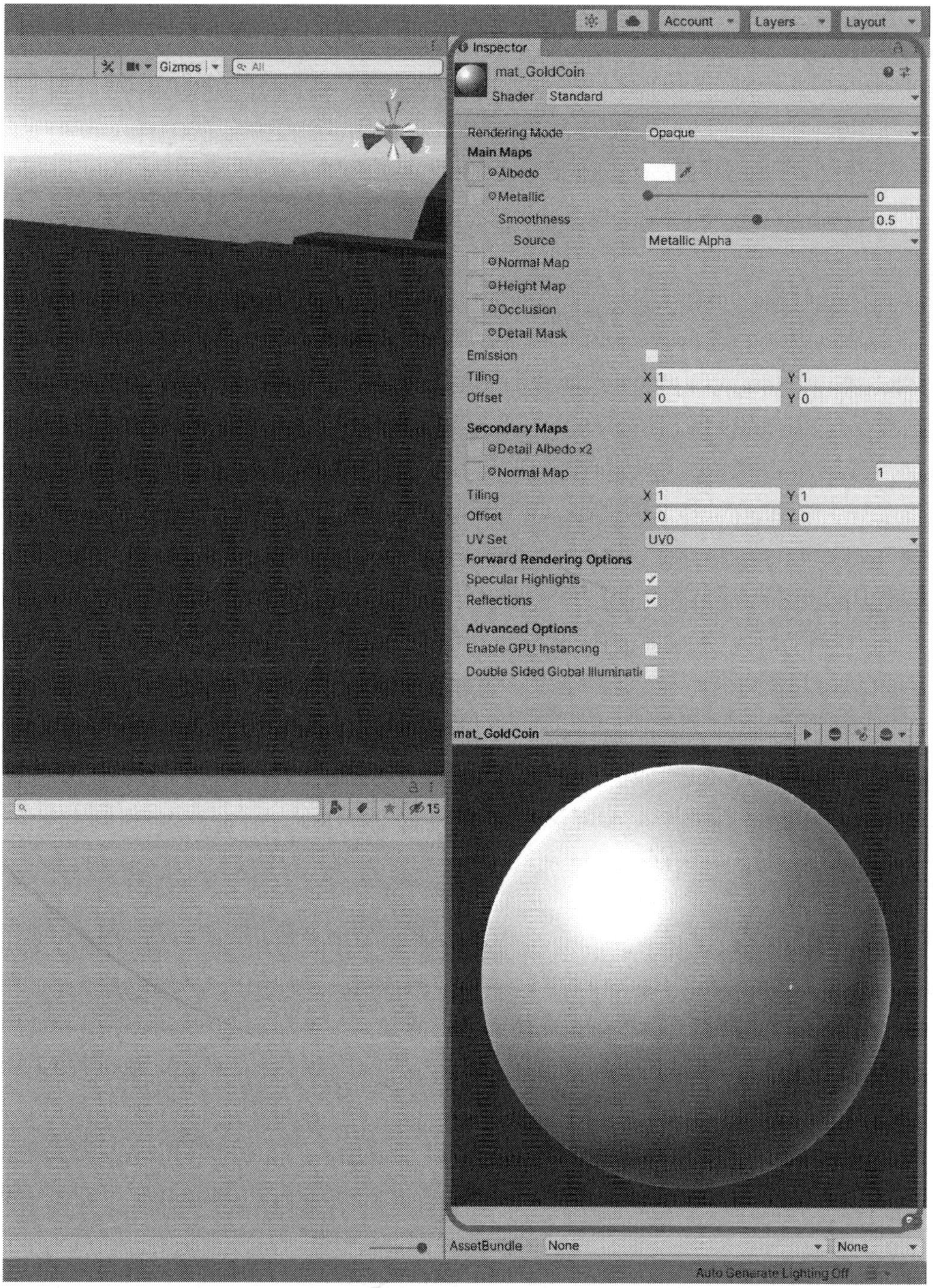

Figure 2.4 – Material properties are changed from the object Inspector

We'll edit these properties to create a gold Material for the coin. When creating any Material, the first setting to choose is the **Shader** type because this setting affects all other parameters available to you. The **Shader** type determines which algorithm will be used to shade your object. There are many different choices, but most Material types can be approximated using either **Standard** or **Standard (Specular setup)**. For the gold coin, we can leave **Shader** as **Standard**:

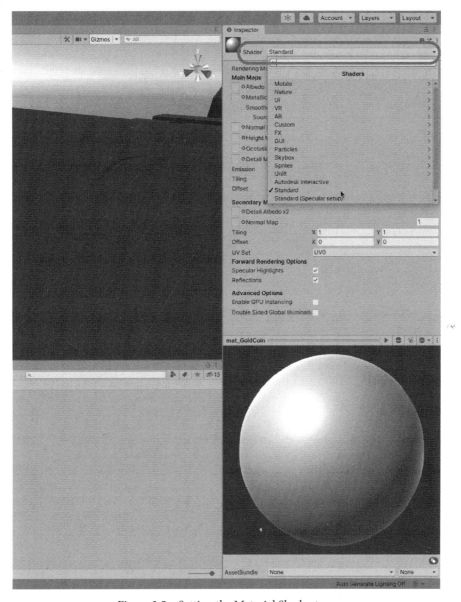

Figure 2.5 – Setting the Material Shader type

Right now, the **Preview** panel displays the Material as a dull gray, which is far from what we need. To define a gold color, we must specify the **Albedo** color. To do this, take the following steps:

1. Click on the **Albedo** color slot to display a color picker.

2. From the color picker dialog, select a gold color. The Material preview updates in response to reflect the changes:

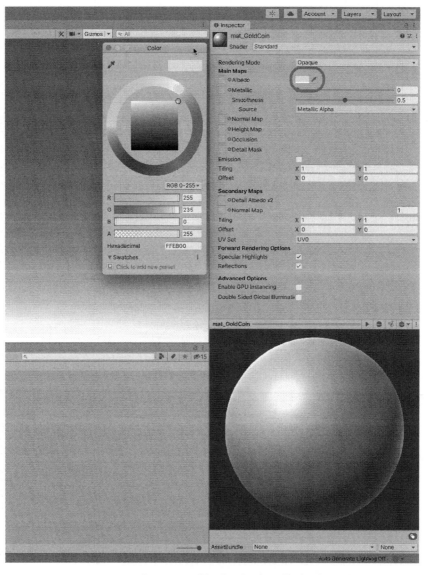

Figure 2.6 – Selecting a gold color for the Albedo channel

The coin Material is looking better than it did but is still not quite right as it is supposed to represent a metallic surface, which tends to be shiny and reflective. To add this quality to our Material, click and drag the **Metallic** slider in the **Inspector** to the right-hand side, setting its value to 1. This value indicates that the Material represents a fully metal surface as opposed to a diffuse surface such as cloth or hair. Again, the **Preview** panel will update to reflect the change:

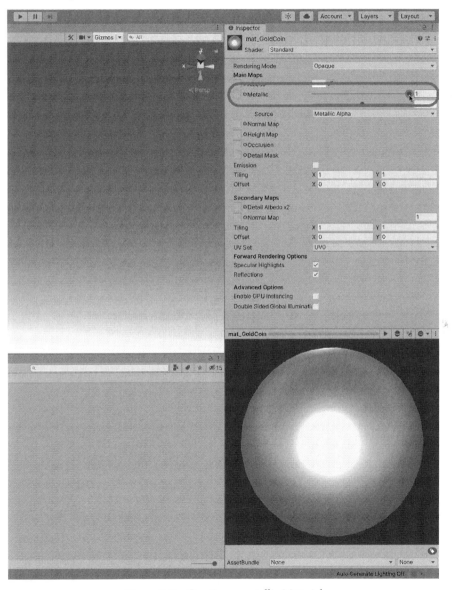

Figure 2.7 – Creating a metallic Material

When you're happy with what is shown in the preview, it's time to assign the Material to the coin object.

Assigning the Material

We now have a gold Material created, and it's looking good in the **Preview** panel. If needed, you can change the kind of object used for a preview. By default, Unity assigns the created Material to a sphere, but other primitive objects are allowed, including cubes, cylinders, and toruses. You can change the object by clicking on the geometry button directly above the **Preview** panel to cycle through them. Viewing different objects will help you preview Materials under different conditions:

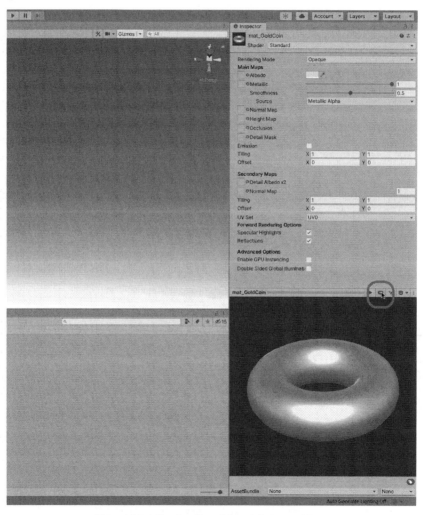

Figure 2.8 – Previewing a Material on an object

When your Material is ready, you can assign it directly to meshes in your scene by dragging and dropping from the **Project** panel to the object (either in the **Scene** view or **Hierarchy** panel). Let's assign the coin Material to the coin. Click and drag the Material from the **Project** panel to the coin object in the scene. On dropping the Material, the coin will change appearance to reflect the change of Material:

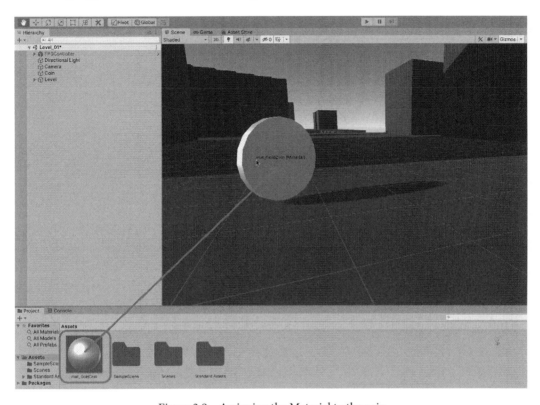

Figure 2.9 – Assigning the Material to the coin

You can confirm that Material assignment occurred successfully and can even identify which Material was assigned by selecting the **Coin** object in the scene and viewing its **Mesh Renderer** component in the **Inspector**. The **Mesh Renderer** component is responsible for making sure that a mesh object is visible in the scene. The **Mesh Renderer** component contains a **Materials** field, which lists all Materials currently assigned to the object. By clicking on the Material name from the **Materials** field, Unity automatically selects the Material in the **Project** panel, making it quick and easy to locate Materials:

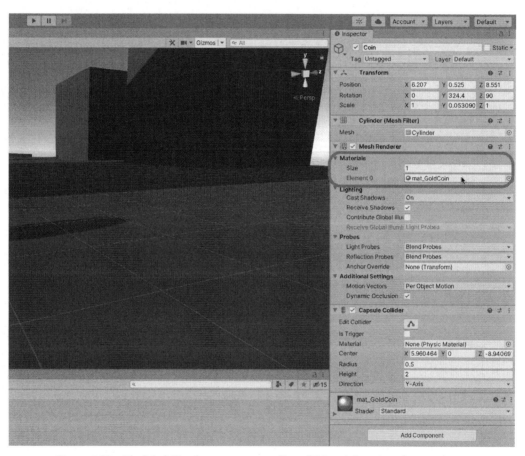

Figure 2.10 – The Mesh Renderer component lists all Materials assigned to an object

> **Tip**
>
> Mesh objects may have multiple Materials, with different Materials assigned to different **faces**. For the best in-game performance, use as few unique Materials on an object as necessary. Make the extra effort to share Materials across multiple objects, if possible. Doing so can significantly enhance the performance of your game. For more information on optimizing rendering performance, see the online documentation at `https://docs.unity3d.com/Manual/OptimizingGraphicsPerformance.html`.

We now have a complete and functional gold Material for the collectible coin. However, we're still not finished with the coin. It may look correct, but it doesn't behave in the way we want. For example, it doesn't disappear when touched, and we don't yet keep track of how many coins the player has collected overall. To address this, we'll need to write a script.

Scripting in Unity

Defining game logic, rules, and behavior often requires scripting. Specifically, to transform a static scene with objects into an environment that does something interesting, a developer needs to code behaviors. It requires the developer to define how things should act and react under specific conditions. The coin collection game is no exception to this. In particular, it requires three main features:

1. To know when the player collects a coin

2. To keep track of how many coins are collected during gameplay

3. To determine whether a timer has expired

Now we have an understanding of the requirements, it's time to create our first script!

Creating a script

There's no default out-of-the-box functionality included with Unity to handle the custom logic we require, so we must write some code to achieve it. Unity's programming language of choice is **C#**. Previous versions had support for **UnityScript** (a language similar to **JavaScript**), but this has been officially deprecated, and you can no longer create new `UnityScript` files. For this reason, this book will use C#. We'll start coding the three features in sequence. To create a new script file, do the following:

1. Right-click on an empty area in the **Project** panel.

2. From the context menu, choose **Create | C# Script**. Alternatively, you can navigate to **Assets | Create | C# Script** from the application menu:

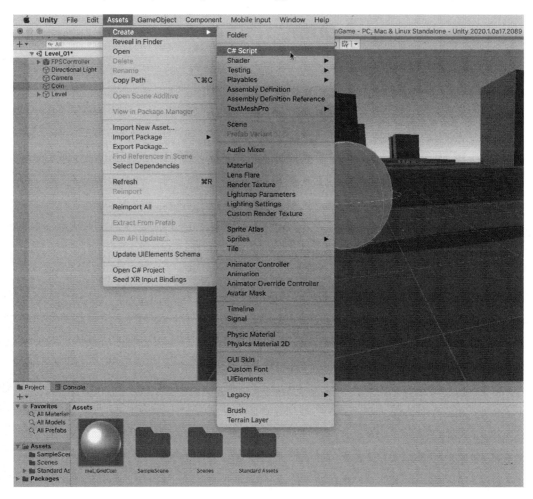

Figure 2.11 – Creating a new C# script

Once the file is created, assign a descriptive name to it. I'll call it `Coin.cs`. By default, each script file represents a single, discrete class with a name matching the filename. Hence, the `Coin.cs` file encodes the `Coin` class. The `Coin` class will encapsulate the behavior of a Coin object and will, eventually, be attached to the Coin object in the scene. However, at the moment, our `Coin` class doesn't do anything, as we'll see shortly.

Understanding the coin script

Double-click on the `Coin.cs` file in the **Project** panel to open it in **Visual Studio (VS 2019 8.4 for Mac)** a third-party **IDE** that ships with Unity. This program lets you edit and write code for your games. Once opened in Visual Studio, the source file will appear, as shown in *Code Sample 2.1*:

```
using UnityEngine;
using System.Collections;


public class Coin : MonoBehaviour
{
    // Use this for initialization
    void Start ()
    {

    }

    // Update is called once per frame
    Void Update ()
    {

    }
}
```

Downloading the example code

Remember, you can download the example code files for this book from GitHub with the link provided in the *Technical requirements* section.

By default, all newly created classes derive from MonoBehavior, which defines a common set of functionality shared by all **components**. The Coin class features two autogenerated functions: Start and Update. These functions are invoked automatically by Unity. Start is called once (and only once) when the GameObject, to which the script is attached, is created in the **Scene**, and Update is called once per frame. Start is useful for initialization code and Update is useful for adding behavior over time, such as motion.

> **Important note**
>
> There are other functions that are called before the Start function. We will examine the Unity event execution order in more detail later in the book as it is an important concept to understand. However, for a sneak peek at the execution order, see Unity's online documentation: https://docs. unity3d.com/Manual/ExecutionOrder.html.

The script is not yet attached to our object, therefore the functions would not be called if we were to play the game now. As you'll see shortly, this is easily remedied.

Running the script

Before the script is run, it needs to be attached to the Coin object in the **Scene**. To do this, drag and drop the Coin.cs script file from the **Project** panel to the **Coin** object. When you do this, a new **Coin** component is added to the object, as shown in *Figure 2.12*:

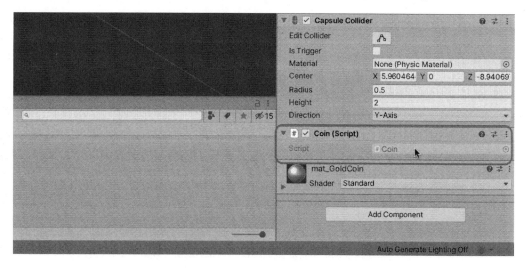

Figure 2.12 – Attaching a script file to an object

When a script is attached to an object, it exists on the object as a component and is instantiated with the object. A script file can usually be added to multiple objects and even to the same object multiple times. Each component represents a separate and unique instantiation of the class. When a script is attached in this way, Unity automatically invokes its events, such as **Start** and **Update**. You can confirm that your script is working normally by including a Debug.Log statement in the Start function:

```
using UnityEngine;
using System.Collections;


public class Coin : MonoBehaviour
{
    // Use this for initialization
    void Start ()
    {
        Debug.Log ("Object Created");
    }

    // Update is called once per frame
    void Update ()
    {
    }
}
```

If you now press play (*Ctrl* + *P*) on the toolbar to run your game, you will see the message **Object Created** printed to the **Console** window—once for each instantiation of the class:

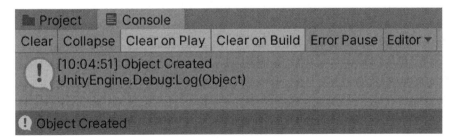

Figure 2.13 – Printing messages to the Console window

Good work! We've now created a basic script for the Coin class and attached it to the coin. Next, let's update our Coin.cs file to keep track of coins as they are collected.

Recording the total coin count

The coin collection game wouldn't be much of a game if there were only one coin. The central idea is that a level should feature many coins, all of which the player should collect before a timer expires. To know when all the coins have been collected, we'll need to know how many coins there are in the scene. After all, if we don't know how many coins there are, then we can't know whether we've collected them all. We'll configure the Coin class to keep track of the total number of coins in the scene at any moment. Consider *Code Sample 2.3*, which adapts the Coin class to achieve this:

```
public class Coin : MonoBehaviour
{
  //Keeps track of total coin count in scene
  public static int CoinCount = 0;

   void Start ()
   {

      //Object created, increment coin count
      ++Coin.CoinCount;
   }

   //Called when object is destroyed
   void OnDestroy()
   {
      --Coin.CoinCount;

      if(Coin.CoinCount <= 0)
      {
         //We have won
      }
   }
}
```

Let's summarize the preceding code:

- The Coin class maintains a **static** member variable, CoinCount, which, being static, is shared across all instances of the class. This variable keeps a count of the total number of coins in the scene, and each instance has access to it.

- The Start function is called once per Coin instance when the object is created in the scene. For coins that are present when the scene begins, the Start event is called at scene startup. This function increments the CoinCount variable by one per instance, thus keeping count of all coins.

- The OnDestroy function is called once per instance when the object is destroyed. This decrements the CoinCount variable, reducing the count for each coin destroyed.

Being able to keep track of the number of coins is a great start, but the player cannot currently collect the coins, so the coin count will never decrement. Let's fix that now.

Collecting coins

Thinking carefully, we know that a coin is considered collected whenever the player walks into it. We can say a coin is obtained when the player and the coin *intersect* or *collide*. To determine when a collision occurs, we must approximate the volume of both objects (coin and player) and then have some way of knowing when the two volumes overlap in space. This is achieved in Unity through **colliders**, which are special physics components attached to objects that can tell us when two GameObjects intersect. When two objects with colliders intersect, a function will be called in our script. In this section, I will walk you step by step through this process, starting with an overview of the colliders that are already present in our scene.

Introducing colliders

The **FPSController** object (first-person controller) already has a collider on it, included as part of the **Character Controller** component. This can be confirmed by selecting the **FPSController** object in the scene and examining the green wireframe cage. It is capsule-shaped and approximates the physical body of a generic person, as shown in *Figure 2.14*:

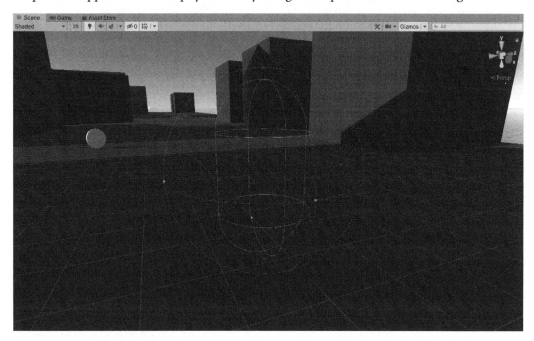

Figure 2.14 – The Character Controller component features a collider to approximate the player's body

> **Important note**
>
> The **Character Controller** inherits from **Collider** and provides specialized movement behavior on top of the functionality offered by the **Collider** component. It is more common (and better practice) to add a collider as a component and then write a script that interacts with the **Collider** component but doesn't inherit from it. We'll follow this pattern when we create the movement for the player's ship in *Chapter 3, Creating a Space Shooter*.

FPSController has a **Character Controller** component attached, which is configured by default with a radius, height, and center. These settings define the physical extents of the character in the scene. These settings can be left unchanged for our game:

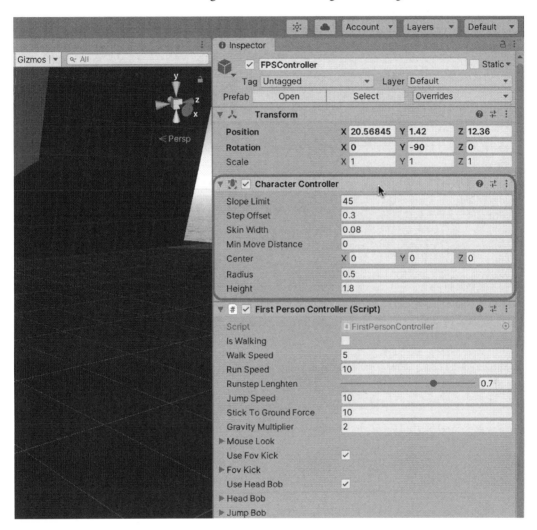

Figure 2.15 – FPSController features a Character Controller component

The **Coin** object, in contrast, features only a **Capsule Collider** component, which was automatically added when we created the cylinder primitive earlier. This collider approximates the coin's physical volume in the scene without adding any additional features specific to characters and motion. This is perfect for our needs as the coin is a static object, not a moving and dynamic object like the FPSController. The **Capsule Collider** is shown in *Figure 2.16*:

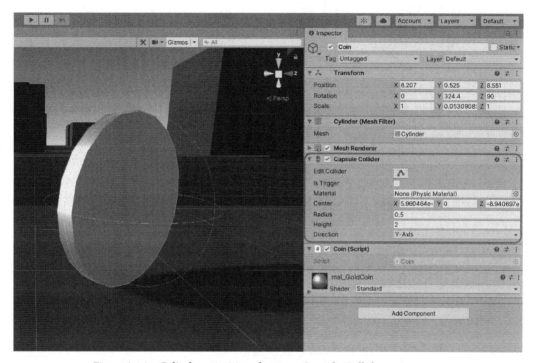

Figure 2.16 – Cylinder primitives feature a Capsule Collider component

For this project, we'll continue to use a **Capsule Collider** component for the Coin object. If you want to change the attached collider to a different shape instead, you can do this by doing the following:

1. Click on the cog icon of the component in the **Inspector**.

2. Select **Remove Component** from the context menu, as shown in *Figure 2.17*:

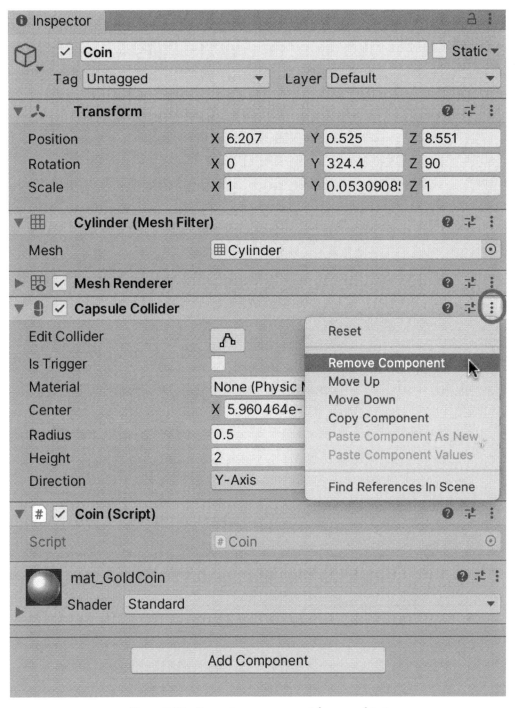

Figure 2.17 – Removing a component from an object

Add a new collider component to the selected object by choosing **Component | Physics** from the application menu and choosing a suitably shaped collider:

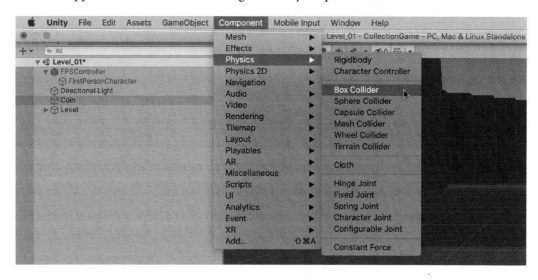

Figure 2.18 – Adding a component to the selected object

Regardless of the collider type used, there's a minor problem. If you play the game now and try to run through the coin, it'll block your path. The coin acts as a solid, physical object through which the FPSController cannot pass. However, for our purposes, this isn't how the coin should behave. It's supposed to be a collectible object—one that we can walk through. To fix this, take the following steps:

1. Select the **Coin** object.

2. Enable the **Is Trigger** checkbox on the **Capsule Collider** component in the **Inspector**:

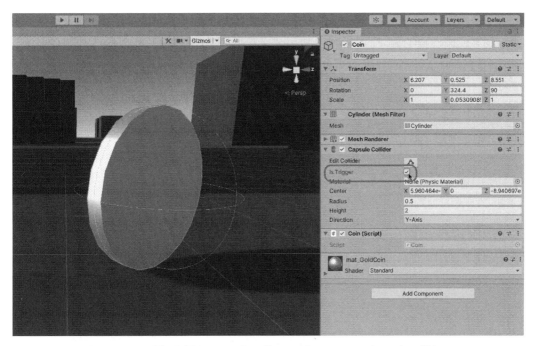

Figure 2.19 – The Is Trigger setting allows objects to pass through colliders

The **Is Trigger** setting appears for almost all collider types. It lets us detect collisions and intersections with other colliders while allowing them to pass through. With the collider attached, and properly configured, we can update the `Coin.cs` script to count the number of coins collected.

Counting coins

If you play the game now, the `FPSController` will be able to walk through the coin objects in the scene. However, the coins don't disappear when touched; they still don't get collected. To achieve this, we'll need to add additional code to the `Coin.cs` file. Specifically, we'll add an `OnTriggerEnter` function. This function is automatically called when an object, like the player, enters a collider. For now, we'll add a `Debug.Log` statement to print a debug message when the player enters the collider for test purposes:

```
public class Coin : MonoBehaviour
{

    ...


    void OnTriggerEnter(Collider Col)
    {
```

```
        Debug.Log ("Entered Collider");
    }
}
```

> **Tip**
> More information on the style function can be found in the online
> Unity documentation here: `https://docs.unity3d.com/`
> `ScriptReference/MonoBehaviour.OnTriggerEnter.html`.

Test *Code Sample 2.4* by pressing play on the toolbar. When you run into a coin, the `OnTriggerEnter` function will be executed and the message will be displayed. However, the question remains as to what object initiated this function in the first place. Something indeed collided with the coin, but what exactly? Was it the player, an enemy, a falling brick, or something else? To check this, we'll use a feature in Unity called **Tags**.

Working with Tags

The **Tag** attribute lets you mark specific objects in the scene with a label. We can then use this label in our code to identify which object is colliding with the coin. After all, it should only be the player that can collect coins. So, firstly, we'll assign the player object a **Tag** called **Player**:

1.   Select the **FPSController** object in the scene.

2.   Click on the **Tag** drop-down box in the **Inspector**.

3.   Select the **Player** Tag:

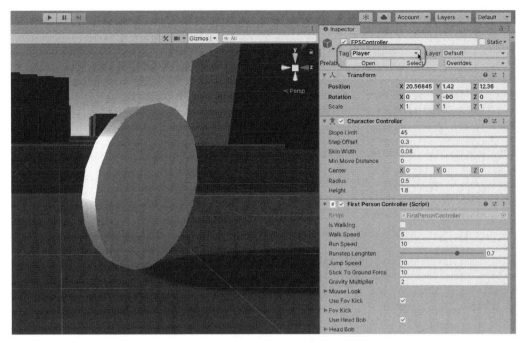

Figure 2.20 – Tagging FPSController as Player

With **FPSController** now tagged as **Player**, we can refine the Coin.cs file, as shown in *Code Sample 2.5*. This change handles coin collection, making coins disappear on touch and decreasing the coin count:

```
using UnityEngine;
using System.Collections;


public class Coin : MonoBehaviour
{
    ...
    void OnTriggerEnter(Collider Col)
    {
        //If player collected coin, then destroy object
        if(Col.CompareTag("Player"))
        {
            Destroy(gameObject);
        }
    }
}
```

The following points summarize the code sample:

- `OnTriggerEnter` is called once automatically by Unity each time an object intersects the `Coin` object.

- When `OnTriggerEnter` is called, the `Col` argument contains information about the object that entered the collider on this occasion.

- The `CompareTag` function determines whether the colliding object is the `Player` as opposed to a different object.

- The `Destroy` function is called to destroy the `Coin` object itself, represented internally by the inherited member variable, `gameObject`. This call removes the coin from the game.

- When the `Destroy` function is called, the `OnDestroy` event is invoked automatically, which decrements the coin count.

When two objects with colliders intersect, several different script events can be called. Factors that affect which (if any) event function is called include the following:

- Does the object have a Rigidbody component attached?

- Is the collider set as a trigger?

- Is the Rigidbody component **kinematic** or not?

- Is the collider 2D or 3D?

We will discuss these combinations and which events they call in more detail as we progress through the book. For now, it's enough to know that because we've haven't added a `Rigidbody` component to our coin object, and the collider is a **Trigger**, the object has a **static trigger collider**. When an object has a static trigger collider, the `OnTriggerEnter` function will be called when colliding with any object that has a 3D `Rigidbody` *and* a 3D Collider component attached, such as the **Character Controller**.

> **Tip**
>
> You can find the complete collision action matrix here: `https://docs.unity3d.com/Manual/CollidersOverview.html`.

Excellent work! You've just created your first working coin. The player can now run into the coin, collect it, and remove it from the scene. Next up: adding additional coins to the scene. We could duplicate the existing coin many times and reposition each duplicate. However, there's a better way, as we'll see shortly.

Working with prefabs

With the basic coin functionality created, it's time to add additional coins to the scene. The problem with simply duplicating a coin arises if we make a change to one of these coins and need to propagate that change to the other coins. We'd then need to delete the former duplicates and manually replace them with newer, amended versions. To avoid this tedious process, we can use **prefabs**. Prefabs let you convert an object in a scene to an asset. The asset can then be instantiated in the scene as frequently as needed, as though it were any other kind of asset. The advantage is that changes made to the prefab can be easily applied to all instances of the object in the project, even across multiple scenes.

Now we know the benefits of prefabs, let's convert the coin object to one now. To do this, select the **Coin** object in the scene and then drag and drop it in the **Project** panel:

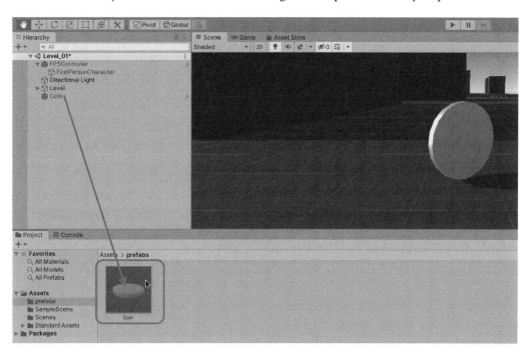

Figure 2.21 – Creating a coin prefab

A new prefab will be created, and the object in the scene will be automatically updated to be an instance of that prefab. This means that if the asset is deleted from the **Project** panel, the instance will become invalidated.

Once the prefab has been created, you can add more instances of the coin to the level by dragging and dropping the prefab from the **Project** panel to the scene. Each instance is linked to the original prefab asset, which means that all changes made to the prefab will propagate to all instances. Add as many **Coin** prefabs to the level as suitable for your coin collection game. Refer to the following figure for my arrangement:

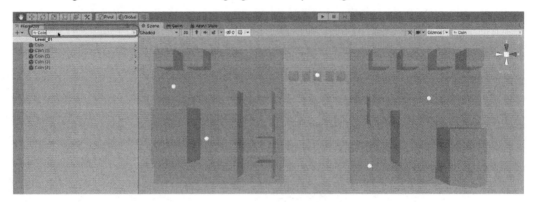

Figure 2.22 – Adding coin prefabs to the level

One question that naturally arises is how you can transform a prefab back into an independent GameObject that is no longer connected to the prefab asset. This is useful to do if you want some objects to be based on a prefab but to deviate from it slightly. To achieve this, right-click a prefab instance in the **Scene**, and then navigate to **Prefab | Unpack Completely**:

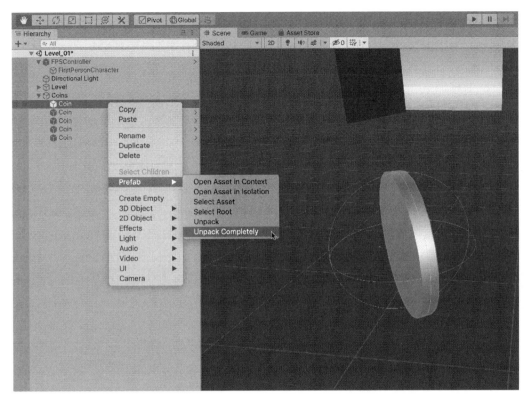

Figure 2.23 – Breaking the prefab instance

You may have noticed that you have two choices, **Unpack** or **Unpack Completely**. Both will return the Coin object to a regular GameObject; however, **Unpack Completely** will also unpack any child objects that are prefabs. As the coin has no child objects that are themselves prefabs, either of these options would be suitable for our purposes.

Conversely, if you wanted to apply changes you made to the Coin object upstream to the prefab asset, you would do the following:

1. Select the **Coin** object.

2. In the **Inspector** panel, click on the **Overrides** drop-down box. The window that appears lists all of the changes made to this instance that will be applied to the prefab.

3. Select **Apply All**:

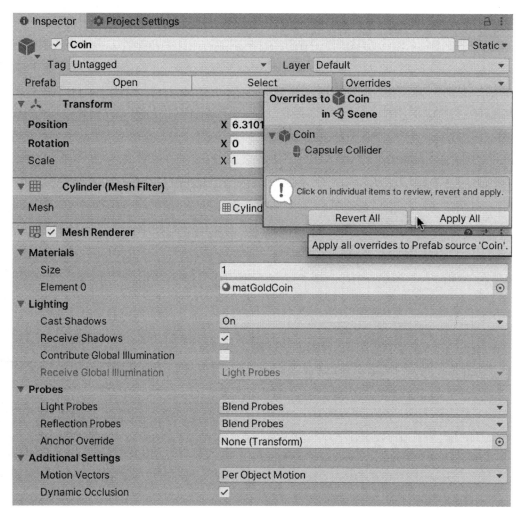

Figure 2.24 – Applying changes to the prefab

One last thing we should discuss regarding prefabs, at least for now, is **Prefab Mode**. Using this tool, you can easily edit a prefab. Enter **Prefab Mode** by clicking on the arrow next to the object's name in the **Hierarchy** panel:

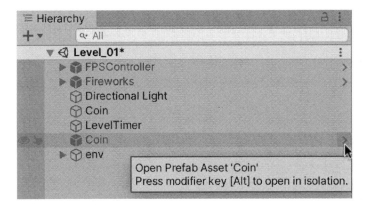

Figure 2.25 – Entering Prefab Mode

When you enter **Prefab Mode**, everything in the scene apart from the prefab will become gray—enabling you to focus on your prefab:

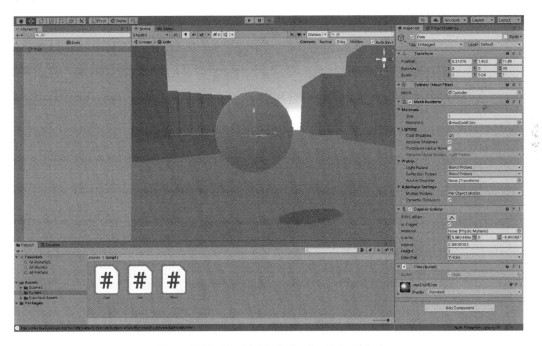

Figure 2.26 – Prefab Mode for the Coin object

> **Important note**
>
> Any changes you make to the prefab in **Prefab Mode** will be applied to all instances of the prefab.

You should now have a level complete with geometry and coin objects. Thanks to our newly added `Coin.cs` script, the coins are both countable and collectible. Even so, the level still poses little or no challenge to the player as there's nothing for the player to achieve. This is why a time limit is essential for the game: it defines a win and loss condition. We'll create a timer now.

Creating a timer

Before we create the timer script, we'll create the object to which we'll attach the script:

1. Create an empty game object by selecting **GameObject | Create Empty**.

2. Name the new object `LevelTimer`:

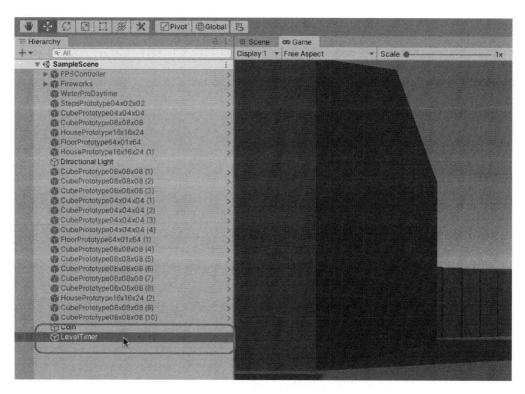

Figure 2.27 – Renaming the timer object

> **Important note**
>
> Remember that the player cannot see empty game objects because they have no Mesh Renderer component. Invisible objects are especially useful to create functionality and behaviors that don't correspond directly to physical and visible entities, such as timers, managers, and game logic controllers.

Next, create a new script file named `Timer.cs` and add it to the `LevelTimer` object in the scene. Make sure that the timer script is only added to one object, and no more than one. Otherwise, there will effectively be multiple, competing timers in the same scene. You can always search a scene to find all components of a specified type by using the **Hierarchy** panel. To do this, take the following steps:

1. Click in the **Hierarchy** search box and type `t:timer`.

2. Press *Enter* on the keyboard to confirm the search. This will display all objects with a Timer component attached in the **Hierarchy** panel. The `t` prefix in the search string indicates a search by type operation:

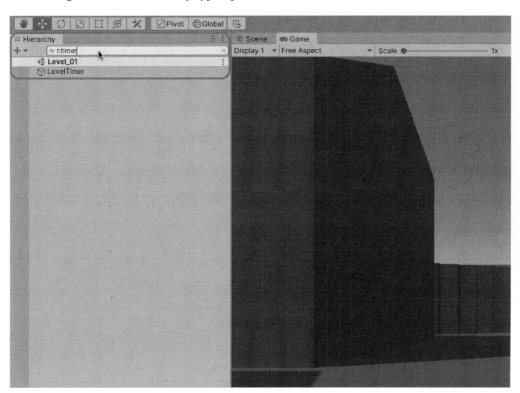

Figure 2.28 – Searching for objects with a component of a matching type

3.   You can easily cancel a search and return the **Hierarchy** panel to its original state by clicking on the small cross icon to the right-hand side of the search field, as shown in *Figure 2.28*.

4.   Now we've added the script to an object, we need to complete the script by writing the code for the timer:

```
public class Timer : MonoBehaviour
{
    //Maximum time to complete level (in seconds)
    public float MaxTime = 60f;

    [SerializeField] private float CountDown = 0;

    void Start ()
    {
        CountDown = MaxTime;
    }

    void Update ()
    {
        //Reduce time
        CountDown -= Time.deltaTime;

        //Restart level if time runs out
        if (CountDown <= 0)
        {
            //Reset coin count
            Coin.CoinCount=0;
            SceneManager.LoadScene(SceneManager.
                GetActiveScene().buildIndex);
        }
    }
}
```

The following points summarize the code sample:

- In Unity, class variables declared as `public` (such as `public float MaxTime`) are displayed as editable fields in the **Inspector** of the Unity editor. These fields enable developers to monitor and set public variables directly from the **Inspector** without the need to recompile the code for every change.
  `Private` variables, in contrast, are hidden from the **Inspector** by default. However, you can force them to be visible, if needed, using the `SerializeField` attribute. Private variables prefixed with this attribute, such as the `CountDown` variable, will be displayed in the **Inspector** just like a public variable, even though the variable's scope remains private.

- The `Update` function is a native Unity event supported by all classes derived from `MonoBehaviour`. `Update` is invoked automatically once per frame for all active GameObjects in the scene, notifying them of frame change events. `Update` is usually called many times per second; the game's **FPS** is a general indicator of how many times each second, but the actual number of calls will vary in practice. `Update` is especially useful to animate, update, and change objects over time. In the case of the `CountDown` class, it'll be used to keep track of time as it passes. More information on the `Update` function can be found here: `http://docs.unity3d.com/ScriptReference/MonoBehaviour.Update.html`.

> **Important note**
>
> In addition to the `Update` function, Unity also supports two other related functions, namely: `FixedUpdate` and `LateUpdate`. `FixedUpdate` is typically used for physics calculations, as we'll see later, and is called a fixed number of times per frame. `LateUpdate` is called once per frame for each active object, but the `LateUpdate` call will always happen after every object has received an `Update` event. There are numerous reasons why we would want to perform an action after `Update`, and a few of them will be explored later in this book.

- The static `Time.deltaTime` floating-point variable describes the amount of time (in seconds) that has passed since the previous frame ended. For example, if your game has a frame rate of 2 FPS (a very low frame rate!), then the `deltaTime` will be `0.5`. This is because, each second, there would be two frames, and thus each frame would be half a second. The `deltaTime` is useful in our game because, if added over time, it tells us how much time has elapsed or passed since the game began. For this reason, the `deltaTime` variable is used in the `Update` function to subtract the elapsed time from the countdown total. More information can be found online at `http://docs.unity3d.com/ScriptReference/Time-deltaTime.html`.

- The static `SceneManager.LoadScene` function can be called anywhere to change the active scene at runtime. It causes Unity to terminate the active scene, destroying all its contents, and load a new scene. It can also be used to restart the active scene by retrieving the current scene's `buildIndex` using `SceneManager.GetActiveScene().buildIndex`. `SceneManager.LoadScene` is most appropriate for games with clearly defined levels that have distinct beginnings and endings.

Once you have created the timer script, select the `LevelTimer` object in the scene, and, using the **Inspector**, set the maximum time (in seconds) that the player is allowed to complete the level, as shown in *Figure 2.29*. I've set the total time to 60 seconds. If the player takes longer than this to collect all of the coins, the level is reloaded.

Figure 2.29 – Setting the level's total time

Great work! You now have a completed level with a countdown that works. You can collect coins, and the timer can expire. Overall, the game is taking shape, but there is still no win condition. We'll address this now.

Creating a win condition

The coin collection game is nearly finished. Coins can be collected, and a timer expires, but the win condition itself is not yet handled. When all coins are collected before the time expires, nothing happens to show the player that they've won; the countdown still proceeds and the level even restarts as though the win condition hadn't been satisfied at all. When the win scenario happens, we should delete the timer object to prevent further countdown and show visual feedback to signify that the level has been completed. For the visual feedback, we'll add some fireworks!

Adding fireworks

You can add these from the Unity Particle System packages:

1. Navigate to the **Standard Assets | ParticleSystems | Prefabs** folder.
2. Drag and drop the **Fireworks** particle system in the **Scene**.

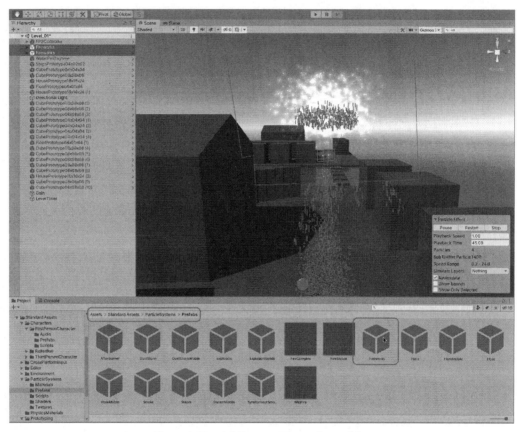

Figure 2.30 – Adding two Fireworks prefabs

As you can see in *Figure 2.30*, I've added a couple of **Fireworks** prefabs to the scene. By default, all **Fireworks** particle systems will play when the level begins. You can test this by pressing play on the toolbar. We only want the fireworks to play when the win condition has been satisfied. To disable playback on level startup, do the following:

1. Select the **Particle System** object in the **Scene**.

2. Disable the **Play On Awake** checkbox on the **Particle System** component in the **Inspector**:

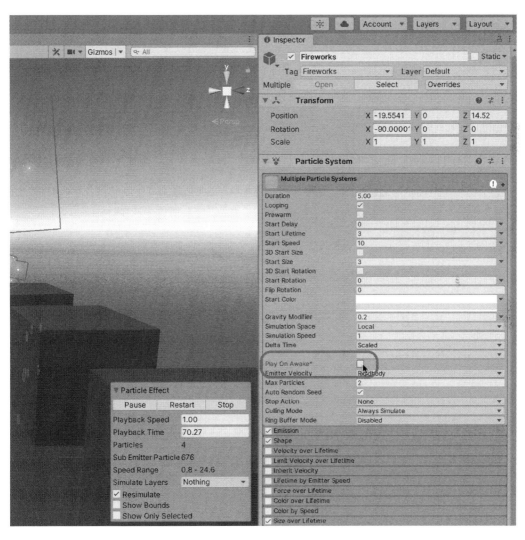

Figure 2.31 – Disabling Play On Awake

Disabling **Play On Awake** prevents particle systems from playing automatically at level startup. This is fine, but if they are ever to play at all, something must manually start them at the right time. We can achieve this through code. However, we'll first mark all firework objects with an appropriate Tag. The reason for this is that, in code, we'll want to search for all firework objects in the scene and trigger them to play when needed. To isolate the firework objects from all other objects, we'll use Tags. So, let's create a new **Fireworks** Tag and assign it to the **Fireworks** objects in the Scene:

1.   Select the **Fireworks** object in the **Hierarchy** panel.

2.   In the **Inspector**, at the top, select the **Tag** drop-down menu.

3.   Select **Add Tag…**:

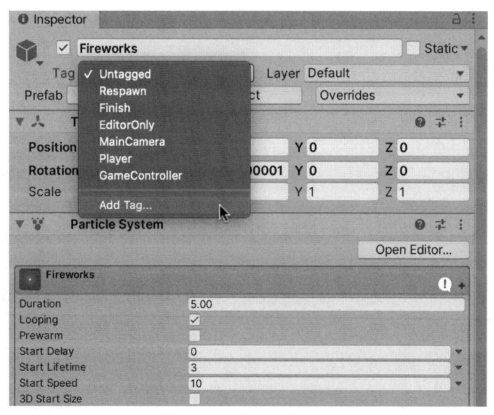

Figure 2.32 – Opening the Tags & Layers settings

4.   Click the plus sign under the **Tags** heading.

5.   Type the name `Fireworks` and click **Save**:

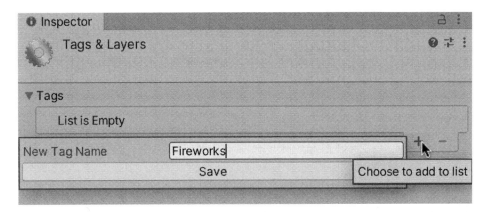

Figure 2.33 – Adding a new Tag

With the Tag created, we can assign it to the **Fireworks** object

6.   Once again, select the **Fireworks** object in the **Hierarchy**.

7.   You'll see our custom Tag in the **Tag** menu; select it:

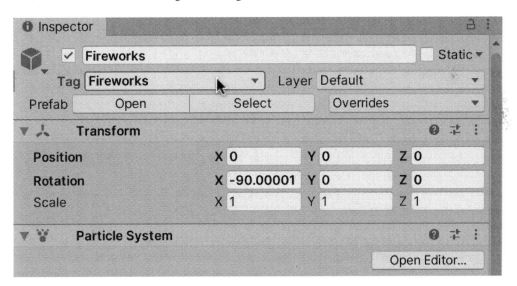

Figure 2.34 – Assigning the custom Tag

The firework object now has a custom Tag that we can use in our code to find the object in the scene, which is exactly what we'll do next to play the fireworks at the right moment.

Lighting the fireworks

With the firework objects now tagged, we can refine the Coin.cs script class to play the
fireworks particle system when the player has collected all of the coins:

```
public class Coin : MonoBehaviour
{
    ...
    void OnDestroy()
    {
        --Coin.CoinCount;

        if(Coin.CoinCount <= 0)
        {
            GameObject Timer = GameObject.Find("LevelTimer");
            Destroy(Timer);
            GameObject[] FireworkSystems =
                GameObject.FindGameObjectsWithTag("Fireworks");
            if (FireworkSystems.Length <= 0) { return; }
            foreach(GameObject GO in FireworkSystems)
            {
                GO.GetComponent<ParticleSystem>().Play();
            }
        }
    }
}
```

Let's summarize the preceding code:

- The OnDestroy function is called automatically whenever the GameObject is
  destroyed. In our game, this occurs when a coin is collected. In the function, an if
  statement is used to determine when all coins are collected (the win scenario).

- When a win scenario happens, the GameObject.Find function is called to
  search the complete scene hierarchy for any active object named LevelTimer. If
  found, the object is deleted. This prevents the countdown from progressing. If the
  scene contains multiple objects with a matching name, then only the first object is
  returned. This is one reason why the scene should have one, and only one, timer.

> **Tip**
>
> Try to avoid using `GameObject.Find` wherever possible as it's relatively slow. Instead, use `FindGameObjectsWithTag`. `GameObject.Find` has been used here only to demonstrate its existence and purpose. Sometimes, you'll need to use it to find a single, miscellaneous object that has no specific Tag.

- In addition to deleting the `LevelTimer` object, the `OnDestroy` function finds all fireworks in the scene, gets their `ParticleSystem` component, and plays the particle animation. It finds all objects using the `GameObject.FindGameObjectsWithTag` function, which returns an array of objects with the **Fireworks** Tag. The `GetComponent` function is used to retrieve a reference to any specified component, giving you direct access to its public properties and methods. The `OnDestroy` function in the preceding code uses `GetComponent` to retrieve a reference to the `ParticleSystem` component attached to the object. `GetComponent` is an important function, which you'll often use as a Unity developer. More information on `GetComponent` can be found online at `https://docs.unity3d.com/ScriptReference/GameObject.GetComponent.html`.

> **Important note**
>
> As mentioned, each GameObject in Unity is really made from a collection of attached and related components. An object is the sum of its components. For example, a standard cube (created using **GameObject | 3D Object | Cube**) is made from a **Transform** component, a **Mesh Filter** component, a **Mesh Renderer** component, and a **Box Collider** component. These components together make the cube what it is and behave how it does.

You've now completed your first game in Unity! It's time to take it for a test run and then finally to compile an executable that can be run from outside of Unity.

Playtesting

The basics of testing in Unity are very straightforward; you press play on the toolbar and play your game to see that it works as intended from the perspective of a gamer. However, there are two tools worth mentioning that will help with this process:

- Inspector debugging
- The game stats panel

Let's look at each of these in more detail.

Enabling Inspector debugging

In addition to playing, you can also enable debugging mode from the **Inspector** to keep a watchful eye on all public and private variables during runtime, making sure that no variable is assigned an unexpected value. To activate the **Debug** mode:

1. Click on the menu icon in the top-right corner of the **Inspector**.

2. From the context menu that appears, select the **Debug** option:

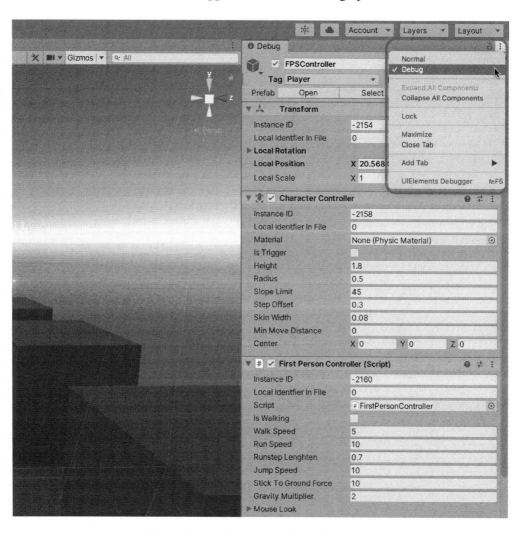

Figure 2.35 – Activating Debug mode from the object Inspector

After activating the **Debug** mode, the appearance of some variables and components in the **Inspector** may change. Typically, you'll get a more detailed and accurate view of your variables, and you'll also be able to see most private variables. See *Figure 2.36* for the **Transform** component in **Debug** mode:

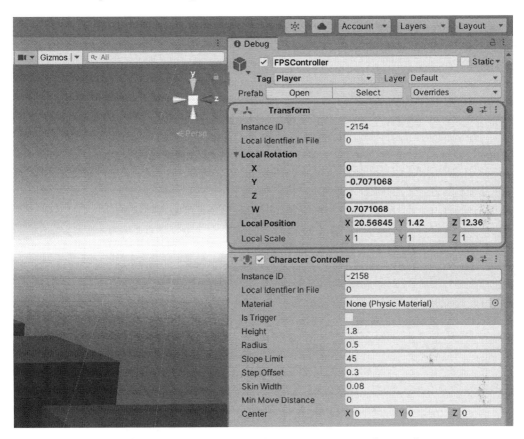

Figure 2.36 – Viewing the Transform component in Debug mode

Debugging individual components can be very useful when you are having problems with specific areas of your game; for example, when your player isn't moving as intended, you can see the private variables of your **Character Controller** script. However, to gain a broader understanding of how your game is performing, you will want to use the **Stats** panel.

Monitoring game stats

Another useful debugging tool at runtime is the **Stats** panel. This can be accessed from the **Game** tab by clicking on the **Stats** button on the toolbar, as shown in *Figure 2.37*:

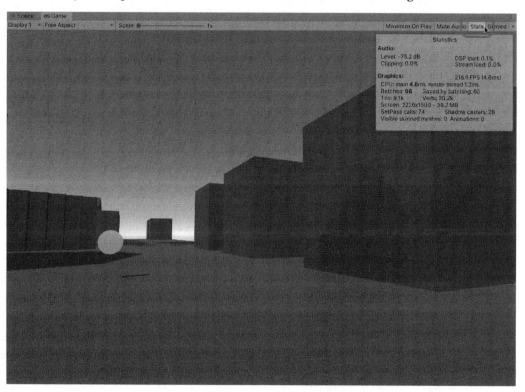

Figure 2.37 – Accessing the Stats panel from the Game tab

The **Stats** panel is only useful during the Play mode. In this mode, it details critical performance statistics for your game, such as **Frame Rate per Second** (**FPS**) and memory usage. With these stats, you can diagnose or determine whether any problems may be affecting your game. The FPS represents the total number of frames (**ticks** or **cycles**) per second that your game can sustain on average. There is no right, wrong, or magical FPS, but higher values are better than lower ones. Higher values represent better performance because it means that your game can sustain more cycles in 1 second. If your FPS falls below 20 or 15, your game will likely appear choppy or laggy. Many variables can affect FPS, some internal, and some external to your game. Internal factors include the following:

- The number of lights in a scene

- The vertex density of meshes

- The number of instructions, and the complexity of the code

Some external factors include the following:

- The quality of your computer's hardware

- The number of other applications and processes running at the same time

- The amount of hard drive space

In short, if your FPS is low, then it indicates a problem that needs attention. The solution to that problem varies depending on the context, and you'll need to use judgment; for example, are your meshes too complex? Do they have too many vertices? Are your textures too large? Are there too many sounds playing?

> **Important note**
> The completed game source code can be found in the book companion files in the `Chapter02/End` folder.

Once you're happy with how your game is performing, it's time to build the game so it can be run without Unity.

Building the game

In this section, I will take you through how to compile and package the game into a standalone and self-executing form that anyone can run and play without requiring the Unity editor. Typically, when developing games, you'll decide your target platform (such as Windows, iOS, Android, and others) during the design phase and not at the end of development. It's often said that Unity is a develop once, deploy everywhere tool. This slogan can conjure up the unfortunate image that, after a game is made, it'll work just as effortlessly on every platform supported by Unity as it does on the desktop.

Unfortunately, things are not so simple; games that work well on desktop systems don't necessarily perform equally well on mobiles and vice versa. This is primarily due to the significant differences in target hardware and industry standards that hold between them. Due to these differences, we'll focus our attention here on the Windows and Mac desktop platforms, ignoring mobiles and consoles and other platforms (for now). To create a build for a desktop platform, take the following steps:

1. Select **File | Build Settings...** from the **Application** menu:

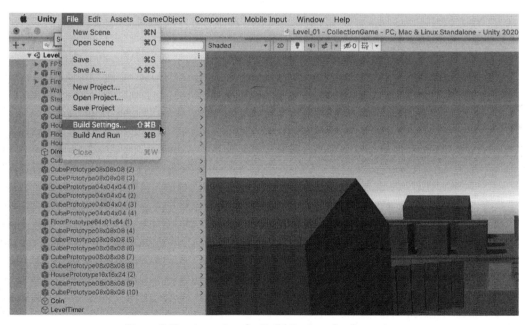

Figure 2.38 – Accessing the Build Settings for the project

2. The **Build Settings** dialog is then displayed. The **Scenes In Build** section contains a list of all scenes to be included in the build, regardless of whether the gamer will visit them in the game. In short, if you want a scene in your game, then it needs to be on this list. If the list is empty, make sure that the game scene is open and then click **Add Open Scenes**:

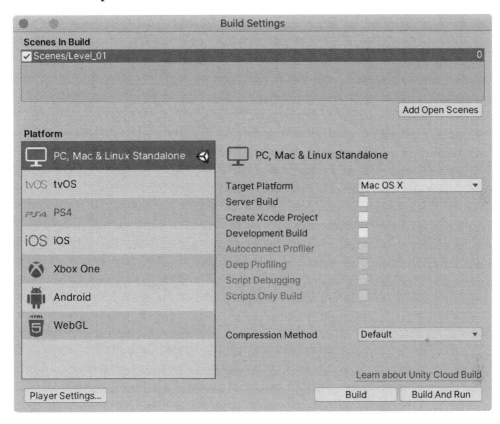

Figure 2.39 – Adding a level to the Build Settings dialog

> **Tip**
> You can also add scenes to the list by dragging and dropping the scene asset from the **Project** panel to the **Scenes In Build** list.

Unity automatically assigns scenes a number, depending on their order in the list. 0 represents the first item, 1 the next item, and so on. The first scene (scene 0) will always be the starting scene. When the build runs, Unity automatically begins execution from scene 0. For this reason, scene 0 will typically be your splash or intro scene.

3. Next, be sure to select your target platform from the **Platform** list on the bottom left-hand side of the **Build Settings** dialog. For desktop platforms, choose **PC, Mac & Linux Standalone**, which should be selected by default. Then, from the options, set the **Target Platform** drop-down list to either **Windows, Linux,** or **Mac OS X**, depending on your system:

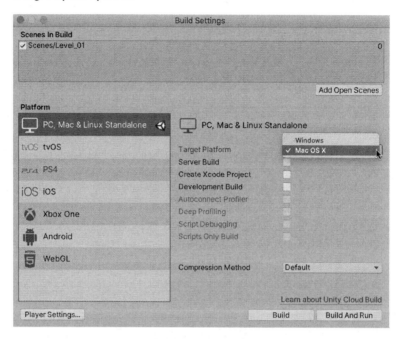

Figure 2.40 – Choosing a target build platform

> **Important note**
>
> If you've previously been testing your game for multiple platforms or trying out other platforms such as Android and iOS, the **Build** button (shown in *Figure 2.40*) may instead say **Switch Platform** when you select the **Standalone** option. If it does, click on the **Switch Platform** button to confirm to Unity that you intend to build for that platform. On clicking this, Unity may spend a few minutes configuring your assets for the selected platform.

4. Before building for the first time, you'll probably want to view the **Player Settings…** options to fine-tune important build parameters, such as game resolution, quality settings, executable icon, and information, among other settings. To access the player settings, click on the **Player Settings…** button from the **Build Settings** dialog or select **Edit | Project Settings** in the application menu and then click on **Player** in the new panel that opens.

5. From the **Player** settings options, set the **Company Name** and **Product Name** as this information is baked and stored within the built executable. You can also specify an icon image for the executable, as well as a default mouse cursor if one is required. For the collection game, however, these latter two settings will be left empty:

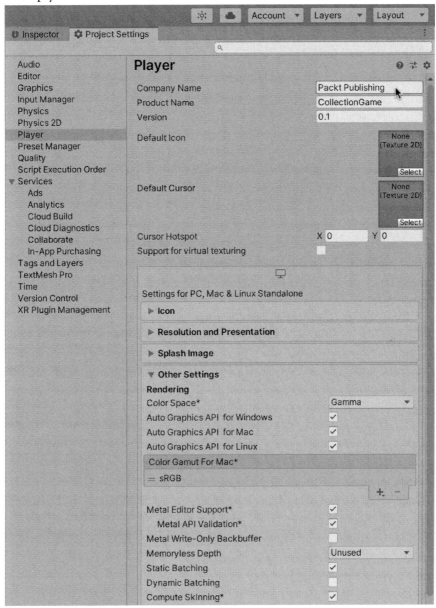

Figure 2.41: Setting Company Name and Product Name

6. The **Resolution and Presentation** tab is especially important as it specifies the game screen size and resolution. From this tab, ensure that **Fullscreen Mode** is set to **Full screen Window**, so that the game will use the total size of the system's screen as opposed to a smaller, movable window:

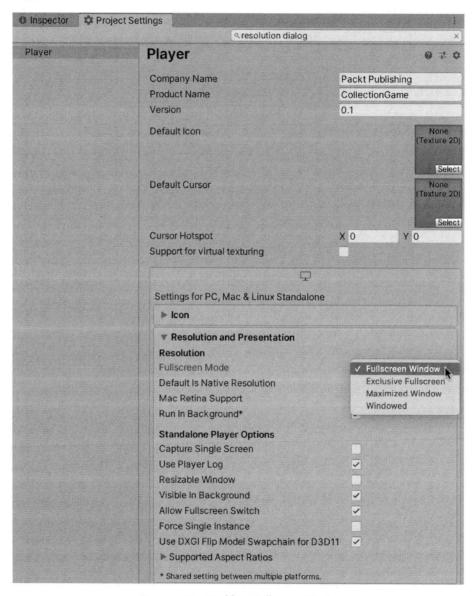

Figure 2.42 – Enabling Fullscreen Mode

7. Now you're ready to compile your first build! Click on the **Build** button from the **Build Settings** dialog or choose **File | Build And Run** from the application menu:

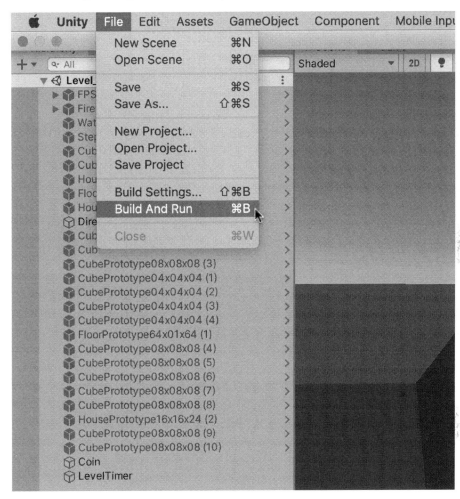

Figure 2.43 – Building and running a game

8. When you do this, Unity presents you with a **Save** dialog, asking you to specify a target location on your computer where the build should be made. Select a location and choose **Save**, and the build process will be completed.

Occasionally, this process can generate errors, which are printed in red in the **Console** window. This can happen, for example, when you save to a read-only drive, have insufficient hard drive space, or don't have the necessary administrative privileges on your computer. However, generally, the build process succeeds if your game runs properly in the editor.

After the build is complete, Unity generates new files at your destination location. On macOS, it generates an **app file** that contains all the necessary data to run the game. On Windows, it will create a folder containing the **executable** and several other files, as shown in *Figure 2.44*:

Figure 2.44 – Unity builds several files

It's worth quickly running through what each file and folder contains:

- The `CollectionGame_Data` folder contains all the data necessary to run the project.

- `CollectionGame.exe` is the executable, the entry point into our game. Run this to play the game.

- `MonoBleedingEdge` contains the C# and `MonoDevelop` libraries required by our game.

- `UnityCrashHandler64.exe` has the same lifetime as your game. It is automatically started and closed with the game and handles any crashes that occur.

- `UnityPlayer.dll` contains the native Unity engine code required by our game.

The files are essential and interdependent. If you want to distribute your game and have other people play it without needing to install Unity, you'll need to send users both the executable file and associated data folders and all their contents.

By running `CollectionGame.exe` on Windows or `CollectionGame.app` on macOS, the game will start:

Figure 2.45 – Running the coin collection game in Fullscreen mode

> **Tip**
> As there's no quit button or main menu option, to quit the game press *Alt + F4* (Windows), *cmd + Q* (macOS), or *Ctrl + Q* (Linux).

Congratulations! Your game is now completed and built, and you can send it to your friends and family for playtesting.

Summary

Excellent work! On reaching this point, you've completed the coin collection game, as well as your first game in Unity. On achieving this, you've seen a wide range of Unity features. While there's a lot more to learn about scripting in Unity (and we'll cover more throughout this book), the information provided in this chapter provides a solid foundation for any future projects.

Taking advantage of prefabs will save you time, reduce the need to duplicate work, and makes spawning custom objects easy. You can even share prefabs between projects as packages or upload them for sale to the Unity Asset Store to kickstart your career as a Unity developer!

You now have a complete overview of a project's lifecycle from initial project creation to compiling the project to be distributed. This process will be the same for all new projects, whether personal or professional. Of course, there's a lot more to be said and explored for all these areas, but we've pulled them together to make a playable game that can be distributed. In the next chapter, we'll start a new 2D project, and in doing so, examine entirely new features of Unity. We'll look at how to write scripts for character movement and enemy AI, as well as discussing issues specific to 2D games.

Test your knowledge

Q1. You can easily find `GameObject` in code using…

    A. Layers

    B. Tags

    C. Components

    D. Integers

Q2. You can search the hierarchy for objects that contain specific component types by using a prefix of...

    A. C

    B. T

    C. W

    D. D

Q3. Static variables are always…

    A. Shared across all instances of a class

    B. Public

    C. Reset on every new frame

    D. The same

Q4. The main color for a Material is defined by the...

    A. Normal channel

    B. Detail channel

    C. Albedo channel

    D. Specular channel

Q5. The main scripting language for Unity is…

    A. C#

    B. JavaScript

    C. UnityScript

    D. C++

Further reading

You can check out these links for more information:

- https://unity3d.com/learn/tutorials/s/scripting
- https://www.packtpub.com/game-development/unity-c-scripting-complete-c-for-unity-game-development-video
- *Mastering Unity Scripting – Alan Thorn*
- https://www.packtpub.com/game-development/mastering-unity-5x-scripting
- http://docs.unity3d.com/ScriptReference/MonoBehaviour.FixedUpdate.html
- http://docs.unity3d.com/ScriptReference/MonoBehaviour.LateUpdate.html
- https://docs.unity3d.com/Manual/CollidersOverview.html

3
Creating a Space Shooter

This chapter enters new territory as we begin development on our second game, a twin-stick space shooter. The twin-stick genre refers to any game in which the player input for motion spans two dimensions or axes, typically one axis for movement and one for rotation. Example twin-stick games include *Zombies Ate My Neighbors* and *Geometry Wars*. Our game will rely heavily on coding in C# to demonstrate just how much can be achieved with Unity procedurally (that is, via script), without using the editor and level-building tools. We'll still use the editor tools to some extent but won't rely on it as heavily as we did in the previous chapters.

Try to see the game created here and its related work in abstract terms, that is, as general tools and concepts with multiple applications. For your own projects, you may not want to make a twin-stick shooter, and that's fine. However, it's essential to see the ideas and tools used here as transferrable, as the kind of things you can creatively use for your games.

In this chapter, we'll learn how to create reusable components that will reduce the amount of work you need to do in the future. By configuring the camera, you'll also learn the differences between a 2D and 3D camera. And we will also learn how to generate objects at **runtime**, which will enable you to spawn any object you want in your own projects.

This chapter covers the following important topics:

- Creating reusable components
- Player controllers and shooting mechanics
- Basic enemy movement and AI
- Configuring a 2D camera
- Selecting and customizing particle systems
- Spawning enemies during gameplay

Now let's roll up our sleeves, if we have any, and get stuck into making a twin-stick shooter.

Technical requirements

This chapter assumes that you have not only completed the game project from the previous two chapters, but also have a good, basic knowledge of C# scripting generally, though not necessarily in Unity.

The completed `TwinStickShooter` project can be found in the book companion files in the `Chapter03/End` folder. Most assets for this game (including sound and textures) were sourced from the freely accessible site, `OpenGameArt.org`. Here, you can find many game assets available through the public domain or creative common licenses.

Looking ahead – the completed project

Before we start work on the twin-stick shooter game, let's see what the completed project looks like and how it works. As shown in *Figure 3.1*, the game will contain one scene where the player controls a spaceship that can shoot oncoming enemies:

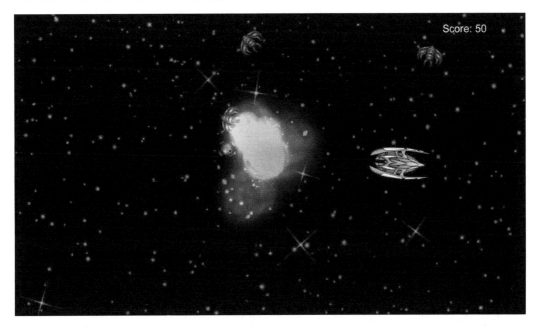

Figure 3.1 – The completed twin–stick shooter game

The directional keyboard arrows, and *WASD*, move the spaceship around the level, and it will always turn to face the mouse pointer. Clicking the left mouse button will fire ammo.

Now that we have an idea of what we're aiming for, we can start the project.

Starting the project

To get started, perform the following steps:

1. Create a new Unity 3D project without any packages or specific assets. Details about creating new projects can be found in *Chapter 1, Exploring the Fundamentals of Unity*.

> **Important note**
>
> The project we create in this chapter will technically be 2D; however, in an attempt to not introduce too many new topics at once, we will start with a 3D project, and configure it to our needs. We'll see that many of the items we relied on to create the collection game can just as easily be used in a 2D game.

2. Create folders to structure and organize the project assets. This is very important to keep track of your files as you work. Create folders for `Textures`, `Scenes`, `Materials`, `Audio`, `Prefabs`, and `Scripts`:

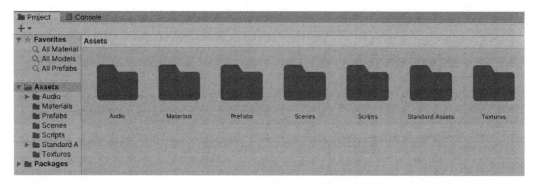

Figure 3.2 – Creating folders for structure and organization

Next, our game will depend on some graphical and audio assets. These are included in the book companion files in the `Chapter03/End/Assets` folder, but can also be downloaded online from `OpenGameArt.org`. Once they are downloaded, we can import them into the project.

Importing assets

Most projects you undertake in Unity will require external resources, and this project is no different. You will often need to import and configure sound, images, 3D models, and even other people's code, and this process will become second nature to you as you create the projects in the book.

> **Important note**
> As a reminder, when we import assets, we are making a copy of the original. During the import process, Unity will create a corresponding `meta` file for each asset. Please do not remove or edit this file yourself as it includes necessary import settings. For information on the import process, see *Chapter 1, Exploring the Fundamentals of Unity*, and Unity's online documentation: `https://docs.unity3d.com/Manual/ImportingAssets.html`.

In this section, we will go through how to import and configure textures and audio.

Importing textures

Let's start with textures for the player spaceship, enemy spaceships, and star-field background. Drag and drop textures from Windows Explorer or Finder to the Unity **Project** panel in the `Textures` folder. Unity imports and configures the textures automatically:

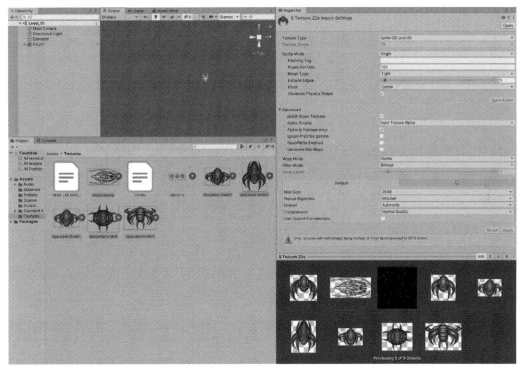

Figure 3.3 – Importing texture assets for the spaceship, enemies, star-field background, and ammo

> **Tip**
>
> The use of the provided assets is optional. You can create your own if you prefer. Just drag and drop your textures in place of the included assets, and you can still follow along with the tutorial.

By default, Unity imports image files as regular textures for use on 3D objects, and it assumes that their pixel dimensions are a power-2 size (4, 8, 16, 32, 64, 128, 256, and so on). If the size is not one of these, then Unity will up-scale or down-scale the texture to the nearest valid size. This is not appropriate behavior, however, for a 2D top-down space shooter game in which imported textures should appear at their native (imported) size without any scaling or automatic adjustment. To fix this, perform the following steps:

1. Select all the imported textures.

2. In **Inspector**, change the **Texture Type** from **Default** to **Sprite (2D and UI)**.

3. Click on **Apply** to update the settings, and the textures will retain their imported dimensions.

4. Remove the checkmark from the **Generate Mip Maps** box if it is enabled:

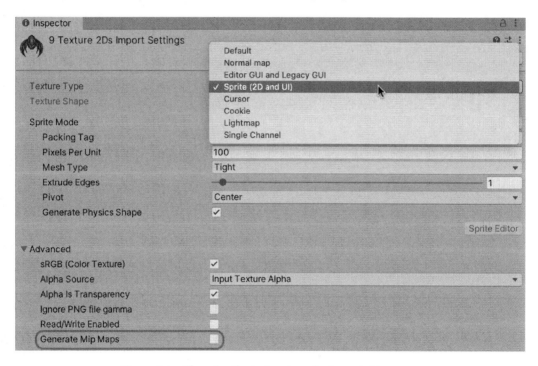

Figure 3.4 – Changing the texture type for imported textures

Disabling generating **Mip Maps** will prevent Unity from automatically downgrading the quality of textures based on their distance from the camera in the scene. This ensures that your textures retain their highest quality. More information on 2D texture settings and Mip Maps can be found at the online Unity documentation: `http://docs.unity3d.com/Manual/class-TextureImporter.html`.

> **Important note**
>
> Later in the chapter, we will drag and drop the textures to the scene, which will add them as sprite objects. You must drag and drop them from the **Project** panel to the **Hierarchy** panel, not to the scene view. When you do this, the texture will be added as a sprite object in the scene. We'll make frequent use of this feature as we create spaceship objects.

With the textures successfully imported, we can move on to importing the audio files.

Importing audio

Music and audio effects are important. They add an extra level of immersion and, on occasion, are a core part of the gameplay experience (think Cadence of Hyrule on the Nintendo Switch). With that in mind, it's important that you familiarize yourself with the process of importing and configuring audio files.

> **Important note**
>
> The assets used in this section can be found in the `Chapter03/End/Assets/Audio` folder and were downloaded from `OpenGameArt.org`.

To import the audio, drag and drop the files from the folder to the **Project** panel. Unity will import and configure the assets. You test the audio from within the Unity Editor by pressing Play on the preview toolbar from the **Inspector**, as shown in *Figure 3.5*:

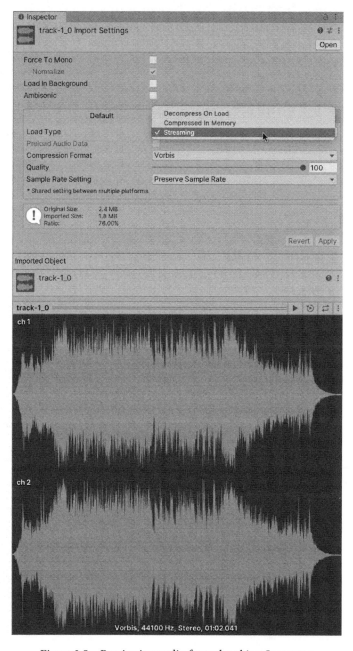

Figure 3.5 – Previewing audio from the object Inspector

As with texture files, Unity imports audio files using a set of default parameters. These parameters are typically suitable for short sound effects such as footsteps, gunshots, and explosions. However, for longer tracks such as music, they can be problematic, causing long level-loading times. To fix this, select the music track in the **Project** panel and, from the **Load Type** drop-down box, select the **Streaming** option, as shown in *Figure 3.5*. This option ensures that the music track is streamed as opposed to loaded wholly in memory at level startup.

> **Important note**
>
> In future projects, we won't go step by step through importing assets. However, you can always refer back to this section, and any differences will be noted.

And that's it! Both the textures and audio files required for this project are ready to use in our game. Now it is time to start creating our own assets, beginning with the player object.

Creating the player object

We've now imported most assets for the twin-stick shooter, and we're ready to create a player spaceship object. This will be the object that the player will control and move around. Creating this might seem a straightforward matter of simply dragging and dropping the relevant player sprite from the Project panel to the scene, but things are not so simple. The player object is a complex object with many different behaviors, as we'll see shortly. For this reason, more care needs to be taken when creating the player. Let's start with the **GameObject**, which will contain our custom **components**.

Creating the GameObject

The GameObject will hold all of the data and components required for our player, including position and collision data, as well as custom functionality we add through writing scripts. To create the player object, perform the following steps:

1. Create an empty GameObject in the scene by navigating to **GameObject | Create Empty** from the application menu.

2. Name the object `Player`.

3. The newly created object may or may not be centered at the world origin of (0, 0, 0), and its rotation properties may not be consistently 0 across X, Y, and Z. To ensure a zeroed transform, you could manually set the values to 0 by entering them directly in the **Transform** component for the object in the Inspector. However, to set them all to 0 automatically, click on the icon with the three dots in the top-left corner of the **Transform** component and select **Reset** from the context menu:

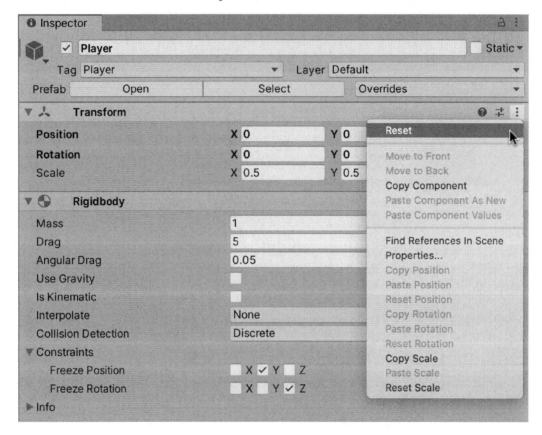

Figure 3.6 – Resetting the Transform component

4. Drag and drop the Player dropship sprite (in the Textures folder) from the **Project** panel to the newly created Player object in the **Hierarchy** panel. Dragging the texture to the player object will make it a **child** of the player object, which becomes the **parent**.

Child/parent hierarchy

In Unity, you'll often add objects as children of other objects. A child object is positioned, scaled, and rotated relative to their parent. But a parent's transform is not affected by their children, so you can move a child without moving a parent, but if you move a parent object, the child will also move.

Rotate this child object ship by 90 degrees on the X-axis, and 90 degrees on the Z-axis. This rotation orientates the sprite in the direction of its parent's **forward vector**. Make sure you have the child object selected and not the parent `Player` object:

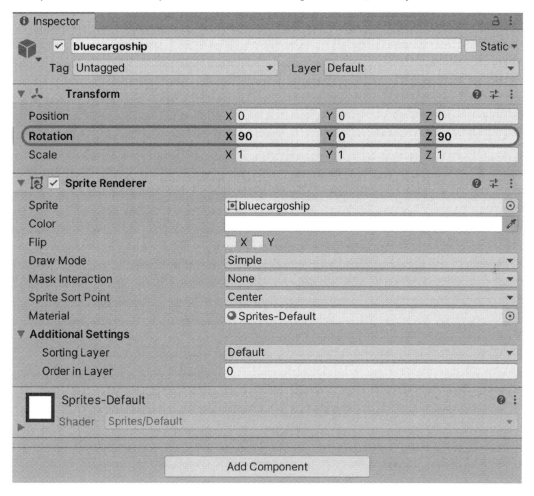

Figure 3.7 – Aligning the player ship

You can confirm that the ship sprite has been aligned correctly in relation to its parent by selecting the Player object and viewing the blue forward vector arrow. The front of the ship sprite and the blue forward vector should be pointing in the same direction. If they're not, then continue to rotate the sprite by 90 degrees until they're in alignment. This will be important later when coding player movement to make the ship travel in the direction it's looking:

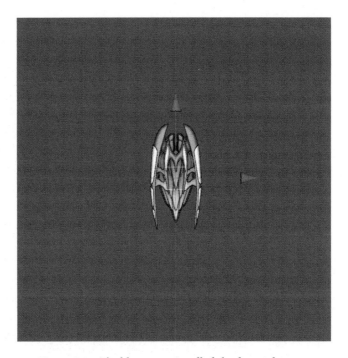

Figure 3.8 – The blue arrow is called the forward vector

With the GameObject created, visible to the player, and rotated to suit our needs, it's time to add functionality by adding components.

Adding components

We'll prepare the Player object so that it is solid and affected by physical forces. It must collide with other solid objects and take damage from enemy ammo when hit. To facilitate this, two additional components should be added to the Player object, specifically a **Rigidbody** and **Collider**:

1. Select the Player object (not the **Sprite** object).

2. Select **Component | Physics | Rigidbody** from the application menu to add a Rigidbody.

3. Select **Component | Physics | Capsule Collider** from the application menu to add a collider.

> **2D components**
>
> You may have noticed that there are 2D counterparts to the components we're adding here specifically, **Rigidbody2D** and **Capsule Collider 2D**. We'll cover them in *Chapter 5, Creating a 2D Adventure Game*.

The **Collider** component approximates the volume of the object, and the **Rigibody** component uses the collider to determine how physical forces should be applied. Let's adjust the capsule collider a little because the default settings typically do not match up with the **Player** sprite as intended. Adjust the **Direction**, **Radius**, and **Height** values until the capsule encompasses the Player sprite and represents the volume of the player:

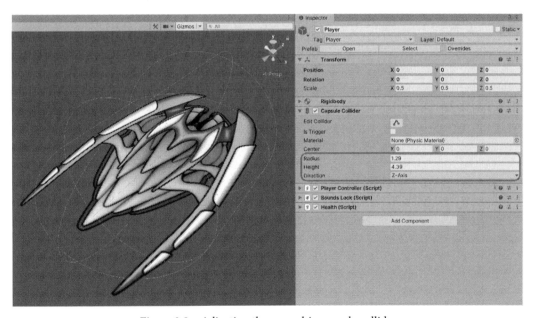

Figure 3.9 – Adjusting the spaceship capsule collider

By default, the **Rigidbody** component is configured to approximate objects that are affected by gravity, which is not appropriate for a spaceship that flies around. To fix this, Rigidbody should be adjusted as follows:

1. Disable the **Use Gravity** checkbox to prevent the object from falling to the ground.

2.   Enable the **Freeze Position Y** checkbox and the **Freeze Rotation Z** checkbox to prevent the spaceship moving and rotating around axes that are undesirable in a 2D top-down game, as shown in *Figure 3.10*:

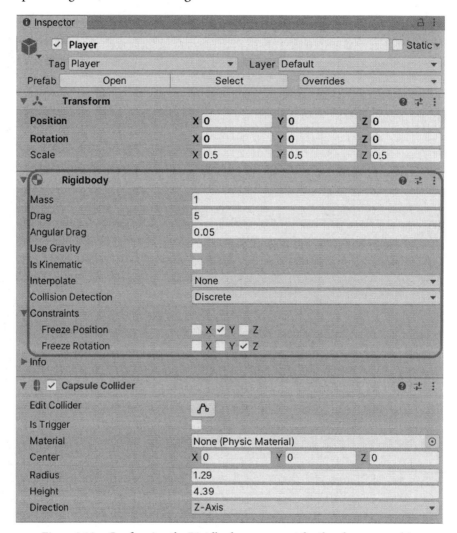

Figure 3.10 – Configuring the Rigidbody component for the player spaceship

On previewing the game thus far, the spaceship probably looks too large. We can fix this quickly by changing the scale of the Player object. I've used a value of 0.5 for the X, Y, and Z axes, as shown in *Figure 3.10*.

Excellent work! We've now configured the player spaceship object successfully. Of course, it still doesn't move or do anything specific in the game because we haven't added any code yet. That's something we'll turn to next by adding logic to react to player input.

Controlling the player

The `Player` object is now created in the scene, configured with both **Rigidbody** and **Collider** components. However, this object doesn't respond to player controls. In a twin-stick shooter, the player provides input on two axes and can typically shoot a weapon. The control scheme for our game is outlined here:

- The keyboard *WASD* buttons guide player movements up, down, left, and right.
- The mouse controls the direction in which the player is looking and aiming.
- The left mouse button fires a weapon.

To implement this, we'll need to create a `PlayerController` script file. Right-click on the **Scripts** folder of the **Project** panel and create a new C# script file named `PlayerController.cs`:

```
public class PlayerController : MonoBehaviour
{
    public bool MouseLook = true;
    public string HorzAxis = "Horizontal";
    public string VertAxis = "Vertical";
    public string FireAxis = "Fire1";
    public float MaxSpeed = 5f;

    private Rigidbody ThisBody = null;

    void Awake ()
    {
        ThisBody = GetComponent<Rigidbody>();
    }
}
```

The following points summarize the code sample:

- The `PlayerController` class should be attached to the `Player` object in the scene. It accepts input from the player and will control the movement of the spaceship.

- The `Awake` function is called once when the object is created and is typically used to retrieve references to objects required by the component. You cannot rely on the order in which objects receive an `Awake` call. During this function, the `Rigidbody` component (used for controlling player movement) is retrieved. The `Transform` component can also be used to control player movement through the `Position` property, but this ignores collisions and solid objects.

Now that we're retrieving the components we require, we can make use of them in the `FixedUpdate` function:

```
public class PlayerController : MonoBehaviour
{
...
    void FixedUpdate ()
    {
        float Horz = Input.GetAxis(HorzAxis);
        float Vert = Input.GetAxis(VertAxis);
        Vector3 MoveDirection = new Vector3(Horz, 0.0f, Vert);
        ThisBody.AddForce(MoveDirection.normalized * MaxSpeed);
        ThisBody.velocity = new Vector3
          (Mathf.Clamp(ThisBody.velocity.x, -MaxSpeed,
             MaxSpeed),
           Mathf.Clamp(ThisBody.velocity.y, -MaxSpeed,
             MaxSpeed),
           Mathf.Clamp(ThisBody.velocity.z, -MaxSpeed,
             MaxSpeed));


        if(MouseLook)
        {
            Vector3 MousePosWorld =
                Camera.main.ScreenToWorldPoint(new
                   Vector3(Input.mousePosition.x,
                     Input.mousePosition.y, 0.0f));
            MousePosWorld = new Vector3(MousePosWorld.x,
                0.0f, MousePosWorld.z);
            Vector3 LookDirection = MousePosWorld -
                transform.position;


            transform.localRotation = Quaternion.LookRotation
```

```
                    (LookDirection.normalized,Vector3.up);
            }
        }
}
```

Let's summarize the preceding code:

- The `FixedUpdate` function is called once before the physics system is updated, which is a fixed number of times per second. `FixedUpdate` differs from `Update`, which is called once per frame and can vary on a per-second basis as the frame rate fluctuates. For this reason, if you ever need to control an object through the physics system, using components such as `Rigidbody`, then you should always do so in `FixedUpdate` and not `Update`.

- The `Input.GetAxis` function is called on each `FixedUpdate` to read the axial input data from an input device, such as the keyboard or gamepad. This function reads from two named axes, `Horizontal` (left-right) and `Vertical` (up-down). These work in a normalized space of `-1` to 1. This means that when the left key is pressed and held down, the Horizontal axis returns `-1` and, when the right key is being pressed and held down, the horizontal axis returns 1. A value of 0 indicates that either no relevant key is being pressed or both left and right are pressed together, canceling each other out. A similar principle applies to the vertical axis. Up refers to 1, down to `-1`, and no keypress relates to 0. More information on the `GetAxis` function can be found online at `http://docs.unity3d.com/ScriptReference/Input.GetAxis.html`.

- The `Rigidbody.AddForce` function applies a physical force to the `Player` object, moving it in a specific direction. The `MoveDirection` vector encodes the direction of movement and is based on player input from both the horizontal and vertical axes. This direction is multiplied by our maximum speed to ensure that the force applied to the object is capped. For more information on `AddForce`, refer to the online Unity documentation at `http://docs.unity3d.com/ScriptReference/Rigidbody.AddForce.html`.

- The `Camera.ScreenToWorldPoint` function converts the screen position of the mouse cursor in the game window to a position in the game world. This code is responsible for making the player always look at the mouse cursor. However, as we'll see soon, some further tweaking is required to make this code work correctly. For more information on `ScreenToWorldPoint`, refer to the Unity online documentation at `http://docs.unity3d.com/ScriptReference/Camera.ScreenToWorldPoint.html`.

The preceding code allows you to control the `Player` object, but there are some problems. One of them is that the player doesn't seem to face the position of the mouse cursor, even though our code is designed to achieve this behavior. The reason is that the camera, by default, is not configured as it needs to be for a top-down 2D game. We'll fix this shortly, but before we move away (no pun intended) from the movement code, let's add one more feature: preventing the player from moving out of the bounds of the game.

Limiting movement

As the game stands now, it's possible to move the player outside the boundaries of the screen. The player can fly off into the distance, out of view, and never be seen again. Not ideal! The player movement should be limited to the camera view or bounds so that it never exits the view.

There are different ways to achieve bounds locking, most of which involve scripting. One way is to clamp the positional values of the `Player` object between a specified range, a minimum, and a maximum. Consider *Code Sample 3.3* for a new C# class called `BoundsLock`. This script file should be attached to the player:

```
public class BoundsLock : MonoBehaviour
{
    public Rect levelBounds;

    void LateUpdate ()
    {
        transform.position = new Vector3
            (Mathf.Clamp(transform.position.x, levelBounds.xMin,
                levelBounds.xMax), transform.position.y,
                Mathf.Clamp(transform.position.z,
                    levelBounds.yMin, levelBounds.yMax));
    }
}
```

There's not a lot new here that we haven't seen in previous code samples, except possibly the `Mathf.Clamp` function, which ensures that a specified value is capped between a minimum and maximum range.

> **Tip**
> Understanding the order of execution of event functions, such as
> `LateUpdate`, is important. I outline the order of execution whenever
> appropriate in this book, but you can find more information here: `https://`
> `docs.unity3d.com/Manual/ExecutionOrder.html`.

To use the `BoundsLock` script, perform the following steps:

1. Drag and drop the file to the **Player** object.

2. Specify the bounds in the Inspector:

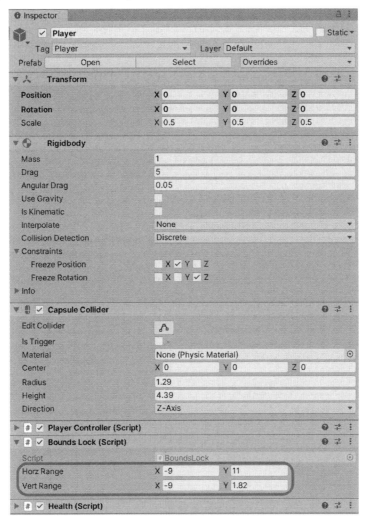

Figure 3.11 – Setting Bounds Lock

You may be wondering how I came up with those numbers. And it's a good question. I could have used trial and error by setting some initially random numbers, playing the game, refining the numbers, and repeating that process until I had the bounds precisely as I want. However, there's a far more productive way to do it by using Unity's **Gizmos**.

As discussed in *Chapter 1, Exploring the Fundamentals of Unity*, we use gizmos all the time in Unity. They add visual representations to GameObjects, imparting additional useful information that will help us develop games. Unity provides many built-in gizmos that make using the editor much easier; for example, the outline of selected objects is a gizmo, if you're using the move tool, that is also a gizmo; even the green outline of a collider is a gizmo. This list goes on, and not only does Unity provide their own gizmos, but we can also write our own.

> **Important note**
>
> Gizmos are only visible in the Unity Editor. They will not be visible to end users, so do not rely on any gizmos for gameplay. For instance, if we wanted the player to see the bounds of the level, a gizmo would not be an appropriate tool for the job.

We'll use a gizmo to visualize the bounds of the level so that we can see in real time how our settings affect the size and position of the bounds. To do this, add a new function to the BoundsLock script:

```
public class BoundsLock : MonoBehaviour
{

...

    void OnDrawGizmosSelected()
    {
        const int cubeDepth = 1;
        Vector3 boundsCenter = new Vector3(levelBounds.xMin +
            levelBounds.width * 0.5f, 0, levelBounds.yMin +
            levelBounds.height * 0.5f);
        Vector3 boundsHeight = new Vector3(levelBounds.
            width, cubeDepth, levelBounds.height);
        Gizmos.DrawWireCube(boundsCenter, boundsHeight);
    }
}
```

In `OnDrawGizmosSelected`, we call `Gizmos.DrawWireCube`, which will draw a wireframe of a cube with a specified center and size. The center and size are calculated using the `levelBounds` rectangle that we created earlier. I've set the `cubeDepth` arbitrarily to 1 as our game is 2D, and we are not concerned about the depth of the level bounds. As the function name hints, the gizmo will be drawn only if the object is selected in the hierarchy. As we only really need the level bounds visible while we edit them, this is perfect for us.

> **Tip**
>
> `OnDrawGizmosSelected` is an event function provided by Unity. We could have also used the `OnDrawGizmos` function. `OnDrawGizmos` is called every frame and will draw the gizmo even when the object isn't selected, whereas `OnDrawGizmosSelected` requires the object to be selected. Which function to use depends on your needs. If you want the gizmo to be visible most of the time, then `OnDrawGizmos` is more appropriate. If, however, you only need it to be shown when a specific object is selected, such as in our level bounds example, then `OnDrawGizmosSelected` is more appropriate.

To test whether the gizmo is working correctly, in the Unity Editor, select the `Player` object. As the `BoundsLock` script is attached to that object, a white cube wireframe should be drawn in the **Scene** view, as shown in *Figure 3.12*:

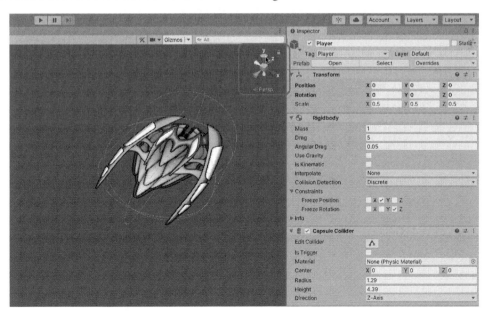

Figure 3.12 – Level bounds displayed using a gizmo

If you edit the **Level Bounds** rectangle on the `Player` object, you'll notice that the gizmo's size is automatically adjusted to reflect the new level bounds. Perfect! Using this, you can easily customize the level bounds to suit your needs.

> **Tip**
> Gizmos can also be viewed in the **Game** tab by selecting the gizmo button on the panels toolbar. However, as previously mentioned, even with this setting turned on, they will not be visible in the final compiled game.

Now take the game for a test run by pressing Play on the toolbar. The player spaceship should remain in view and be unable to move offscreen. Splendid!

As stated earlier, you may have an issue where the player object does not face the cursor correctly. Because the project was initially created as a 3D project, the camera is not configured correctly for our needs, so we will need to change that now and, in the process, learn how easy it is to switch a camera from a 3D to a 2D perspective.

Configuring the cameras

In this section, we'll configure the scene and game camera. Remember that any changes to the scene camera won't change the playable game. It is only used to navigate the scene to help you create it, whereas changing the game's camera will change how the player views the game.

We'll start with the scene camera:

1. Switch the **Scene** viewport to a top-down 2D view by clicking on the up arrow in the top-right corner of the **Scene** viewport:

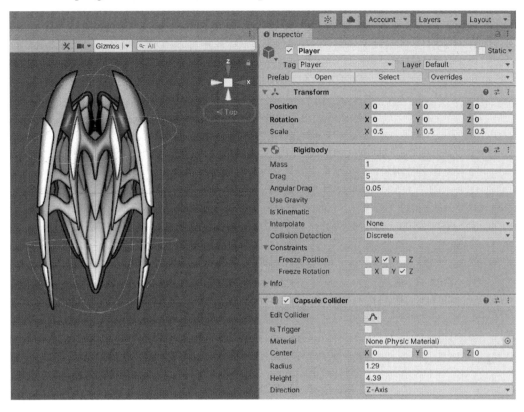

Figure 3.13 – Changing the viewport perspective

You can confirm that the viewport is in a top view because it will list **Top** as the current view:

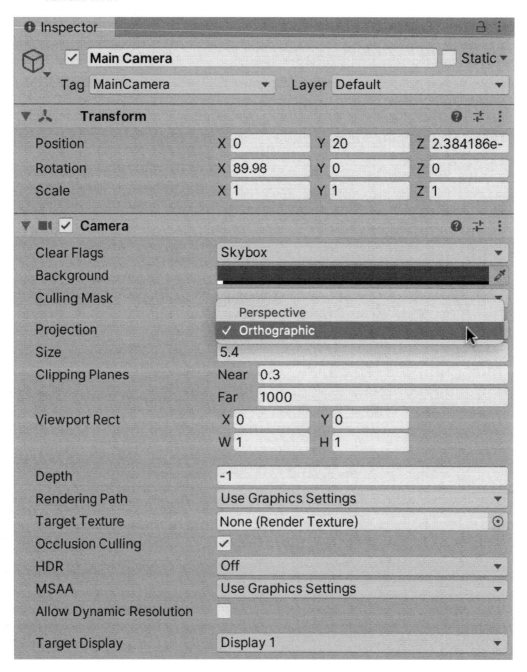

Figure 3.14 – Top view in the Scene viewport

2. From here, you can have the scene camera conform to the viewport camera exactly, giving you an instant top-down view for your game. Select the camera in the scene (or from the **Hierarchy** panel and choose **GameObject | Align With View** from the application menu).

This makes your game look much better than before, but there's still a problem. When the game is running, the spaceship still doesn't look at the mouse cursor as intended. This is because the camera is a **Perspective** camera, and the conversion between a screen point and world point is leading to unexpected results. We can fix this by changing the camera to an **Orthographic** (2D) camera:

1. Select the camera in the scene.

2. In the Inspector, change the **Projection** setting from **Perspective** to **Orthographic**:

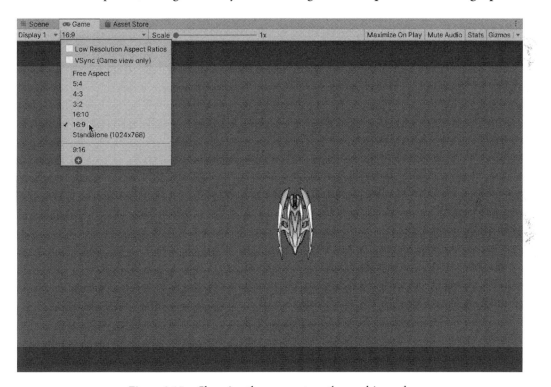

Figure 3.15 – Changing the camera to orthographic mode

Every orthographic camera has a **Size** field in the **Inspector**, which is not present for perspective cameras. This field controls how many units in the world view correspond to pixels on the screen. We want a 1:1 ratio between world units to pixels to ensure that our textures appear at the correct size, and that any cursor movement has the intended effect. The target resolution for our game will be **Full HD**, which is 1920 x 1080, and this has an aspect ratio of 16:9. For this resolution, set the orthographic size to 5 . 4, as shown in *Figure 3.15*.

> **Important note**
>
> The formula used to calculate the orthographic is *screen height (in pixels) / 2 / 100 (Pixels per Unit)*. Don't worry if this isn't very clear at this stage; it is covered in detail in *Chapter 5, Creating a 2D Adventure Game*. For now, it is enough to know that our assets use a pixel per unit value of 100, hence *1080 / 2 / 100 = 5.4.*

3. Finally, make sure that your **Game** tab view is configured to display the game at a 16:9 aspect ratio. If it isn't, click on the aspect drop-down list at the top-left corner of the **Game** view and choose the **16:9** option:

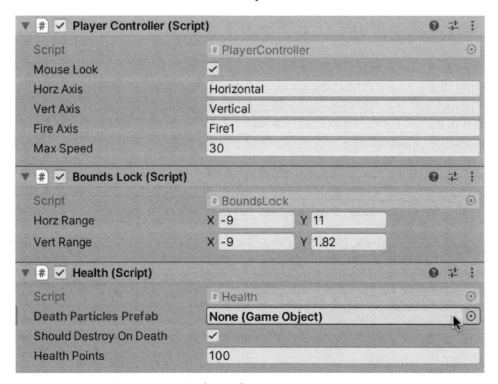

Figure 3.16 – Displaying the game at a 16:9 aspect ratio

Now try running the game, and you have a player spaceship that moves based on *WASD* input and also turns to face the mouse cursor. Great work! The game is taking shape. However, there›s lots more work to do, including creating our first reusable component: the **Health** component.

Creating a Health component

Both the player spaceship and enemies need health. Health is a measure of a character's presence and legitimacy in the scene, typically scored as a value between 0-100. 0 means death, and 100 means full health. Health is, in many respects, specific to each instance: the player has a unique health rating, and the enemy theirs. There are nevertheless many things in common, in terms of behavior, between player and enemy health, that it makes sense to code health as a separate component and class that can be attached to all objects that need health. Create a new class called `Health`, which should be attached to the player and all enemies or objects that need health:

```
public class Health : MonoBehaviour
{
    public GameObject DeathParticlesPrefab = null;
    public bool ShouldDestroyOnDeath = true;
    [SerializeField] private float _HealthPoints = 100f;
}
```

The `Health` class maintains object health through a **private** variable, `_HealthPoints`. The `_HealthPoints` variable is declared as a `SerializedField`, allowing its value to be visible in the Inspector while maintaining a **private scope**, in other words, not accessible by other scripts. The `prefab` variable, on the other hand, is **public**, allowing its value to be both seen in the Inspector and changeable from elsewhere in the code if needed.

We want to be able to change the `_HealthPoints` variable from another script and have some logic to check for when it reaches zero. We could create a **setter** function to accomplish this, but instead, we'll make use of **C# properties**:

```
public class Health : MonoBehaviour
{

    ...

    public float HealthPoints
    {
        Get
```

```
        {
            return _HealthPoints;
        }

        Set
        {
            _HealthPoints = value;
            if(HealthPoints <= 0)
            {
                SendMessage("Die",
                    SendMessageOptions.DontRequireReceiver);
                if(DeathParticlesPrefab != null)
                {
                    Instantiate(DeathParticlesPrefab,
                        transform.position, transform.rotation);
                }
                if(ShouldDestroyOnDeath)
                {
                    Destroy(gameObject);
                }
            }
        }
    }
}
```

Let's summarize the preceding code:

- `_HealthPoints` is now accessible through a C# property, `HealthPoints`. This property features both `get` and `set` accessors to return and set the health variable.

- The `Health` class is an example of **event-driven programming**. The class could have continually checked the health of the object in an `Update` function. Instead, the check for death is made during the C# property set method. This makes sense because the properties **mutator** is the only place where health will ever change. Not having to check the health of every object on every frame saves a lot of work. Imagine if you had thousands of objects on screen at once, and each one was constantly checking its own health! You'd see a significant performance increase by writing event-driven code.

- The `Health` class uses the `SendMessage` function that lets you call any other function on any component attached to the object by specifying the function name as a string. In this case, a function called `Die` will be executed on every component attached to the object (if such a function exists). If no function of a matching name exists, then nothing happens for that component. This is a quick and easy way to run customized behavior on an object in a **type-agnostic** way without using **polymorphism**. The disadvantage of `SendMessage` is that it internally uses a process called **Reflection**, which is slow and performance-prohibitive. For this reason, `SendMessage` should be used infrequently. More information can be found online at `https://docs.unity3d.com/ScriptReference/` `GameObject.SendMessage.html`.

When the health script is attached to the player spaceship, it appears as a component in the **Inspector**. As shown in *Figure 3.17*, it contains a field for **Death Particles Prefab**:

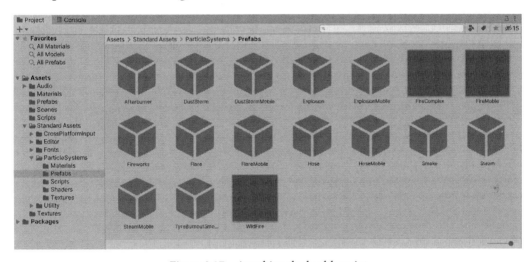

Figure 3.17 – Attaching the health script

This field is optional (it can be null), and is used to specify a particle system to be **instantiated** when the health of the object reaches zero. This will let us instantiate an explosion particle effect when the player dies. But first, we have to create one.

Creating the explosive particle system

In this twin-stick shooter game, both the player and enemies are spaceships. Therefore, a suitable particle effect for their destruction would be an explosive fiery ball. To achieve explosions, we can use a particle system. This refers to a special kind of object that features two main parts, namely, a **Hose** (or **Emitter**) and **Particles**. The emitter spawns or generates new particles into the world, and the particles are many small objects or pieces that, once spawned, move and travel along a trajectory. Particle systems are ideal for creating rain, snow, fog, sparkles, or, in our case, explosions!

With that in mind, let's select and customize a particle system for our game.

Selecting the particle system

We can create our own particle systems from scratch using the menu option **GameObject | Particle System**, or we can use any pre-made particle system included with Unity. In this game, we'll use some of the premade particle systems. To do this, perform the following steps:

1. First import the Unity Standard Assets package. I won't go into detail how to do this here as it was covered in *Chapter 1, Exploring the Fundamentals of Unity*, so please refer back to that chapter for a step-by-step guide.

2. Once the Standard Asset Package has been imported, the particle systems will be added to the **Project** panel in the **Standard Assets | ParticleSystems | Prefabs** folder:

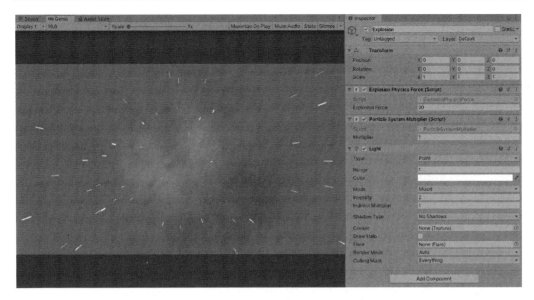

Figure 3.18 – Particle systems imported to the Project panel

> **Tip**
> Note that the preview for a particle system is only played in the **Scene** view while it is selected in **Hierarchy**.

3. You will observe from *Figure 3.18* that an explosion system is included among the default assets. To make sure it is fit for our purposes, you can test it by dragging and dropping the explosion to the scene and pressing play on the toolbar to see the explosion in action, as shown in *Figure 3.19*.

Great! We're almost done, but there's still a bit more work to do. We've now seen that an appropriate particle system is available, and we could drag and drop this system to the **Death Particles Prefab** slot in the **Health** component in the **Inspector**. This will work technically: when a player or enemy dies, the explosion system will be spawned, creating an explosion effect. However, the particle system will never be destroyed! This is problematic because, with every enemy death, a new particle system will be spawned. This raises the possibility that, after many deaths, the scene will be full of disused particle systems. We don't want this; it's bad for performance and memory usage to have a scene full of unused objects lingering around. To fix this, we'll modify the explosion system slightly, creating an altered prefab that will suit our needs. In future, we'll look at more advanced object management techniques, such as **object pooling**, but now we will simply destroy the objects after a specified time.

Customizing the particle system

To begin altering the particle system, drag and drop the existing explosion prefab anywhere to the scene and position it at the world origin, as shown in *Figure 3.19*:

Figure 3.19 – Adding an explosion system to the scene for modification

Next, we must refine the particle system to destroy itself soon after instantiation. To accomplish this, we'll create a new C# script called `TimedDestroy.cs`:

```
public class TimedDestroy : MonoBehaviour
{
    public float DestroyTime = 2f;

    void Start ()
    {
        Destroy(gameObject, DestroyTime);
    }
}
```

The `TimedDestroy` class destroys the object to which it's attached after a specified interval (`DestroyTime`) has elapsed. The script is simple: in the `Start` function, a call to `Destroy` is made, passing the script's `gameObject` and the desired `DestroyTime`. This call holds no surprises and will destroy the object after the desired amount of time has passed.

> **Tip**
>
> You can also destroy a particle system on completion by setting **Stop Action** to **Destroy** in the Inspector. This setting will destroy the particle system without the need to write a single line of code. However, this is not entirely suitable for our explosion particle, as it actually consists of several particle systems that are all children of a parent object. We could have set **Stop Action** for each particle system individually, but this would not have destroyed the parent object. These parent objects would accumulate over time, thereby reducing the performance of our game.

Drag and drop the `TimedDestroy` script to the explosion particle system in the scene and then press Play on the toolbar to test that the code works and that the object is destroyed after the specified interval. Remember that, as `DestroyTime` is a public variable, it can be adjusted in the Inspector.

The `TimedDestroy` script should remove the explosion particle system after the delay expires. So, let's create a new and separate prefab from this modified version. To do this, perform the following steps:

1. Rename the explosion system in the **Hierarchy** panel to `ExplosionDestroy`.

2. Drag and drop the system from **Hierarchy** to the **Project** panel in the **Prefabs** folder. Unity will automatically create a new prefab, representing the modified particle system.

3. Now, drag and drop the newly created prefab from the **Project** panel to the **Death Particles Prefab** slot on the **Health** component for the player in the **Inspector**. Setting this field means that the prefab is instantiated when the player dies:

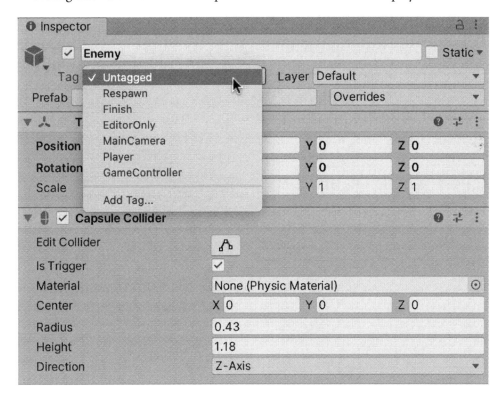

Figure 3.20 – Configuring the health script

If you run the game now, you'll see that you cannot initiate a player death event to test the particle system generation. Nothing exists in the scene to destroy or damage the player, and if you set the **Health** points to 0 in the Inspector, it doesn't use the **C# property set** function. For now, however, we can write temporary code that triggers an instant kill when the spacebar is pressed. Refer to *Code Sample 3.7* for the modified health script:

```
public class Health : MonoBehaviour
{
...
    void Update()
    {
        if(Input.GetKeyDown(KeyCode.Space))
        {
            HealthPoints = 0;
        }
    }
}
```

Run the game now and press the *Spacebar* to trigger an instant player death. You should see the player object removed from the game and the particle system generated until the timer destroys that too.

Excellent work! We now have a playable, controllable player character that supports health and death functionality. We'll introduce enemies to the game next.

Creating the enemy object

The enemies in our game will take the form of roaming spaceships that will be spawned into the scene at regular intervals and will follow the player, drawing nearer and nearer. Essentially, each enemy represents a combination of multiple behaviors working together, and these should be implemented as separate scripts. Let's consider them in turn:

- **Health**: Each enemy supports health functionality. They begin the scene with a specified amount of health and will be destroyed when that health falls below 0. We already have a health script created to handle this behavior.

- **Movement**: Each enemy will continuously be in motion, traveling in a straight line along a forward trajectory.

- **Turning**: Each enemy will rotate and turn toward the player even as the player moves. In combination with the movement functionality, this will ensure that the enemy is always moving toward the player.

- **Scoring**: Each enemy rewards the player with a score value when destroyed.

- **Damage**: Enemies cannot shoot but will harm the player on collision.

Now that we've identified the range of behaviors applicable to an enemy, let's create an enemy in the scene.

Creating the GameObject

We'll make one specific enemy, create a prefab from that, and use it as a basis to instantiate multiple enemies:

1. Start by selecting the player character in the scene and duplicating the object with *Ctrl + D* or select **Edit | Duplicate** from the application menu. We will edit this duplicate to become our enemy.

2. Rename the object to **Enemy** and ensure that it is not tagged as **Player**, as there should be one and only one object in the scene with the Player tag. Set the tag to **Untagged**, as shown in *Figure 3.21*:

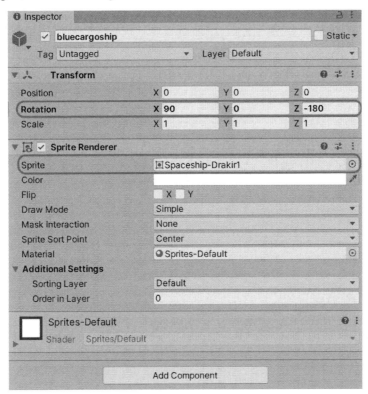

Figure 3.21 – Removing a Player tag from the enemy, if applicable

3.   Temporarily disable the **Player** GameObject, allowing us to focus more clearly on the **Enemy** object in the **Scene** tab.

4.   Select the child object of the duplicated enemy and, from the **Inspector**, click on the **Sprite** field of the **Sprite Renderer** component to pick a new sprite. Pick one of the darker imperial ships for the enemy character, and the sprite will update for the object in the viewport:

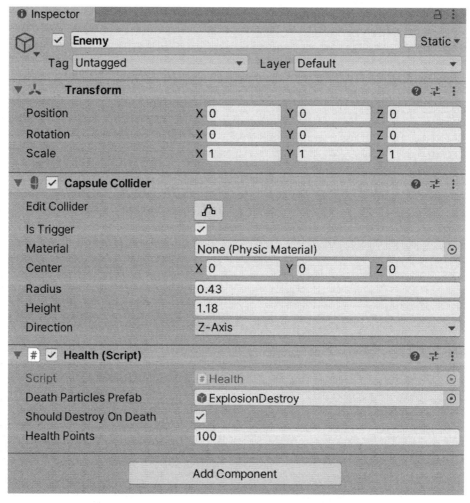

Figure 3.22 – Selecting a sprite for the Sprite Renderer component

5.   After changing the sprite to an enemy character, you may need to adjust the **Rotation** values to align the sprite to the parent forward vector, ensuring that the sprite is looking in the same direction as the forward vector, as shown in *Figure 3.22*.

6. Lastly, select the parent object for the enemy and remove the `Rigidbody`, `PlayerController`, and `BoundsLock` components, but keep the Health component as the enemy should support health. See *Figure 3.23* for the updated component list. Also, feel free to resize the **Capsule Collider** component to better approximate the `Enemy` object:

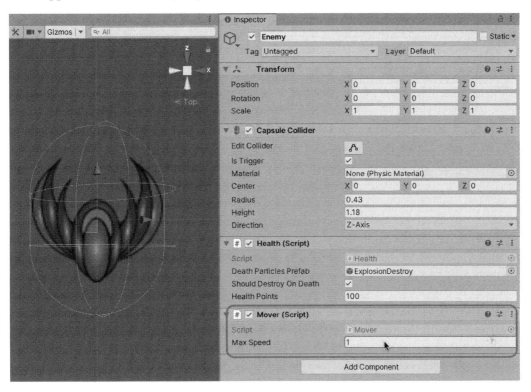

Figure 3.23 – Adjusting enemy sprite rotation

> **Tip**
>
> When designing scripts for your games, try to create them in such a way that they can be reused as much as possible, such as our Health component. If we had added logic specific to the player in the Health component, we wouldn't have been able to add it to both our enemy and player objects. We would most likely have ended up writing duplicate code for the enemy objects.

Now that we have the base enemy object, we can start adapting its behavior with custom scripts, starting with moving the enemy to chase the player.

Moving the enemy

As a reminder, the enemy should continually move in the forward direction at a specified speed. To achieve this, create a new script called `Mover.cs` and add it to the Enemy object:

```
public class Mover : MonoBehaviour
{
    public float MaxSpeed = 10f;

    void Update ()
    {
        transform.position += transform.forward * MaxSpeed *
            Time.deltaTime;
    }
}
```

The following points summarize the code sample:

- The script moves an object at a specified speed (`MaxSpeed` per second) along its forward vector. To do this, it uses the `Transform` component.

- The `Update` function is responsible for updating the position of the object. It multiplies the forward vector by the object speed and adds this to its existing position to move the object further along its line of sight. The `Time.deltaTime` value is used to make the **motion frame rate independent** style moving the object per second as opposed to per frame. More information on `deltaTime` can be found at `http://docs.unity3d.com/ScriptReference/Time-deltaTime.html`.

It's always good practice to frequently test your code. Your enemy may move too slow or too fast. So, we'll do that now by pressing Play on the toolbar. If the enemy's speed isn't correct, perform the following steps:

1. Stop playback to exit game mode.
2. Select the enemy in the scene.

3. From the **Inspector**, adjust the **Max Speed** value of the **Mover** component:

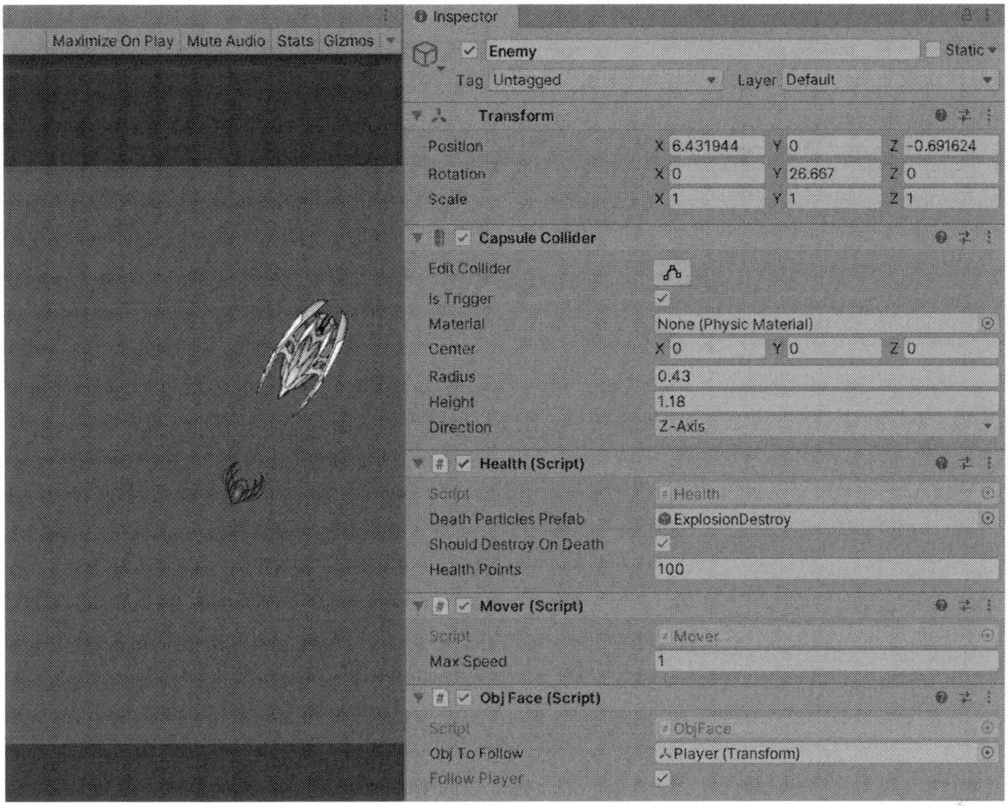

Figure 3.24 – Adjusting enemy speed

The enemy will now move forward, but this won't be much of a challenge for the player, as it will be effortless to avoid. To increase the difficulty, let's make the enemy turn toward the player. Turning toward the player, combined with moving in its forward direction, will create a suitable chase mechanic.

Turning the enemy

In addition to moving in a straight line, the enemy should also continually turn to face the player. To achieve this, we'll write another script that works in a similar manner to the player controller script, but instead of turning to face the cursor, the enemy turns to face the player. This functionality should be encoded in a new script file called `ObjFace.cs` and, once again, be attached to the enemy object:

```csharp
public class ObjFace : MonoBehaviour
{
    public Transform ObjToFollow = null;
    public bool FollowPlayer = false;

    void Awake ()
    {
        if(!FollowPlayer)
        {
            return;
        }

        GameObject PlayerObj =
            GameObject.FindGameObjectWithTag("Player");
        if(PlayerObj != null)
        {
            ObjToFollow = PlayerObj.transform;
        }
    }

    void Update ()
    {
        if(ObjToFollow==null)
        {
            return;
        }

        //Get direction to follow object
        Vector3 DirToObject = ObjToFollow.position -
            transform.position;
```

```
        if(DirToObject != Vector3.zero)
        {
            transform.localRotation = Quaternion.LookRotation
                (DirToObject.normalized,Vector3.up);
        }
    }
}
```

The following points summarize the code sample:

- The ObjFace script will always rotate an object so that its forward vector points toward a destination point in the scene.

- In the Awake event, the FindGameObjectWithTag function retrieves a reference to the only object in the scene tagged as Player, which should be the player spaceship. The player represents the default look-at destination for an enemy object.

- The Update function is called automatically once per frame and will generate a displacement **vector** from the object location to the destination location. This vector represents the direction in which the object should be looking. The Quaternion. LookRotation function accepts a direction vector and will rotate an object to align the forward vector with the supplied direction. This keeps the object looking toward the destination. More information on LookRotation can be found at http://docs.unity3d.com/ScriptReference/Quaternion. LookRotation.html.

Before testing the code, make sure of the following:

- The Player object in the scene is tagged as **Player**.

- The Player object is enabled (we previously disabled the object for testing).

- The enemy's position is offset from the player.

- The **Follow Player** checkbox on the **Obj Face** component is enabled in the **Inspector**.

Figure 3.25 shows these settings in practice:

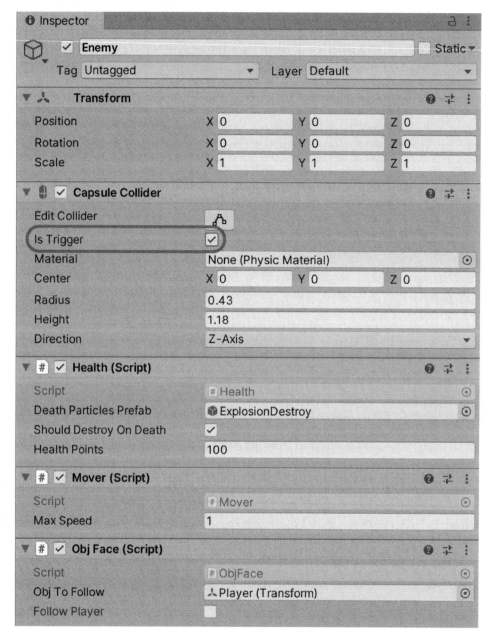

Figure 3.25 – Enemy spaceship moving toward the player

This is looking excellent! However, it's not very challenging if the enemy doesn't damage the player when they collide, so we will resolve that next.

Dealing damage to the player

If and when the enemy finally collides with the player, it should deal damage and potentially kill the player. To achieve this, a collision between the enemy and player must be detected. Let's start by configuring the enemy. Select the Enemy object and, from the **Inspector**, enable the **Is Trigger** checkbox on the **Capsule Collider** component, as shown in *Figure 3.26*:

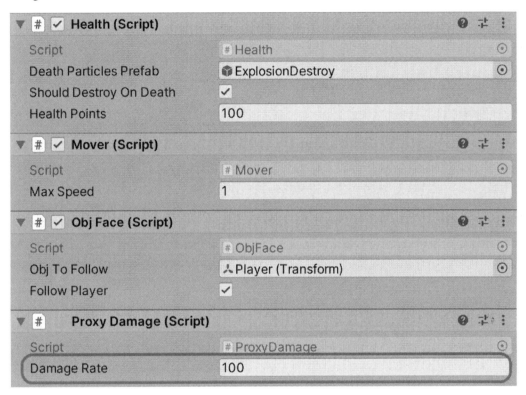

Figure 3.26 – Changing the enemy collider to a trigger

Setting a collider as a trigger means that we can still respond to collision events, but Unity will not try to resolve (separate) the collisions.

Next, we'll create a script that detects collisions and deals damage to the player for as long as the collision state remains. Refer to the following code (`ProxyDamage.cs`), which should be attached to the enemy character:

```
public class ProxyDamage : MonoBehaviour
{
    //Damage per second
    public float DamageRate = 10f;

    void OnTriggerStay(Collider Col)
    {
        Health H = Col.gameObject.GetComponent<Health>();
        if(H == null)
        {
            return;
        }
        H.HealthPoints -= DamageRate * Time.deltaTime;
    }
}
```

The following points summarize the code sample:

- The `ProxyDamage` script will deal damage to any colliding object with a Health component.

- The `OnTriggerStay` event is called once every frame for as long as an intersection state persists. During this function, the `HealthPoints` value of the Health component is reduced by the `DamageRate`, which is multiplied by `Time.deltaTime` to get the **damage per second (DPS)**.

After attaching the `ProxyDamage` script to an enemy, you can use the **Inspector** to set the `Damage Rate` of the **Proxy Damage** component. The **Damage Rate** represents how much health should be reduced on the player, per second, during a collision. For a challenge, I've set the value to 100 health points:

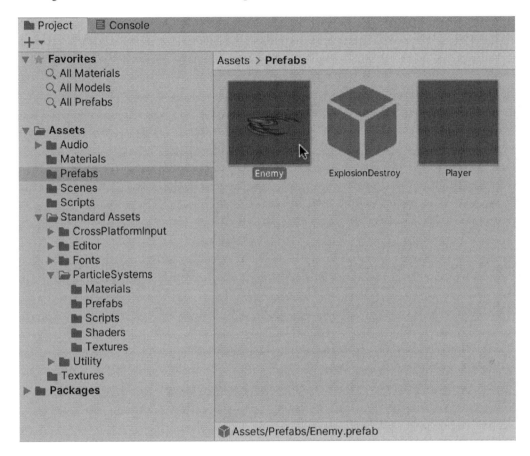

Figure 3.27 – Setting Damage Rate for a Proxy Damage component

Time for a test run: press Play on the toolbar and attempt a collision between the player and enemy. After 1 second, the player should be destroyed. Things are coming along well. However, we'll need more than one enemy to make things challenging.

Spawning enemies

To make the level fun and challenging, we'll need more than simply one enemy. In fact, for a game that's essentially endless, we'll need to add enemies continually and gradually over time. Essentially, we'll need either regular or intermittent spawning of enemies, and this section will add that functionality. Before we can do this, however, we'll need to make a prefab from the enemy object. The steps are the same as for previously created prefabs: select the enemy in the **Hierarchy** panel and then drag and drop it to the **Project** panel in the **Prefabs** folder:

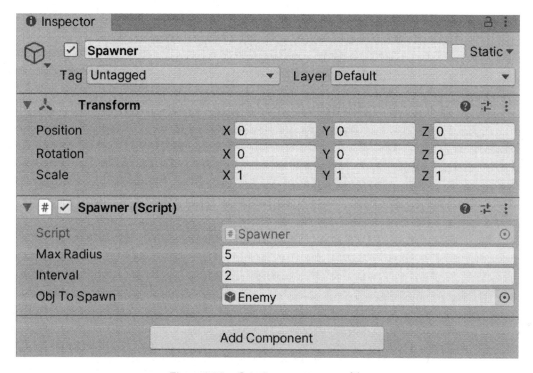

Figure 3.28 – Creating an enemy prefab

Now, we'll make a new script, called `Spawner.cs`, that spawns new enemies in the scene over time within a specified radius from the player spaceship. This script should be attached to a new, empty GameObject in the scene:

```
public class Spawner : MonoBehaviour
{
    public float MaxRadius = 1f;
    public float Interval = 5f;
    public GameObject ObjToSpawn = null;
    private Transform Origin = null;
```

```
void Awake()
{
    Origin = GameObject.FindGameObjectWithTag
      ("Player").transform;
}

void Start ()
{
    InvokeRepeating("Spawn", 0f, Interval);
}

void Spawn ()
{
    if(Origin == null)
    {
        return;
    }
    Vector3 SpawnPos = Origin.position + Random.
      onUnitSphere * MaxRadius;
    SpawnPos = new Vector3(SpawnPos.x, 0f, SpawnPos.z);
    Instantiate(ObjToSpawn, SpawnPos, Quaternion.
      identity);
}
}
```

During the `Start` event, the `InvokeRepeating` function will spawn instances of `ObjToSpawn` (a prefab) repeatedly at the specified `Interval`, measured in seconds. The generated objects will be placed within a random radius from a center point, `Origin`.

The `Spawner` class is a global behavior that applies scene-wide. It does not depend on the player, nor any specific enemy. For this reason, it should be attached to an empty GameObject. Create one of these by selecting **GameObject | Create Empty** from the application menu. Name the new object something memorable, such as `Spawner`, and attach the `Spawner` script to it.

Once added to the scene, from the **Inspector**, drag and drop the **Enemy** prefab to the **Obj To Spawn** field in the **Spawner** component. Set the **Interval** to 2 seconds and increase the **Max Radius** to 5, as shown in *Figure 3.29*:

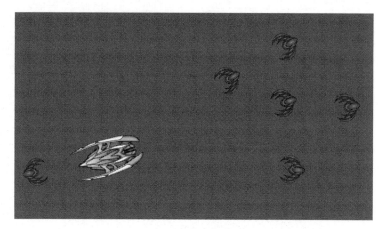

Figure 3.29 – Configuring Spawner for enemy objects

Now (drum roll), let's try the level. Press Play on the toolbar and take the game for a test run:

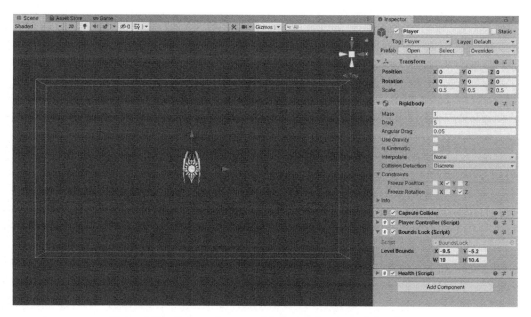

Figure 3.30 – Spawned enemy objects moving toward the player

You should now have a level with a fully controllable player character surrounded by a growing army of tracking enemy ships! Excellent work!

Summary

Good job on getting this far! The space shooter is really taking shape now, featuring a controllable player character that relies on native physics, twin-stick mechanics, enemy ships, and a scene-wide spawner for enemies. All these ingredients together still don't make a game: we can't shoot, we can't increase the score, and we can't destroy enemies. These issues will need to be addressed in the next chapter, along with other technical issues that we'll undoubtedly encounter. Nevertheless, we now have a solid foundation.

By writing a `health` script and adding it to both the player and the enemy object, we've reduced the amount of code we need to write. Of course, there will always be times when you need to write code that is specific to one object, but whenever possible, you should design code that can be reused. By converting the 3D camera to a 2D camera, we've learned the differences between the two, and how to configure them. This information will prove useful in the future as even in 3D games, you may want a 2D camera for certain features, such as the UI.

In the next chapter, we'll create the projectiles for the player to shoot, and in doing so, we'll look at several important topics, including object management techniques and physics. We'll discuss **object pooling**, a method of preventing unnecessary object creation and destruction, a tool that you'll end up using frequently in your future projects. We'll also create a scoring system, where each enemy defeated awards the player a specific number of points, and we'll develop a UI to display the score. Lastly, we'll add some final touches to improve the overall experience, including adding a background image and some sound effects.

Test your knowledge

Q1. `SerializableField` renders...

> A. public variables hidden in the Inspector
>
> B. private variables visible in the Inspector
>
> C. protected variables hidden in the Inspector
>
> D. public variables visible in the Inspector

Q2. Importing audio with the **Streaming Load** type means...

> A. the audio will be loaded in its entirety at startup
>
> B. the audio will be loaded in segments
>
> C. the audio will be muted
>
> D. the audio will be deleted

Q3. Orthographic cameras remove...

    A. perspective effects

    B. distant objects

    C. post-processing

    D. MeshRenderers

Q4. The `Input.GetAxis` function lets you read input from...

    A. horizontal and vertical axes

    B. VR touch controllers

    C. mobile touches

    D. mouse clicks

Further reading

Refer to the following links for more information:

- `https://unity3d.com/learn/tutorials/s/scripting`
- `https://docs.unity3d.com/Manual/2Dor3D.html`
- `https://docs.unity3d.com/Manual/ParticleSystems.html`

4
Continuing the Space Shooter Game

This chapter continues on from the previous one by completing the twin-stick space shooter game. At this point, we already have a working game. The gamer can control a spaceship using two axes: movement and rotation. The *WASD* keys on the keyboard control movement and the spaceship rotates to face the mouse cursor. In addition to player controls, the level features enemy characters that spawn at regular intervals and move toward the player. Finally, both the player and enemies support a **Health component**, which means both objects are susceptible to damage. Right now, however, the game lacks two essential features: the player cannot fight back against the enemies and there is no system to keep track of and display the score. This chapter tackles these issues and more.

Once you've completed this chapter, you should have a solid understanding of the following topics:

- Creating a projectile
- Spawning the projectile at runtime
- Memory management and pooling
- Configuring background audio
- Creating a score system and a basic UI to display the score

- Debugging and testing
- Profiling the game's performance

Generating projectiles, as we'll see, presents a particularly interesting problem regarding memory management. However, before we get to that, let's look at the technical requirements for this chapter and create the projectile prefab.

Technical requirements

As this chapter is a continuation of the previous one, it assumes that you have completed and are comfortable with the information provided in the last chapter, specifically how to create a new script and add it to an object as a **component**, and creating **prefabs** from objects in the scene.

The project so far can be found in the book's companion files in the `Chapter04/Start` folder. You can start there and follow along with this chapter if you don't have your own project already. If you want to test the final game, you can find the completed project in the `Chapter04/End` folder.

Creating the projectile system

Currently, the level contains a player and an enemy ship, which the player must shoot, as shown in *Figure 4.1*:

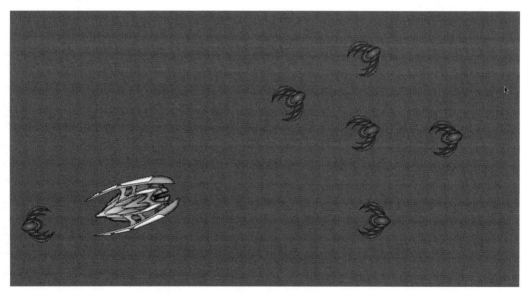

Figure 4.1 – The game so far

The player doesn't yet have any method of killing the enemy, so we'll start the chapter by implementing the last significant system missing from the game: the projectile system. Thinking carefully about how we want our weapon systems to behave, we can identify a few concepts that need development:

- The projectile spawn location: We need a way to spawn projectiles at a position relative to the player or enemy ships.

- We need the projectile itself. If you've read the previous chapters, you won't be surprised to hear that we'll create this as a prefab.

- We need a system to spawn the projectiles. This system will be slightly more complex than simply instantiating and destroying the missiles when required, for reasons that will become apparent.

- Lastly, we will need to configure Unity's physics system to prevent collisions between the projectiles shot by the player and the player's ship.

Any future projectile system you create may have different requirements and therefore require you to implement different systems.

We'll tackle each of these areas in order, starting with the projectile spawn location.

Implementing the projectile spawn location

We'll call the points where bullets are spawned and fired "turrets." For this game, the player will have only one turret, but ideally, the game should support easily adding more turrets if desired. Let's jump right in and create the first turret:

1. Add a new empty GameObject to the scene by selecting **GameObject | Create Empty** from the application menu.

2. Name the new object `Turret`.

3. Position the `Turret` object to the front of the spaceship, making sure that the blue forward vector arrow is pointing ahead in the direction that the projectile will be fired.

4. Make the turret a child of the spaceship by dragging and dropping it in the **Hierarchy** panel.

Once you've followed these steps, you'll have a setup similar to *Figure 4.2*:

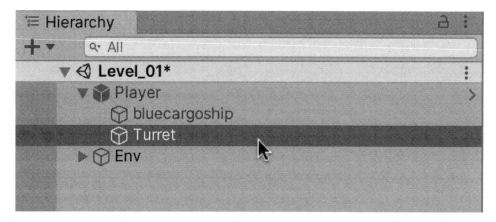

Figure 4.2 – Positioning a Turret object as a child of the spaceship

Creating a `Turret` object for the ammo as a spawn location is an excellent start, but for ammo to be fired, we'll need an ammo object. Specifically, we'll create an **Ammo** prefab that can be instantiated as ammo when needed. We'll do this next.

Creating the projectile prefab

When the player presses the fire button, the spaceship should shoot projectile objects. These objects will be based on an **Ammo** prefab. As part of the prefab creation, we will configure the projectile's texture, reuse a previously written script to enable projectile movement, and add new logic to handle collisions with enemies. We'll start by configuring the projectile's texture; that way, we can more easily see the projectile move and collide with enemies, which will help us debug any issues when we get to that stage.

Configuring the projectile's texture

To start, we'll configure the texture to be used as the projectile graphic:

1. Open the `Textures` folder in the **Project** panel, and select the **Ammo** texture. This texture features several different versions of an ammo sprite, aligned in a row. When ammo is fired, we don't want to show the complete texture; instead, we want to show either just one of the images or the images played as an animation sequence, frame by frame:

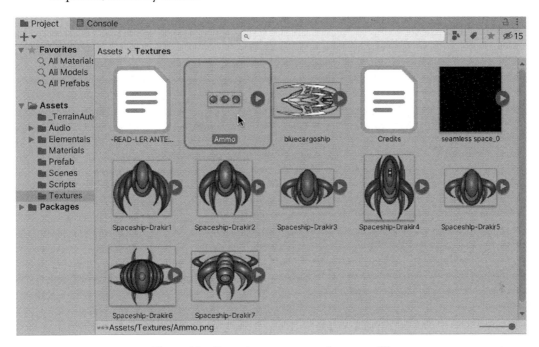

Figure 4.3 – Preparing to create an Ammo prefab

Currently, Unity recognizes the texture (and each ammo element) as a complete unit. We can use the Sprite Editor, however, to separate each part.

2.   Select the texture in the **Project** panel.

3.   From the **Inspector**, change the **Sprite Mode** dropdown from **Single** to **Multiple**, which informs Unity that more than one sprite is contained within the texture space:

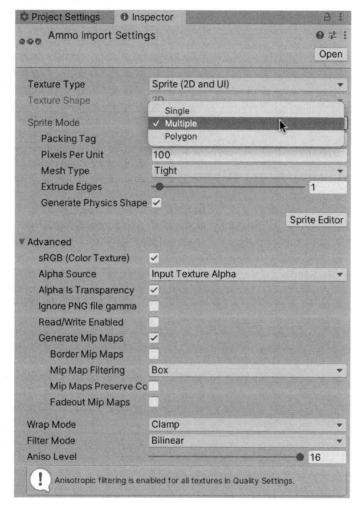

Figure 4.4 – Selecting Multiple as the texture type

4.   Click on the **Apply** button to apply the changes so far.

5.   Click on the **Sprite Editor** button from the **Inspector**, which will open the **Sprite Editor** window, allowing you to isolate each sprite.

6.   Click and drag your mouse to select each sprite, making sure that the **Pivot** setting is aligned to the object's center, as shown:

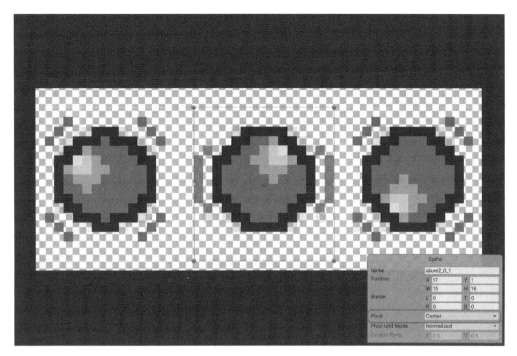

Figure 4.5 – Separating multiple sprites in the Sprite Editor

7. Lastly, click on **Apply** to accept the changes.

After accepting the changes in the **Sprite Editor**, Unity automatically cuts the relevant sprites into separate units, each of which can now be selected as an object in the **Project** panel by clicking on the left arrow to the side of the texture:

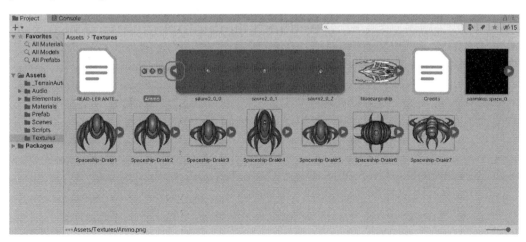

Figure 4.6 – Expanding all sprites within a texture

Now that we've separated the sprites, drag and drop one of them from the **Project** panel to the scene via the **Hierarchy** panel. On doing this, it will be added as a **Sprite** object. This object represents the beginning of our **Ammo** prefab. The sprite itself may not initially be oriented to face the game camera. Rename the object to Ammo_Sprite and, if required, rotate the sprite by 90 degrees on the **X** axis, as shown in *Figure 4.7*:

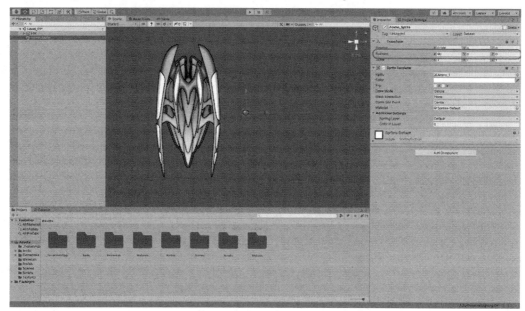

Figure 4.7 – Rotating the ammo sprite

With the initial projectile object created, correctly rotated, and visible to the player (and us), we can move on to configuring the object so that it moves through the scene when spawned by the player.

Adding projectile movement

As we've previously created a movement script, enabling movement for the projectile will be quick and easy. However, before we can attach the Mover script, we'll create a parent object to attach the script to:

1. Create a new empty GameObject in the scene (**GameObject | Create Empty** from the application menu), and rename it **Ammo**.

2. Make this new object a parent of Ammo_Sprite and ensure that its local forward vector is pointing in the direction that the ammo should travel, as shown in *Figure 4.8*:

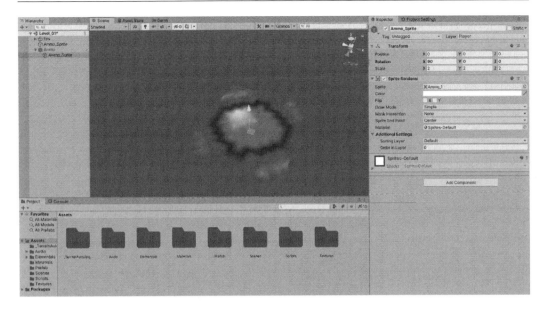

Figure 4.8 – Configuring an ammo object

3. Drag and drop the `Mover.cs` script from the **Project** panel to the **Ammo** parent object via the **Hierarchy** panel to add it as a component.

4. Select the **Ammo** object and, in the **Inspector**, change the ammo's **Max Speed** value in the **Mover** component to 7.

5. Finally, add a **Box Collider** to the object to approximate its volume (**Component | Physics | Box Collider** from the application menu).

6. Press play on the toolbar. The **Ammo** object should shoot forward as though fired from a weapon.

> **Tip**
> If the projectile moves up or down incorrectly, then make sure that the parent object is rotated so that its blue forward vector is pointing forward, as shown in *Figure 4.8*.

Great! Now that the projectile is moving through the scene, we can set up collisions so that it destroys any enemies in its path.

Handling projectile collisions

Any objects that we want to collide in Unity should have a **Rigidbody** component attached so that they are included in Unity's physics system. We'll add and configure a **Rigidbody** component for the ammo now:

1. Select the **Ammo** object.

2. Select **Component | Physics | Rigidbody** from the application menu.

3. On the **Rigidbody** component in the **Inspector**, disable the **Use Gravity** checkbox to prevent the ammo from falling to the ground during gameplay:

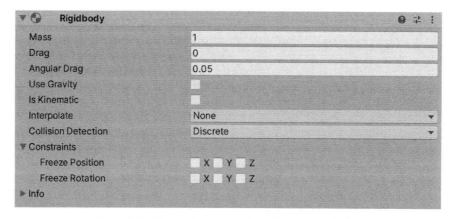

Figure 4.9 – Removing gravity from the Ammo object

For our purposes, gravity does not need to apply to the ammo as it should simply travel along and eventually be destroyed. This highlights an essential point in game development generally: real-world physics need not apply to every object accurately. We only need physics to make objects appear correct to the player when they're looking.

In addition to adding a Mover script and physics components, we also need the ammo to damage objects and destroy or disable itself on collision. To achieve this, create a new script file called Ammo.cs. The entire code for this is included in the following code block, as follows:

```
public class Ammo : MonoBehaviour
{

    public float Damage = 100f;
    public float LifeTime = 2f;


    void OnEnable()
    {
```

```
            CancelInvoke();
            Invoke("Die", LifeTime);
    }


    void OnTriggerEnter(Collider Col)
    {
        Health H = Col.gameObject.GetComponent<Health>();
        if(H == null)
        {
            return;
        }
        H.HealthPoints -= Damage;
        Die();
    }


    void Die()
    {
        gameObject.SetActive(false);
    }
}
```

The following points summarize the preceding code:

- The Ammo class should be attached to the **Ammo** prefab object and will be instantiated for all ammo objects created. Its primary purpose is to damage any objects with which it collides.

- The OnTriggerEnter function is invoked for the ammo when it enters a trigger attached to a movable entity, such as the player or enemies. It retrieves the Health component attached to the object, if it has one, and reduces its health by the Damage amount. The **Health component** was created in the previous chapter.

- Notice that each ammo object will have a LifeTime value. This represents the amount of time in seconds for which the ammo should remain alive and active after it is generated in the scene. After the lifetime expires, the ammo should either be destroyed entirely or deactivated (more on this shortly).

- The Invoke function is used to disable the ammo object after the LifeTime interval. The function call is scheduled in the OnEnable event, which is called automatically by Unity each time an object is activated (changed from disabled to enabled).

To apply the new script to the ammo object, take the following steps:

1. Drag and drop the **Ammo** script file from the `Scripts` folder in the **Project** panel to the **Ammo**.

2. Drag and drop the whole **Ammo** object in the scene back to the **Project** panel in the `Prefabs` folder to create a new **Ammo** prefab, as shown in *Figure 4.10*:

Figure 4.10 – Creating an Ammo prefab

Congratulations! You've now created an **Ammo** prefab, which we will spawn from the turret location we previously set up. However, before we can start work on the spawn system, we need a method of creating and storing projectiles efficiently, which is where the object pool design pattern comes in.

Creating an object pool

The **Ammo** prefab created so far presents us with a technical problem that, if not taken seriously, has the potential to cause serious performance issues in our game. When the spaceship weapon is fired, we'll need to generate ammo that launches into the scene and destroys the enemies on collision. This is fine in general, but the problem is that the player could potentially press the fire button many times in quick succession, and could even hold down the fire button for long periods of time, thereby spawning potentially hundreds of **Ammo** prefabs. We could use the **Instantiate** function to generate these prefabs dynamically, but this is problematic because instantiating is computationally expensive. When used to instantiate many items in succession, it will typically cause a nightmarish slowdown that'll reduce the **frames per second** (**FPS**) to unacceptable levels. We need to avoid this!

The solution is known as **Pooling**, **Object Pooling**, or **Object Caching**. In essence, it means that we must spawn a large and recyclable batch of ammo objects at the level startup (a pool of objects) that initially begin hidden or deactivated, and we activate the objects as and when needed. When the ammo collides with an enemy, or when its lifetime expires, we don't destroy the object entirely; we deactivate it again, returning it to the pool for reuse later if needed. In this way, we avoid all calls to instantiate, apart from the initial pool creation, and recycle the ammo objects that we have.

To get started with coding the object pool, we'll make an `AmmoManager` class. This class will be responsible for two things:

- Generating a pool of ammo objects at scene startup
- Giving us a valid and available ammo object from the pool on demand, such as on weapon-fire

Consider the following `AmmoManager` code block created to achieve this:

```
public class AmmoManager : MonoBehaviour
{
    public static AmmoManager AmmoManagerSingleton = null;
    public GameObject AmmoPrefab = null;
    public int PoolSize = 100;
    public Queue<Transform> AmmoQueue = new Queue<Transform>();

    private GameObject[] AmmoArray;

    void Awake ()
```

```
    {
        if(AmmoManagerSingleton != null)
        {
            Destroy(GetComponent<AmmoManager>());
            return;
        }

        AmmoManagerSingleton = this;
        AmmoArray = new GameObject[PoolSize];

        for(int i = 0; i < PoolSize; ++i)
        {
            AmmoArray[i] = Instantiate(AmmoPrefab, Vector3.zero,
                Quaternion.identity, transform) as GameObject;
            Transform ObjTransform = AmmoArray[i].transform;
            AmmoQueue.Enqueue(ObjTransform);
            AmmoArray[i].SetActive(false);
        }
    }

    public static Transform SpawnAmmo (Vector3 Position,
        Quaternion Rotation)
    {
        Transform SpawnedAmmo =
            AmmoManagerSingleton.AmmoQueue.Dequeue();

        SpawnedAmmo.gameObject.SetActive(true);
        SpawnedAmmo.position = Position;
        SpawnedAmmo.localRotation = Rotation;

        AmmoManagerSingleton.AmmoQueue.Enqueue(SpawnedAmmo);
        return SpawnedAmmo;
    }
}
```

The following points summarize the code block:

- `AmmoManager` features an `AmmoArray` member variable, which holds a complete list (a sequential **array** of **references**) of all ammo objects to be generated at startup (during the `Awake` event).

- `AmmoArray` will be sized to `PoolSize`. This is the total number of ammo objects to be generated. The `Awake` function generates the ammo objects at the beginning of the level and adds them to the queue using `Enqueue`.

- Once generated, each ammo object is deactivated with `SetActive(false)` and held in the pool until needed.

- `AmmoManager` uses the `Queue` class from the **Mono library** to manage how specific ammo objects are selected from the pool. The queue is a **First-In, First-Out (FIFO)** structure. The object removed from the queue is always the object at the front. More information on the `Queue` class can be found online at `https://msdn.microsoft.com/en-us/ library/7977ey2c%28v=vs.110%29.aspx`.

- The `Enqueue` function of the `Queue` object is called during `Awake` to add objects initially to the queue, one by one, as they are generated.

- The `SpawnAmmo` function generates a new item of ammo in the scene. This function does not rely on the `Instantiate` function but uses the `Queue` object instead. It removes the first ammo object from the queue, activates it, and then adds it to the end of the queue again behind all the other ammo objects. In this way, a cycle of generation and regeneration happens, allowing all ammo objects to be recycled.

- `AmmoManager` stores a **singleton** object, meaning that one, and only one, instance of the object should exist in the scene at any one time. This functionality is achieved through the **static** member, `AmmoManagerSingleton`.

To use this class, take the following steps:

1. Create a new GameObject in the scene called `AmmoManager` by selecting **GameObject | Create Empty** from the application menu.

2. Drag and drop the `AmmoManager` script from the **Project** panel to the new object in the Hierarchy.

3. Drag and drop the **Ammo** prefab from the `Prefabs` folder to the **Ammo Prefab** slot for the **Ammo Manager** component in the object's Inspector:

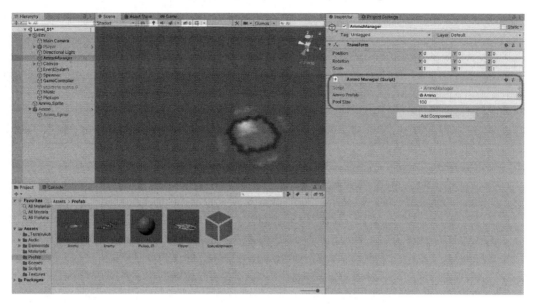

Figure 4.11 – Adding AmmoManager to an object

The scene now features an `AmmoManager` object to maintain an ammo pool. However, nothing in our existing functionality connects a fire button press from the gamer with the generation of a projectile in the scene. Let's fix that now.

Spawning projectiles

The game now has an efficient way of storing projectiles that we can retrieve when required. We'll put this system to the test soon as we create the logic to spawn the projectiles whenever the player presses a specific button. The functionality we require will sit nicely in the `PlayerController` script that we started in the previous chapter. The amended `PlayerController` class is included in the following code block. Only the changes are included in the following code; for the full class, please refer to the `Chapter04/End/Assets/Scripts` folder:

```
public class PlayerController : MonoBehaviour
{
    public string FireAxis = "Fire1";
    public float ReloadDelay = 0.3f;
    public bool CanFire = true;
    public Transform[] TurretTransforms;
```

```
Void Awake ()
{
    ThisBody = GetComponent<Rigidbody>();
}

Void FixedUpdate ()
{
    ...
    if(Input.GetButtonDown(FireAxis) && CanFire)
    {
        foreach(Transform T in TurretTransforms)
        {
            AmmoManager.SpawnAmmo(T.position, T.rotation);
        }

        CanFire = false;
        Invoke ("EnableFire", ReloadDelay);
    }
}

void EnableFire()
{
    CanFire = true;
}
}
```

In summary, we have the following:

- `PlayerController` now features a `TurretTransform` array variable, which will list all the children to be used as turret spawn locations.

- During the `Update` function, `PlayerController` checks for a fire button press. If detected, the code cycles through all turrets and spawns one ammo object at each turret location.

Once the ammo is fired, `ReloadDelay` is engaged (set to `true`). This means that the delay must first expire before new ammo can be fired again later.

After adding this code to `PlayerController`, select the **Player** object in the scene, enter 1 in the **Size** field of **Turret Transforms**, and then drag and drop the empty object onto the **Turret Transforms** slot. This example uses only one turret, but you could add more if desired:

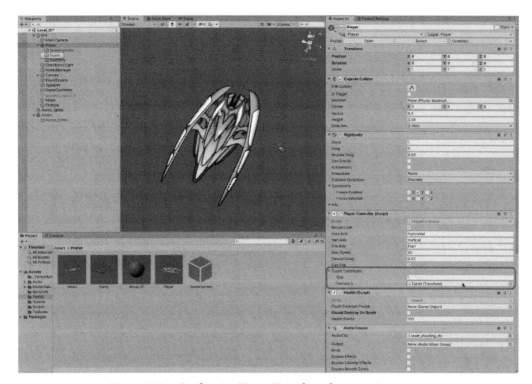

Figure 4.12 – Configuring Turret Transform for spawning ammo

Now you're ready to playtest and fire ammo. By playing the scene and pressing fire on the keyboard or mouse (left-click), projectiles will be generated. Excellent! However, when testing, you may notice two main problems. First, the ammo is the incorrect size. Second, the ammo sometimes bounces, flips, or reacts to the player's spaceship. Fixing the size issue is simple:

1. Select the **Ammo** prefab in the **Project** panel.

2. In the **Inspector**, enter a new scale in the **Transform** component.

However, fixing the second issue, where the projectile collides with the player ship, is slightly more complex, and involves editing Unity's physics settings, which is what we'll look at next.

Configuring projectile physics

If the ammo appears to bounce or react to the player's spaceship, then we'll need to make the ammo immune or unresponsive to the `Player` object. To achieve this, we can use **physics layers**:

1. Select the `Player` object in the scene.

2. From the **Inspector**, click on the **Layer** dropdown, and choose **Add Layer** from the context menu.

3. Name the layer **Player** to indicate that all objects attached to the layer are associated with the player:

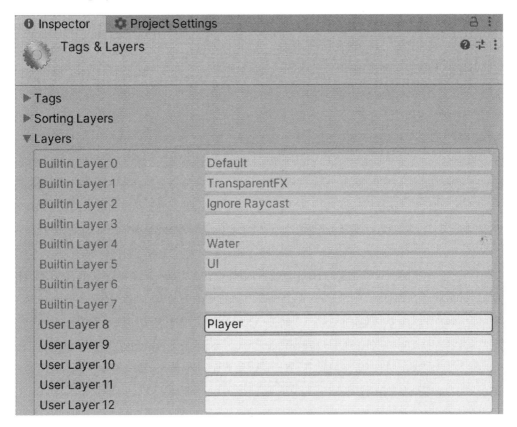

Figure 4.13 – Creating layers

4. Assign both the `Player` object in the scene and the **Ammo** prefab in the **Project** panel to the newly created **Player** layer by selecting each in turn, clicking on the **Layer** dropdown, and choosing the **Player** option:

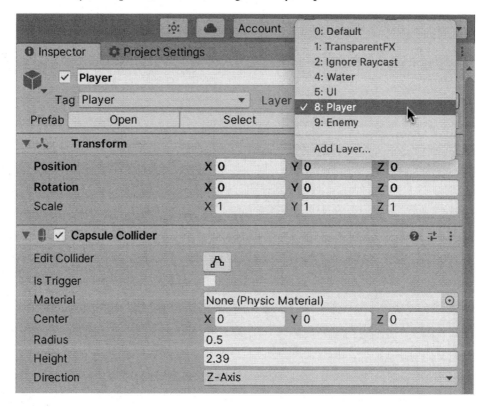

Figure 4.14 – Assigning the player and ammo to the Player layer

5. If prompted with a pop-up dialog, choose to change the children also. This ensures that all child objects are also associated with the same layer as the parent.

    Both **Player** and **Ammo** have now been assigned to the same layer. From here, we can make all objects in the same layer ignore each other.

6. Navigate to **Edit | Project Settings** from the **Application** menu.

7. In the window that appears, select **Physics**.

8. The global **Physics** settings appear in the **Project Settings** window. At the bottom of the window, **Layer Collision Matrix** displays how layers interact with each other. Intersecting layers with a checkmark can and will affect each other. For this reason, remove the checkmark for the **Player** layer to prevent collisions from occurring between objects on this layer, as shown in *Figure 4.15*:

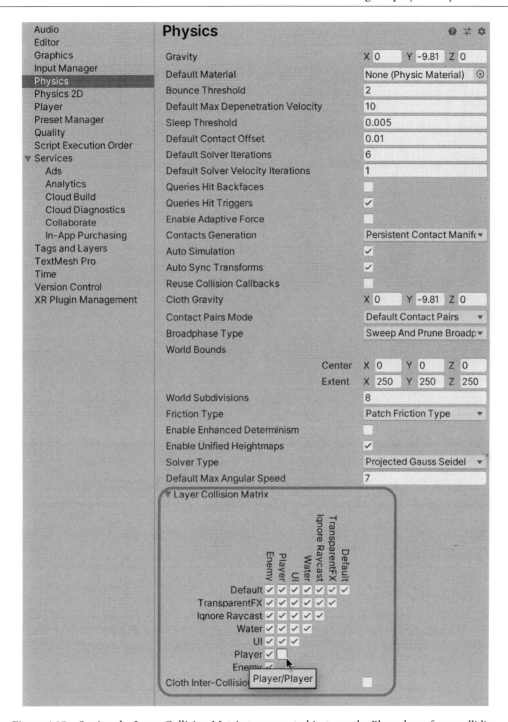

Figure 4.15 – Setting the Layer Collision Matrix to prevent objects on the Player layer from colliding

With **the Layer Collision Matrix** set, test the game again by pressing Play on the toolbar. When you do this and press fire, the projectiles should no longer react to the player spaceship. The projectile should, however, still collide with and destroy the enemies:

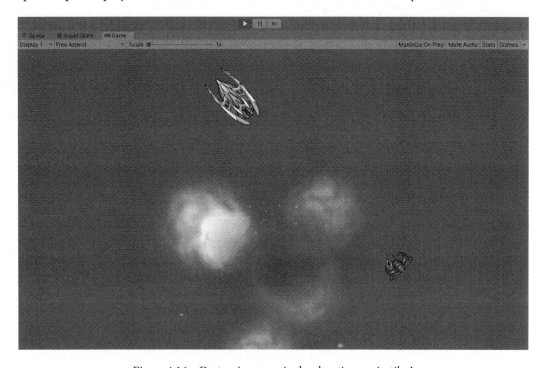

Figure 4.16 – Destroying enemies by shooting projectiles!

Excellent work! We now have a spaceship that can fire weapons and destroy enemies, and the physics works as expected. Maybe you'd like to customize the player controls a little, or perhaps you want to use a gamepad. The next section will explore this further.

Customizing controls

You may not like the default controls and key combinations associated with the input axes—**Horizontal**, **Vertical**, and **Fire1**. Perhaps you want to change them. Even if you don't want to change the controls for this game, you most certainly will in a future project, so it's good to know how.

The input axes are read using the `Input.GetAxis` function (shown earlier) and are specified by human-readable names, but it's not immediately clear how Unity maps specific input buttons and devices to these virtual axes. Here, we'll see how to customize them. To get started, do the following:

1. Access the input settings by navigating to **Edit | Project Settings** from the **Application** menu.

2. Select **Input Manager** in the **Project Settings** window that opens.

On selecting this option, a collection of custom-defined input axes appears as a list. This defines all the axes used by the input system. The **Horizontal** and **Vertical** axes should be listed here:

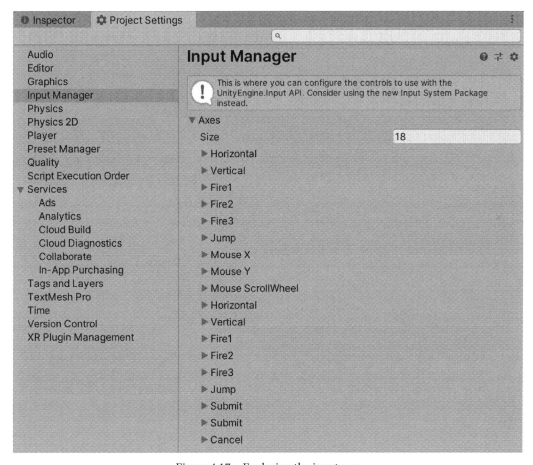

Figure 4.17 – Exploring the input axes

By expanding each axis in the **Project Settings** panel, you can specify how specific keys and controls on hardware devices, such as a keyboard and mouse, will map to an axis. The **Horizontal** axis, for example, is defined twice. For the first definition, **Horizontal** is mapped to the left, right, and *A* and *D* keys on the keyboard. Right and *D* are mapped as **Positive Button** because, when pressed, they produce positive **floating-point** values from the `Input.GetAxis` function (0–1). Left and *A* are mapped as **Negative Button** because, when pressed, they result in negative floating-point values for `Input.GetAxis`. This makes it easy to move objects left and right using negative and positive numbers:

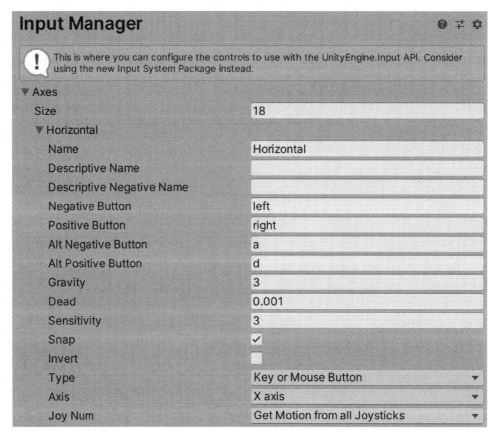

Figure 4.18 – Configuring an input axis

As mentioned, the **Horizontal** input is defined twice—once near the top of the list and again near the bottom. These two definitions are accumulative and not contradictory— they stack on top of one another. They allow you to map multiple devices to the same axis, giving you cross-platform and multidevice control over your games.

By default, **Horizontal** is mapped in the first definition to the left, right, *A*, and *D* keys on the keyboard, and in the second definition, to joystick motion. Both definitions are valid and work together. You can have as many definitions for the same axis as you need, depending on the controls you need to support.

> **More Information**
>
> More information on player input and customizing controls can be found in the online Unity documentation at `https://docs.unity3d.com/Manual/class-InputManager.html`.

For this project, the controls will remain at their defaults, but go ahead and change or add additional controls if you want to support different configurations.

With the player now controlled precisely as we want, and able to shoot projectiles that collide with and destroy our enemies, there's one last thing missing from our core gameplay loop—keeping track of and displaying the score.

Creating the score system

We want to be able to assign a point value to each enemy and have a visible score increase with each kill. This goal can be split into two tasks: first, we need the UI to display the score and second, we need logic to track the current score and push any changes to the UI. As the second task (the score logic) requires the UI, we'll start by creating an interface to display the score before moving on to the logic.

Implementing the score UI

UI is an acronym for **user interface** and refers to all the 2D graphical elements that sit atop the game window and provide information to the player:

1. Create a new UI **Canvas** object by selecting **GameObject | UI | Canvas** from the application menu.

2. The **Canvas object** defines the total surface or area in which the UI lives, including all buttons, text, and other **widgets**. Initially, the **Canvas object** may be too large or too small to be seen clearly in the viewport, so select the **Canvas object** in the Hierarchy panel and press the *F* key on the keyboard to focus the object. It should appear as a sizeable, vertically aligned rectangle, as shown in *Figure 4.19*:

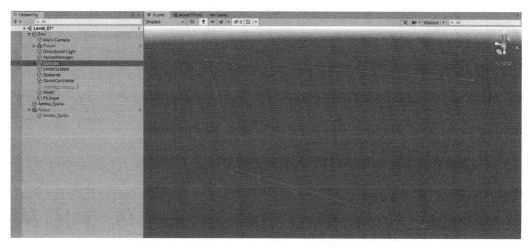

Figure 4.19 – Examining the **Canvas object** in the viewport

The **Canvas object** is not visible itself in the **Game** tab. Instead, it acts as a container. Even so, it strongly influences how contained objects appear on the screen in terms of size, position, and scale. For this reason, before adding objects and refining the design of an interface, it's helpful to configure your **Canvas object** first. To do this, take these steps:

1. Select the **Canvas object** in the scene.

2. From the **Inspector**, click on the **UI Scale Mode** drop-down option under the **Canvas Scaler** component.

3. From the drop-down list, choose the **Scale With Screen Size** option.

4. For the **Reference Resolution** field, enter 1920 for the X field and 1080 for the Y field, as shown in *Figure 4.20*:

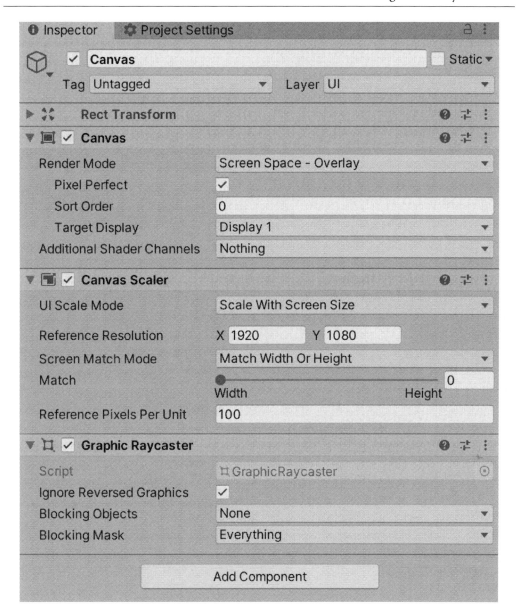

Figure 4.20 – Adjusting the Canvas Scaler component

By adjusting the **Canvas Scaler** component to **Scale With Screen Size**, the UI for the game will automatically stretch and shrink to fit the target resolution, ensuring that each element is scaled to the same proportions, maintaining the overall look and feel. This is a quick and easy method to create a UI once and have it adjust its size to fit nearly any resolution. It may not always be the best solution to maintaining the highest quality graphical fidelity, but it's functional and suitable for many applications.

In any case, before proceeding with the UI design, it's helpful to see both the **Scene** viewport and **Game** tab side by side in the interface (or across two monitors, if you have a multi-monitor configuration). This allows us to build the interface in the **Scene** viewport, and then preview its effects in the **Game** tab. You can rearrange the **Scene** and **Game** tabs by dragging and dropping the **Game** tab beside the **Scene** tab in the Unity Editor. Your Unity Editor should then look similar to the one in *Figure 4.21*:

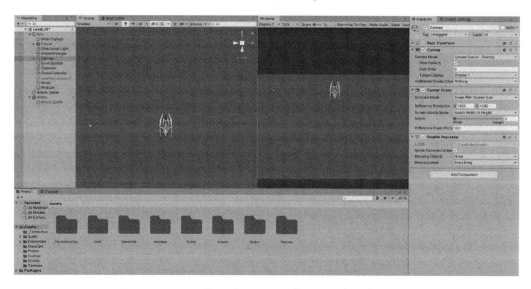

Figure 4.21 – Docking the Scene and Game tabs side by side

Next, let's add the text widget to the UI to display the game score:

1. Right-click on the **Canvas object** in the **Hierarchy** panel.

2. Select **UI | Text** from the context menu that appears.

This creates a new text object as a child of the **Canvas object**, as opposed to a top-level object with no parent. The text object is useful to draw text on screen with a specific color, size, and font setting.

By default, the text object may not initially appear visible in either the scene or viewport, even though it's listed as an object in the Hierarchy panel. However, look more closely at the scene, and you're likely to see a very small and dark text object, which appears both in the Canvas and the **Game** tab, as shown in *Figure 4.22*:

Figure 4.22: Newly created text objects can sometimes be difficult to see

By default, new text objects feature black text with a small font size. For this project, these settings will need to be changed:

1. Select the **Text** object in the **Hierarchy** panel, if it's not already selected.

2. From the **Inspector**, on the **Text** component, change the text color to white and the font size to 20:

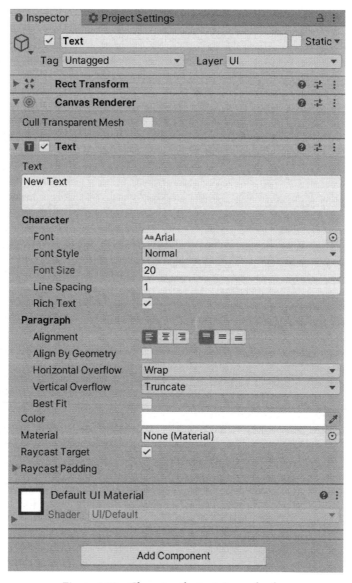

Figure 4.23 – Changing the text size and color

The text still appears too small, even after changing its size. If you increase the size further, however, the text may disappear from view. This happens because each text object has a rectangular boundary defining its limits. When the font size increases beyond what can fit in the boundary, the text is hidden altogether. To fix this, we'll expand the text boundary:

1. Switch to the **Rect Transform** tool with *T* or select the tool from the toolbar.

2. On activating the **Rect Transform** tool, a clearly defined boundary will be drawn around the selected text object in the **Scene** viewport, indicating its rectangular extents. To increase the boundary size to accommodate larger text, click and drag on the boundary edges with the mouse to adjust them as needed.

3. Adjusting the rectangle will not change the text size but will increase the boundary size, and now you can increase **Font Size** to improve text readability:

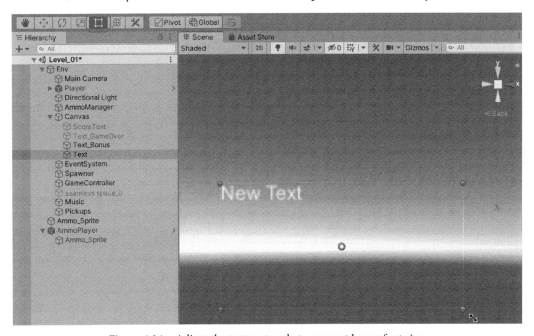

Figure 4.24 – Adjust the text rectangle to support larger font sizes

4. In addition to setting the text boundary size, the text can also be vertically aligned to the boundaries' center by clicking on the center alignment button for the vertical group. For horizontal alignment, the text should remain left-aligned to allow for the score display, as shown in *Figure 4.25*:

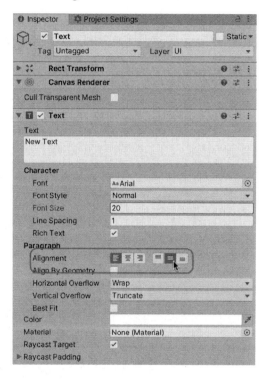

Figure 4.25 – Aligning text within the boundary

Although the text is now aligned vertically within its containing boundary, we'll still need to align it as a whole to the canvas container to ensure that it remains on screen at the same position and orientation, even if the **Game** window is resized and realigned. To do this, we'll use **Anchors**:

1. Select the transform tool (*W*).

2. Reposition the text object to the top-right corner of the screen at the location where the score should appear. The object will automatically move within a 2D plane as opposed to 3D space.

As you move the text object in the **Scene** viewport, check its appearance in the **Game** tab to ensure that it looks correct and appropriate. To better understand what it will look like in-game, you can set the **Text** field in the **Inspector** to Score :, as shown in *Figure 4.26*. However, this is not essential as we will update this text programmatically soon::

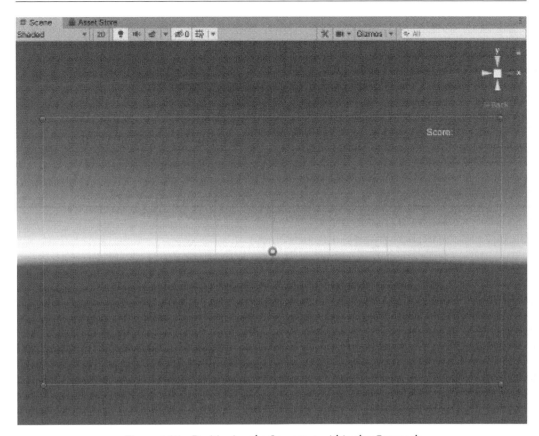

Figure 4.26 – Positioning the Score text within the Game tab

To secure the position of the text object on screen (preventing it from sliding or moving), even if the user resizes the **Game** tab, we can set the object's Anchor position to the top-right corner of the screen. Using an Anchor ensures that the text is always positioned as a constant, proportional offset from its Anchor. To configure an Anchor for the text object, do the following:

1.   Click on the **Anchor Presets** button under the **Rect Transform** component in the Inspector. When you do this, a preset menu appears from which you can choose a range of alignment locations. Each preset is graphically presented as a small diagram, including a red dot at the location of anchor alignment.

2. Select the **top-right** preset, as shown in *Figure 4.27*:

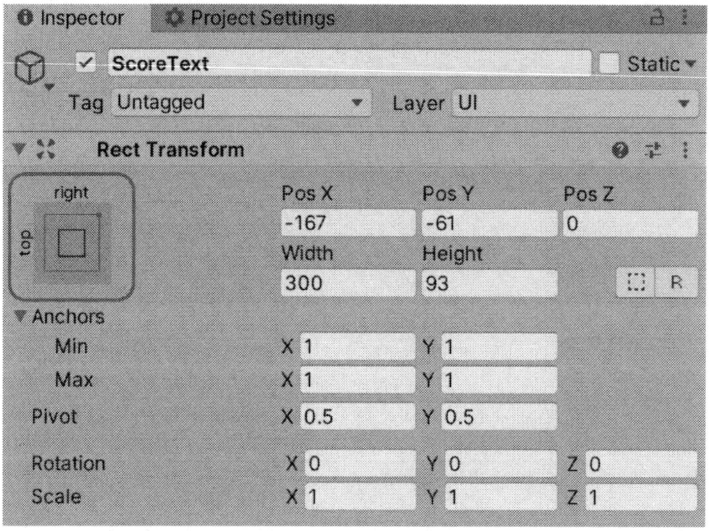

Figure 4.27 – Aligning the text object to the screen

Excellent work! The text object is now ready to use. Of course, in play mode, the text remains unchanged and doesn't display a real score. That's because we need to add some code. However, overall, the text object is in place, and we can move on to writing that code.

Scripting the score logic

To display a score in the newly created UI, we'll first need to create a scoring system in code. The score functionality will be added to a general, overarching `GameController` class, responsible for all game-wide logic and features. The code for `GameController` is included in the following code block:

```
public class GameController : MonoBehaviour
{

    public static GameController ThisInstance = null;


    public static int Score;
    public string ScorePrefix = string.Empty;
    public Text ScoreText = null;
    public Text GameOverText = null;


    void Awake()
```

```
        {
            ThisInstance = this;

        }

    void Update()
        {
            if(ScoreText!=null)
            {
                ScoreText.text = ScorePrefix + Score.ToString();

            }

        }

    public static void GameOver()
        {
            if(ThisInstance.GameOverText!=null)
            {
                ThisInstance.GameOverText.gameObject.
                    SetActive(true);

            }

        }

}
```

In summary, we have the following:

- The GameController class uses the UnityEngine.UI namespace. This is important because it includes access to all the UI classes and objects in Unity. If you don't include this namespace in your source files, then you cannot use UI objects in that script

- The GameController class features two public Text members—namely, ScoreText and GameOverText. These refer to two text objects, both of which are optional as the GameController code will work just fine even if the members are null. ScoreText is a reference to a text UI object to display score text, and GameOverText will be used to display a message when a game-over condition occurs.

To use the new script, take the following steps:

1. Create a new, empty object in the scene named GameController.
2. Drag and drop the GameController script file to that object.

3. Drag and drop the `ScoreText` object to the **Score Text** field for `GameController` in the **Inspector**.

4. In the **Score Prefix** field, enter the text that should prefix the score itself. The score, on its own, is simply a number (such as 1,000). The prefix allows you to add text to the front of this score, indicating to the player what the numbers mean:

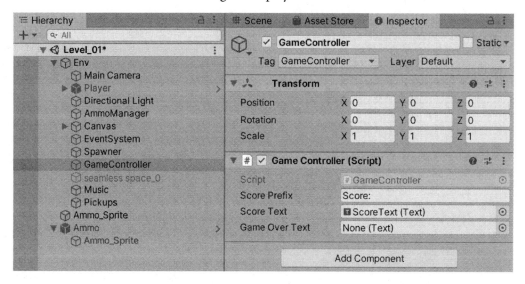

Figure 4.28 – Creating a GameController object to maintain the game score

Now, take the game for a test run, and you'll see the score display at the top-right corner of the **Game** tab using the UI text object. The score will always remain at 0 because we are yet to write the functionality to increase it. For our game, the score should increase when an enemy object is destroyed. To achieve this, we'll create a new script file, `ScoreOnDestroy`:

```
public class ScoreOnDestroy : MonoBehaviour
{
    public int ScoreValue = 50;

    void OnDestroy()
    {
        GameController.Score += ScoreValue;
    }
}
```

The script should be attached to any object that assigns you points when it's destroyed, such as the enemies. `ScoreValue` specifies the total number of points awarded. To attach the script to the enemy prefab, take the following steps:

1. Select the `Prefabs` folder in the **Project** panel.

2. From the **Inspector**, click on the **Add Component** button.

3. Type `ScoreOnDestroy` into the search field to add the component to the prefab:

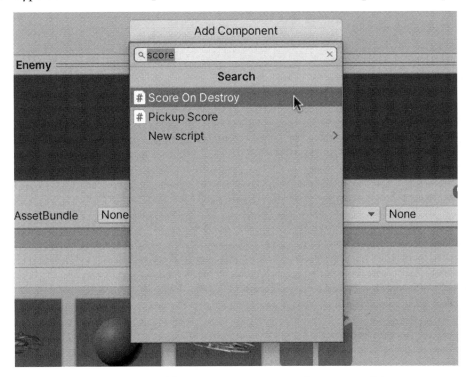

Figure 4.29 – Adding a score component to the enemy prefab

4. Once added, specify the total number of points to be allocated for destroying an enemy. For this game, a value of 50 points is assigned.

Great work! You now have destroyable enemies that assign you points on destruction. This means that you can finally have an in-game score and could even extend gameplay to include high-score features and leaderboards. This also means that our game is almost finished and ready to build, but before that, we'll add a couple of small final touches.

Adding the final touches

In this section, we'll add the final touches to the game. We'll start by adding a background image to fit the space theme, and then we'll move on to adding background music. These small additions should have a significant impact on the feel of the game.

Adding a background image

First on the agenda is fixing the game background! Until now, the background has displayed the default background color associated with the game camera. However, as the game is set in space, we should display a space background. To do this, take the following steps:

1. Create a new **Sprite** object in the Scene that'll display a space image by navigating to **GameObject | 2D Object | Sprite** from the menu.

2. Drag and drop the space texture from the **Project** panel to the **Sprite** field on the **Sprite Renderer** component in the scene.

3. Rotate the object 90 degrees on the **X** axis.

4. Position the object at the world origin (0, 0, 0).

5. Scale the object until it fills the viewport. I used a scale of 3 on the *X* and *Y* axes.

The correctly configured background is shown in *Figure 4.30*:

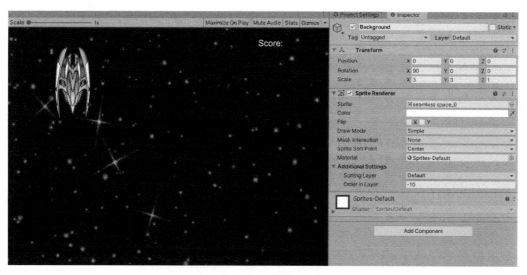

Figure 4.30 – Configuring the background

With those steps completed, you should now have an appropriate background for your space game!

> **UI Image**
>
> There are several different methods of implementing a background image. We could, for example, have created the background as a **UI image**. We could then use the rectangle and **Anchors** tools, outlined in the *Implementing the score UI* section, to make it fullscreen.

With the background looking the part, let's make it sound the part too by adding background music, an integral component of many games.

Implementing background music

Now that the level has a suitable background, let's add some background music, which will play on a loop. To do this, take the following steps:

1. Select the music track in the **Project** panel from the Audio folder.

2. In the **Inspector**, set the music **Load Type** option to **Streaming**, and ensure **Preload Audio Data** is disabled. These audio settings improve loading times as Unity will not need to load all music data to memory as the scene begins:

Figure 4.31 – Configuring audio data ready for playback

3. Next, create a new empty GameObject in the scene and name it `Music`.

4. Drag and drop the **Music** track from the **Project** panel to the **Music** object, adding it as an **Audio Source** component. **Audio Source** components play sound effects and music.

5. Under the **Audio Source** component in the **Inspector**, enable the **Play On Awake** and **Loop** checkboxes. These settings ensure the music starts at the level's beginning and loops seamlessly for the lifetime of the scene.

6. Lastly, the **Spatial Blend** field should be set to 0, which represents 2D:

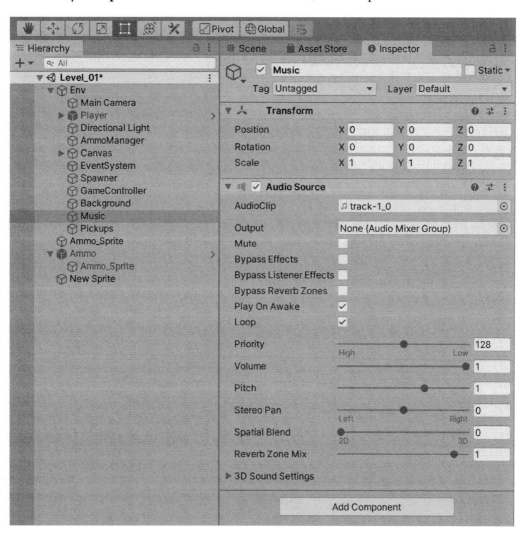

Figure 4.32 – Creating a GameObject with an Audio Source component

2D sounds have a consistent volume throughout the level regardless of the player's position because 2D sounds are not **spatially** located. 3D sounds, in contrast, are used for gunshots, footsteps, explosions, and other sounds that exist in 3D space and whose volume should change based on how close the player is standing to them when they play.

Now, let's take the game for a test run! Click on the Play button on the toolbar and test it out. If the music doesn't play, check that the **Mute Audio** button is disabled in the **Game** tab:

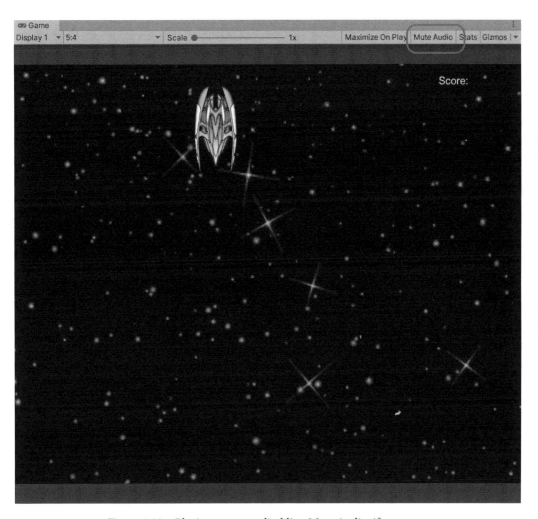

Figure 4.33 – Playing a game – disabling Mute Audio, if necessary

And that's almost a wrap! We've implemented every feature we desired in our space game. However, before we move on to the next project, we'll look at the tools Unity provides to help you test and diagnose potential performance issues.

Testing and diagnosis

With practically all games, you'll need to spend considerable time testing and **debugging** to reduce bugs and errors as much as humanly possible. With this sample program, very little debugging and testing has been required by you, but that's not just because the game is simple. It's because I've already prechecked and pretested most of the code and functionality before presenting the material to you in this book, ensuring that you get a smooth learning experience. For your own projects, however, you'll need to do lots of testing. One way to get started is by using the **Stats** panel. To open this panel, click on the **Stats** button in the **Game** tab:

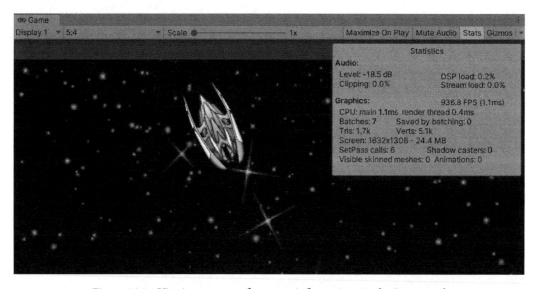

Figure 4.34 – Viewing game performance information via the Stats panel

> **More Information**
>
> More details on the **Stats** panel are included in *Chapter 2, Creating a Collection Game*, and more information can be found online in the Unity documentation at `http://docs.unity3d.com/Manual/RenderingStatistics.html`.

Another debugging tool is the **Profiler**. This tool is useful when the **Stats** panel has already helped you identify a general problem, such as a low FPS, and you want to dig deeper to find where the problem might be located.

> **More Information**
>
> More details on the Profiler are included later in *Chapter 6, Continuing the 2D Adventure.*

To use the Profiler tool, do the following:

1. Select **Window | Analysis | Profiler** from the **Application** menu.

2. With the **Profiler** window open, click on Play on the toolbar to playtest your game. When you do this, the **Profiler** window fills with color-coded performance data in a graph, as shown in *Figure 4.35*:

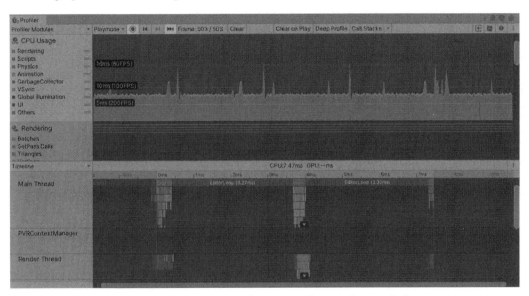

Figure 4.35 – During gameplay, the Profiler populates with data

> **Important Note**
>
> Reading and understanding the graph requires some experience, but as a general rule, watch out for mountains and peaks (sharp fluctuations) in the graph as this could indicate a problem, especially when it roughly coincides with frame rate drops.

3. If you want to investigate further, pause the game and then click in the graph. The horizontal axis (the *x* axis) represents the most recent frames, and the vertical axis represents workload. When you click in the graph, a line marker is added to indicate the frame under investigation:

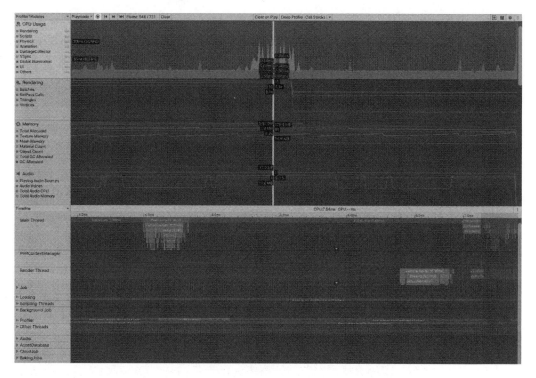

Figure 4.36 – Investigating performance data with the Profiler

Beneath the graph, you'll find detailed information on the currently selected module. In *Figure 4.36*, the **CPU Usage** module is selected, so this area will show a timeline of CPU instructions.

> **More Information**
>
> More information on the Profiler can be found in the online Unity documentation at `https://docs.unity3d.com/Manual/Profiler.html`.

Now, finally, we're ready to build a standalone version of our game to send off to friends, family, and testers! The process to do this is the same as detailed in *Chapter 2, Creating a Collection Game*, to build the coin collection game.

Summary

Great work! We're really on a roll now, having completed two Unity projects. Both the coin collection game and twin-stick shooter are, ultimately, simple games in that they don't rely on advanced mechanics or display sophisticated features. However, even complicated games, when boiled down to their fundamental ingredients, can be found to rest on a similar foundation of essential concepts such as the ones that we've covered so far. That's why our projects are so critical to understanding Unity from the ground up. In this project alone, we've learned how to spawn prefabs at runtime, import textures and audio, create a basic UI, implement reusable components, and determined how to cache objects using an object pool. No matter what project you are working on, some or all of these techniques will be useful.

In this chapter, while we created a game with a 2D perspective, we used mostly 3D components. In the next chapter, we'll be going fully 2D and creating a 2D platform game. Moving from 3D to 2D brings a few changes in our workflow, and these will be discussed in detail, as well as important 2D topics such as sprites, environmental physics, and 2D movement. We'll also look at adding **post-processing effects**. These effects can help improve the look of the game and are applied to the image before it appears onscreen.

Test your knowledge

Q1. Static variables are...

   A. Hidden variables for static objects

   B. Shared variables across all instances of a class

   C. Protected variables

   D. Constants

Q2. The Profiler is useful for...

   A. Pausing gameplay

   B. Identifying performance issues

   C. Removing objects

   D. Checking audio levels

Q3. UI objects are useful for...

A. Creating interface elements

B. Making animations

C. Sorting objects by name

D. Editing mesh objects

Q4. The **Layer Collision Matrix** lets you…

A. Prevent groups of objects from colliding

B. Make objects collide

C. Remove all collisions

D. Activate low-quality collisions

Further reading

For more information, take a look at the following links:

- `https://unity3d.com/learn/tutorials/s/scripting`
- `https://www.packtpub.com/game-development/mastering-ui-development-unity`
- `https://www.packtpub.com/game-development/learning-c-developing-games-unity-2019-fourth-edition`

5
Creating a 2D Adventure Game

In this chapter, we will start an entirely new project: a 2D adventure game where the player controls an alien character and explores and navigates a dangerous world, complete with a quest to collect a gem. Platform games have been hugely popular since their inception in the 1980s with the first platforming game *Space Panic*. Since then, the genre has grown drastically to include the likes of *Super Mario*, *Mega Man*, *Crash Bandicoot*, and *Limbo*.

This project will build on the ideas we introduced in previous chapters but will also introduce new techniques, such as complex collisions, 2D physics, singletons, and more. Learning these techniques will empower you to create your own 2D games. In this chapter alone, we will cover the following topics:

- Configuring the game view by adjusting the camera's vertical size to ensure our **sprites** are shown at the correct size

- Creating an environment including a 2D level with a background and foreground

- Adding **post-processing effects** to improve the look of our game

- Creating a 2D player consisting of several GameObjects

- Moving the player using 2D physics and collision detection

- Optimizing rendering using Unity's **Sprite Packer**

Let's get started!

Technical requirements

This chapter assumes that you have not only completed the projects from the previous chapters but also have a good, basic knowledge of C# scripting in general, though not necessarily in Unity.

The starting assets can be found in this book's companion files, in the `Chapter05/Assets` folder. You can start here and follow along with this chapter. The end project can be found in the `Chapter05/End` folder.

Getting started

Adventure games require the player to use their cunning, dexterity, mental sharpness, and acumen to make progress. Such games feature dangerous obstacles, challenging missions, and character interaction, as opposed to all-out action like many first-person shooter games. Our adventure game will be no exception. The following is a screenshot of the game that we'll be creating:

Figure 5.1 – The 2D adventure game we'll be creating

In this game, the player moves around using the keyboard arrows or *W*, *A*, *S*, and *D* keys. Furthermore, they can jump with the *spacebar* and interact with other characters by approaching them. During the game, the player will be tasked with a mission from an NPC character to collect an ancient gem hidden somewhere within the level. The player must then navigate dangerous obstacles in search of the gem before returning to the NPC, completing the game.

To get started, do the following:

1. Create a new Unity project using the *2D Project Template*. The project creation process was outlined in *Chapter 1, Exploring the Fundamentals of Unity*.

2. Import the *Standard Assets Package* (once again, this process is outlined in *Chapter 1, Exploring the Fundamentals of Unity*). This package includes particle effects, character control, and cross-platform input systems that we'll use in our game.

3. Next, we'll import the texture assets we'll be using, both for the player character and the environment. The assets to import are included in this book's companion files, in the the `Chapter05/Assets` folder. From here, select all the textures and drag and drop them into the Unity Project panel in a designated `Textures` folder (create one if you haven't already!). This will import all the relevant textures into the active project, as shown in the following screenshot:

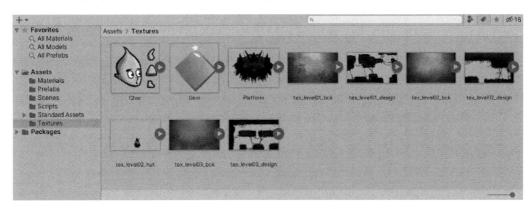

Figure 5.2 – Importing texture assets into the active project

---

Tip

Remember that you can always use the Thumbnail Size Slider (at the bottom-right corner of the **Project** panel) to adjust the size of thumbnail previews in order to get an easier view of your texture assets.

Now that we've created the project using the 2D template, the textures should be imported as sprites rather than as textures for a 3D model. To confirm this, do the following:

1. Select all the imported textures.

2. From the **Inspector**, make sure that the **Texture Type** field is set to **Sprite (2D and UI)**.

3. If enabled, remove the checkmark from the **Generate Mip Maps** box.

4. Lastly, if you made any changes, click on the **Apply** button to save your changes:

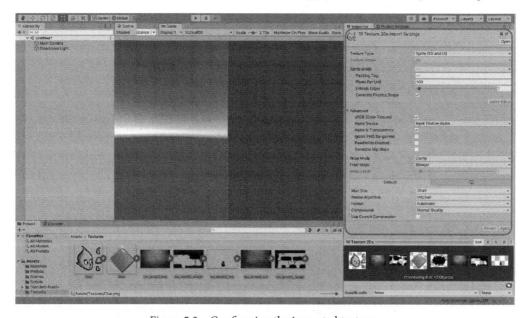

Figure 5.3 – Configuring the imported textures

With the changes applied, Unity flags the assets as having a 2D usage internally. This allows transparent backgrounds to be used where applicable (such as for PNG sprites) and also has important performance implications for graphics rendering, as we'll see later in this chapter. Before that, we'll configure the game view in preparation for creating the environment and player objects.

Configuring the game view

Now that we've imported all the essential textures for the project, let's configure the Game panel resolution and game camera. We should configure the game view correctly at the beginning of the project as it controls how we and, consequently, the end user sees the game. This, believe it or not, will help us when we come to creating the environment. We'll start with the Game panel's resolution, before moving on to configuring the game's camera.

Changing the Game panel's resolution

We'll use a resolution of **1024 x 600** for our game, which works well across many devices. To do this, follow these steps:

1. Click on the **Free Aspect** button from the **Game** tab on the toolbar.

2. Select **1024 x 600** from the drop-down menu.

If the required resolution is not available, then do the following:

1. Click on the + button from the bottom of the list.

2. Enter a custom name in the **Name** field.

3. Select **Fixed Resolution** from the **Type** dropdown.

4. Type your resolution dimensions into the **Width** and **Height** fields.

5. Click on **OK**.

Your target resolution should then be added as a selectable option from the **Game** tab, as shown in the following screenshot:

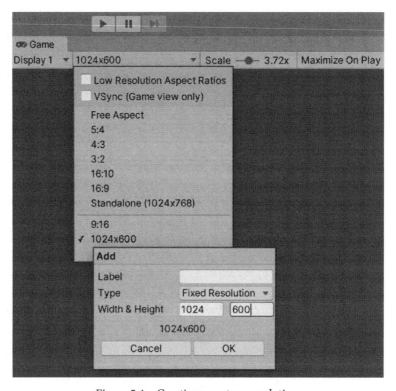

Figure 5.4 – Creating a custom resolution

The resolution for the **Game** panel is not necessarily the resolution of the final game. You can set the resolution of the compiled game using the **Project Settings** panel. For more details, see *Chapter 2, Creating a Collection Game.*

With the correct game resolution, we can move on to configuring the game camera in preparation for creating our first 2D level.

Adjusting the scene camera's size

In this section, we'll configure the scene camera for use in a 2D game so that our textures, when added as sprites, will display onscreen at a 1:1 ratio, **Texel** (texture pixel) for **pixel**. The camera will already be configured with an **orthographic projection** because we used the 2D template. The alternative (**perspective projection**) is often used with 3D games and would be the default configuration if we had selected any of the 3D project templates.

> **Important Note**
>
> Orthographic projection removes any sense of perspective and is often used for 2D games. For more information on the perspective and orthographic projections, see *Chapter 3, Creating a Space Shooter*.

In our game, we want the sprites to appear onscreen exactly the same size as they are in the texture files. To achieve this, we need to adjust the **Size** field of the **Main Camera** object in the **Inspector** window. The **Size** field defines the viewing volume of the camera. A larger size results in a larger viewing volume, making all visible objects appear smaller, and vice versa.

The formula we'll use for this field to ensure that the sprites are the same size as they appear in their image files is *Screen Height / 2 / Pixel to World*. The **pixel to world** ratio details how many pixels in the texture will be mapped to 1 unit in the world. A Unity unit is an arbitrary length measurement, usually interpreted as equaling a meter. Therefore, 1 unit is equal to 1 meter in our game. This value can be viewed by doing the following:

1. Selecting a sprite in the **Project** panel.

2. Inspecting the **Pixels Per Unit** field in the **Inspector** window. You can also change the value here.

The sprites in our game are configured with the default value of 100 pixels to units. Now that we know the pixel per unit value, we can use the aforementioned formula to calculate the required camera size:

- We previously set the screen height to 600 so 600 / 2 = 300.

- We know that our pixel to world ratio is set to 100 so 300 / 100 = 3.

We now know the value we should use for the **Camera Size** field, so let's set it:

1. Select **Main Camera** from the **Hierarchy** window.

2. In the **Inspector** window, on the **Camera** component, enter 3 in the **Size** field.

3. To test the camera and scene settings, drag and drop a background texture from the **Project** panel to the **Scene**. The background textures are sized at precisely **1024 x 600** to fit the scene's background. Therefore, when added to a scene with a correctly configured camera, the background textures should fill the screen, as shown in the following screenshot:

Figure 5.5 – Testing the camera settings with a texture

Looking good! In the next section, we'll create something interesting for the player to view using our newly configured 2D camera.

Creating an environment

Our adventure game will feature three separate but connected scenes that the player can explore, moving from one scene to the next. The player may travel between scenes by traversing the edge of a scene. Each scene consists primarily of platforms and ledges and, in some cases, obstacles that must be overcome. In terms of graphical assets, each scene is made up from two textures or sprites: the background and foreground. The preceding screenshot shows the background of the first scene, while the following screenshot shows the foreground, which includes a complete layout of all the platforms and ledges that the player must traverse:

Figure 5.6 – Scene foreground

> **Important Note**
>
> These files are included in this book's companion files, in the `Chapter05/ Assets` folder.

Let's create the first level:

1. Drag and drop both the background (`tex_level01_bck`) and foreground (`tex_ level01_design`) sprites from the **Project** panel into the **Scene**. Both will be added to the scene as separate sprite objects.

2. Position them at the world origin by setting the **Position** to `0, 0, 0`, as shown here:

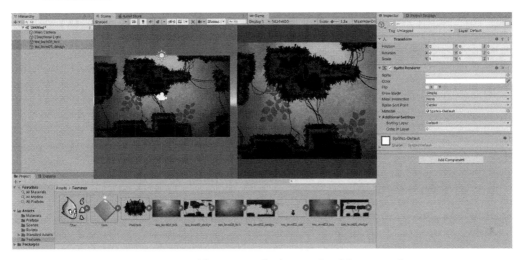

Figure 5.7 – Adding a scene background and foreground

> **Important Note**
>
> If you drag and drop both the background and foreground textures together as one selection from the **Project** panel to the scene, Unity may ask you to create an Animation when you release your mouse. In such cases, Unity assumes that you want to create an animated sprite in which each selected texture becomes a frame of animation played in a sequence. You don't want to do this; instead, drag and drop each sprite individually.

With both sprites added to the scene at the same world position, the question arises now as to which sprite Unity should display on top, given that both sprites overlap one another. Left as it is right now, there is a conflict and ambiguity about **depth order**, and we cannot rely on Unity consistently showing the correct sprite on top. We can solve this problem with two methods: one is to move the sprite forward on the Z-axis, closer to the Orthographic camera, while the other is to change its Order setting from the **Inspector** window. High values for Order result in the sprite appearing atop lower-order sprites. Here, I'll use both methods, and that's fine too!

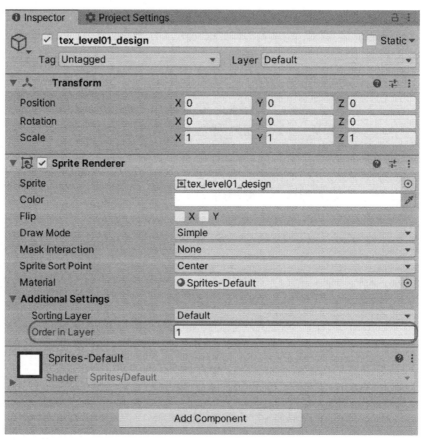

Figure 5.8 – Ordering sprite layers in a scene

Note, however, that order always takes precedence over position. Objects with a higher order value will always appear on top of objects with lower order values, even if higher-order objects are positioned behind lower-order objects.

Before moving further, let's organize the scene hierarchy to prevent overcomplication and confusion occurring later:

1. Select each environment object and name them appropriately. I named the background `scene_background` and the foreground `scene_foreground`.

2. Create a new, empty GameObject, which will be the **parent** object of all **static** (non-movable) objects in the scene, by selecting **GameObject | Create Empty** from the application menu.

3. Rename the object `Env` (for environment).

4. Position the object at the world origin by setting the **Position** to `0, 0, 0`.

5. Drag and drop the background and foreground objects onto the newly created **GameObject** to convert them into **child** objects.

> **Important Note**
> Having an empty parent object like this is a standard method of grouping all related objects easily.

Our game is already looking great. However, by adding **post-processing effects**, we can further improve the appearance of the game. Let's look at how to do that.

Adding post-processing effects

By switching to the **Game** tab, we can get an early preview of the level as it will appear to the gamer in terms of mood and emotional resonance. This feeling can be enhanced further by adding some camera **post-process effects** with the **post-processing stack**. These refer to pixel-based effects that can be applied to the camera in order to improve the atmosphere for the final, rendered image on a per-frame basis. Let's take a look:

1. Import the **Post Processing** package using the **Package Manager** by searching for **Post-processing Stack**.

2. Once imported, you can add image effects to the selected camera using a **Post-processing Profile**. To create a profile, right-click in the **Project** panel and select **Create | Post-processing Profile**. This will generate a new asset for saving all post-processing data:

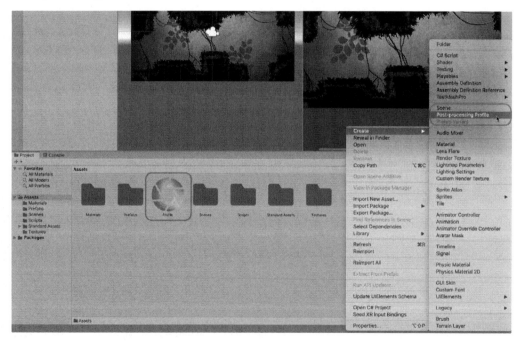

Figure 5.9 – Adding Image Effects to the selected camera

3. Next, let's create a new **Post-process Volume** in the scene to define a volume inside which the effect will apply whenever the camera enters. Select **GameObject | 3D Object | Post-process Volume** from the main menu to create a new **Post-process Volume** object in the scene.

4. Adjust the **Size** field of the **Box Collider** to 13, 8, 1 to enclose the entire scene, as we want the effects to apply throughout the game.

5. Drag and drop the **Post-processing Profile** from the **Project** panel into the **Profile** slot of the **Post-process Volume** component. This associates the profile, and its effects, with the volume:

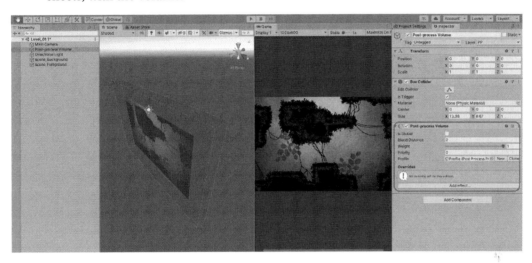

Figure 5.10 – Defining a Post-process Volume

6. You'll need to add a **Post-process Layer** component to the main camera for the effects to work as intended. To do this, select the camera and choose **Component | Rendering | Post-process Layer** from the application menu.

7. Once added, you'll need to define post-process effects using the profile. Select the **Profile** asset in the **Project** panel and choose **Add Effect** to bring up a menu.

8. Using this menu, add both **Unity | Bloom** and **Unity | Grain**.

9. Configure each using the settings shown in the following screenshot:

Figure 5.11 – Image Effects applied to the game camera

Good work. The scene so far features a background and foreground taken from texture files with enhanced visual effects by using the **Post-processing stack** package. This is a great start, but there's still much to do. For instance, while the levels now look the part, if we did have a player, they would fall straight through them as we have no environmental physics. We'll fix this now by adding colliders to the levels and creating a temporary character to test the colliders.

Implementing environmental physics

The main problem with our level, as it stands, is that it lacks interactivity. If we dragged and dropped a player object into the level and pressed play on the toolbar, the player would fall through the floor and walls because Unity doesn't recognize the foreground texture as a solid object. It's just a texture and exists only in appearance and not in substance. In this section, we'll correct this using **Physics** and **Colliders**. To get started, we'll create a player object (not the final version but just a temporary *White Box* version used only for testing purposes). Let's get started:

Generate a capsule object in the scene by navigating to **GameObject | 3D Object | Capsule** from the application menu.

1. Once generated, remove the **Capsule Collider** from the object by clicking on the three dots icon on the **Capsule Collider** component in the **Inspector** window and choosing **Remove Component** from the menu, as shown here:

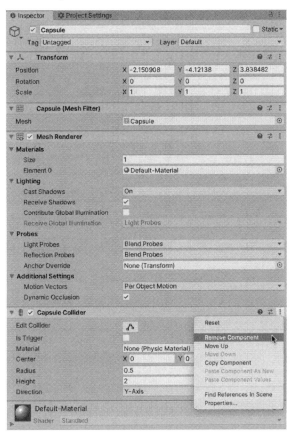

Figure 5.12 – Removing the Capsule Collider component

2. Set the *Z* position of the **Transform** so that it matches the foreground texture (for me, this is -2).

By default, the Capsule is assigned a 3D collider (such as the **Capsule Collider**), which is useful primarily for 3D physics. However, our game will be in 2D, hence the need to remove the existing collider.

To make the object compatible with 2D physics, add a **Circle Collider** component:

1. Select **Component | Physics 2D | Circle Collider 2D** from the application menu.

2. Use the **Offset** and **Radius** settings on the **Circle Collider** component in the **Inspector** window to adjust the size and position of the circle to approximate the feet of a player character.

3. Next, to make the **Circle Collider** work with 2D physics, add a **RigidBody2D** component to the Capsule by selecting **Component | Physics 2D | RigidBody 2D** from the application menu.

To aid you in positioning the **Circle Collider**, you can switch the **Scene** viewport mode to **Wireframe** and **2D**, as shown in the following screenshot:

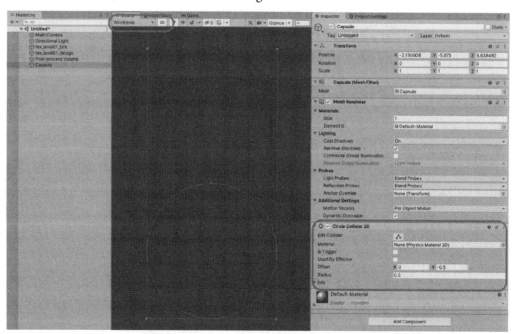

Figure 5.13 – Adjusting the Circle Collider for the player character

You can confirm that this has worked by previewing the game in Play mode. When you click on the Play icon, the **Capsule** object should fall down and through the foreground floor under the effect of gravity.

Now, it's time to configure the foreground texture so that it works as a unified whole with physics. Right now, our test player character falls through the floor, and this is not what we want. To fix this, we'll need to also add a collider to the foreground environment. One method to accomplish this is to use Edge Collider 2D. The edge collider lets you draw out a low polygon mesh collider around your ground image manually, approximating the terrain. To get started, follow these steps:

1. Select the foreground in the scene.

2. Choose **Component | Physics 2D | Edge Collider 2D** from the application menu to add a collider.

3. Position the player above the horizontal line and press Play on the toolbar to see the player character fall downward and treat the horizontal edge as a solid platform:

Figure 5.14 – The Edge Collider is useful to approximate platforms and solid surfaces

By default, adding an **Edge Collider 2D** appears to have little effect on the selected object or any other objects, except for a single horizontal line drawn across the width of the scene. As with all colliders, it can be seen in the **Scene** tab when the foreground object is selected and in the **Game** tab if the Gizmos tool button is enabled.

Of course, our terrain isn't merely a straight-edged surface. Instead, it has elevations, bumps, and platforms. These can be approximated closely with the **Edge Collider 2D** component using the Collider Edit mode. Let's take a look:

1. To access this mode, click on the **Edit Collider** button in the **Inspector** window:

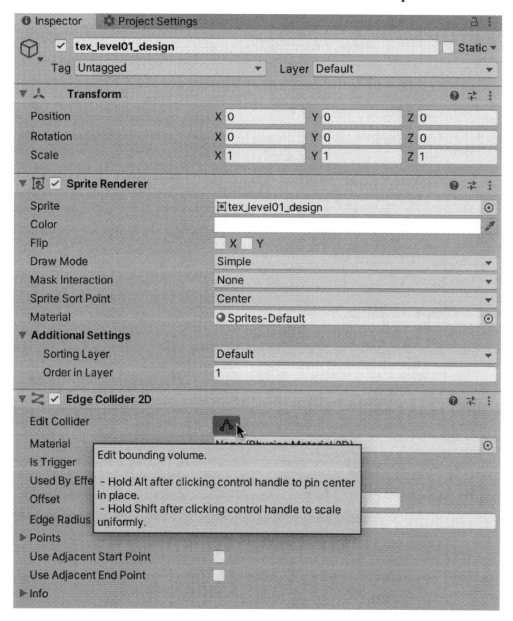

Figure 5.15 – The Edit Collider lets you change the shape of an Edge Collider 2D

2. With **Edit Collider** mode active, you can reshape the collider so that it conforms to the terrain. Let's focus on one area, such as the bottom-right-hand side of the terrain. By moving your mouse cursor over the edge points of the Edge Collider (the green line), you can click and drag to reposition them. To approximate the bottom-right island of the terrain, click and drag the rightmost edge point to the right-hand side of the scene, as shown in the following screenshot:

Figure 5.16 – Starting to reshape the Edge Collider to approximate the terrain

3. Next, click and drag the left point of the collider so that it matches with the leftmost edge of the right-hand island:

Figure 5.17 – Positioning the leftmost edge of the right-hand island

4. Now that the left and right edge points are positioned, add some additional points on the line between them to reshape it so that it conforms to the right-hand island. Move your cursor anywhere on the line, click and drag to insert a new point, and reposition it so that it matches the island. Repeat this process, adding additional points to reshape the line as needed, until it looks similar to what can be seen in the following screenshot:

Figure 5.18 – Shaping the Edge Collider to the rightmost island

5. You now have a shaped line that matches the terrain's rightmost island. Having created this, exit **Edit Collider** mode by once again clicking on the **Edit Collider** button in the **Inspector** window.

6. To create colliders for the remaining islands of the terrain, add a new **Edge Collider** to the same object. You can then add any number of **Edge Colliders** to a single object, and each collider should be used to approximate the topology of an individual, isolated island in the complete terrain. See the following screenshot for the completed island collider:

Figure 5.19 – Multiple Edge Colliders on one object can be used to approximate complex terrain

With multiple Edge Collider components being used to approximate the complete terrain for the scene, we can now test play collisions against the **Player Capsule** object. You'll notice that, this time, the capsule will collide and interact with the ground as opposed to passing through it. This interaction confirms that the terrain has been configured appropriately with the physics system.

Congratulations! In this section, we've created a complete terrain for a single scene using Edge Collider components. This terrain not only fits the screen and appears as intended but acts as a physical obstacle for the player character and other physics-based objects. So far, we've only been using a rough approximation of the player. Now, it's time to expand upon this by implementing the final version of the player character.

Creating a 2D player

The player character is a small, green alien-looking creature that can be controlled and guided by the gamer through a level using many conventional platforming game mechanics, such as walking and jumping. In the previous section, we built a white box (prototype) character to test physical interactions with the environment, but here, we'll develop the player character in more depth. We'll look at the following aspects:

- Using Unity's **Sprite Editor** to unpack the player sprite sheet, thus creating multiple sprites from one texture.

- Creating the player GameObject. The process of creating a GameObject has been shown several times in this book already, as it's a core concept for any Unity game. However, the player object will be slightly more complex than previous objects, as we need to add different sprites for each limb of the player.

- Adjusting the sorting order of the player's sprites so that they are drawn in the correct order.

- Finally, we'll add the player object to the physics engine so that it can interact with our level.

That's a lot to cover, so let's jump right in with creating the player sprites using the Sprite Editor.

Using the Sprite Editor

The following image illustrates our character texture, which we imported earlier in this chapter, representing all the limbs and parts of the player:

Figure 5.20: Character Sprite Sheet

This player texture is called an **Atlas Texture** or **Sprite Sheet** because it contains all the frames or parts of a character in a single texture space. The problem with this texture, as it stands, is that when dragged and dropped from the **Project** panel into the scene, it'll be added as a single sprite, as shown in the following screenshot:

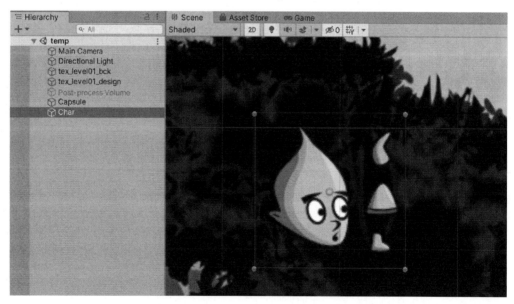

Figure 5.21: The player sprite texture needs to be divided into separate parts

To divide the character texture into separate parts on a per-limb basis, we'll use the Sprite Editor:

1. Select the character texture in the **Project** panel.

2. From the **Inspector** window, change **Sprite Mode** from **Single** to **Multiple**.

3. Click on **Apply**.

4. Click on the **Sprite Editor** button to open the **Sprite Editor** tool. This allows you to cut the texture into specific slices:

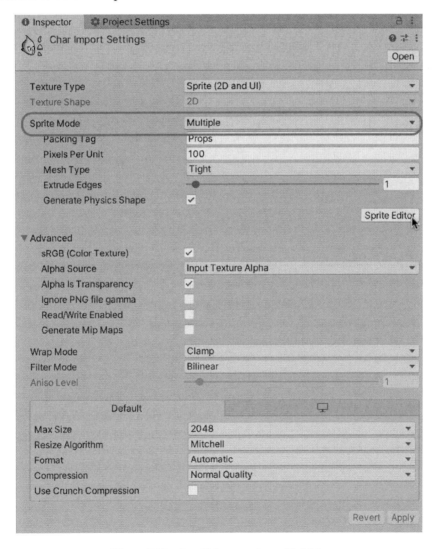

Figure 5.22 – Specifying a sprite as Multiple

With the **Sprite Editor** tool, you can separate different parts of a texture into discrete and separate units. One method to achieve this is by drawing a rectangle around each image area that should be separate, and then clicking and dragging your mouse to draw a texture region, as shown in the following screenshot:

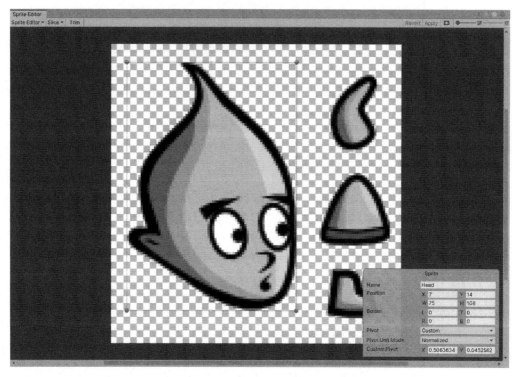

Figure 5.23 – Slicing a sprite manually

Although a sprite can be separated manually, as we've just seen, Unity can often cut apart the texture automatically, identifying isolated areas of pixels and saving us time. We'll do that here for the player character:

1. Click on the **Slice** button listed in the top-left corner of the **Sprite Editor** window.

2. From the **Slice** tool window, ensure that **Type** is set to **Automatic**, which means that Unity will auto-detect the location of separate sprites. **Pivot** can be left as **Center**, which determines the pivot point for each sprite.

3. Set **Method** to **Delete Existing**, meaning that any existing sprites or slices in the texture space will be erased and replaced entirely by the newly autogenerated slices, as shown in the following screenshot:

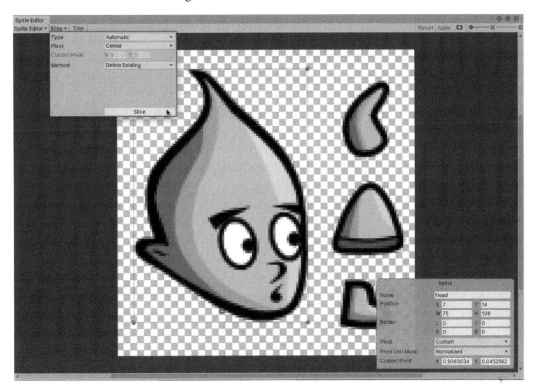

Figure 5.24 – Accessing the Slice tool

4. Click on the **Slice** button to confirm the operation, and the texture will be sliced into separate sprites with a clear border drawn around each sprite.

The texture is now divided into several sprites: head, body, arm, and leg. The final character in-scene will have two arms and two legs, but these will be formed from duplicated sprites. The next step is to set the pivot point for each sprite – the point around which the sprite will rotate. This will be important later to animate the character correctly, as we'll see. Let's start by setting the pivot for the head:

1. Select the head sprite in the **Sprite Editor** window.

2. Click and drag the pivot handle (blue circle) to the bottom middle of the head, roughly where the head would connect to the neck, to reposition the sprite's center of rotation. This position makes sense because the head will rotate and hinge from around this point. The exact location is shown in the following screenshot:

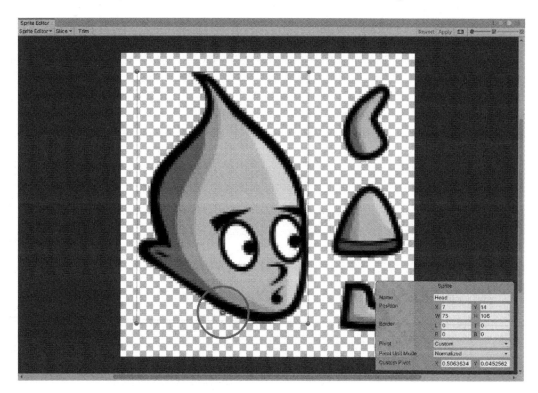

Figure 5.25 – Repositioning the sprite pivot

Important Note

As you move the pivot around, you should see the X and Y values change in the **Custom Pivot** field in the **Sprite Properties** dialog, shown in the bottom-right-hand corner of the **Sprite Editor** window.

---

3. Position the pivot for the arm, which should be at the shoulder joint where the arm connects to a torso.

4. Position the leg pivot near the hip where the leg connects to the torso.

5. Finally, position the torso itself, whose pivot should be at the hip joint, as shown in the following screenshot:

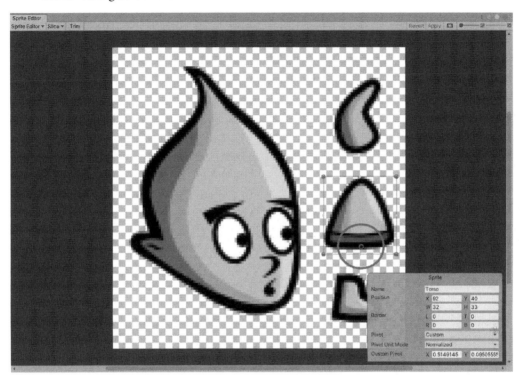

Figure 5.26 – Positioning the pivot for the torso

6. When completed, click on the **Apply** button to confirm changes and then close the **Sprite Editor** window.

On returning to the main Unity interface, the appearance of the character texture will have changed in the **Project** panel. The character texture should now feature a small arrow icon attached to the right-hand side. When you click this, the texture expands to review all the separate sprites in a row, which can be dragged and dropped individually into the scene:

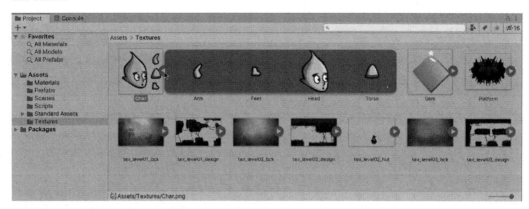

Figure: 5.27 – Previewing character sprites

Now that we've isolated all the player sprite textures, we can start building a game character in the scene.

Creating the player GameObject

As mentioned previously, the player object for this game will be slightly more complicated than the objects that we have created previously. For the player, we need to create several child objects to represent the limbs of the player:

1. Create an empty GameObject. This will be the parent object.

2. Name the object **Player** and assign it a **Player Tag** from the **Inspector** window. This object will act as the ultimate or topmost parent object for the player character.

3. Drag and drop the **Torso** sprite from the **Project** panel into the **Hierarchy** panel and make it a child of the **Player** object, as shown in the following screenshot:

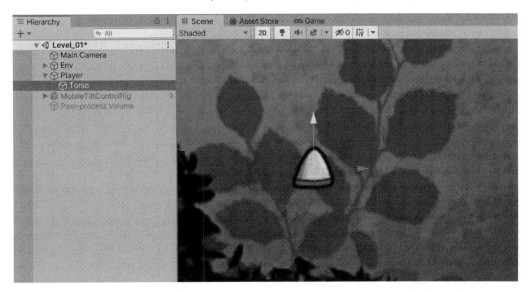

Figure 5.28 – Starting the player character

4. Add the arms as children of the torso since the torso determines where the arms will be.

5. Add the legs as children of the **Player** object since the torso can rotate independently of the legs.

6. Offset the position of each limb so that it appears correctly in relation to the other limbs – the head should appear above the feet and so on.

The following screenshot shows the complete hierarchical arrangement:

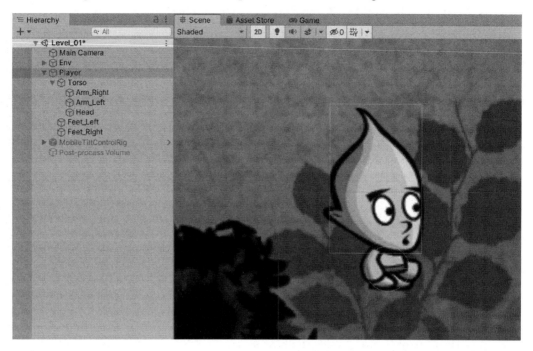

Figure 5.29 – Building a character

Even though all of the player's limbs have now been correctly positioned, the rendering order of the body parts may not be correct yet, as each item will have an identical order in the Sprite Renderer component. We'll look at this next.

Adjusting the sorting order

With the limbs having the same draw order, Unity could potentially render them in any order, thereby allowing arms to appear in front of the head, legs to appear in front of the body, and so on. To correct this, do the following:

1. Select each limb.

2. In the **Inspector** window, on the **Sprite Renderer** component, assign an appropriate value to the **Order in Layer** field, taking care that it's higher than the world background order and less than the world foreground order.

I've assigned the following values:

- **Body** = 103
- **Head** = 105
- **Left arm** = 102
- **Right arm** = 104
- **Left leg** = 100
- **Right leg** = 101

> **Tip**
> When assigning a sorting order to objects in your game, it's a good idea to leave gaps in-between the orders. For example, we may, in the future, want to add a scarf to the player. Ideally, the scarf should be drawn in-between the body and head. As the body is assigned a sort order of 103 and the head a value of 105, we can assign the scarf a sorting order of 104, and it will fit in nicely. If there were no gap between the numbers, we would then have to adjust the sorting value of the head and body to accomplish the same task. This isn't the end of the world for smaller projects, such as this one, but as your project's complexity grows, you may find that having that gap between the sorting order can save you significant time in the future.

Now that the player looks the part, let's make sure they also act the part by adding them to the game's physics engine.

Adding the player to the physics engine

The rendering order for limbs has now been configured successfully. Now, let's set up collisions and physics for the player:

1. Add two colliders – a **Circle Collider 2D** to approximate the character's feet, allowing us to determine when the character is in contact with the ground, and a **Box Collider 2D** to approximate most of the body, including the head, as shown in the following screenshot:

Figure 5.30 – Adding two colliders to the Player object – Circle Collider and Box Collider

The Circle Collider is of particular importance because it's the primary means to determine whether the character is touching the ground. For this reason, a Physics Material should be assigned to this collider to prevent friction effects from stopping or corrupting character motion as it moves around the scene.

2. Create a new physics material by right-clicking in the empty space in the **Project** panel and selecting **Create | Physics 2D Material** from the context menu.

3. Name the material **Low Friction**.

4. Select the **Physics2D** material in the **Project** panel, and from the **Inspector** window, change the **Friction** setting to **0.1**.

5. Drag and drop the **Physics2D** material from the **Project** panel into the **Material** slot for the **Circle Collider 2D** component on the **Player** object, as shown in the preceding screenshot.

By using this material, the character will interact with the level more realistically. Lastly, add a Rigidbody 2D to our character:

1. Select the **Player** object.

2. Add the component using the application menu; that is, **Component | Physics 2D | Rigidbody 2D**.

3. Set both **Linear Drag** and **Gravity Scale** to 3.

4. Set **Collision Detection** to **Continuous** for more accurate collision detection.

5. Freeze the rotation of the object on the Z-axis because the player character should
    never rotate:

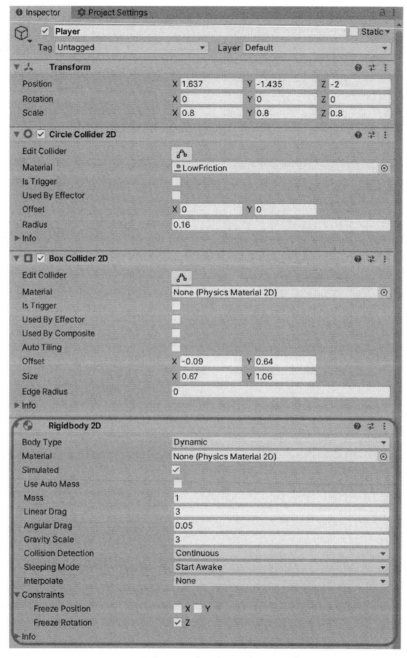

Figure 5.31 – Configuring the player character for physics

Now, you have a fully completed physical object representing the player. Great work! As the player can now interact with the world, it's a good time to look at moving the player using a custom script.

Moving the player

The game, as it currently stands, features an environment with collision data and a multipart player object that interacts and responds to this environment. The player, however, cannot yet be controlled. We'll correct this situation now as we explore controller functionality further by writing and implementing a player control script.

Writing the movement script

The user will have two main input mechanics; namely, movement (walking left and right) and jumping. This input will be read using **CrossPlatformInputManager**, which is a native Unity package that was imported during the project creation phase. Let's take a look:

1. Open the **Assets | Standard Assets | CrossPlatformInput | Prefabs** folder and drag and drop the **MobileTiltControlRig** prefab into the scene. This prefab lets you read input data across a range of devices, mapping directly to the horizontal and vertical axes that we've already seen in previous chapters.

2. Create a new C# script named `PlayerControl.cs` and attach it to the **Player** character. This script will use the cross-platform input object we just added to the scene:

```csharp
public class PlayerControl : MonoBehaviour
{
    private bool GetGrounded()
    {
        Vector2 CircleCenter = new
            Vector2(transform.position.x, transform.
            position.y)+ FeetCollider.offset;
        Collider2D[] HitColliders =
            Physics2D.OverlapCircleAll(CircleCenter,
            FeetCollider.radius, GroundLayer);
        return HitColliders.Length > 0; true;
    }
    private void Jump()
    {
```

```
    if(!isGrounded || !CanJump) return;


        ThisBody.AddForce(Vector2.up * JumpPower);
        CanJump = false;
        Invoke ("ActivateJump", JumpTimeOut);
    }
}
```

The following points summarize this code sample:

- The `PlayerControl` class is responsible for handling all player input, making the character move left and right and jump.

- The `GetGrounded` function detects where any `CircleCollider` intersects and overlaps with any other collider in the scene on a specific layer. This function indicates whether the player character is touching the ground, and if they are, the player can jump; otherwise, the player cannot jump as they are already airborne. Double-jumping is not allowed in this game!

We're still missing the function that actually reads and applies input. Let's add it now:

```
public class PlayerControl : MonoBehaviour
{

...

void FixedUpdate ()
{
    if(!CanControl || Health <= 0f)
    {
        return;
    }
    isGrounded = GetGrounded();
    float Horz = CrossPlatformInputManager.
        GetAxis(HorzAxis);
    ThisBody.AddForce(Vector2.right * Horz * MaxSpeed);


    if(CrossPlatformInputManager.GetButton(JumpButton))
    {
        Jump();
    }
    ThisBody.velocity = new
```

```
                Vector2(Mathf.Clamp(ThisBody.velocity.x,
                  -MaxSpeed, MaxSpeed),

                Mathf.Clamp(ThisBody.velocity.y, -Mathf.Infinity,
                  JumpPower));


            if((Horz < 0f && Facing != FACEDIRECTION.FACELEFT)
                || (Hor > 0f && Facing != FACEDIRECTION.
                  FACERIGHT)
            {
                FlipDirection();
            }
    }
```

Let's summarize the preceding code:

- The movement and motion of the player are set using the `RigidBody2D.Velocity` variable. More information on this variable can be found online at `http://docs.unity3d.com/ScriptReference/Rigidbody2D-velocity.html`.

- The `FixedUpdate` function is used instead of Update to update the movement of the player character because we're working with RigidBody2D – a physics-based component. All physics functionality should be updated in `FixedUpdate`, which is invoked at a fixed interval each second as opposed to every frame. More information can be found in the Unity online documentation at `http://docs.unity3d.com/ScriptReference/MonoBehaviour.FixedUpdate.html`.

> **Important Note**
> Often, it makes sense to show a snippet of the code, rather than the full listing, as the full code listing may be irrelevant or too long. The previous code listing excludes many of the variables required for it to run, so if you copied it verbatim, you would run into compiler errors. You can always find the full code listings in the relevant chapter folders. For example, `PlayerControl.cs` can be found in the `Chapter05/End/Assets/Scripts` folder.

Before we can use our new `PlayerControl` script, we need to configure the environment as the script expects, which involves adding the level object to a specific layer and adding a collider to the player object. We'll do this now.

Implementing the movement script

For the preceding code to work correctly, a few tweaks must be made to both the scene and player character. Specifically, the GetGrounded function requires that the floor area of the level is grouped as a single layer. This means that the level foreground should be on a distinctive layer from other objects. Let's do this now:

1. Create a new layer named **Ground**. For more information on how to create a layer, see *Chapter 4, Continuing the Space Shooter Game.*

2. Assign the foreground object to the **Ground** layer.

3. After the foreground object has been assigned to the **Ground** layer, the PlayerControl script requires us to specify the **Ground** layer. Select the **Player** object and, from the **Inspector** window, select the **Ground** layer for the **Ground Layer** field, as shown in the following screenshot:

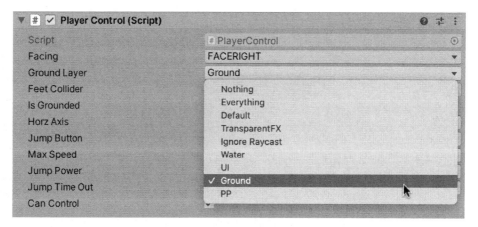

Figure 5.32 – Selecting the Ground layer for collision detection

4. In addition, we need to assign a collider to the **Feet Collider** variable on the PlayerControl script to indicate which collider object should be used for ground collision detection. Drag and drop the **Circle Collider 2D** component into the **Feet Collider** slot, as shown in the following screenshot:

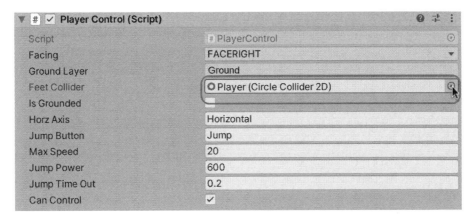

Figure 5.33 – The Feet Collider detects when the character is in contact with the ground

5. Now, give the player character a test run. The *W*, *A*, *S*, and *D* keys (or the arrow keys) will move the player character around, while the spacebar will make the character jump. An example of this can be seen in the following screenshot:

Figure 5.34 – Play testing with the player character

The player character is an ideal candidate for a prefab because it must feature in all the other scenes we create. Let's create a prefab from the player. To do this, drag and drop the **Player** object into the **Project** panel in a separate folder called `Prefabs` (create the folder if it doesn't exist already).

Our work so far has produced a stimulating environment and a character that can traverse that environment. Before moving forward, let's turn our attention to *optimization* – an issue that should be considered early during development. Optimization refers to the tips and tricks that we can apply to improve runtime performance, as well as our workflow in general. In the next section, we'll look at an optimization technique that's specific to 2D sprites called **sprite packing**.

Optimizing using sprite packing

Right now, when running the game, Unity will perform a separate **draw call** for every unique texture or sprite on screen at the time. A draw call refers to a step or process cycle that Unity must run through to correctly display a graphic on-screen, such as a mesh, material, or texture. Draw calls represent a computational expense, and so it's a good idea to reduce them wherever possible.

For 2D games, we can reduce draw calls by **batching** together related textures, such as all the props for a scene, all the enemies, or all the weapons. By indicating to Unity that a group of textures belong together, Unity can perform internal optimizations that increase render performance. Unity will add all related textures to a single internal texture that it uses instead. To achieve this optimization, follow these steps:

1. Select all prop textures: **Player**, **House**, **Platform**, and **Gem**. These textures are all featured in the **Project** panel, though not all are used in the game yet.

2. From the **Inspector** window, assign them the same name in the **Packing Tag** field (`Props`), as shown in the following screenshot:

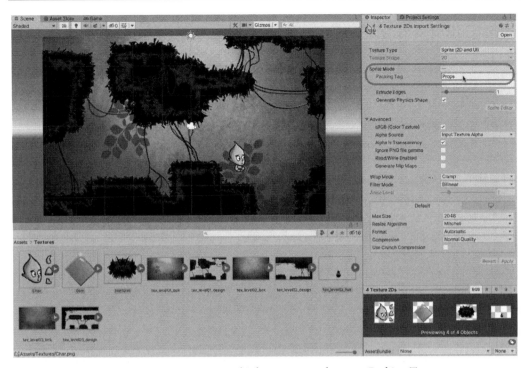

Figure 5.35 – Assigning multiple textures to the same Packing Tag

3. Click on **Apply**.

4. Repeat this process for the backgrounds by selecting all the backgrounds and assigning them to the Background packing tag.

When you Play the game next, Unity will automatically batch and organize the textures for optimal performance based on your groupings. This technique can significantly reduce draw calls. On pressing the play button, you may see a loading or progress bar while Unity internally generates a new texture set.

You can view how Unity has organized the textures through the **Sprite Packer** window. To access this window, select **Window | 2D | Sprite Packer** from the application menu:

Figure 5.36 – Unity organizes all textures with the same tag into the same texture space as an Atlas

And it's as simple as that. Now, Unity can batch the sprites, thereby reducing the number of draw calls dramatically and increasing the performance of the game.

Summary

Superb work! We've come a long way in this chapter, from a new project to a working 2D game. The player character can navigate a complete 2D environment with 2D physics by moving left, right, and jumping. The player's sprite will dynamically update to match the direction of travel, and by using sprite packing, we've improved runtime performance, which is useful for mobile devices.

By completing this chapter, you've learned the fundamentals of 2D sprites, movement, and physics. By building on this foundation, you will have the required knowledge to create any 2D game, not just a platformer, of your own design.

The next chapter is a big one: in it, we'll complete the game by adding additional levels, obstacles (including moving platforms), a friendly character that assigns a quest – oh, and the quest system itself!

Test your knowledge

Q1. Edge Colliders let you...

    A. Create pretty patterns

    B. Draw out collider edges

    C. Create 3D volumes

    D. Create physics animations

Q2. The Sprite Packer is useful for...

    A. Creating sprites in rows and columns

    B. Grouping sprites onto a single atlas texture

    C. Animating sprites

    D. Creating multiple color sprites

Q3. Physics Materials can...

    A. Help you define how 2D objects behave

    B. Scale 2D objects

    C. Rotate objects

    D. Edit object vertices

Q4. The Sprite Editor lets you...

>   A. Divide an image into multiple sprites

>   B. Animate textures

>   C. Create mesh objects

>   D. Edit material properties

Further reading

For more information on Unity scripting, take a look at the following links:

- `https://learn.unity.com/tutorials`
- `https://www.packtpub.com/game-development/unity-2d-game-development-cookbook`
- `http://docs.unity3d.com/ScriptReference/Rigidbody2D-velocity.html`
- `http://docs.unity3d.com/ScriptReference/MonoBehaviour.FixedUpdate.html`

6
Continuing the
2D Adventure

In the previous chapter, we started work on a 2D adventure game. On reaching this point, we've now created a controllable character that can navigate a level using 2D physics.

Sprite shaping allows you to create freeform 2D environments in the Editor. Dynamic and exciting environments that would otherwise require custom sprite work can instead be generated from within the Editor by tiling sprites along **spline** paths. We'll go step by step through how to install the Sprite Shape Unity package, create custom shape profiles, and create several platforms to form a level for our 2D adventure game.

Up to this point, our levels have been relatively static. The only moving element (apart from particles) is that of the player. In this chapter, we'll fix that by adding moving platforms that the player can jump on. By implementing platforms in this game, you'll be able to do the same in any future game you develop, whether 2D or 3D.

By implementing a health system, including the UI, you can then create a similar system for any game, no matter the genre. Need a health system for your units in a **real-time strategy** (**RTS**) game or for a base on an alien planet in your next space game? After completing this chapter, you'll gain the necessary skills to implement this functionality.

This chapter will provide a crash course into these topics and act as a springboard for future projects.

This chapter continues the game by adding the following features:

- Constructing additional scenes using **sprite shaping** – a dynamic method to create 2D environments
- Adding moving platforms – a more dynamic method of travel for the player
- Implementing the first hazard for the player in the form of a kill zone – an area that will kill the player if they enter it
- Implementing a health system and UI to display a health bar

Technical requirements

This chapter assumes that you have not only completed the projects from the previous chapters but also have a good, basic knowledge of C# scripting generally, though not necessarily in Unity. In this chapter, you will continue the project started in *Chapter 5, Creating a 2D Adventure Game*, so you should read that chapter first if you haven't already.

The starting project and assets can be found in the book's companion files in the Chapter06/Start folder. You can start there and follow along with this chapter if you don't have your own project already. The end project can be found in the Chapter06/End folder.

Constructing additional scenes

Unlike the other games created in the book so far, our adventure game will span multiple scenes, which the player can move between freely. Supporting this functionality introduces us to some new and exciting problems in Unity that are well worth exploring, as we'll see later. In this section, we'll briefly introduce two levels that have been created using premade assets, and then detail how you can create a custom level using Unity's new **sprite shaping** tool. We'll start with the first two premade levels.

Introducing levels two and three

For now, let's make a second and third scene for the game, using the remaining background and foreground objects. The details to create a level are covered in depth in *Chapter 5, Creating a 2D Adventure Game*, and the completed levels can be found in Chapter06/End, so we won't go into detail here but rather briefly introduce them before moving on to exciting new topics.

Important Note

When testing the project from the GitHub repo, start the game at the Scenes/scene_start scene. This scene sets the correct player position and includes the QuestManager (more on quests later), which is required by the other scenes.

Level two is divided across two vertically arranged ledges, which will shortly be gapped by a set of moving platforms that we will create in the next section. The upper ledge is, for now, non-hazardous, but this will also be changed later as we add gun turrets that can shoot at the player. This level can be reached from the first level by walking off the left edge of the screen:

Figure 6.1 – Scene two: dangerous ledges and moving platforms

Level three can be reached from the first level by walking off the right edge of the screen. It consists of one ground-level plane featuring a house. It will be home to an NPC character that the player can meet and receive a quest to collect an item. This character will be created in the next chapter:

Figure 6.2 – Scene three: a lonely house for an NPC

Both of these levels were created entirely with the techniques covered in the previous chapter using premade textures. However, Unity also provides tools to sculpt levels directly in the Editor. We'll look at one of these tools next as we create the last level of the game using Unity's **sprite shaper**.

Creating platforms using sprite shaping

We've just created two levels using existing assets. But what if you want to sculpt your own levels? There are several options available to you; for example, you could do the following:

- Position individual platform textures in the scene.

- Write a script that procedurally generates the levels for you.

- Use a tool designed to help you create custom levels.

Of course, there are many more options available, but these are some of the most common ones.

> **Tip**
>
> For more information on procedural generation in Unity, refer to https://www.packtpub.com/game-development/procedural-content-generation-unity-game-development.

In this section, we'll go with the third option and use Unity's new **Sprite Shape** tool to create a custom level. The **Sprite Shape** package allows us to shape platforms by dragging points in the **Scene** view. Unity will automatically generate a tiled platform along a **spline** path between the positions we specify.

> **Important Note**
>
> If you're not familiar with splines, that's fine. A quick internet search will bring up numerous, generally complicated definitions. For our specific purpose (that is, creating platforms using the sprite shaper), it is enough to know that a spline is a curve that connects two points. The actual implementation is handled internally by Unity, as you will see shortly.

Constructing platforms using the Sprite Shape package involves these steps:

- Importing the package – we can't use the tool if it is not in our project.

- Creating the **Shape Profile** – this defines how the platforms will look.

- Finally, creating the platforms themselves – with the package imported and the profile created, we can start creating the platforms.

We'll work through these in order, beginning with importing the package.

Importing the Sprite Shape package

Importing the Sprite Shape package works in the same way as the packages we imported earlier:

1.   Select **Window | Package Manager** from the application menu to open the **Package Manager** window.

2.   Ensure all packages are displayed by selecting the **Unity Registry** option in the **Packages** menu:

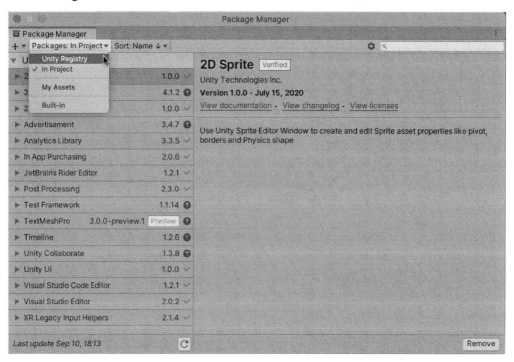

Figure 6.3 – Showing all the packages in Unity's Package Manager

3. Install the **2D SpriteShape** package by selecting it in the package explorer and clicking **Install**:

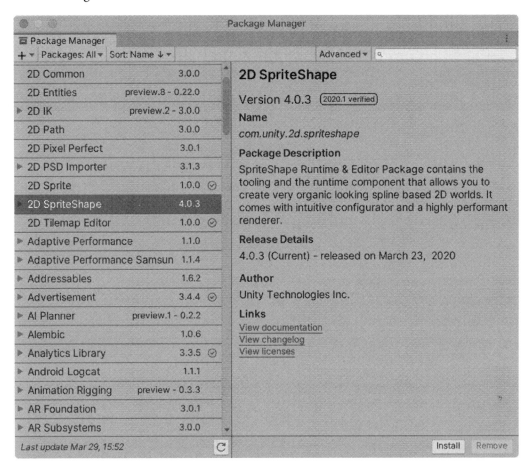

Figure 6.4 – Installing the 2D SpriteShape package

Unity will then import the package to your project. We're now ready to create the Shape Profile, which will define how our platforms look.

Creating the Shape Profile

As previously mentioned, the Sprite Shape tool works by tiling a texture along a path created by us and relies on a **Shape Profile**. The Shape Profile stores information on which tile to display and whether to fill the space in between the platform with a texture. You can also set different tiles to be drawn based on the angle of the tile, among other things.

Creating a new profile is simple:

1. By installing the Sprite Shape package, a number of new entries were added to the application menu, including the option to create Shape Profiles. To do this, select **Assets | Create | Sprite Shape Profile | Open Shape**.

    > **Important Note**
    >
    > You may have noticed that you have two options when creating a profile; you could have created a **Closed Shape** or **Open Shape** profile. We selected the Open Shape Profile as this is the recommended choice for smaller platforms. It enables us to create single-edged platforms if we desire and initially has only one **angle range** to implement (more on this shortly), meaning that we can start creating platforms quicker. The Closed Shape Profile will enable the creation of shapes that enclose an area. Unity recommends this profile for larger platforms. For more information on the differences between the two, see the online documentation at `https://docs.unity3d.com/Packages/com.unity.2d.spriteshape@2.0/manual/SSProfile.html`.

2. Once created, name the profile something informative, such as `Platform`. Now, create a folder called `sprite shape` in the `Assets` folder and drag the profile to that folder:

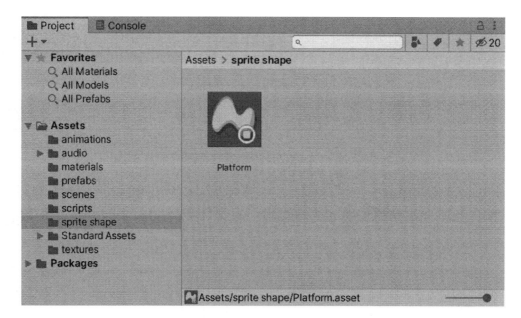

Figure 6.5 – Creating a Shape Profile

3. Select the newly created profile.

4. Assign the `black_square` texture (located in the `Chapter05/Assets` folder) as the **Fill** texture in the **Inspector,** as shown in *Figure 6.6*. This texture will be used in the center of the platforms we create:

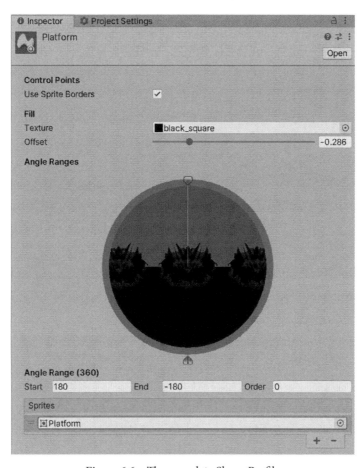

Figure 6.6 – The complete Shape Profile

5. Assign the **Platform** sprite to the **Sprites** field under the **Angle Range (360)** heading.

An open platform profile defaults to only one angle range – 180 to -180 – which covers the full 360 degrees. You can rotate the image in the circle for a preview of what the tile will look like at various angles. For more detailed platforms, we could create several angle ranges and add unique textures for those angles. For example, we could add a specific texture that would only be shown if the tile was facing down. You can also add multiple textures for one angle range, and a random texture will then be selected.

> **Important Note**
> Creating new angle ranges and using multiple textures is not shown here as
> we only need the one texture regardless of the tiles' facing direction. For more
> information on creating new ranges, refer to the resources listed in the *Further
> reading* section of this chapter.

You may have noticed that the preview doesn't look quite right as there are gaps between
each tile. To remove the gaps and enable the correct tiling of the sprite, we'll need to edit
the border of the sprite:

1. Select the **Platform** texture in the **Project** panel.

2. In the **Inspector**, select **Sprite Editor**:

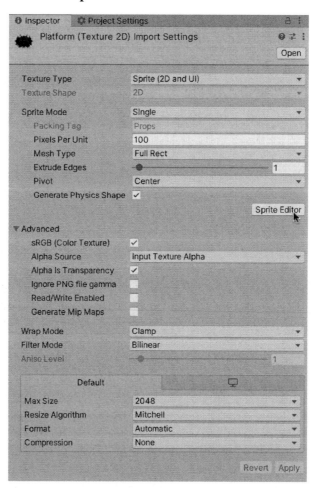

Figure 6.7 – Opening the Sprite Editor

3. Adjust the sprite's **Border** value to 41 for **L** and **R** so that its left and right borders are the same as shown in *Figure 6.8*:

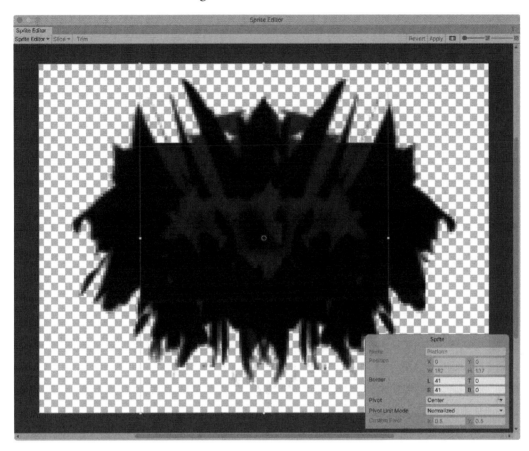

Figure 6.8 – The platform sprite border settings

You can play around with the location of this border to create drastically different-looking platforms.

4. Close the **Sprite Editor** and click on **Apply** in the **Inspector**.

If you now go back to the **Platform** sprite shaping profile, you'll notice that the preview has been updated and looks much better:

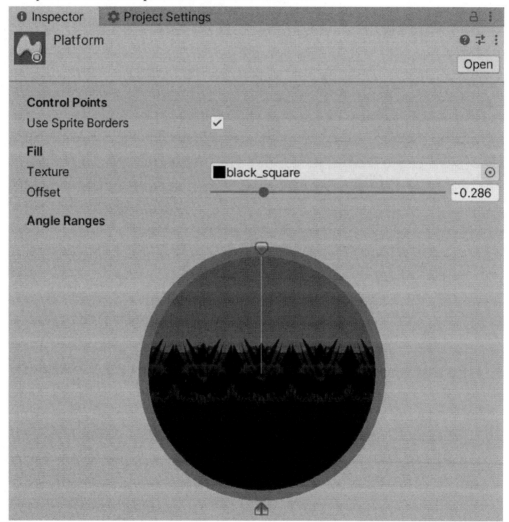

Figure 6.9 – Updated preview with correct texture tiling

This is all the setup we need to do for our level. We're now ready to create the platforms using our newly created profile.

Shaping the platforms

For our level, we'll want several different platforms, each with a unique look. We can accomplish this easily using the profile created in the last section:

1. Create a new scene by selecting **File | New** Scene from the Application menu

2. Save the scene by pressing *Ctrl + S* and call it `scene_Level04`.

3. Start by right-clicking in the **Hierarchy** panel and selecting **2D Object | Sprite Shape**. This will create a new object that, for now, looks like a white square. The new object will have a **Sprite Shape Controller** component attached. We'll edit this component to create the platform:

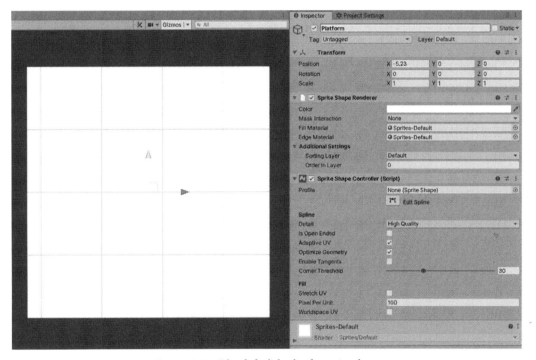

Figure 6.10 – The default look of a sprite shape

4. Name the new object `Platform`.

5. Assign the Platform profile to the **Profile** field on the **Sprite Shape Controller** component:

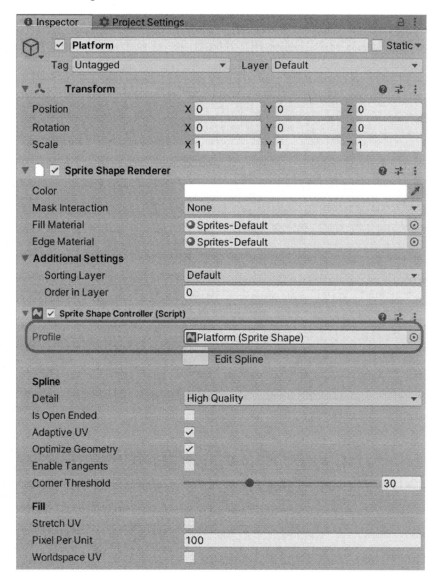

Figure 6.11 – Assigning a profile to the shape controller

With that done, you'll notice that the white square transforms. While it is still a square, it will now be using the textures we previously assigned to the profile. With this groundwork complete, now comes the fun bit – shaping the platforms.

6. Select the **Platform** object in the **Hierarchy**.

7. Click **Edit Spline** in the **Inspector**:

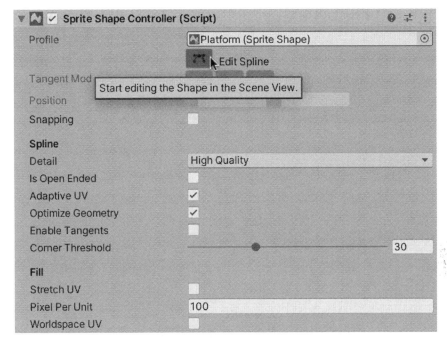

Figure 6.12 – Enabling the Spline Editor

8. As the tooltip explains, this will let you edit the shape of the platform directly in the **Scene** view by dragging the designated points. Do this now to create a platform that looks similar to the one shown in *Figure 6.13*:

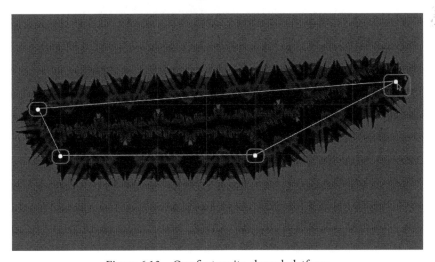

Figure 6.13 – Our first sprite-shaped platform

You can change the **Tangent Mode** setting to create uniquely shaped platforms by selecting a new mode in the Inspector, just below the **Edit Spline** button. **Linear** (the default option) does not create curves between the selected points. This is the option used to create the platform in *Figure 6.13*. **Continuous** mode creates a curve between the control point and its neighbors. In this mode, the angle between the points is always at 180 degrees. The last option is **Broken Mirrored**; this mode also creates curves between the selected point and its neighbors. However, the angle of the curve can be adjusted and is not necessarily always 180 degrees.

9. Continue to experiment with the different **Tangent Mode** options to create a number of platforms. The platforms I've created are shown in *Figure 6.14*. I have used close-ended platforms here to add a bit of depth, but you can select the **Is Open Ended** option on the **Sprite Shape Controller** component to create flat, open platforms:

> Tip
> You can delete a point by selecting it and pressing the *Delete* button.

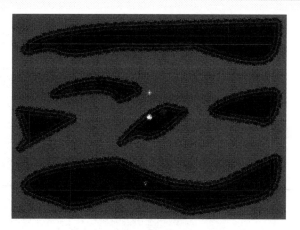

Figure 6.14 – The platforms for level four

10. Add colliders to the platforms by selecting all of them in the **Hierarchy** panel and choosing **Component | Physics 2D | Edge Collider 2D** in the **Inspector**. This will automatically create colliders with the correct shape, as shown in *Figure 6.14* by the green outlines.

11. Drag the tex_level02_bck texture from the **Project** panel to the **Scene** and assign it the **Position** of 0, 0, 0 in the **Inspector**. This will be the background for the level:

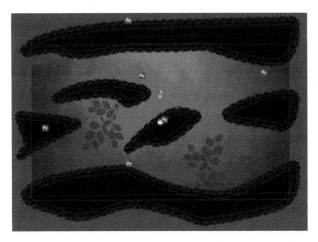

Figure 6.15 – Adding a background

12. To differentiate the background from other levels, make the background semitransparent and add a color tint by selecting the **Color** field on the **Sprite Renderer** component and entering 153, 255, 155, and 186 for the **red, green, blue, and alpha** (**RGBA**) values, respectively:

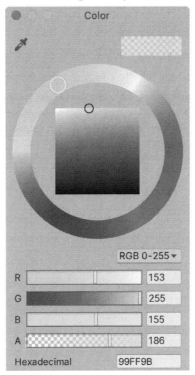

Figure 6.16 – Background color settings

13. By making the background translucent, we can control the level's color scheme using the camera's **Background** color. Select the camera in the **Hierarchy** and change **Projection** to **Orthographic** (if not already), **Clear Flags** to **Solid Color**, and **Background** to a color of your choice. I've selected blue, as shown in *Figure 6.17*:

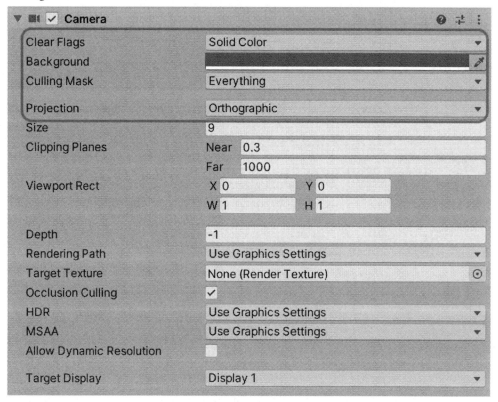

Figure 6.17 – Camera settings for level four

14. Add the `vine` textures from the `textures` folder to add depth to the scene. Position and scale them as you see fit. You will now have a level that looks something like *Figure 6.18*:

Figure 6.18 – The completed level

15. Save the scene by selecting **File | Save** from the application menu and call it `Level04`.

And that's it, we've added three new levels to the game. The levels as they stand are relatively static, there are particle effects that add movement, but there are no moving interactive elements. We'll fix that now by adding moving platforms.

Implementing moving platforms

While the level structure is complete, they are relatively static environments. The only moving element is that of the player. We'll rectify this situation by creating a moving platform. The platform should move up and down continuously, and the player should be able to jump on it anytime to hitch a ride. We'll construct the object as a prefab so that it can be reused across multiple scenes. See *Figure 6.19* for the result:

Figure 6.19 – Create a moving platform

Now that we have an idea of the end goal, let's start by creating the platform GameObject.

Creating the platform object

To create the platform object, take the following steps:

1. Select the **Platform** texture in the **Project** panel.

2. Select the **Sprite (2D and UI) Texture Type** option in the **Inspector**:

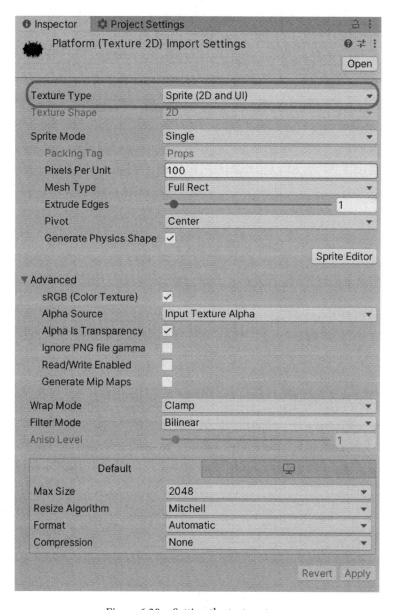

Figure 6.20 – Setting the texture type

3. Set **Sprite Mode** to **Single**.

4. Drag and drop the **Platform** texture to the scene.

5. Set the **Scale** of the new object to (0.7, 0.5, 1):

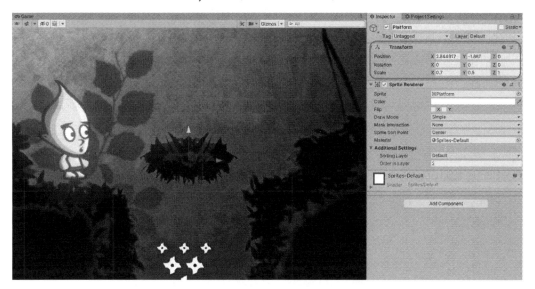

Figure 6.21 – Building a moving platform

6. Next, the platform should be a solid object, as we'll want the player to be able to stand on it, so we'll add a collider component. Select the **Platform** object in the scene and choose **Component | Physics 2D | Box Collider 2D** in the **Inspector**.

7. Adjust the collider's **Offset** and **Size** values to make the collider match the size of the platform:

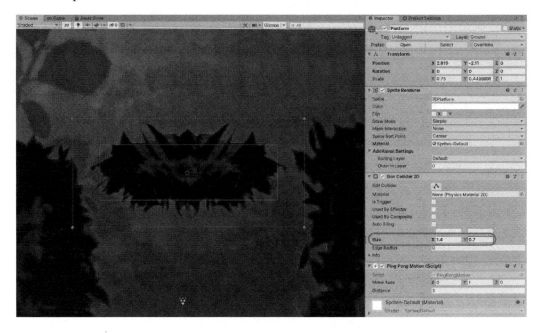

Figure 6.22 – Estimating the platform's physical size

8. Finally, test the platform by entering Play mode and moving the player character to the platform. As you can see in *Figure 6.23*, the player should be able to stand on the platform:

Figure 6.23 – Testing platform collisions

Great, we have a platform that behaves mostly as expected. I say mostly because, for a moving platform, it's not very mobile. We'll fix that next by writing the scripts that will animate the platform.

Scripting platform movement

The platform so far is static and motionless. To fix this, we could create a predefined animation sequence using the **Animation Editor**. However, instead, we'll write a script. Frequently, when making animations, you'll often need to make decisions about which option is best: *C# animations* or *baked animations*. Typically, you'll tend to use a script when an animation is simple and must apply to many objects with slight variations. Create and add the following `PingPongMotion.cs` script to the platform object:

```
public class PingPongMotion : MonoBehaviour
{
    public Vector3 MoveAxes = Vector2.zero;
    public float Distance = 3f;

    private Vector3 OrigPos = Vector3.zero;

    void Start ()
    {
        OrigPos = transform.position;
    }
    void Update ()
    {
        transform.position = OrigPos + MoveAxes *
            Mathf.PingPong(Time. time, Distance);
    }
}
```

The following points summarize the preceding code block:

- The `PingPongMotion` class is responsible for moving a GameObject back and forth from an original starting point.

- The `Start` function uses the `OrigPos` variable to record the starting position of the GameObject.

- The `Update` function relies on the `Mathf.PingPong` function to transition a value smoothly between a minimum and maximum. This function fluctuates a value between minimum and maximum repeatedly and continuously over time, allowing you to move objects linearly. For more information, see the Unity online documentation at `http://docs.unity3d.com/ScriptReference/Mathf.PingPong.html`.

Attach the completed script to the platform object in the scene. It can also be reused easily for any other object that should move up and down regularly (or left and right).

As you test the new platforms, you may notice that if the player falls off the platform and down one of the holes at the bottom of the level, nothing happens. We would expect the player to lose a life when they fall down these pits, and that's what we'll implement next.

Implementing player kill zones

A common scripted feature required by all scenes, but not yet implemented, is the kill zone. This is the functionality to mark out a region of 2D space in the level that, when entered by the player, will kill or damage them. This is an especially useful tool to kill the player whenever they fall down a hole in the ground. The kill zone will be required in most levels because nearly every level created so far contains pits and holes in the ground. To implement this functionality, take the following steps:

1. Create a new and empty GameObject in any scene. It doesn't matter which scene because we'll be making a prefab object that can be reused anywhere. As previously mentioned, new GameObjects are created with the menu option, **GameObject | Create Empty**.

2. Once created, name the object `KillZone`.

3. Position the object at the world origin (`0,0,0`).

4. Attach a **Box Collider 2D** component using the menu command, **Component | Physics 2D | Box Collider 2D**. The Box Collider will define the kill zone area.

5. Make sure that the collider is configured as a trigger by checking the **Is Trigger** checkbox in the **Inspector** from the **Box Collider 2D** component, as shown in *Figure 6.24*:

Figure 6.24 – Creating a kill zone object and trigger

A trigger differs from a collider; colliders prevent objects from passing through, and triggers detect when objects pass through, allowing you to perform custom behaviors.

Next, create a new script called `KillZone.cs`, which should be attached to the kill zone object in the scene. This script will be responsible for damaging the player's health for as long as they are in the kill zone. At this stage, there are several ways to approach implementation. One way is to destroy the player as soon as they enter the zone. The other is to damage the player for as long as they are in the zone. The second method is preferred here because of its versatility and contribution toward code reuse. Specifically, we get the option to damage the player by reducing their health at a particular rate (if we need to), as well as killing the player instantly by increasing the rate at which it is reduced. Let's see this at work in the following code block:0

```
public class KillZone : MonoBehaviour
{
    public float Damage = 100f;

    void OnTriggerStay2D(Collider2D other)
    {
```

```
        if(!other.CompareTag("Player"))return;

        if(PlayerControl.PlayerInstance!=null)
        {
            PlayerControl.Health -= Damage * Time.deltaTime;
        }
    }
}
```

The following points summarize the preceding code block:

- The KillZone class is responsible for continually damaging the player's health when a GameObject, tagged as Player, enters and remains within a trigger volume.

- The OnTriggerStay2D function is called automatically by Unity, once per frame, when an object with a Rigidbody enters and remains within a trigger volume. Thus, when a physics object enters the kill zone trigger, the OnTriggerStay2D function will be called as frequently as the Update function. More information on OnTriggerStay2D can be found in the online Unity documentation at http://docs.unity3d.com/ScriptReference/MonoBehaviour.OnTriggerStay2D.html.

- The Damage variable encodes the reduction of health per second for the player by adjusting the public static property, Health, which is part of the PlayerControl class. When Health reaches 0, the player will be destroyed.

To use the new script, do the following:

1. Add the KillZone script to the **KillZone** object.

2. To ensure that the player is killed instantly, increase the **Damage** to a very high number, such as 9000.

3. Create a prefab from the KillZone object by dragging and dropping it from the scene's **Hierarchy** panel to the **Project** panel in the Prefab folder.

4. Then, add the **KillZone** prefab to each level, adjusting the collider's size as needed.

We now have a method of reducing the player's health, yet the eventual player of our game has no way of knowing the current health status of the character. To fix this, we'll implement a UI health bar.

Creating the UI health bar

In the previous section, we introduced the first danger and hazard to the game: a zone that can damage and potentially kill the player. As a result, their health has the potential to reduce from its starting state. It's therefore useful both to us as developers and to gamers to visualize the health status. For this reason, let's focus on rendering the player's health to the screen as a UI health bar. *Figure 6.25* offers a glimpse into the future, displaying the result of our work to come:

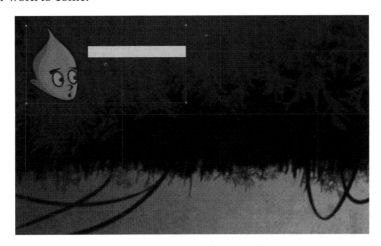

Figure 6.25 – Preparing to create the player health bar

We'll start by configuring a canvas object that will contain our new UI.

Preparing the scene for the UI

To get started, we'll create and configure a canvas object and associated UI camera:

1. Create a new UI Canvas in the scene (any scene) by choosing **GameObject | UI | Canvas** from the application menu. The newly created Canvas object represents the surface on which the UI will be drawn.

> **Important Note**
>
> Adding a canvas object to a scene will automatically create an **EventSystem** object if one does not exist already. This object is essential for the proper use of the UI system; without it, interaction with the UI will not work. If you accidentally delete it, the EventSystem can be recreated by choosing **GameObject | UI | Event System** from the application menu.

2. Next, we'll create a separate camera object for the UI, adding it as a child of the newly created Canvas. By creating a camera for UI rendering, we can apply camera effects and other image adjustments separately to the UI, if we need to. To create a camera as a child, right-click on the **Canvas** object in the **Hierarchy** panel and, from the context menu, choose **Camera** and rename the object as HUD_Cam:

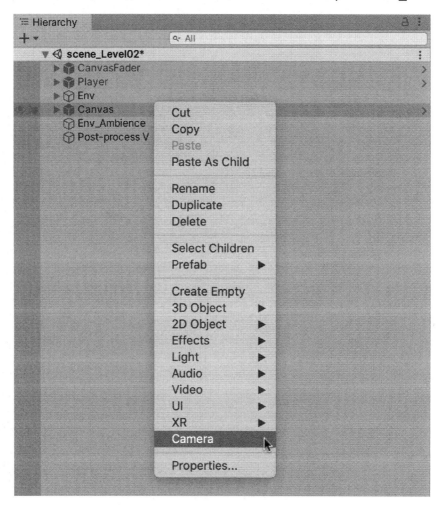

Figure 6.26 – Creating a camera as a child object

3. Now, configure the UI camera to be an **Orthographic** camera. We saw how to do this in the previous chapter, as well as earlier chapters too. *Figure 6.27* displays the camera settings for an orthographic camera. Remember that an orthographic camera removes perspective and foreshortening effects from the render result, which is appropriate for UIs and other objects that live and work in screen space.

4. The camera's **Depth** field, in the **Inspector**, should be higher than the main game camera to ensure that it renders on top of everything else. Otherwise, the UI could potentially render beneath and be ineffective in the game. Set it to 0 (the main camera depth defaults to -1):

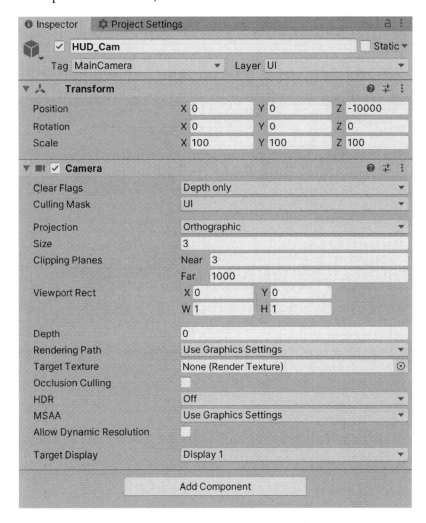

Figure 6.27 – Configuring an orthographic camera for UI rendering

The created camera is almost ready to go! However, right now, it's configured to render everything in the scene, just like any other camera. This means that the scene is effectively being rendered twice by two cameras. This is not only wasteful and poor for performance, but it also makes the second camera redundant. Instead, we want the first original camera to show everything in the scene, in terms of characters and environments, but to ignore UI objects, and the newly created UI camera should only show UI objects.

To fix this, do the following:

1. Select the main game camera.

2. From the **Inspector**, click on the **Culling Mask** drop-down list on the **Camera** component. From here, remove the checkmark for the **UI** layer. This drop-down list allows you to select layers to be ignored for the rendering from the selected camera:

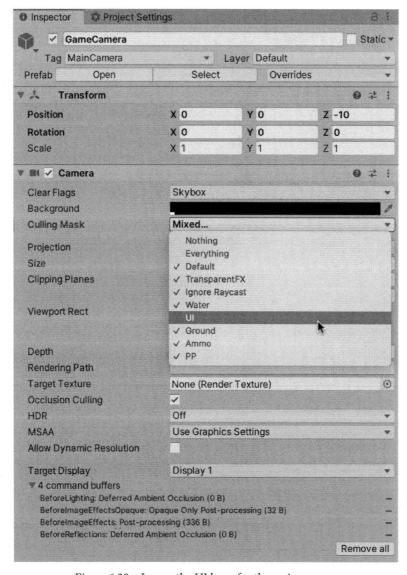

Figure 6.28 – Ignore the UI layer for the main camera

3. Now, select the UI camera object and, for the **Culling Mask** field in the **Camera** component, select the **Nothing** option to deselect all options, and then enable the **UI** layer to render UI layer objects only, as shown in *Figure 6.29*:

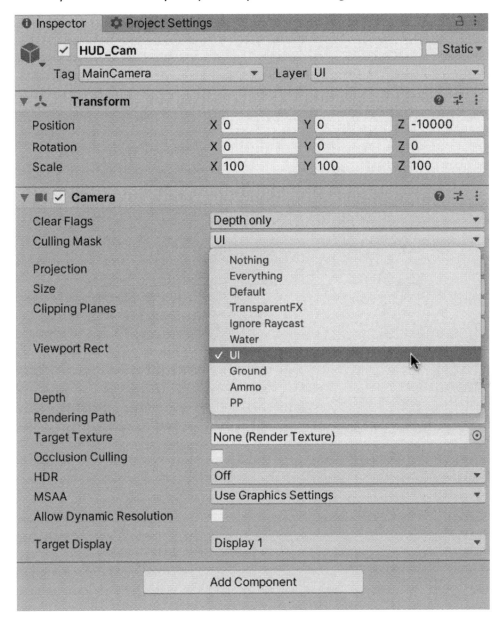

Figure 6.29 – Ignoring all layers except the UI layer for the UI camera

By default, any newly created canvas is configured to work in the **Screen Space Overlay** mode, which means it renders on top of everything else in the scene that is not associated with any specific camera. In addition, all the UI elements will be sized and scaled based on this. To make our work simpler, let's start creating the UI by first configuring the **Canvas** object to work with the newly created UI camera:

1. Select the **Canvas** object and, from the **Canvas** component in the **Inspector**, change **Render Mode** from **Screen Space - Overlay** to **Screen Space - Camera**.

2. Drag and drop the UI camera object to the **Render Camera** field, as shown in *Figure 6.30*:

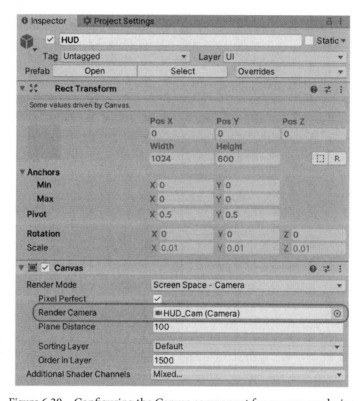

Figure 6.30 – Configuring the Canvas component for camera rendering

Next, let's configure the **Canvas Scaler** component, which is attached to the **Canvas** object. This component is responsible for how the UI appears when the screen size is changed. For our game, the UI should scale relative to the screen size:

1. Change the **UI Scale Mode** dropdown to **Scale With Screen Size**.

2. Enter a resolution of 1024 x 600 in the **Reference Resolution** field, as shown in *Figure 6.31*:

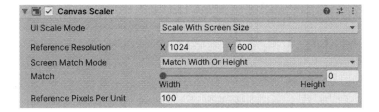

Figure 6.31 – Adjusting the Canvas Scaler component for responsive UI design

With the scene prepared for our game's UI, we can start creating and adding the elements required for our health interface.

Adding UI elements

Now we know that the UI elements will display correctly we can start creating them. We'll first add an image of the player:

1. Create a new **Image** object by right-clicking on the **Canvas** object from the **Hierarchy** panel and choosing **UI | Image** from the context menu:

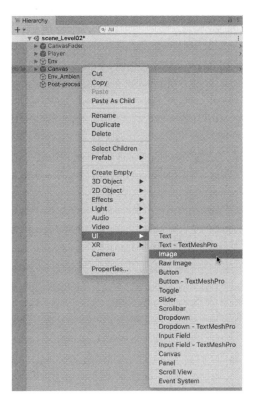

Figure 6.32 – Creating an image as a child object

2. Select the new **Image** object.

3. From the **Inspector**, on the **Image** component, drag and drop the player head sprite (**spr_Head**) from the **Project** panel to the **Source Image** field.

4. Then, use the **Rect Transform** tool (*T* on the keyboard) to resize the image in place at the top-left corner of the screen, as shown in *Figure 6.26*:

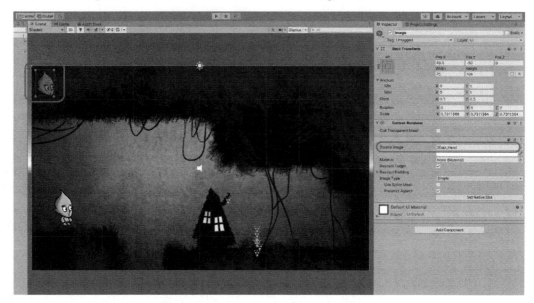

Figure 6.33 – Adding a head image to the UI Canvas

If you cannot see the added head image, remember to assign the UI layer to render by the UI camera. In addition, you may need to offset the UI camera back along the *z* axis to include the head sprite within the camera frustum (viewing area).

5. Finally, anchor the head sprite to the top-left of the screen by clicking on the **Anchor Presets** button on the **Rect Transform** component from the Inspector and selecting **top-left** alignment. This locks the head sprite to the top left of the screen, ensuring that the interface will look consistent at multiple resolutions:

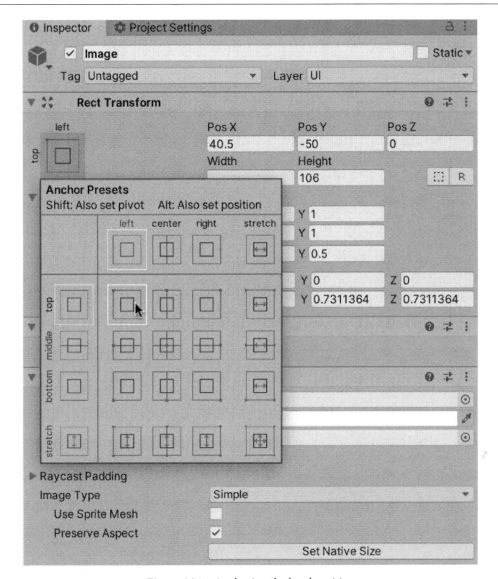

Figure 6.34 – Anchoring the head position

To create the health bar, take the following steps:

1. Add a new **Image** object to the UI Canvas by right-clicking on the Canvas and selecting **UI | Image** from the context menu.

2. For this object, leave the **Source Image** field empty and choose red for the **Color** field, RGB (255,0,0). This will represent the background or **red status** for the health bar when it's fully depleted.

3. Then, use the **Rect Transform** tool to resize the bar as needed, once again anchoring it to the top-left corner of the screen, as shown in *Figure 6.35*:

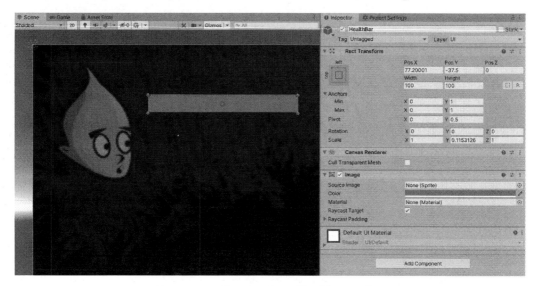

Figure 6.35 – Creating the red health status bar

The UI as it stands is static and doesn't update as the player takes damage. To fix this, we'll need to write a new script.

Scripting the health bar

To implement the health bar functionality, we're going to overlap two identical health bars on top of each other, one red and one green. We'll then scale the green bar as the health reduces so that it reveals the red bar underneath. Before scripting this behavior, further configuration is necessary. Let's change the pivot of the health bar away from the center and to the middle-left point—the point from which the health bar should scale as it reduces and increases. To do this, take the following steps:

1. Select the **HealthBar** object in the **Hierarchy** panel.

2. From the **Inspector**, enter a new **Pivot** value of 0 for **X** and 0.5 for **Y**, as shown in *Figure 6.35*.

Before we jump into writing code, there's one more thing we need to do: create the green overlay for the health bar. This can be accomplished by duplicating the current health bar:

1. Duplicate the red health bar by right-clicking on the object in the Hierarchy panel and selecting **Duplicate**.

2. Name the duplicate `Health_Green` and drag and drop it to appear beneath the red version in the Hierarchy panel list. This will render the object on top of the red health bar as the ordering of objects in the Hierarchy relates to the draw order for UI elements—lower-order objects are rendered on top of higher-order objects:

Figure 6.36 – Creating a duplicate green bar

Now, we need to make a new script file linking the width of the green bar to the health of the player. This means that reductions in health will reduce the width of the green bar, revealing the red bar beneath. Create a new script file named `HealthBar.cs` and attach it to the green bar:

```
public class HealthBar : MonoBehaviour
{
    public float MaxSpeed = 10f;
    private RectTransform ThisTransform = null;
    ...
    void Update ()
    {
        float HealthUpdate = 0f;
        if(PlayerControl.PlayerInstance!=null)
```

```
        {
                HealthUpdate = Mathf.MoveTowards(ThisTransform.
            rect.width, PlayerControl.Health, MaxSpeed);
        }

        ThisTransform.sizeDelta = new Vector2(Mathf.
            Clamp(HealthUpdate,0,100),ThisTransform.sizeDelta.y);

    }
}
```

The following points summarize the preceding code block:

- The `HealthBar` class is responsible for reducing the width of the green health bar, based on the player's health. The green health bar is overlaid on top of the red health bar. Therefore, as the green bar's width decreases, more of the red health bar is exposed.

- We use the `SizeDelta` property of `RectTransform` to set the width of the health bar. More information on this property can be found online at `https://docs.unity3d.com/ScriptReference/RectTransform-sizeDelta.html`.

- The `Mathf.MoveTowards` function smoothly transitions the health bar's width from its existing to its destination width over time. The health bar width will decrease gradually, as opposed to instantly. More information can be found in the online Unity documentation at `https://docs.unity3d.com/ScriptReference/Mathf.MoveTowards.html`.

To use the script, do the following:

1. Attach the `HealthBar` script to the green bar.

2. Make a prefab of the UI objects by dragging and dropping the topmost **Canvas** object from the **Hierarchy** panel to the **Project** panel in the `Prefab` folder. Creating a prefab allows us to reuse the UI system across multiple scenes.

Now whenever the player takes damage, the UI will update accordingly! With every point of damage the player takes, the green bar will shrink, and more of the red bar will be shown. To properly test the UI, it would be useful to have something else in the game that can damage the player (I know we currently have kill zones, but they kill the player too quickly). Luckily for us, in the next chapter, we'll create gun turrets that will do precisely that.

Summary

By learning how to take advantage of sprite shaping, you have added a new tool to your game development belt. If you're not so artistically minded (I'm certainly not), the ability to use a small set of tiles to create a diverse range of environments is hugely useful. Even if you are terrific at creating game art (lucky you!), sprite shaping can help bring your art to life in ways that weren't possible before.

Many games rely on a health system of some variety, and the knowledge gained by implementing the system in this chapter will be useful for a long time to come, no matter what genre of game you're working on (although there are some exceptions; a health system in most sports games wouldn't make much sense, for example). By building on this system by creating a custom health UI, you've laid the foundation for creating a dynamic UI for games in the future. While we focused on creating a health bar in this chapter, using the same principles, you could just as easily create a UI for your score, or the number of collectibles obtained.

By adding platforms to the game, you've introduced the first dynamic element. This dynamism will be extended in the next chapter as we complete the game by adding gun turrets, an NPC, and a quest system.

Test your knowledge

Q1. `OnTriggerExit2D` is a function that runs...

   A. Every frame

   B. When an object leaves a trigger

   C. When the player completes the level

   D. When the level exits

Q2. To interact with the UI, you need a(n)…

   A. EventSystem

   B. Animation System

   C. Collider

   D. Component

Q3. Enumerations are good for...

    A. Storing lists of values

    B. Counting objects

    C. Searching for objects

    D. Sorting objects by name

Q4. You can pick a random number using...

    A. `Random.Range`

    B. `SelectRandomNumber`

    C. `ChooseRandom`

    D. `GetRandomNumber`

Further reading

For more information on Unity serialization, sprite shaping, and more, take a look at the following links:

- `https://unity3d.com/learn/tutorials/s/scripting`
- `https://docs.unity3d.com/Manual/script-Serialization.html`
- `https://www.packtpub.com/game-development/mastering-ui-development-unity`
- `https://blogs.unity3d.com/2018/09/20/intro-to-2d-world-building-with-sprite-shape/`

7
Completing the 2D Adventure

In the previous chapter, we continued to work on a 2D adventure game. We added additional scenes, created a dynamic element in the form of a moving platform, added player kill zones, and created a health system including a UI health bar. This chapter completes the game by adding the remaining features:

- Adding gun turrets that damage the player—as we have a health system, we need something to test it

- Creating a friend for the player—the game's first **Non-Player Character** (**NPC**)

- Giving the NPC something to talk about by creating a quest system—useful knowledge for many game genres

An NPC is any character not controlled by the player. They are usually friendly or at least ambivalent toward the player and, when used correctly, can help bring a game to life. The NPC we create here will be very basic but will have many of the characteristics of NPCs from RPG games. You know, those characters that stand around with an exclamation point over their head and tell you to kill 100 rats. Our NPC will use the quest system (more on that shortly) to assign a quest to the player using onscreen dialog—a straightforward one-sided conversation system that we'll also create.

For our NPC to have anything to talk about, we'll create a quest system. Nowadays, a quest system is not only useful for RPGs. You'll find that many games include a quest-like structure, including 2D platformers (such as the one we're working on here), and shooter games (although the quests may be called "missions"). Even the ever-growing number of simulation games include some method for the player to receive and complete quests.

By the end of this chapter, you will have a better understanding of how to develop systems related to quests and NPC dialog in Unity, information that should prove useful in many future projects.

Technical requirements

This chapter assumes that you have not only completed the projects from the previous chapters but also have a good, basic knowledge of C# scripting generally, though not necessarily in Unity. In this chapter, you will complete the project started in *Chapter 5, Creating a 2D Adventure Game*, so you should read that chapter if you haven't already.

The starting project and assets can be found in this book's companion files in the Chapter07/Start folder. You can start here and follow along with this chapter if you don't have your own project already. The end project can be found in the Chapter07/End folder.

Adding gun turrets

Creating a gun turret involves creating several objects and scripts. We can't just create the turret object. We also need to create the projectiles that will be fired from the turret, script the projectiles so that they move when spawned, and finally create a script for the turret to spawn the projectiles at regular intervals. Let's start by creating the turret object.

Constructing the gun object

Instead of using an image file for our turrets, as we have previously for the player and level objects, we'll create the turret using a primitive shape:

1. Double-click scene_Level03 in the **Project** panel to open it The Scene_ Level03 can be found in the project included in the Chapter07/Start folder at https://github.com/PacktPublishing/Unity-2020-By- Example-Third-Edition.

2. Create a new cube object (**GameObject | 3D Object | Cube**) and name it as Turret:

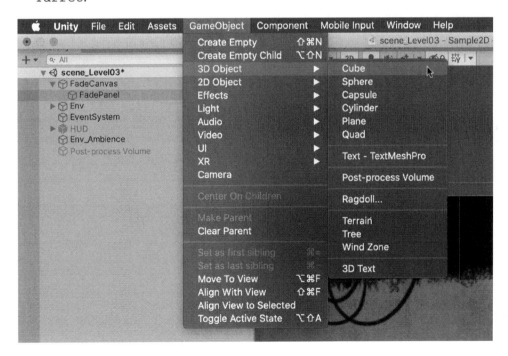

Figure 7.1 - Creating a cube

3.   Adjust the object's scale to approximate a gun turret.

> **Tip**
> You can also use the Rect Transform tool to resize primitives.

Position it on the upper ledge in the scene where it will appear as part of the scenery, as shown in *Figure 7.2*:

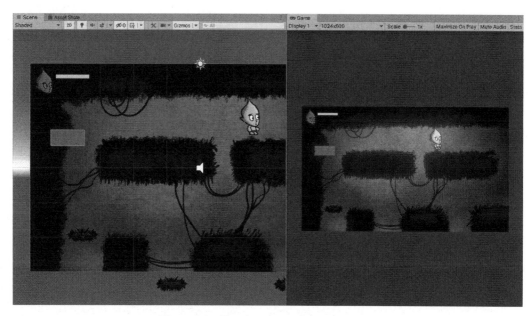

Figure 7.2 - Creating a prop for a gun turret

The gun turret created so far is a conspicuous and prominent gray color, but we want it to blend in with the level. To solve this, we do the following:

1. Create a new material by right-clicking in the **Project** panel and selecting **Create | Material** from the context menu and name it as `Dark`:

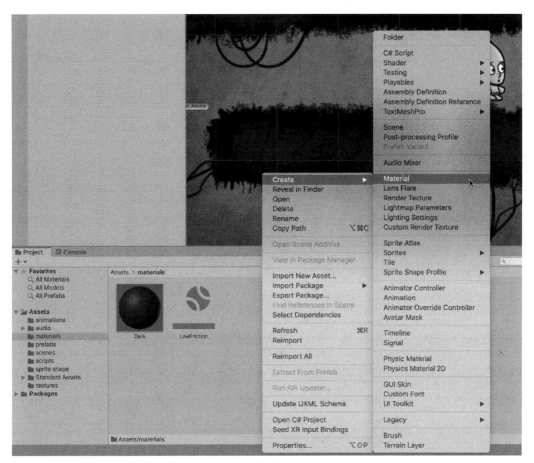

Figure 7.3 - Creating new material for the turret

2. Assign the material a black color from the **Inspector** in the **Albedo** field:

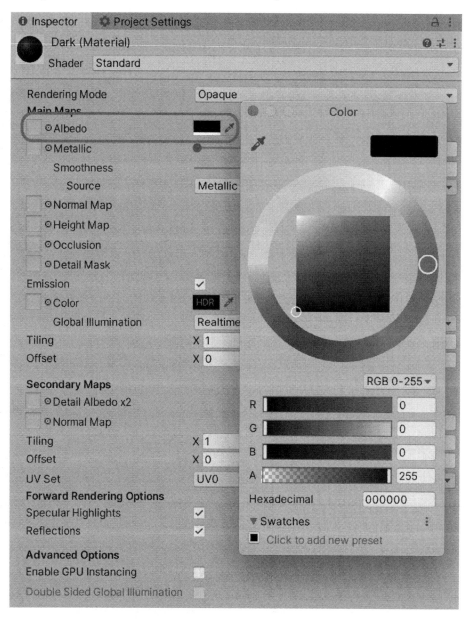

Figure 7.4 - Assigning a color to the turret material

3. Make sure that the **Metallic** field for the black material is reduced to 0 to prevent a shiny or glowing appearance:

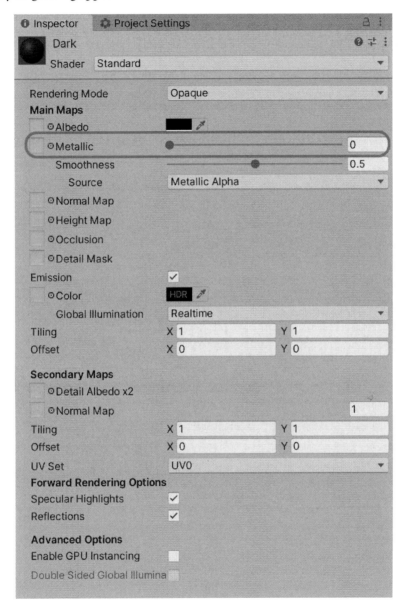

Figure 7.5 - Creating a black material for the turret

4. Drag and drop the material from the **Project** panel to the Turret object in the scene.

After the material is assigned, the turret will more consistently match the level's color scheme—perfect! Now we have the turret object ready to be added to our levels; we next need to create the projectiles that the turrets will shoot.

Creating projectiles

With the turret looking the part, let's create the projectiles that will be fired by the turret. To achieve this, we'll need an empty child object to position the newly spawned projectiles correctly. Let's create this now:

1. Select **GameObject | Create Empty** from the **Application** menu and name it as `SpawnPoint`.

2. Drag and drop the newly created object to the **Turret** cube in the **Hierarchy** panel to make it a **child** of the turret:

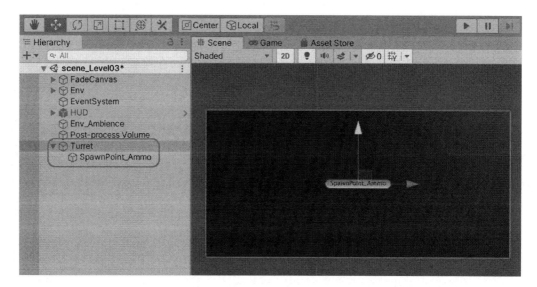

Figure 7.6 - Creating a spawn location

3. Position the empty object at the tip of the cannon:

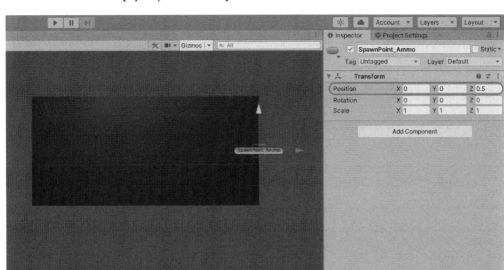

Figure 7.7 - Positioning the turret spawn point relative to its parent

4. Once positioned, assign an icon to represent the empty object visually by clicking on the cube icon (beside the object name) in the **Inspector**, as shown in *Figure 7.8*:

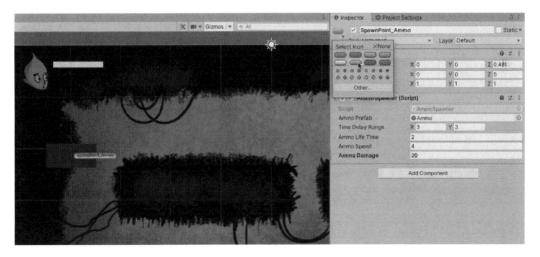

Figure 7.8 - Assigning an icon to the turret's spawn point

Before moving further with ammo spawning, we'll need some ammo to spawn. For the platform game, the ammo should appear as a glowing and pulsating plasma ball. To build this, we do the following:

1. Create a new particle system by choosing **GameObject | Effects | Particle System** from the **Application** menu and name it as Ammo.

> **Tip**
>
> Remember that a particle system is useful to create special effects such as rain, fire, dust, smoke, sparkles, and more. When you create a particle system, a new object is created in the scene. When selected, you can preview how the particle system works and looks in the Scene viewport. By default, small blob-like particles spawn.

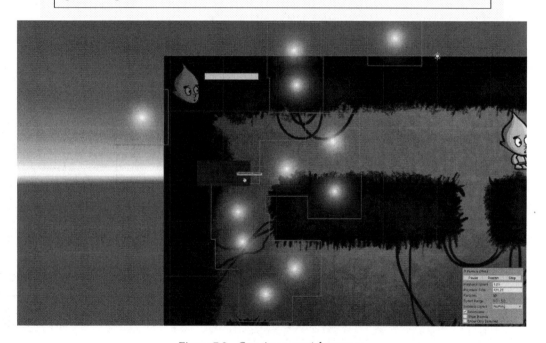

Figure 7.9 - Creating a particle system

2. Sometimes, on creating a particle system for a 2D game, the particles themselves may not be visible because they appear behind other 2D objects in the scene, such as the background and characters. You can control the depth order of the particle system from the **Inspector**. Click on the **Renderer** roll-out title to expand options relating to rendering:

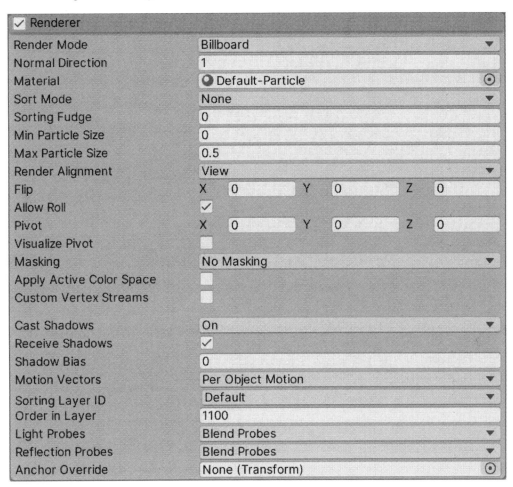

Figure 7.10 - Adjusting render properties

3. From the **Renderer** group, set the **Order In Layer** field to a higher value, above the order of other objects to render the particles in front, as shown in *Figure 7.11*:

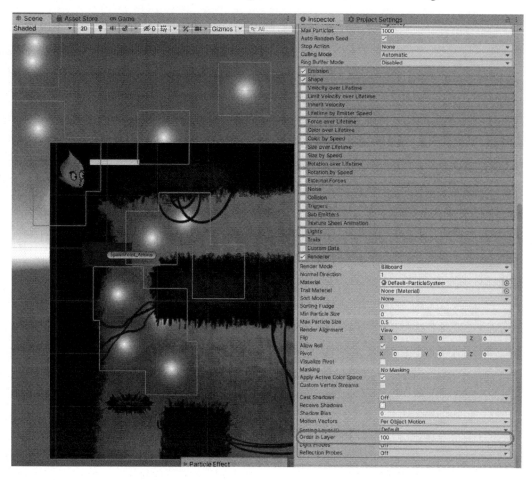

Figure 7.11 - Controlling the render order of particles

Excellent, we should now see particles in the viewport. Getting a particle system to look and behave correctly takes some tweaking and trial and error. It involves testing settings, previewing their effects in the viewport, making judgments about what is needed, and then tweaking and amending as required. To start creating a more believable Ammo object, I want particles to spawn slowly in multiple directions and not just one direction:

1. Expand the **Shape** field in the **Inspector**, which contains settings relating to the shape of the spawn surface.

2. Change the **Shape** from **Cone** to **Sphere**.

3. Set the **Radius** value to 0.01:

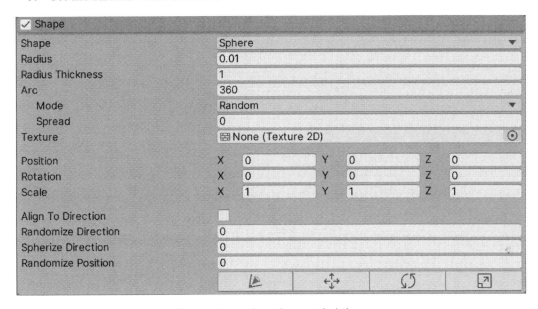

Figure 7.12 - Adjust the particles' Shape

4. On doing this, particles will spawn and travel in all directions emitted from a Sphere's surface. Next, adjust the main particle system properties to create the energy-ball effect. From the **Inspector**, set the **Start Lifetime** to 0.19, **Start Speed** to 0.88, **Start Size** to 0.59, and **Start Color** to teal (light blue).

The settings are shown in *Figure 7.13*:

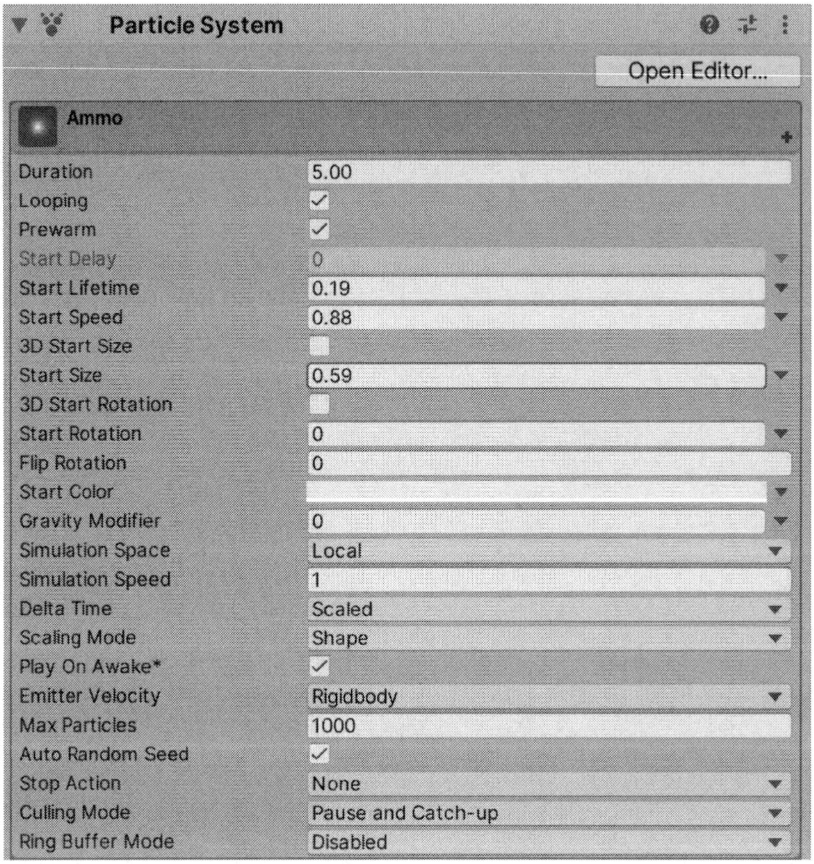

Figure 7.13 - Configuring the particle system's main properties

Great! The particle system should now look just as we need it. However, if we press Play on the toolbar, it doesn't move. A projectile should, of course, hurtle through the air and collide with its target. We'll work on that next.

Scripting projectile movement

The movement of the projectiles will be simple. We want them to move forward at a constant speed specified by us. To accomplish this, create a `Mover.cs` script that will be attached to the object:

```
public class Mover : MonoBehaviour
{
    public float Speed = 10f;
```

```
void Update ()
{
    transform.position += transform.forward * Speed *
        Time.deltaTime;
}
}
```

The `Mover` script features nothing that we haven't seen many times already so won't be discussed in detail here. It moves whichever object it is attached to in the direction of its forward vector.

In addition to moving through the level, the Ammo object must collide with and damage the player character on impact:

1. Attach a Rigidbody component to the ammo by selecting the **Ammo** object in the scene and, from the **Application** menu, choosing **Component | Physics 2D | Rigidbody 2D**.

2. Once added, set the **Body Type** of the Rigidbody to **Kinematic** in the **Inspector**. A kinematic Rigidbody ensures that the object will travel based on the `Mover` script and still interact with physical objects without being affected by gravity, collisions, or other forces:

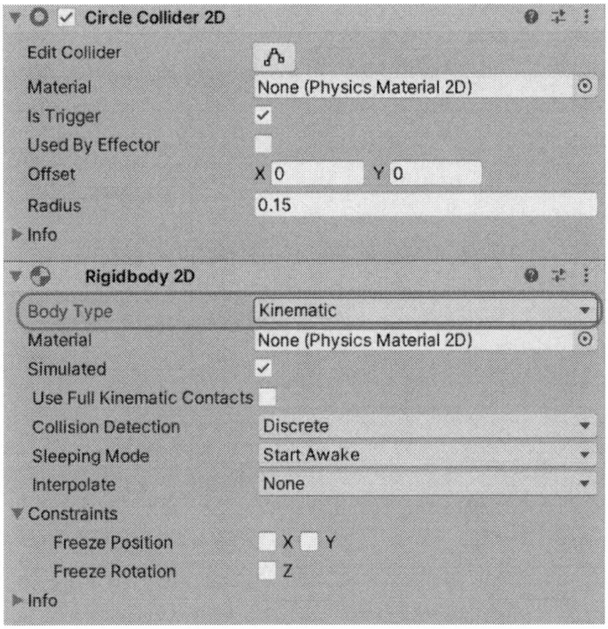

Figure 7.14 - Marking Rigidbody as Kinematic

3. Next, add a **Circle Collider 2D** to the Ammo object to allow detectable collisions between the ammo and its target by selecting **Component | Physics 2D | Circle Collider 2D** from the Application menu.

4. Once added, enable the **Is Trigger** field and change the **Radius** until it approximates the size of the **Ammo** object. Configuring the collider as a trigger prevents any collision resolution from occurring as we don't want the projectile to bounce off of the player or level:

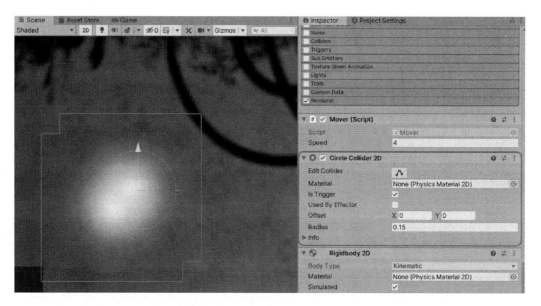

Figure 7.15 - Configuring the Circle Collider for the Ammo object

The ammo should support two final behaviors. First, the ammo should damage and perhaps destroy any target it collides with, and second, the ammo should destroy itself, both after an elapsed time and if it hits a target. Two additional scripts will be created to handle these conditions: CollideDestroy.cs and Ammo.cs. The following code lists the Ammo.cs file, which will handle collisions with the player object:

```
public class Ammo : MonoBehaviour
{

    public float Damage = 100f;
    public float LifeTime = 1f;


    void Start()
    {
        Destroy(gameObject, LifeTime);
```

```
        }

        void OnTriggerEnter2D(Collider2D other)
        {
            if(!other.CompareTag("Player"))return;
            PlayerControl.Health -= Damage;
        }

        public void Die()
        {
            Destroy(gameObject);
        }
}
```

The following code lists the CollideDestroy.cs file:

```
public class CollideDestroy : MonoBehaviour
{
        public string TagCompare = string.Empty;

        void OnTriggerEnter2D(Collider2D other)
        {
            if(!other.CompareTag(TagCompare))return;

            Destroy(gameObject);
        }
}
```

The code in these files includes functionality that we encountered before when making the Twin-stick Space Shooter. So, please refer to *Chapter 3, Creating a Space Shooter*, and *Chapter 4, Continuing the Space Shooter Game*, for detailed information if required.

To complete the Ammo object, do the following:

1. Attach both the Ammo and CollideDestroy scripts to the **Ammo** object in the scene.
2. Drag and drop the **Ammo** object from the scene viewport to the **Project** panel in the Prefabs folder to make an **Ammo** prefab, ready to add to any scene.

Excellent work! You now have an Ammo object that moves and collides with the player. By setting the **Damage** setting high enough, you will be able to destroy the player on impact. Give this a test now by adding an **Ammo** object to the scene and pressing Play. You'll notice straight away that nothing in the scene fires the ammo yet. We'll explore that next.

Completing the turret

We've now created an **Ammo** object, and we've started to engineer a gun turret, but it doesn't yet spawn ammo. Let's build this functionality now.

We already have a spawn point positioned in front of the turret parented to it as a child object. We'll attach a new script file called `AmmoSpawner.cs` to this object, which will be responsible for generating ammo at regular intervals:

```
public class AmmoSpawner : MonoBehaviour
{
    public GameObject AmmoPrefab = null;
    public Vector2 TimeDelayRange = Vector2.zero;
    public float AmmoLifeTime = 2f;
    public float AmmoSpeed = 4f;
    public float AmmoDamage = 100f;


    void Start()
    {
        FireAmmo();
    }

    public void FireAmmo()
    {
        GameObject Obj = Instantiate(AmmoPrefab,
            transform.position, transform.rotation) as
                GameObject;
        Ammo AmmoComp = Obj.GetComponent<Ammo>();
        Mover MoveComp = Obj.GetComponent<Mover>();
        AmmoComp.LifeTime = AmmoLifeTime;
        AmmoComp.Damage = AmmoDamage;
        MoveComp.Speed = AmmoSpeed;

        Invoke("FireAmmo", Random.Range(TimeDelayRange.x,
```

```
                TimeDelayRange.y));
    }
}
```

The preceding code relies on the `Invoke` function called at random intervals using `Random.Range` to instantiate a new ammo prefab into the scene. This code could be improved using **Object Pooling** (or **Caching**), as discussed in the previous chapter, but in this case, it performs acceptably.

To complete the turret, follow these steps:

1. Attach the script to the **SpawnPoint_Ammo** object we created previously:

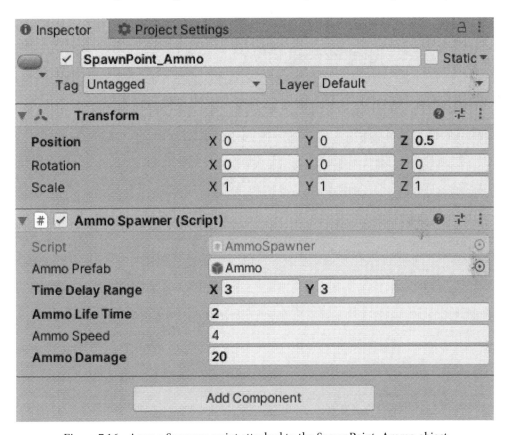

Figure 7.16 - Ammo Spawner script attached to the SpawnPoint_Ammo object

2. Create a prefab of the **Turret** by dragging and dropping the object from the
    Hierarchy to the `Prefabs` folder:

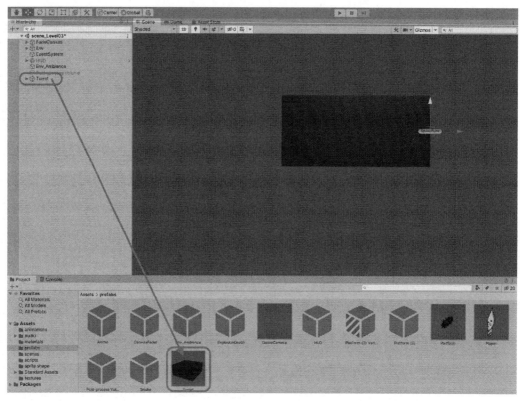

Figure 7.17 - Creating a turret prefab

We can now use the **Turret** in other scenes by reversing this process and dragging
the prefab to the **Hierarchy**.

3. Press Play to test the **Turret**. As shown in *Figure 7.18*, it should regularly
    fire projectiles:

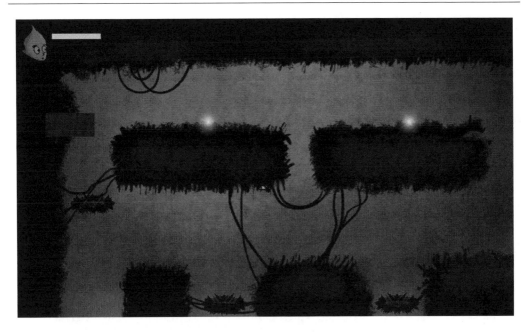

Figure 7.18 - Turret shooting projectiles

Excellent! We've now created a gun turret. Go ahead and position more turrets, if wanted, to increase the difficulty of the level.

> **Tip**
>
> Make sure that the Time Delay range (the time between ammo spawns) has a value higher than zero; otherwise, ammo will be continually generated and become practically impossible for the player to avoid.

Next, we'll create the last system for our platformer game: the questing system and a friendly NPC to provide the player with the first quest of the game.

Creating an NPC

As stated earlier, **NPC** stands for **Non-Player Character** and typically refers to any friendly or neutral characters other than the player-controlled character. In our adventure, Level three will feature an NPC character standing outside their house, who will provide us with a quest to collect a gem from Level two. To create the NPC character, we'll duplicate the player and adjust the character color, making them appear distinct:

1. Drag and drop the `Player` prefab from the **Project** panel to the `Level02` scene and position it near the house area:

Figure 7.19 - Creating an NPC Prefab

2. Name the object `NPC`.

3. To prevent any changes we make to the NPC object to propagate back to the prefab, remove the association between the two by right-clicking on the object and selecting **Prefab | Unpack Completely**.

> **Important note**
> Prefabs are discussed in detail in *Chapter 1, Exploring the Fundamentals of Unity*.

4. Remove all additional components (such as the **Player Controller** and collider) to return this character to a standard sprite that is not player controlled:

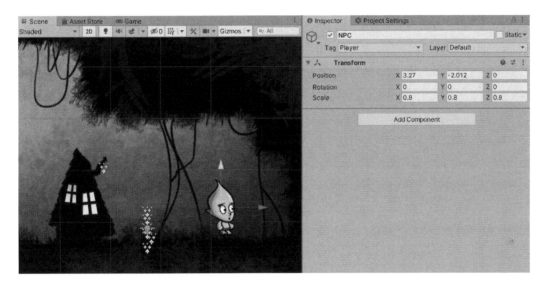

Figure 7.20 - Creating an NPC from the player character prefab

5. Invert the character's **X** scale to make them face left instead of right by selecting the parent NPC object (not the child limb objects) and making the **X** scale negative. All child objects will flip to face the direction of their parent:

Figure 7.21 - Flipping the X scale for a character NPC

6. Change the **Color** property of the **Sprite Renderer** of the NPC object from green to red to distinguish it from the player. The NPC object is a multi-part object composed of several **Sprite Renderers**. We could select each object and change its color individually via the Inspector. However, Unity supports multi-object editing for common properties, so it's easier to select all of the objects and change their colors together, as shown in *Figure 7.22*:

Figure 7.22 - Setting the NPC color

The NPC should talk to the player on approach by displaying a dialog text
be displayed will vary, depending on the status of their quest. On a first
give the player a quest. On a second visit, the NPC's response will depend
quest has been completed. We'll write the quest functionality in the next section.
we can start creating this functionality now by adding the ability to determine when
player approaches the NPC. We can achieve this by using a collider:

1. Select the **NPC** object in the scene.

2. Choose **Component | Physics 2D | Box Collider 2D** from the **Application** menu.

3. Adjust the **Size** field on the collider to approximate the area around the **NPC** object
   in which the player should enter to have a conversation.

4. Mark the collider as a **Trigger** object, allowing the player to enter the zone:

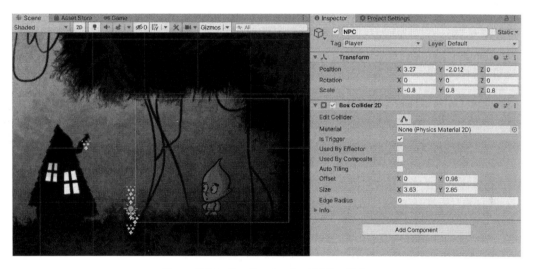

Figure 7.23 - Configuring the NPC collider

Now that we have an NPC and a method of interacting with the player using a trigger
collider, we need to create something meaningful for the NPC to say and, in doing so,
create a questing system.

Implementing a quest system

Implementing a quest system is a large topic, so it's a good idea to split it into several separate chunks of work that are a more manageable size. To create a system that works for our game and is easily extendable, we'll need to complete the following tasks:

1. Create a data structure to hold individual quest information. This information will include the current quest status (whether it is unassigned, assigned, or completed) and the name of the quest.

2. Design a method of managing the quest status of all of the quests in the game. We need to be able to query the status of a quest at any time.

3. Create a way to assign quests to the player.

4. Place a quest item in the game world. The goal of the quest in this game will be to find an object, so we'll need to create and place that item in one of the levels.

We'll start by creating the structure to store quest items and then build on top of this basic structure by creating a quest manager.

Starting a quest

The quest data structure will be simple. For each quest, we need to store the current quest status (unassigned, assigned, and complete) and the name of a quest, which we'll use to identify each quest in the manager class (we'll write this shortly).

Create a new class called Quest.cs to hold quest-related data:

```
[System.Serializable]
public class Quest
{
    public enum QUESTSTATUS {UNASSIGNED, ASSIGNED ,COMPLETE};
    public QUESTSTATUS Status = QUESTSTATUS.UNASSIGNED;
    public string QuestName = string.Empty;
}
```

The Quest class defines the name and status for a single and specific quest. We store the quest's status as an **enum** with the following possible values:

- UNASSIGNED (the player has not received this quest yet)

- ASSIGNED (the player has received the quest but has not yet completed it)

- COMPLETE (the player has received and completed the quest)

We mark the class as **Serializable** by adding the `System.Serializable` attribute just before the class implementation. Serialization automatically transforms the `Quest` object into a format Unity can store and reconstruct. You may rightfully be wondering how this is useful to us. Well, we generally edit script variables using the Inspector window. The Inspector does not directly interact with our scripts but, rather, it asks the object to serialize itself, transforming it into data, which is then displayed in the Inspector window. When you play the game in the editor or compile the game for release, this data is de-serialized, maintaining any edits we made.

Adding the `Serializable` attribute does not guarantee that our custom class can be serialized and displayed in the Inspector. It also shouldn't be static (it's not), abstract (nope), or generic (no again). As it meets all of these requirements, when we add this class as a member variable, we will be able to edit the public variables in the Inspector window, just as if it was a built-in Unity type (which is automatically serialized for us).

> **Tip**
> If there is an accessor or mutator for a variable, they will not be called when editing the variable using the Inspector.

Serialization is a huge topic in Unity and is used for many other tasks, including the following:

- Instantiating objects: When you call `Instantiate` on an object, Unity serializes the object, creates a new empty object, and then de-serializes the data onto the new object.
- Prefabs: A prefab is just serialized data, ready to be de-serialized as required.
- Other tasks include the saving (serialization) and loading (de-serialization) of a scene.

> **Important note**
> Similar to serializing classes, there are also rules to follow to ensure that your field can be serialized. It needs to be `public` (or have the `SerializeField` attribute), and it cannot be `readonly` or static. Variables that follow these rules are automatically serialized and displayed in the Inspector.

We can test whether the serialization is working correctly shortly, as we'll create a class to manage the quests next and add the `Quest` class as a member variable.

Managing the quests

With the quest structure complete, we can create `QuestManager.cs`, which will be responsible for maintaining and providing access to a collection of quest data. We want this class to be accessible in every scene, so let's start by adding logic that will ensure that the script's GameObject persists between scenes:

```
public class QuestManager : MonoBehaviour
{
private static QuestManager ThisInstance = null;

void Awake()
{
    if (ThisInstance == null)
    {
        DontDestroyOnLoad(this);
        ThisInstance = this;
    }
    else
    {
        DestroyImmediate(gameObject);
    }
}
}
```

The `Awake` function accomplishes two tasks. It ensures that the object that `QuestManager` is attached to persists between scenes, and it makes sure that there is only ever one instance of the script in a scene.

Calling DontDestroyOnLoad tells Unity to keep this object alive when transitioning scenes. By calling this function, we know that when we transition to a new level in our game, we will still be able to access the quest manager. However, it can cause issues if we're not careful. For example, say we have this object in a scene called scene1, and then we transition to scene2. The object persists through the scene transition and is available in scene2. So far, so good. But then what happens if we transition back to scene1? The object is created all over again, and we now have two copies of the same script. This process can be repeated over and over until we have numerous copies when we only wanted one. That's where the ThisInstance variable comes in. By storing a static reference to an instance of QuestManager, it is shared between all instances of a class. If ThisInstance has already been assigned to, then we know there is already an instance of QuestManager in the scene so we can safely destroy this copy, preventing more than one from existing in a level.

Now we have the functionality in place for keeping QuestManager around for as long as needed, let's write the functions to retrieve and set a quest status:

```
public class QuestManager : MonoBehaviour
{
    public Quest[] Quests;

    public static Quest.QUESTSTATUS GetQuestStatus(string
        QuestName)
    {
        foreach(Quest Q in ThisInstance.Quests)
        {
            if(Q.QuestName.Equals(QuestName))
            {
                return Q.Status;
            }

        }

        return Quest.QUESTSTATUS.UNASSIGNED;
    }

    public static void SetQuestStatus(string QuestName,
        Quest.QUESTSTATUS NewStatus)
    {
```

```
            foreach(Quest Q in ThisInstance.Quests)
            {
                if(Q.QuestName.Equals(QuestName))
                {
                    Q.Status = NewStatus; return;
                }
            }
        }
    }
```

The following points summarize the code sample:

- The GetQuestStatus function returns QUESTSTATUS of the quest with the specified quest name. If a quest with the specified name is not found, then a status of UNASSIGNED is returned.

- The SetQuestStatus function assigns a new status to the specified quest.

- The get and set functions are **static** and consequently are callable from any other script, without needing to instantiate a QuestManager object.

Lastly, let's add a reset function to the QuestManager class:

```
public class QuestManager : MonoBehaviour
{
    ...
    public static void Reset()
    {
        foreach(Quest Q in ThisInstance.Quests)
        {
            Q.Status = Quest.QUESTSTATUS.UNASSIGNED;
        }
    }
}
```

The Reset function loops through every quest and sets its status to UNASSIGNED. This is handy if we want to revert the status of every quest, for example, if the player receives a game over, and we need to reset the world's state.

To use the new `QuestManager` component, we do the following:

1. Create an empty object in the first scene of the game and rename it as `QuestManager`.

2. Add the `QuestManager` component.

3. In the **Inspector**, define all of the quests that can be collected. In our game, there is only one quest available: the quest given by an NPC character to obtain a stolen gemstone. Remember, we can see and edit the quest data directly in the **Inspector** as we assigned the `Serializable` attribute to our `Quest` class.

The `QuestManager` settings are shown in *Figure 7.24*:

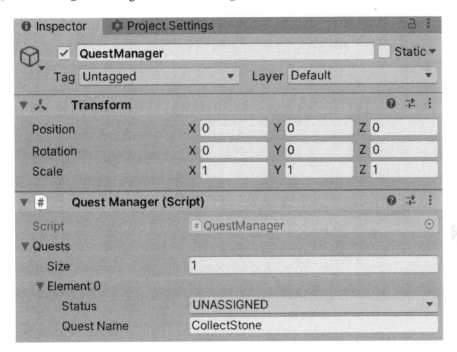

Figure 7.24 - Defining in-game quests using the QuestManager component

`QuestManager` maintains a pool of all possible quests in the game, whether the player has received them or not. However, the NPC still needs to assign the quest to the player on approach. We'll accomplish this next.

Assigning quests to the player

Before we write the script to display the quest, we need a UI element to act as the panel to display conversational text when the NPC speaks. We'll use a UI Canvas with a `Text` object as a child. To create the canvas, follow these steps:

1. Create the canvas object by navigating to **GameObject | UI | Canvas** in the **Application** menu:

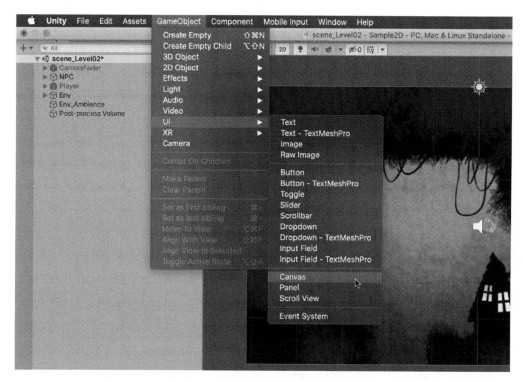

Figure 7.25 - Creating the Quest UI

2. Right-click on the canvas and select **UI | Text**.

3. Add a **Canvas Group** component to the canvas by selecting **Component | Layout | Canvas Group** from the **Application** menu. This component lets you set the alpha transparency for the panel and child objects as one complete unit. You can change the **Alpha** member from the **Inspector**. A value of 1 means fully visible, and a value of 0 is fully transparent:

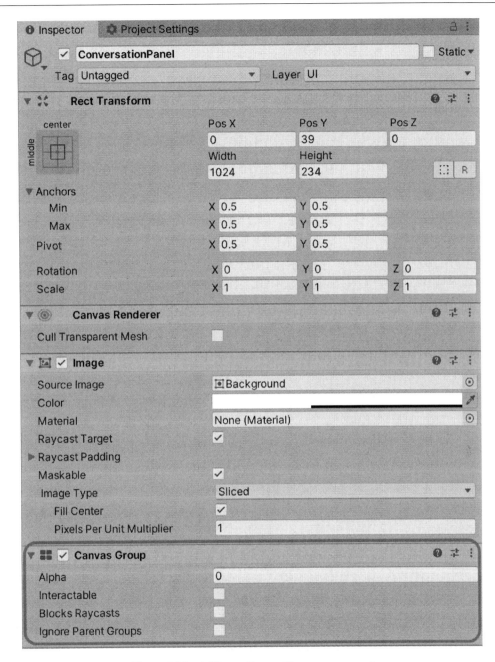

Figure 7.26 - Adding a Canvas Group component

Now that we have the `Text` object, we can create the script that assigns the quest to the player and displays the quest information. Create a script file, `QuestGiver.cs`:

```
public class QuestGiver : MonoBehaviour
{
    public string QuestName = string.Empty;
    public Text Captions = null;
    public string[] CaptionText;

    void OnTriggerEnter2D(Collider2D other)
    {
        if(!other.CompareTag("Player"))return;

        Quest.QUESTSTATUS Status = QuestManager.
            GetQuestStatus(QuestName);
        Captions.text = CaptionText[(int) Status];
    }

    void OnTriggerExit2D(Collider2D other)
    {
        Quest.QUESTSTATUS Status =
            QuestManager.GetQuestStatus(QuestName);
        if (Status == Quest.QUESTSTATUS.UNASSIGNED)
        {
            QuestManager.SetQuestStatus(QuestName,
                Quest.QUESTSTATUS.ASSIGNED);
        }
        else if(Status == Quest.QUESTSTATUS.COMPLETE)
        {
            SceneManager.LoadScene(5);
        }
    }
}
```

Attach this script to the **NPC**. In the future, if you create additional objects that assign quests, you should also attach this component to them.

To use the script, follow these steps:

1. Attach the script to the **NPC** object.

2. Assign the previously created `Text` object to the **Captions** field in the **Inspector**.

3. Write captions for the `UNASSIGNED`, `ASSIGNED`, and `COMPLETED` quest statuses, as shown in *Figure 7.27*:

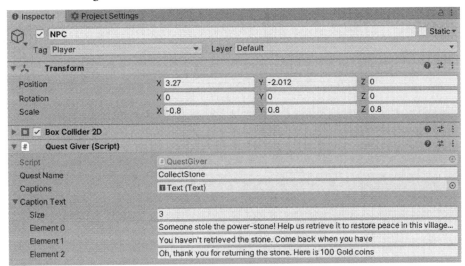

Figure 7.27 - Defining the QuestGiver component

After attaching the script to the **NPC**, test the game by pressing the Play button on the toolbar. When you approach the NPC, the UI text should change to the specified quest as defined for the `QuestName` field on the `QuestGiver` component:

Figure 7.28 - NPC quest text

If you play the game now and talk to the **NPC**, you'll receive the quest but have no way to complete it. There is no *power-stone* for the player to collect. Let's add one now.

Creating the quest item

The assigned quest is to collect a gemstone, but our levels lack said stone. Let's add one for the player to collect:

1. Drag and drop the GemStone texture from the Texture folder in the **Project** panel to scene_Level03 on the topmost ledge so that the player has to climb to reach it.

2. Attach a **Circle Collider 2D** component.

3. Enable the **Is Trigger** option in the collider component so that it registers collisions but does not attempt to resolve them:

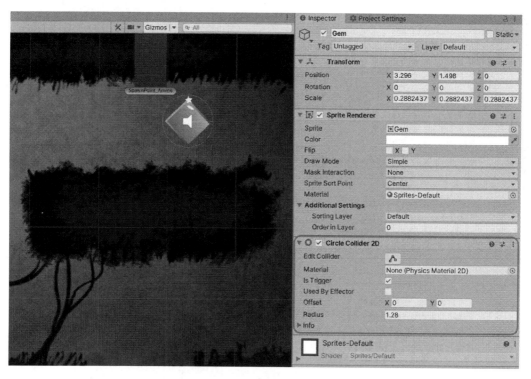

Figure 7.29 - Creating a quest object

4. Finally, we'll need a `QuestItem` script to set the quest status on the `QuestManager` class when the item is collected, allowing `QuestGiver` to determine whether the gem has been collected:

```
public class QuestItem : MonoBehaviour
{
    ...
    void Start ()
    {
        gameObject.SetActive(false);

        if(QuestManager.GetQuestStatus(QuestName) ==
            Quest.QUESTSTATUS.ASSIGNED)
        {
            gameObject.SetActive(true);
        }
    }

    void OnTriggerEnter2D(Collider2D other)
    {
        if(!other.CompareTag("Player"))return;
        if(!gameObject.activeSelf)return;
        QuestManager.SetQuestStatus(QuestName,
            Quest.QUESTSTATUS.COMPLETE);
        ThisRenderer.enabled=ThisCollider.enabled=false;
        if(ThisAudio!=null)ThisAudio.Play();
    }
}
```

The preceding code is responsible for setting the quest status to be completed when the **Gem** (quest item) object is collected as the player enters the trigger volume.

Attach the QuestItem script to the **Gem** object, and make sure you playtest the completed game:

Figure 7.30 - The completed game!

Excellent work! You now have a completed integrated quest system and an NPC character. That's the final addition we'll make in this project, but feel free to extend and add new features as you see fit. For example, you could add a second controllable character, additional levels, or even enemies that attack the player (we discuss enemy AI in the next chapter).

Summary

Great work! We've now completed the 2D adventure game. The game contains 2D physics over multiple levels, moving platforms, a gun that can damage the player with the damage updating a UI, a quest system, and an NPC that assigns a quest to the player. The knowledge gained in creating this game will prove useful in a wide variety of future projects, not just in this book, but in your professional career. It's always handy to know how to create a UI, a quest system, and 2D environmental physics.

Some minor details were not covered in this chapter for the sake of clarity and conciseness because we've seen the methods or content already in earlier chapters. Hence, it's essential to open the course files and check out the completed project, hence seeing how the code works. Overall, in having reached this far in this book, you have three completed Unity projects to your name—not bad at all!

The next chapter is something special, as we move away from general game development to focus on one particular area—**Artificial Intelligence (AI)**. As I'm sure you're aware, AI is an important topic that continues to be popular with the development community. Over the next few chapters, we'll discuss creating navigation meshes, pathfinding, **Finite State Machines (FSM)**, machine learning, and more.

Test your knowledge

Q1. NPC stands for…

    A. Not Player Character

    B. Non-Player Character

    C. No Person Controlling

    D. New Playable Character

Q2. A Canvas Group lets you…

    A. Play UI Animations

    B. Change the Alpha of multiple UI objects

    C. Deletes many objects together

    D. Adjust objects for different resolutions

Q3. You can preview a particle system by…

    A. Selecting the particle system and viewing the Game panel

    B. Going to the editor panel, no need to select the particle system

    C. Selecting the particle system and viewing the Editor panel

    D. Pressing play and view the editor panel

Q4. To keep an object alive when transitioning scenes, you call…

    A. `DestroyOnLoad(false);`

    B. `gameObject.keepAlive = true;`

    C. `DontDestroyOnLoad();`

    D. `Invoke(DestroyGameObject, 1000);`

Further reading

For more information on the topics in this chapter, take a look at the following links:

- https://unity3d.com/learn/tutorials/s/scripting

- https://docs.unity3d.com/Manual/script-Serialization.html

- https://docs.unity3d.com/ScriptReference/Object.DontDestroyOnLoad.html

- https://www.packtpub.com/game-development/hands-game-development-patterns-unity-2019

8
Creating Artificial Intelligence

In this chapter, we'll start looking at specific gameplay elements rather than game genres. This project, unlike the previous three, will not be a game with a clear win and lose condition but will be a functional prototype that highlights a range of important coding techniques and ideas prevalent in the game development.

In the complete project, we'll have a **Non-Player Character** (**NPC**) that will patrol the level searching for the player using Unity's pathfinding tools, and when it finds the player, it will chase the player down until it is within range and mercilessly attack the player. Its behavior will be controlled using a **Finite State Machine** (**FSM**).

In this chapter, we'll cover the following:

- Importing assets from the **Unity Asset Store** (**UAS**)
- Creating the world that the player and NPC will cohabitate
- Generating a navigation mesh using **NavMesh**
- Animating the NPC using Unity's **Mecanim** system
- Writing a custom first-person controller
- Creating an animated waypoint system for the NPC to follow

To achieve our goals, we'll build on packages that we import from the **Unity Asset Store**. The UAS is an excellent resource that enables us to hit the ground running. By importing a terrain package, we don't need to construct the environment from scratch. Instead, we can change an existing terrain to fit our needs; and we'll do the same for the NPC by building on an existing package.

Once we've created the terrain, added an animated NPC, and created a waypoint system, we'll add the player to the world. In the previous chapters, we've relied on the first-person character included with the standard assets. However, by creating a customized version in this chapter, we will gain an understanding of what goes into creating a character controller and have a solid foundation that we can extend in future projects.

We'll start by examining the complete project before importing the required assets for the UAS.

Technical requirements

In this chapter, you will start a new project that is not a direct continuation of previous projects. However, as with previous chapters, this chapter assumes that you have not only completed the previous projects but also have a good and basic knowledge of C# scripting generally, though not necessarily in Unity.

You can download the example code files for this book from GitHub at `https://github.com/PacktPublishing/Unity-2020-By-Example`. Once downloaded, you can find the AI project in the `Chapter08/End` folder.

This chapter uses two assets from the Unity Asset Store, which, along with their author details, can be found at the following links:

- `https://assetstore.unity.com/packages/3d/characters/animals/meshtint-free-chick-mega-toon-series-152777`
- `https://assetstore.unity.com/packages/3d/environments/landscapes/low-poly-simple-nature-pack-162153`

Looking ahead – an overview of the project

In this chapter, we'll start by working on a first-person game in which the player character can explore an environment. The terrain features hills, valleys, and varied terrain elements.

The player will not be alone in the world. An NPC in the form of a baby chicken, tha a chick, will also move around the environment. The **Artificial Intelligence (AI)** for the NPC will operate using an FSM with three states: Patrol, Chase, and Attack. The chick will wander around (Patrol mode) searching for the player. If the player is sighted, the NPC will chase and pursue the player (Chase mode). If, during the chase, the enemy loses sight of the player, they will return to patrolling. On the other hand, if the enemy approaches the player during the chase, the enemy will attack the player (Attack mode).

See *Figure 8.1* for a sneak peek of the completed project:

Figure 8.1 - Building a world with intelligent NPCs

Now that we have an idea of what we want to achieve, we can take the first step toward the goal by importing external assets to jump-start our project.

Importing assets

As with all of the previous projects, there will be some assets we don't create ourselves. For this project, we will import packages for the terrain and character models as creating them is not crucial for understanding AI. We'll import those assets into an empty project:

1. Create a new 3D project. The details on this are covered in *Chapter 1, Exploring the Fundamentals of Unity*.

2. Navigate to the UAS online at https://assetstore.unity.com.

3. Search for `Low-Poly Simple Nature Pack`. This pack will become the terrain for our AI agents.

4. Select **Add to My Assets** as shown in *Figure 8.2*:

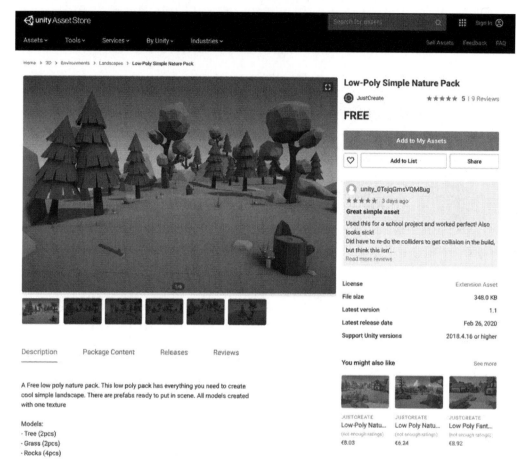

Figure 8.2 - Adding the terrain pack to your asset collection

We also need a terrifying enemy that will patrol and chase the player—striking fear into anyone that enters its territory. Once again, we'll use a premade asset for this, although you could create your own by using the 3D modeling software.

5. In the UAS, search for `Chick Mega Toon Series` and once again click on **Add to My Assets**:

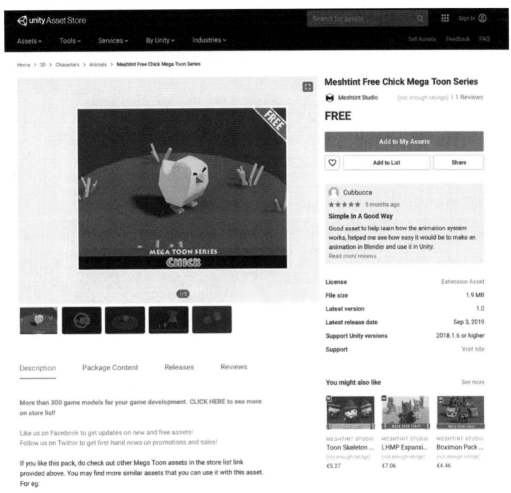

Figure 8.3 - Adding the character pack to your asset collection

It may not look so scary now, but wait until this chick is chasing you down in-game!

6. Back in Unity, we need to import the packages into our project. Open the **Package Manager** by selecting **Window | Package Manager** from the **Application** menu.

7. Find the terrain package in the package explorer and click on **Import**:

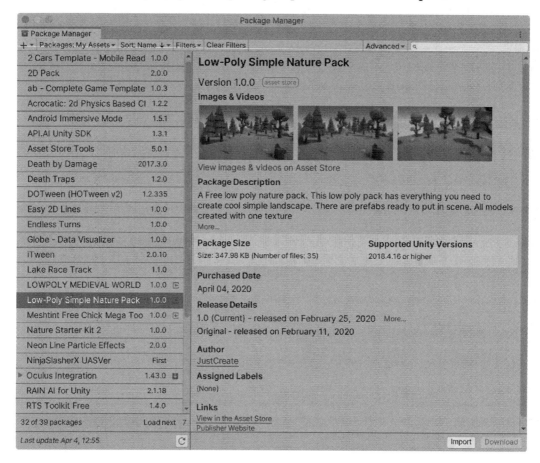

Figure 8.4 - Importing the terrain pack

8. Repeat the process for the character package, which should also be visible in the package list.

We have now imported all of the external packages that we require for now. It's time to start molding them to make them our own. We'll start by creating the terrain that will be our NPC's home.

Constructing the terrain

Now that we've imported all of the assets we require, we can start preparing the scene for our AI agent (also known as the *terrifying chick* for reasons that will become apparent):

1. The nature pack provides an example scene that we can alter to suit our needs. Navigate to `Assets/NaturePackLite/Scenes` in the **Project** panel.

2. Double-click the **Demo** scene to open it:

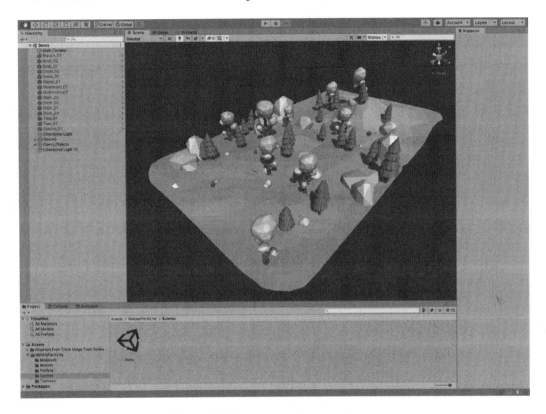

Figure 8.5 - The nature pack example scene

3. You will most likely have noticed that the scene consists of two separate islands. We only require one. Select all items associated with the smaller island from the **Hierarchy** as shown in *Figure 8.6* and delete them:

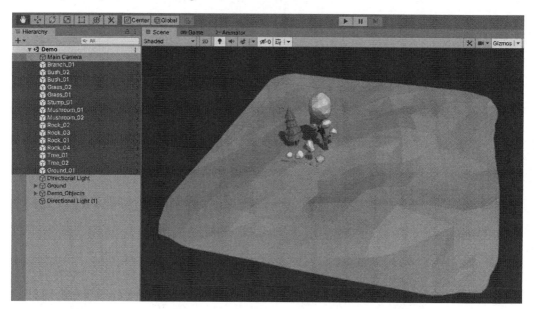

Figure 8.6 - Deleting all items associated with the smaller island

Next, we want to increase the size of the terrain to provide more space for the terrifying chick and the player to walk around.

4. Select `Ground_01` from the **Hierarchy** and duplicate it by pressing *Ctrl* + *D* (Windows) or *cmd* + *D* (macOS). It is a child object of the `Ground` object.

5. Move the new object to **Position** `-25.57, -3.76, 21`. You can do this with the **Move Tool** but will most likely find it easier to type the values manually in the Inspector.

6. Reset the **Rotation** of the new object to `0, 0, 0`:

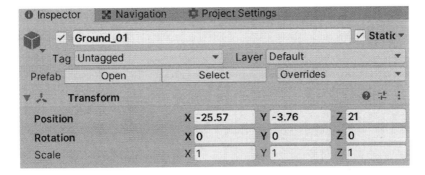

Figure 8.7 - Duplicated ground settings

7. Select `Ground_02` from the Hierarchy (again, it is a child object of the `Ground` object).

8. Duplicate the object.

9. Position the object at `-25.57, -3.47, -1.83`.

10. Set the object's **Rotation** to `0, 180, 0`.

You should now have a scene that looks similar to *Figure 8.8*:

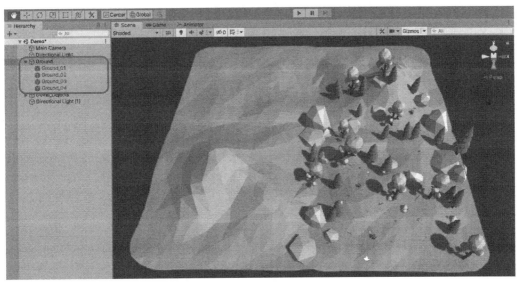

Figure 8.8 - The scene with extended terrain

11. Any player of our game will notice pretty quickly that half the terrain does not have any trees or other decorative objects. The next step is to re-arrange the objects so they're spread out over all four terrain objects. Feel free to duplicate objects as you see fit. My arrangement is shown in *Figure 8.9*:

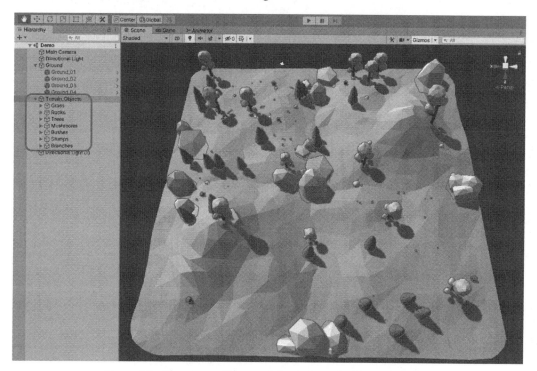

Figure 8.9 - The scene with extended terrain and additional objects

By creating empty parent objects, I've also arranged the objects into the following categories in the Hierarchy:

- Grass
- Rocks
- Trees
- Mushrooms
- Bushes
- Stumps
- Branches

This arrangement will make it easier to define which objects should block the NPC movement (trees, rocks, and stumps) and which objects the terrifying chick should be able to walk through (grass, mushrooms, bushes, and branches).

You may wish to continue to experiment with the terrain tool or look on the UAS for assets to improve the level aesthetically. However, the world terrain is now fit for our purposes, and we can now start implementing features that will help us to achieve the main aim of this project. As a reminder, our goal is to create an enemy character that can wander freely around the terrain and will chase and attack the player whenever the player enters their field of view.

Now that we've created the level, we get one step closer to that goal by configuring the level for pathfinding using a navigation mesh.

Generating the navigation mesh

The terrain is bumpy and features several hills, mountains, dips, and inclines. For an NPC character to navigate this terrain successfully, there are many complexities involved. For example, an NPC cannot necessarily travel in a straight line from point A to point B because doing so would cause the NPC to pass through solid objects and over terrain that should be impassable. The NPC needs to maneuver intelligently around, under, and over appropriate parts of the terrain. This illusion of intelligence is essential to create believable characters that inhabit a world. The computational processes involved in calculating a suitable path for an NPC is called **pathfinding**, and the method of making the character travel the calculated route is called **navigation**. Unity comes with built-in pathfinding and navigation features, making it easy for NPCs to calculate and travel paths.

To prepare our characters for navigation, a **Navigation Mesh** must be generated. This mesh is a special asset included in the scene, which uses non-rendered geometry to approximate the total walkable surface of a scene. This geometry, rather than the one visible to the player, is then used to calculate possible routes.

> **Important note**
> The navigation mesh is usually a much-simplified version of the actual geometry to reduce the complexity of the pathfinding calculations. The trade-off of this approach is that occasionally the navigation and terrain meshes can diverge to the extent that a character can walk a path that doesn't exist or won't take a route that they should. For this reason, it is vital that if the terrain is changed, the navigation mesh is regenerated.

For this process to work effectively, all non-movable floor meshes in the scene should be marked as **Navigation Static**. To do this, follow these steps:

1. Select the terrain (Ground_01, Ground_02, Ground_03, and Ground_04) from the **Hierarchy** panel.

2. From the **Inspector**, click on the **Static** checkbox, as shown in *Figure 8.10*:

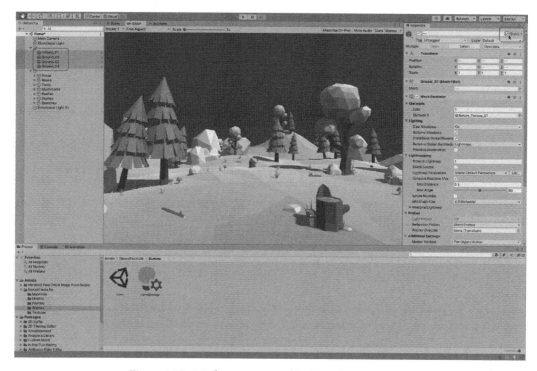

Figure 8.10 - Marking non-movable floor objects as static

By ticking the **Static** checkbox, you're enabling several options. If you click the arrow next to the **Static** label, it will list the options and allow you to enable and disable them individually. For our needs, we only need the **Navigation Static** option selected. However, as the object will not be moving at all in the scene, enabling all of the options provides several benefits, including a possible reduced rendering cost and the ability to precalculate lighting data for improved runtime performance. For these reasons, it is a good practice to mark all of the non-moving objects as static.

> **Tip**
>
> For more information on the individual static options, see the online documentation at https://docs.unity3d.com/Manual/StaticObjects.html.

Now that we've marked our terrain as static, we can now generate a navigation mesh by doing the following:

1. Select **Window | AI | Navigation** from the **Application** menu. The purpose of the **Navigation** window is to generate a low-fidelity terrain mesh that approximates the level floor.

2. Click on the **Bake** tab to access the main navigation settings. From this panel, you can control a range of settings to influence Navigation Mesh (`NavMesh`) generation:

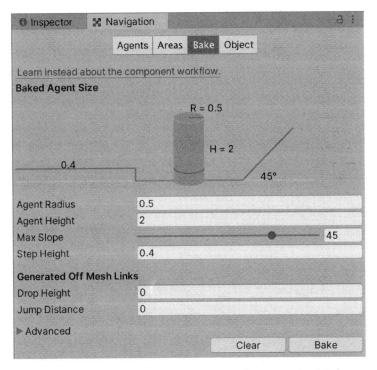

Figure 8.11 - The Bake tab contains the main settings for Navigation Mesh generation

The **Bake** tab contains a number of settings related to generating the navigation mesh:

*   **Agent Radius** is the average radius of an agent. This setting defines how close an agent can get to the rocks, trees, and other obstacles in our map. It also determines how close the agent can get to the edge of the world without falling off.

*   **Agent Height** is the average height of an agent. This setting currently does not affect us as it is used to define how low a space (for example, a tunnel) the agent can enter, and our terrain does not have any overhead obstacles. Even though it doesn't relate to us currently, it is a good practice to set a suitable value here in case we introduce such obstacles in the future.

- **Max Slope** defines the maximum angle of a slope that an agent can comfortably walk up.

- **Step Height** defines the maximum height of an obstacle that the agent can step on.

> **Important note**
>
> The **Generated Off Mesh Links** settings can safely be ignored as they are used to define how an agent can move between two disconnected meshes, and our terrain meshes are connected.

To get started, let's generate an initial Navigation Mesh to see how the default settings look. We can easily erase and regenerate the mesh under new settings if needed.

1. Click on the **Bake** button (not the tab). When you do this, a default Navigation Mesh is generated and appears in blue above the terrain from the Scene viewport, as shown in *Figure 8.12*:

Figure 8.12 - A default Navigation Mesh

The blue area is the navigable terrain. You'll probably notice straight away that we have one problem: the navigation mesh doesn't take into account any of our other objects such as the rocks and trees. To fix this, we also need to mark them as **Static**:

1. Select all of the objects that should hinder movement in the **Hierarchy** panel. This includes trees, rocks, and stumps.

2. Once again, enable the **Static** checkbox in the **Inspector**.

3. Go back to the **Navigation** panel and click **Bake** again. You'll now have a navigation mesh that looks similar to *Figure 8.13*:

Figure 8.13 - A Navigation Mesh with obstacles

The NavMesh asset itself is stored in a folder matching the scene name. When selected from the **Project** panel, you can preview various read-only properties describing the Navigation Mesh, such as the **Height** and **Walkable Radius** settings:

Figure 8.14 - Previewing Navigation Mesh properties from the Project panel

Next, we'll adjust the agent specific settings as our agent is relatively short and has a small radius. The **Agent Radius** setting is particularly important as it controls how large an average agent (NPC) is, and it affects how close the Navigation Mesh can expand toward the surrounding mesh floor and its edges. Lower settings allow the mesh to encroach nearer to the mesh edges, resulting in an expanded navigation mesh:

1. Set **Agent Radius** to 0.3.

2. Set **Agent Height** to 0.5.

3. Set **Max Slope** to 30.

4. Set **Step Height** to 0.5.

5. Click on **Bake** again to observe the result. It should not vary too much from the previous navigation mesh but should have more appropriate paths for our small chick.

> **Tip**
>
> There are many tools available that extend or improve the NavMesh system. A popular one is `NavMeshComponents`. It's simple to use and is released and maintained by Unity. With `NavMeshComponents`, you can have multiple agent profiles, create dynamic navigation meshes that can be updated during play, and generate meshes during runtime for procedurally generated levels. For more information, see the GitHub page at `https://github.com/Unity-Technologies/NavMeshComponents`.

Congratulations! You have now constructed a Navigation Mesh for the level that our NPC will eventually use to traverse the environment either following waypoints or chasing the player down. Before the NPC can do this, we first need to add it to the scene, which we will do now.

Implementing the NPC

With the foundation complete, we can now add the character that will eventually patrol the area and chase the player. As previously mentioned, we have picked an asset that will strike terror into the heart of the player as they are stalked mercilessly by the `Toon Chick`:

1. Locate the `Toon Chick` prefab in the `Assets/Meshtint Free Chick Mega Toon Series/Prefabs` folder in the **Project** panel. This folder was added when we imported the **Toon Chick** package:

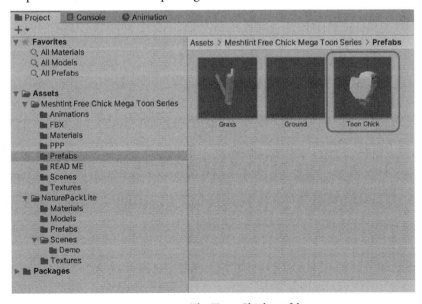

Figure 8.15 - The Toon Chick prefab

We'll refine this prefab by adding our own pathfinding logic.

2. Drag and drop the prefab to the **Scene** view:

Figure 8.16 - The Toon Chick in the scene, looking at us ominously

3. Select the `Toon Chick` from the **Hierarchy**.

4. As the chick will be moving around the environment, we'll add a Rigidbody. In the Inspector, select **Add Component | Physics | Rigidbody**.

5. On the **Rigidbody** component, under the **Constraints** heading, **Freeze Rotation** on the **X** and **Z** axes. Freezing these axes will prevent the chick from rolling over while still allowing for the chick to face different directions by rotating the **Y** axis.

6. To prevent the chick from falling through the floor, we need to add a collider. Select **Add Component | Physics | Capsule Collider**.

7. Adjust the colliders **Center** to 0, 0.2, 0, its **Radius** to 0.15, and its **Height** to 0.4:

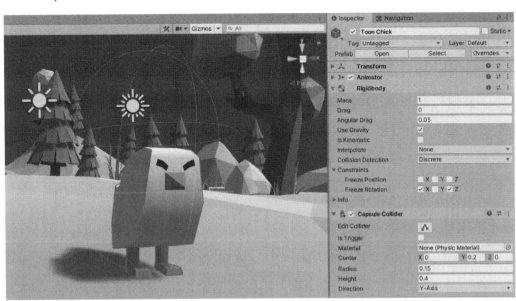

Figure 8.17 - The collider and Rigidbody settings

8. The NPC should navigate and walk around the terrain intelligently using the Navigation Mesh generated for the level. For this, a Nav Mesh Agent component should be attached to the character. Select **Add Component | Navigation | Nav Mesh Agent**. The Nav Mesh Agent component contains both **pathfinding** and **steering** (navigation) behaviors that allow a GameObject to move around a Navigation Mesh.

By default, the Navigation Mesh assigns a **Cylinder Collision** volume to the Agent—the object that will navigate and move around. This volume is not a collider that acts with the physics system, but a pseudo-collider used to determine when the character nears the edge of a navigation mesh and how they collide with other agents in the scene. We don't have any other agents yet, but we could always add more in the future. Let's configure that collider now, on the Nav Mesh Agent component:

1. Set the **Height** to 0.4.

2. Set the **Radius** to 0.2.

3. Set the **Base Offset** to -0.09. This setting moves the collider up slightly, so the chick doesn't look like it is floating.

We should also update the settings related to how quickly the chick moves through the environment:

1. Set the **Speed** to 1.5 to cap the chick's maximum movement speed.

2. Set the **Acceleration** to 2 to define how quickly the chick can go from stationary to maximum speed.

3. Set the **Angular Speed** to 60 to determine how quickly the chick can turn around.

These settings (shown in *Figure 8.18*) better approximate the chick's small stature:

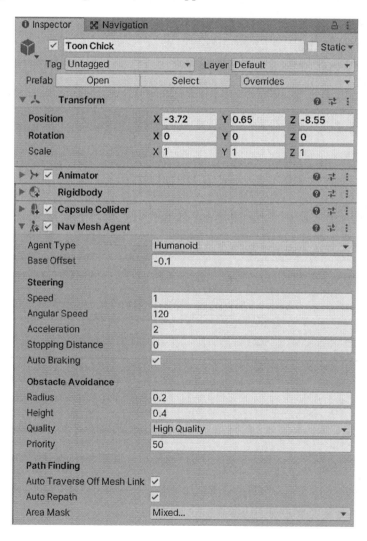

Figure 8.18 - The Agent Nav Mesh Agent

Great! We have everything that we need for the NPC to move through the environment apart from a destination. Let's fix that now.

Testing navigation

To test that our navigation mesh and settings are working correctly, we'll create an object for the chick to seek in the environment, using pathfinding and steering to reach the goal. To implement this behavior, we'll also need to write a new script:

1. Select **GameObject | Create Empty** from the Application menu to create a new empty object, which will act as a target object.

2. Name the new object `Destination`.

3. Assign it a Gizmo icon to make it visible in the viewport by clicking on the cube icon at the top-left of the **Inspector** and then choose an icon representation:

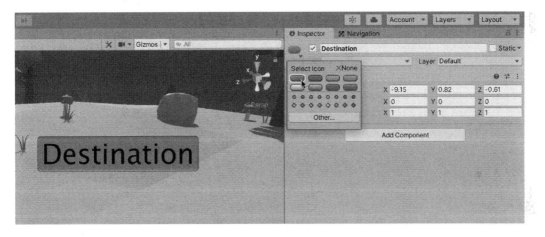

Figure 8.19 - Assigning an icon to the Destination object

4. Next, create a new C# script file called `FollowDestination.cs`:

```
using UnityEngine;
using UnityEngine.AI;


[RequireComponent(typeof(NavMeshAgent))]
public class FollowDestination : MonoBehaviour
{
    public Transform Destination = null;
    private NavMeshAgent ThisAgent = null;
```

```
void Awake()
{
    ThisAgent = GetComponent<NavMeshAgent>();
}

void Update()
{
    ThisAgent.SetDestination(Destination.position);
}
}
```

The following points summarize the code sample:

For the script to work, a `NavMeshAgent` component is required, without which it would throw a runtime error. The `RequireComponent` attribute is useful to prevent these types of errors from happening. Because we've added the `RequireComponent` attribute, if the object does not already have a `NavMeshAgent` component, Unity will add one for us.

> **Important note**
>
> The `RequireComponent` attribute does not work retroactively. For example, if this script (minus the attribute) was already attached to an object without a `NavMesh` component, then we added the `RequireComponent` attribute, Unity would not attempt to add the missing component to the existing object.

The `Destination` variable maintains the destination object.

In every frame `SetDestination` is called on the `NavMeshAgent` component. This function will update the agent's destination and trigger the calculation of a new path, which can take a few frames to complete. While we're not doing it here for the sake of simplicity, we should first check whether the destination has moved before calling the `SetDestination` function to reduce unnecessary path calculations.

5. Attach the script to the **Toon Chick** object in the scene.

6. Drag and drop the **Destination** object to the **Destination** slot on the `FollowDestination` component in the **Inspector**, as shown in *Figure 8.20*:

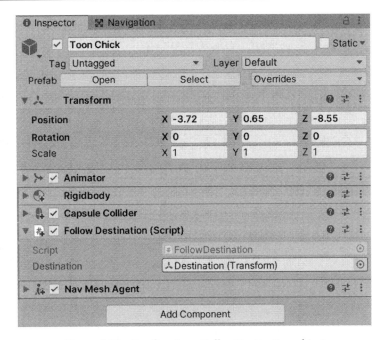

Figure 8.20 - Configuring a FollowDestination object

During gameplay, move the destination object around via the **Scene** tab and see how the chick responds. The **NPC** should continually chase the **Destination** object. In addition, if you play the game with the **Navigation** window open and the **NPC** selected in the **Hierarchy** panel, the **Scene** view will display diagnostic information and gizmos, allowing you to preview and visualize the route calculated by the chick:

Figure 8.21 - Testing NPC navigation

You may have noticed that the environment in which the chick moves is not animated. No matter what speed the chick travels, its feet remain stationary. We'll rectify this now.

Animating the NPC

At the moment, the chick floats around the scene without a walking or running animation. We'll change that now by animating the chick as it walks around the scene. The chick will transition between a walking and running animation depending on its movement speed. Luckily for us, the package we imported comes with several premade animations, so we don't need to start from scratch. Instead, we'll focus on how to apply these animations to the chick, in two different ways. First, we will create separate states to represent each animation, switching between a walking and running animation based on the chick's movement speed. Then, we will look at a method of seamlessly transitioning between these two animations using a **Blend Tree**.

Creating animation states

Unity's animation system (also known as **Mecanim**) has two main panels to help us to develop animations, that is, the **Animator** and **Animation** panel. In this section, we'll look at the Animator panel, which controls how and when animations play.

Let's start by examining the animations currently associated with the chick object:

1. With the **Toon Chick** object selected, open the **Animator** panel by selecting **Window | Animation | Animator** from the **Application** menu:

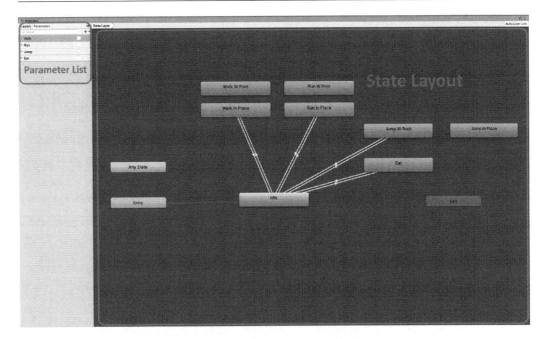

Figure 8.22 - Animator window

The **Animator** window has two main sections: The **State Layout** area and the **Parameters** or **Layers** view. Mecanim uses an FSM to manage its animation states, and this screen is a visual representation of that.

> **Important note**
>
> We'll go into more detail on FSMs in the next chapter when we write a custom FSM for the chick's behavioral states, that is, the Patrol, Chase, and Attack states. For now, it's enough to know that a state machine provides several distinct states and a method of transitioning between them based on specific conditions. It's a versatile pattern used for many different applications.

The rectangles in the state layout area represent a distinct animation state for a particular object (the object doesn't necessarily have to be a character, as we'll see later in this chapter). They are building blocks we can use to create complex animations. The white arrows between the states are user-defined transitions. One state can only transition to another if we define a conditional transition; there will be more on this very shortly when we create our own transitions.

The parameters in the **Parameters** list can be of the `float`, `int`, `bool`, or `trigger` type and are used as conditions for the transitions between animations. Based on whether a parameter is set to `true` or **false (bool)** or is greater or less than a specified amount (`int` and `float`), a transition can occur. As mentioned, you can also transition to an animation based on a trigger. You can think of a trigger as being similar to a Boolean, except that when we set it to `true` (that is, triggered), it is automatically reverted to `false` and stays in that state until triggered again. We'll discuss these parameters in more detail later in this chapter when we write a script that will set a parameter based on the chick's movement speed.

2. Delete all user-created states we don't require by right-clicking on each one and selecting **Delete**. Delete the **Walk W Root, Run W Root, Jump In Place, Idle**, and **Eat** states. We will be left with the **Walk In Place, Run In Place**, and **Jump W Root** animations as shown in *Figure 8.23*. The walk and run animations will be selected based on the movement speed of the NPC, and the jumping animation will be used as an attack animation in the next chapter:

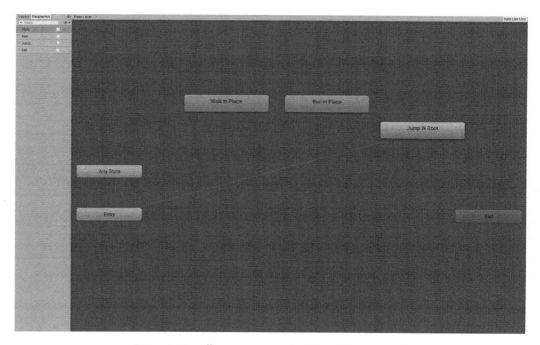

Figure 8.23 - All unnecessary animation states removed

You can't delete the states provided by Unity, that is, **Any State**, **Entry**, and **Exit**. They provide unique functionality:

- By creating a transition from the **Entry** state to another state, the state is marked as the entry point for the animation system and will be the first one played. You can have several entry states, each with different conditions. We'll see how to create a default state shortly.

- By creating a transition from a state to the **Exit** state, if that condition is met, the animation system will exit and then somewhat surprisingly re-enter the state machine at the **Enter** state, effectively creating a looping structure.

- By creating a transition from **Any State** to another state, you are stating that if this condition is met, no matter which state we are currently in, transition to this new state.

- As well as deleting unneeded states, we'll also remove any unnecessary parameters. As previously stated, we use parameters as criteria for transitioning from one state to another. Currently, we are only concerned with the transition between walking and running. We'll look at attacking in the next chapter and then add a new parameter, but for now, we only need one parameter. Delete all parameters apart from **Run** by right-clicking each item from the **Parameters** list and selecting **Delete** as shown in *Figure 8.23*:

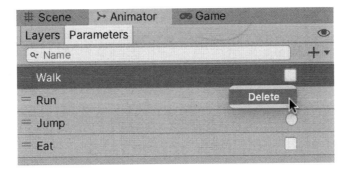

Figure 8.24 - Deleting parameters

Now that we have the minimum number of states and parameters that we require, we can start modifying the functionality to meet our needs. Depending on the order in which the states were deleted, Unity may have changed the default state. The default state is the first state entered and is highlighted in orange. As shown in *Figure 8.23*, the default state is **Jump W Root**. As we don't want our chick to jump as soon as the game starts, let's change the initial state to something more suitable:

1. Right-click the **Walk In Place** state.

2. Select **Set as Layer Default State**.

The chick will start the game moving toward the Destination object, so having the walking animation also playing at the start of the game suits our needs perfectly:

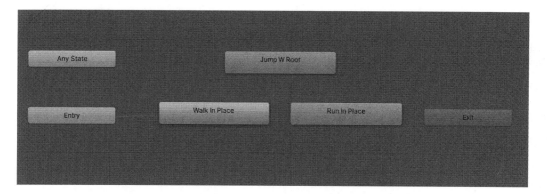

Figure 8.25 - New default state

You will most likely have noticed that we were setting this state as the default state for this *layer*. Unity allows you to create different state machines for different layers. This functionality could be used, for example, if we had a complex character with different animations for different body parts. Layers are a big topic in themselves and one that is not required for this or any other project in this book. For more information on layers, see the *Further reading* section, where links to additional resources on this topic are included.

Tip
You can rearrange the states by clicking and dragging. This functionality comes in very handy as you add more states.

If you test the game now, you will see that the walking animation does indeed play as the chick moves around the environment, but you'll also notice that the run animation never plays. Depending on the speed of the chick, the running animation will be more appropriate, so we need to create a transition from the walking to the running animation:

1. Right-click **Walk In Place** and select **Make Transition**. This will attach an arrow to your cursor, as shown in *Figure 8.26*:

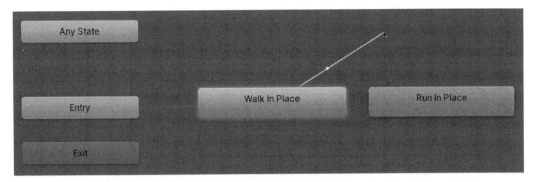

Figure 8.26 - Creating a transition between animation states

2. Drag the arrow to the **Run In Place** state and left-click to assign the transition. The arrow will now point from **Walk In Place** to **Run In Place**.

3. We'll also want the chick to be able to transition from running to walking, so repeat the process but start from **Run In Place** to make two arrows, as shown in *Figure 8.27*:

Figure 8.27 - Two-way transition between the Walk and Run states

We've now created a two-way transition. By default, a transition will happen whenever the animation has played a specified amount. Therefore, as our two-way transition now stands, the chick would walk a bit before running and then go back to walking with the cycle repeating indefinitely. We'll want to control this transition through code, but before we can do that, we will need to configure the conditions:

1. Select the arrow pointing from **Walk In Place** to **Run In Place** (the bottom arrow in *Figure 8.27*).

    We can then use the **Inspector** panel to configure the settings for this transition. The window (shown in *Figure 8.28*) has several settings related to transitions, which include the following:

    Has Exit Time: If checked, the transition can only happen after a specified time. If not selected, a transition condition must be specified.

    Exit Time: This value specifies the normalized time at which the transition should occur. If there are conditions specified, they must also be met before the transition can happen.

    Fixed Duration: If checked, the **Transition Duration** value is interpreted in seconds. If not checked, the **Transition Duration** value represents a fraction of the normalized time of the animation, for example, 0.25 equals 25 percent.

    Transition Duration: This is the length of the transition in either seconds or as a normalized percentage.

    Transition Offset: This is the normalized start time in the target state. For example, if you set a value of 0.5 when the transition occurs, the new animation will start playing halfway through.

    Conditions: You can set conditions based on parameters specified in the **Parameters** list as shown in *Figure 8.24*. We'll see how to do this shortly.

2. In the **Inspector**, untick **Has Exit Time** as we don't want the transition to occur when the animation has played a specified amount.

3. Now that the transition won't occur based on an exit time, we need to specify a condition. Under **Conditions**, select the + sign to add a new condition:

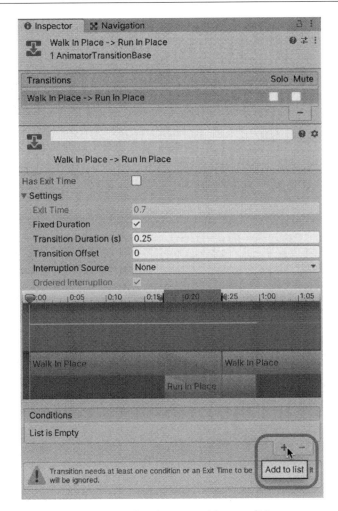

Figure 8.28 - Creating a transition condition

4.   Select the condition **Run** and ensure the state is set to **true**.

The list of possible conditions here matches the parameter list. As we only have the **Run** parameter, this will be the only option. Configuring the condition as **true** here signifies that we need to set this parameter to true in our code for this transition to take effect. We'll see how to do that shortly.

> **Tip**
>
> We could have used a `float` parameter to store the chick's velocity. We could have then transitioned from walking to a running animation if this velocity parameter was greater than a specified amount (and transitioned back to walking when it becomes less than that amount).

We need to repeat the process but for the transition from **Run In Place** to **Walk In Place**:

1. Select the other arrow pointing from **Run In Place** to **Walk In Place**.

2. Once again, untick **Has Exit time** and add the **Condition** as **Run**. However, this time, set it to **false**, as shown in *Figure 8.29*. Now, whenever we set the **Run** parameter to **false** in our code, the chick will transition from a running to a walking animation:

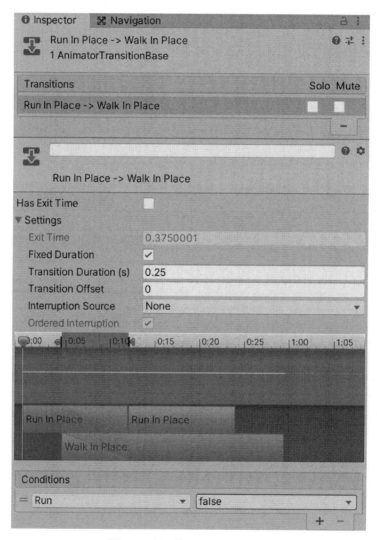

Figure 8.29 - Transition settings

We now have two animations and two transitions. The walk animation will play first, and when the parameter **Run** is set to `true`, then the run animation will play. Once in the run state, if the **Run** parameter is then set to `false`, the run state will transition back to the walking state. Setting this parameter is the last thing we need to do to set up our animation system. We'll do this now using a script:

1. Create a new script called `AnimationController` in the `Script` folder:

```
using UnityEngine;
using UnityEngine.AI;


[RequireComponent(typeof(NavMeshAgent),
    typeof(Animator))]
public class AnimationController : MonoBehaviour
{
    public float RunVelocity = 0.1f;
    public string AnimationRunParamName = "Run";


    private NavMeshAgent ThisNavMeshAgent = null;
    private Animator ThisAnimator = null;


    void Awake()
    {
        ThisNavMeshAgent = GetComponent<NavMeshAgent>();
        ThisAnimator = GetComponent<Animator>();
    }


    void Update()
    {
        ThisAnimator.SetBool(AnimationRunParamName,
        ThisNavMeshAgent.velocity.magnitude >
            RunVelocity);
    }
}
```

The following points summarize the code sample:

The script requires access to the `NavMeshAgent` and `Animator` components, so the `RequireComponent` attribute is added before the class declaration. As you can see, you do not need separate attribute calls for each component.

The `RunVelocity` variable controls the running speed cut off. If the velocity of the NPC is above this value, then the `Run` animation parameter is set to `true`.

The object's velocity is checked in the `Update` function by retrieving the `magnitude` of the `NavMeshAgents` velocity and comparing that to `RunVelocity`. For more information on the magnitude of a vector, see the online documentation at `https://docs.unity3d.com/ScriptReference/Vector3-magnitude.html`.

Calling `SetBool` on the animation component and passing in `AnimationRunParamName` sets the state of the `Run` parameter. If the agent's velocity is greater than the predefined `RunVelocity` variable, then the `Run` parameter is set to `true`, and the run animation is played. Otherwise, it is set to `false`, and the walk animation is played.

2. Add script to the `Toon Chick` object in the **Hierarchy**.

Great! Now the chick will walk rather than float around the environment. To properly test that our animation changes are working as intended and to extend the chick's behavioral repertoire, we will soon add the ability to patrol the environment, leaving no stone unturned in its search for the player. However, before we move away from discussion animations, we will briefly go over how to use Blend Trees, a useful tool for creating natural-looking animation transitions.

Using Blend Trees

In the next chapter, we'll be setting the animation state based on which AI state we are in, for example, if we're in a chase state, we'll tell the animator to play the run animation. Having distinct animation states, such as the ones we created in the previous section, works perfectly for us. However, there is also another way of transitioning between animations that is worth covering. You have probably guessed from the title of this section, but I'm talking about Blend Trees. Using a Blend Tree, we can blend two (or more) animations to create a more natural transition. For the chick, we will create a Blend Tree that combines its walk and run animations according to its current speed. As the chick gains momentum, they will move from playing the walking animation to playing a mix of the walking and running animations, until finally just playing the running animation.

> **Important note**
>
> If you are eager to move on, then feel free to skip this section as the rest of this book will rely on the states we created in the previous section. The steps here are to help you to understand the subject, but for this project, they do not need to be completed.

To create a Blend Tree, follow these steps:

1. Open the **Animator** window with the `Toon Chick` object selected in the **Hierarchy**.

2. Add a new **Parameter** called **Speed** using the steps outlined in the previous section.

3. Right-click in the **State Layout** panel and, from the context menu, select **Create State | From New Blend Tree**. This option creates a new state with a **Blend Tree** as its motion rather than a single animation:

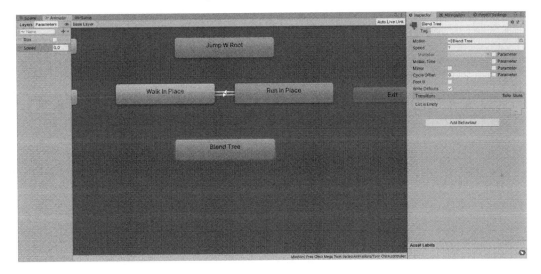

Figure 8.30 - Creating a Blend Tree

To edit the newly created **Blend Tree**, follow these steps:

1. Double-click the **Blend Tree** state. This will change the view from the Layer view to the Blend Tree view, as shown in *Figure 8.31*:

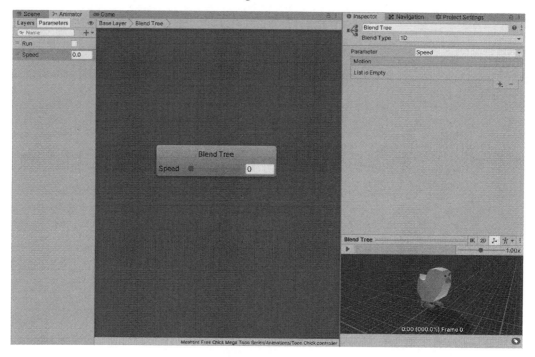

Figure 8.31 - Blend Tree view

2. Select the **Blend Tree**. This will allow you to change the settings in the **Inspector**.

> **Tip**
> The breadcrumb at the upper-left corner shows that we're working on the Blend Tree. You can click on **Base Layer** to exit the Blend Tree.

3. The **Blend Type** is the number of parameters used to control how each of its animations should be played. Leave this as the default setting of **1D** to use a single parameter to control the motions.

4. For the parameter, set **Speed**. Depending on the value of **Speed**, either the walk animation, run animation, or a mixture of the two will play.

5. Select the + button under the **Motion** heading.

6. In the menu that appears, select **Add Motion Field**. Each motion field can represent an animation or another Blend Tree:

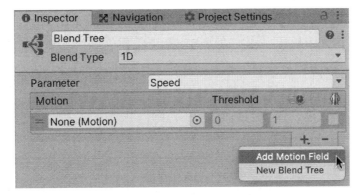

Figure 8.32 - Adding a Motion Field

Each motion field has three properties:

The threshold value represents the value of the **Speed** parameter required for that particular animation to have full influence.

Time Scale is the speed at which the animation plays.

Mirrored defines whether the animation is mirrored left to right.

7. Drag the **Walk In Place** animation from the **Project** panel to the **Motion** field.

8. Add another **Motion** field but this time drag the **Run In Place** animation to the **Motion** field, as shown in *Figure 8.33*:

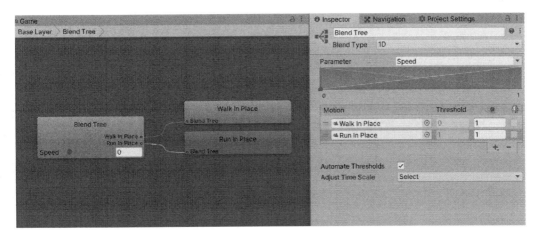

Figure 8.33 - Adding the walk and run animation

After adding the motion fields, you'll notice that a diagram appears above the list, as shown in *Figure 8.33*. This diagram is a visual representation of where the different animations lie on the scale of the Speed parameter— lowest on the left, highest on the right. You can drag the red scrubber, shown in *Figure 8.34*, to preview the animation for various values. The preview is shown at the bottom of the **Inspector** panel:

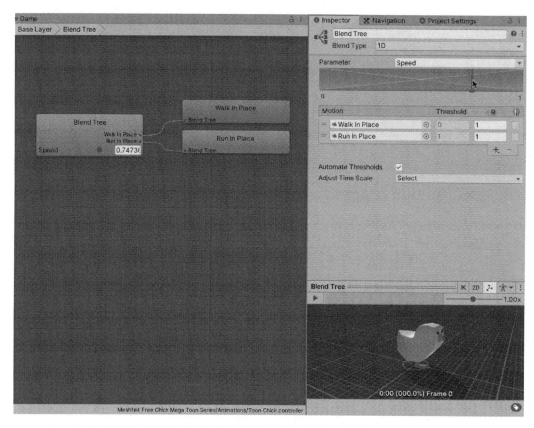

Figure 8.34 - Previewing the animation blend

If you untick **Automate Thresholds** in the **Inspector,** it will give you an additional option: **Compute Thresholds**. **Compute Thresholds** will calculate and set values for each of your motion fields. It will do this based on a property of root motion that you select; the options include the **Speed** parameter that we created earlier and other pre-built options including **Velocity** (on all three axes) and **Angular speed** (in radians and degrees).

> **Tip**
>
> When adding the motions, they were also added to the **Blend Tree** panel. You can click on the animations in that panel to see read-only information about the animation, including length and whether the animation is looped.

Underneath the **Automate Thresholds** option, there is the option to **Adjust Time Scale**. Using this option, you can make the speed for each animation **Homogeneous**, which means that each of the animations will result in the same speed of root motion. This option is only available if all of the motions are animations, not other Blend Trees.

> **Tip**
>
> 2D Blend Trees work in a very similar way to 1D trees but blend on two dimensions.

Next, we need to set the newly created **Blend Tree** as the default state:

1. Ensure the **Automate Thresholds** box is ticked. We'll let Unity calculate the threshold values for us.

2. In the breadcrumb at the top of the **Animator** panel, click on the **Base Layer** to return to our animation state overview:

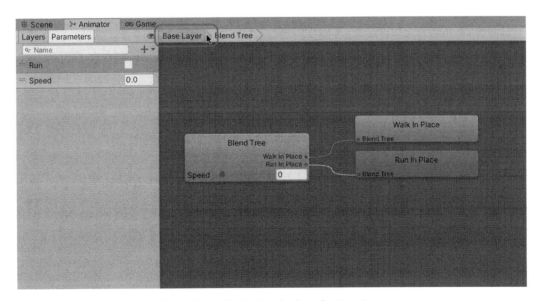

Figure 8.35 - Navigating back to the Base Layer

3. Right-click on the **Blend Tree** you created.

4. Select **Set as Layer Default State**. As explained in the previous section, this means the chick's animation will move to this state at the start of the game:

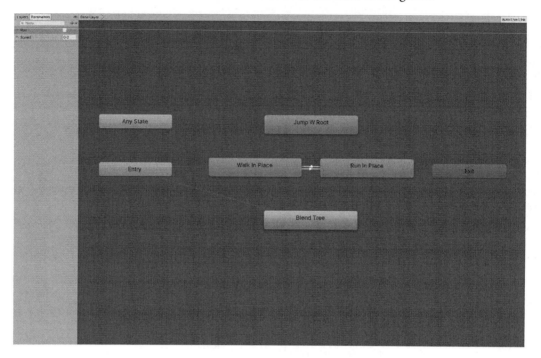

Figure 8.36 - Setting the Blend Tree as the default layer

The last step is to set the **Speed** parameter based on the chick's movement speed:

1. Open the AnimationController class that we created in the *Creating animation state section*.

2. Add the following:

```
public class AnimationController : MonoBehaviour
{
    ...
    public string AnimationSpeedParamName = "Speed";
    private float MaxSpeed;

    void Awake()
    {
        ...
        MaxSpeed = ThisNavMeshAgent.speed;
```

```
        }


    void Update()
    {
        ...
        ThisAnimator.SetFloat(AnimationSpeedParamName,
            ThisNavMeshAgent.velocity.magnitude / MaxSpeed);
    }
}
```

This code is very similar to what we wrote in the previous section to update the **Run** animation parameter, with the small change that we're no longer updating a Boolean but a float value instead. We divide the agent's velocity magnitude by MaxSpeed (obtained from the NavMeshAgent component) to get a normalized value between 0 and 1.

As this script is already attached to the Toon Chick object, there are no further steps required. Press the Play button to see the new blended animation in action.

That's it for the whistle-stop tour through Blend Trees. Remember that the rest of this chapter will use the animation states we created in the previous section. If you would like to do the same, you can reset the animations by doing the following:

1. Select the Toon Chick in the **Hierarchy**.

2. In the **Animator** panel, right-click the **Walk In Place** animation.

3. Select **Set as Layer Default State**.

We've now looked at two methods of adding animations to the chick. In the next section, we'll take a look at how animations can be used for a different purpose, namely, creating a waypoint system for the chick to follow because there's no point in having created walking and running animations if the chick doesn't move anywhere!

Patrolling the environment

We now have an animated NPC that follows a destination object using Unity's built-in pathfinding and steering behavior. This functionality is a solid foundation for creating the next component in our terrifying chicks' behavioral repertoire: the ability to patrol a specified area.

If you break down a patrol, it's just moving from one destination to another in a sequence. We have most of that functionality already. We only need to implement a sequence of destinations. Multiple approaches could be taken to achieve this. One method is through scripting. We could write a script that maintains an array of different waypoint objects and allows the chick to iterate through them on a loop so that when the NPC reaches one destination, they'll move on to the next one. This approach can be very efficient and is easily customizable, but there's also another method we could use. Instead of using a script, we can create an animation to move a single destination object to different waypoint locations over time. As the NPC continually follows the destination wherever it moves, it will continuously patrol.

We'll take the second approach here for several reasons, one of the most crucial being that while we've recently examined Unity's Animator flow, we haven't yet created custom animations using Unity's Animation system:

1. Start by opening the **Animation** window by selecting **Window | Animation | Animation** from the Application menu.

2. Dock the **Animation** window into a horizontal view next to the **Project** panel for ease of viewing:

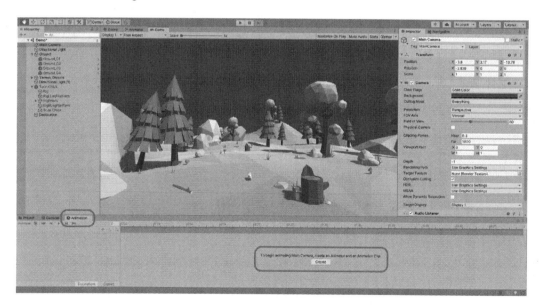

Figure 8.37 - The Animation window docked

3. Select the object to animate (the Destination object) from the **Hierarchy** panel.

4. From the **Animation** window, click on the **Create** button, as shown in *Figure 8.37*.

5.   From here, you will be asked to name and save the animation. I've called the
     animation DestPatrol and saved it to the Animations folder (create the folder
     as a subfolder of the Assets folder if it doesn't already exist):

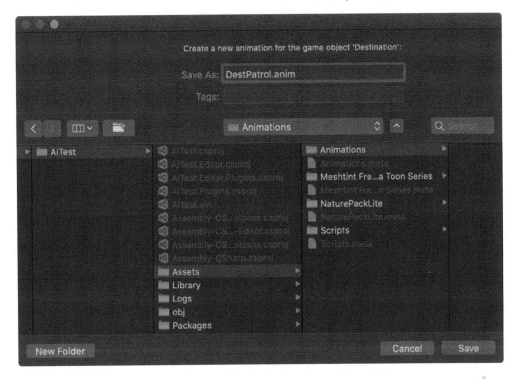

Figure 8.38 - Creating a new animation

6.   With the animation created, you can proceed to define animation properties. For
     the destination object, we'll need to add a property for the position field as the
     object should change position around the scene. Click on the **Add Property** button
     from the **Animation** window, and then choose **Transform | Position** as shown in
     Figure 8.39 to add a new position property.

> **Important note**
> A keyframe marks a transitional point. As you will see shortly, the intermediate
> points between keyframes are interpolated between these points to create a
> smooth animation.

Adding a property will automatically create starting and ending keyframes in the timeline, which are identical and hold the object's current position:

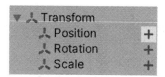

Figure 8.39 - Adding an animation property

1. Click and drag the vertical slider across the timeline in the **Animation** window to the 0:20 mark.

2. Click on the **Record** button. The timeline and any relevant fields on the object (in our case, the object's **Position** value) will then turn red. Unity will now record the position of the object to use as a keyframe:

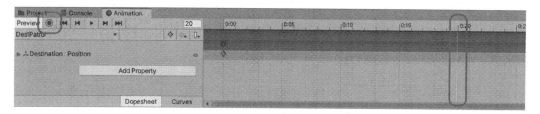

Figure 8.40 - Recording a new keyframe

3. Move the **Destination** object in the **Scene** tab to the position of the second patrol point (the first point is where the **Destination** object currently sits). When you do this, Unity records the object position for that keyframe. Wherever a keyframe has been recorded, Unity will add a diamond shape to the timeline and to any property that's been changed:

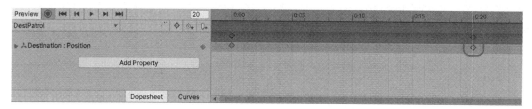

Figure 8.41 - Recording mode activated and new keyframe recorded

4. Repeat this process for the 0:40 mark by pressing the record button and moving the **Destination** object to a different position.

This completes the patrol animation with three patrol points. We leave the start and end of the animation with the same position to create a loop.

You can scrub through the timeline or press Play in the **Animation** panel to watch the Destination object move in the Scene view to test your patrol route. The animation will most likely playback too fast as we've only set 20 seconds between each waypoint. Don't worry, that will be easy to fix as we'll see shortly. However, you may have also noticed that the destination object position has been *tweened* between keyframes. The Unity animation interpolates between the keyframes in the timeline causing the destination object to move smoothly between waypoints. For an animation like this, however, we want the destination to snap between the waypoints immediately without any transition. To achieve this, we need to adjust the interpolation mode of the animation curves:

1. Click on the **Curves** button at the bottom-left corner of the **Animation** window. By default, the **Animation** window is in the **DopeSheet** mode, which enables us to see keyframes easily and reposition them. The **Curve** mode, however, lets us adjust the interpolation between keyframes:

Figure 8.42 - Accessing Animation Curves

2. Click and drag a selection box across all keyframes (diamond shapes) in the graph view to select them all.

3. Right-click on any keyframe to display the keyframe context menu.

4. From the context menu, choose **Right Tangent | Constant** to change all handles to a constant flat shape.

> **Important note**
>
> A point has a left and right tangent. Editing the left tangent changes the incoming curve to the left of the position, and changing the right tangent changes the outgoing curve to the right of the point.

The flat shape shown in *Figure 8.43* signifies that all frames retain their values until the next keyframe, removing inter-frame interpolation:

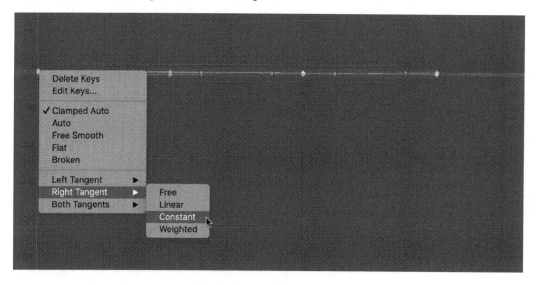

Figure 8.43 - Changing keyframe handles for interpolation

Test whether the change has taken effect by pressing Play on the toolbar. When you do this, the Destination object should jump between waypoints as the animation progresses, and the NPC will try to move toward the destination. Due to the default speed of the animation, the NPC may seem a bit confused as they can never quite reach the rapidly changing destinations. To fix this, follow these steps:

1. Select the Destination object from the **Hierarchy** panel.

2. From the **Inspector**, double-click on the **Controller** field of the **Animator** component to open the animation graph attached to the object, which, as we've seen, controls when and how animations should play:

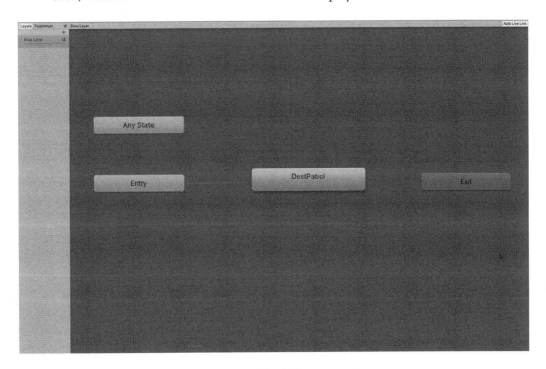

Figure 8.44 - The Animator panel

In the **Animator** window, the default node is highlighted in orange. As a reminder, the default node defines which animation (if any) will play when the object is added to the scene, which for our Destination object is on level startup. As you can see from *Figure 8.44*, the default node for our object is the DestPatrol node, which plays the DestPatrol animation.

3. Select the DestPatrol node in the graph.

4. Reduce its Speed in the **Inspector**. In my case, I've used a value of 0.014, which works well. You may need to test different values before you land on one that works well for you:

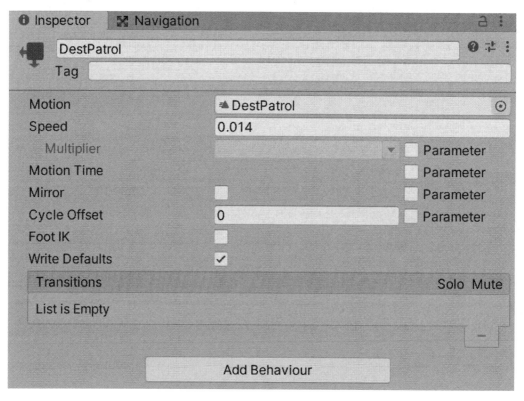

Figure 8.45 - Reducing the animation speed

5. With speed reduced, replay your game to observe the effect.

The chick should now move between destinations at a believable speed, moving from one waypoint to the next. If the NPC moves too fast or too slow between waypoints, increase or decrease the animation speed to get the result you need. You may also need to change NPC's steering speed on its `NavMeshAgent` component:

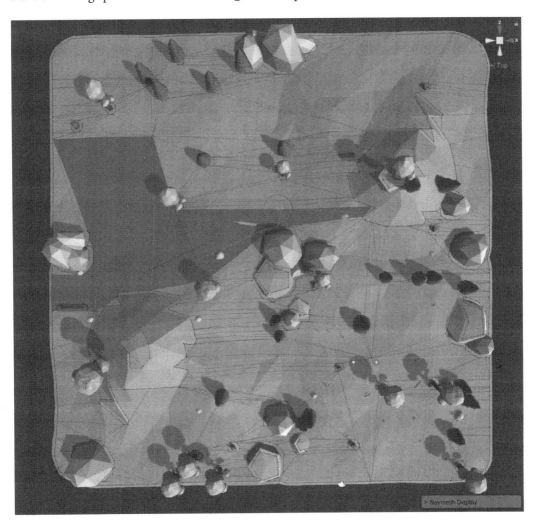

Figure 8.46 - The waypoint system in action

Congratulations! You now have a complete, animated waypoint system. The chick will happily patrol between points. At the moment, it can be quite challenging to get a close up of the chick in action as you need to catch them in the Scene view. We'll change this now by adding a controllable player to the scene.

Entering the world

In previous projects, we've relied on a first-person controller included with the Unity standard assets package. In this section, instead of relying on that package, we'll write our own functionality to accomplish the same task. We'll write a script to control the player's movement through the environment and another to control where the player looks. However, before we write the scripts, we'll create the required player object:

1. Create an empty GameObject.
2. Name the new object as Body.
3. To include the player object in the physics system and prevent them from falling through the floor, add a **Rigidbody** and **Capsule Collider** component.
4. Set the **Height** of the collider to 2 to better represent the height of the player.
5. On the **Rigidbody** component, **Freeze Rotation** on the **X**, **Y**, and **Z** axes. Freezing the rotation on all axes will prevent the player from falling over as they collide with the environment. We will shortly write scripts that will manually rotate the player based on user input:

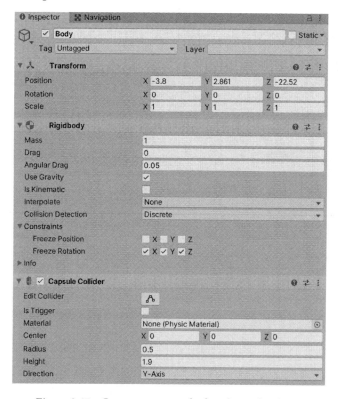

Figure 8.47 - Components attached to the Body object

6. Drag the `Main Camera` to the `Body` object to make it a child object.

7. The camera will act as the eyes and ears of the player; consequently, rename `Main Camera` to `Head`.

8. Reposition the `Head` object to `0, 0.6, 0`, so that it resides at the top of the Body's collider, as shown in *Figure 8.48*:

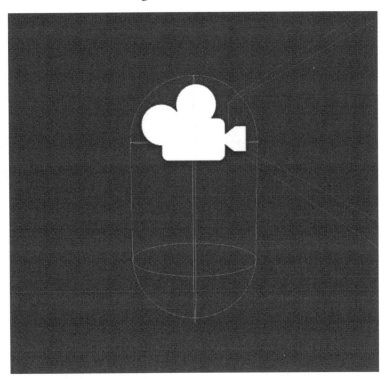

Figure 8.48 - Camera position as a child of the Body object

That's all the setup required for the GameObject. Next, we will script the movement:

1. Create a new script called `PlayerController`:

```
public class PlayerController : MonoBehaviour
{
    public float MovementSpeed = 3f;

    void Update()
    {
        float horiz = Input.GetAxis("Horizontal");
```

```
float vert = Input.GetAxis("Vertical");
Vector3 translation = new Vector3(horiz, 0,
    vert);
translation *= MovementSpeed * Time.deltaTime;
transform.Translate(translation);
        }
    }
```

The following points summarize the code:

- The `Horizontal` and `Vertical` axes are queried using `Input.GetAxis`. This was covered in depth in *Chapter 3, Creating a Space Shooter*.

- A new `translation` vector is created using the results returned.

- The `translation` vector is scaled by the `MovementSpeed` multiplied by `Time.deltaTime` to create a translation vector for this frame. More information on framerate independent movement can be found in *Chapter 2, Creating a Collection Game*.

- Finally, the scaled `translation` vector is added to our current position using `transform.Translate`. `Translate` can accept a second parameter of type `Space`. `Space` is an enum with two possible values, either `World` of `Self`. As we haven't passed in a value, it defaults to `Space.Self`. This means that the translation is applied relative to the transform's local axis. As we'll be adding this script to a GameObject with no parents, it doesn't matter if we use the `World` or `Self` space here. However, it's something to bear in mind: if we were to add the player object as a child of another object, we may need to pass `Space.World` here to achieve the correct result. For a hands-on example of the `Self` versus `World` space, see https://docs.unity3d.com/ScriptReference/Space.Self.html.

2. Attach the script to the `Body` object.

3. Although we are not finished yet, you should test our current progress by pressing the Play button. You should be able to move the character around the environment using the *W, A, S, D,* or *arrow* keys.

   You'll quickly notice that while we can move around, we still can't rotate the camera to look around the environment. We'll fix this now by creating another script:

4. Create a new script called `CameraLook`:

```
public class CameraLook : MonoBehaviour
{
```

```
    public float LookSpeed = 3f;
    public Transform Body;
    public Camera LookCamera;


    private Vector2 Rotation = Vector2.zero;


    void Update()
    {
        Rotation.y += Input.GetAxis("Mouse X");
        Rotation.x -= Input.GetAxis("Mouse Y");
        Vector2 RotThisStep = Rotation * LookSpeed;
        Body.eulerAngles = new Vector2(0, RotThisStep.y);
        LookCamera.transform.localRotation =
            Quaternion.Euler(RotThisStep.x, 0, 0);
    }
}
```

The following points summarize the code sample:

Rotation values are retrieved by calling Input.GetAxis in the Update function.

The Mouse Y axis is subtracted from the current X rotation as the X axis controls horizontal rotation.

The Mouse X axis is added to the Y rotation, which controls vertical rotation.

The Body transform is rotated left and right, and the LookCamera is rotated up and down based on mouse movement.

The Body transform is rotated left and right instead of the camera to replicate traditional first-person controls so that the camera is always facing the forward direction. If we rotated the camera instead of the body, for example, we would end up not facing in the forward direction, so pressing forward could move you backward.

> **Important note**
> A new script was created instead of extending the functionality of the PlayerController script to help create modular, re-usable, logical units. Separating the functionality in this manner will enable us to re-use either script without having to use the other. For example, we may have a stationary turret that we want the player to control, so we add the MouseLook script without the PlayerController script.

5.   Attach the script to the Body object.

6.   Drag the Body object from the **Hierarchy** to the **Body** field on the **Camera Look** script.

7.   Drag the Head object from the **Hierarchy** to the **Look Camera** field:

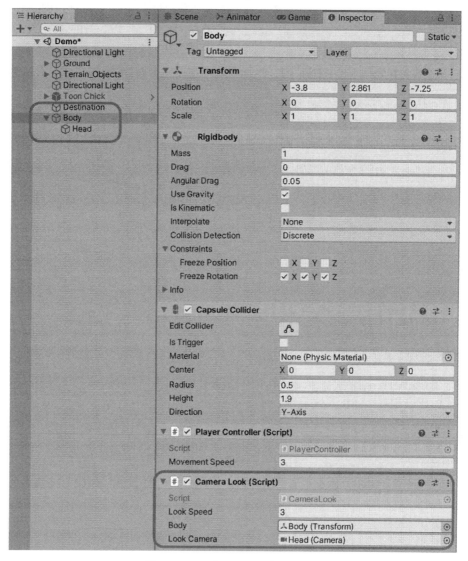

Figure 8.49 - Camera Look settings

Once again, test the game and you will now be able to move freely through the environment. See if you can find the chick, as shown in *Figure 8.50*:

Figure 8.50 - Walking around the environment to find the chick

While this is only the basic moving functionality, it is adequate for our needs and can be extended for future projects.

Summary

Great work! We've now completed the first part of the AI project: constructing a terrain, generating a navigation mesh, and creating a basic waypoint system that an animated chick follows. We hit the ground running by importing 3D models for the terrain and NPC but also extended ourselves by writing a custom first-person controller instead of relying on the controller from the previous chapters.

This is an excellent beginning to simulating intelligence. However, as the project currently stands, there is no way for the chick to decide which action to take at any given moment; it is stuck patrolling in perpetuity. We'll fix this in the next chapter by constructing an FSM with distinct Patrol, Chase, and Attack states. We'll also look at how we can test to see whether the player is in the chick's line of sight using **Raycasting**. This check will act as a condition to transition between specific states, just as we used the **Run** parameter as a condition to switch between animation states in this chapter.

Test your knowledge

Q1. You can generate a walkable surface of the level for AI by using...

    A. Pathfinding

    B. A Collision Box

    C. Navigation Mesh

    D. A Path Tree

Q2. The Animator window of Mechanim is useful for...

    A. Controlling when and how animations play

    B. Creating loopable animations

    C. Editing characters

    D. Applying inverse kinematics

Q3. To walk on a Navigation Mesh, an object needs...

    A. Pathfinding

    B. A Collision Box

    C. A NavMesh agent component

    D. A Collider component

Q4. You can edit animation interpolation by changing...

    A. High poly meshes

    B. Keyframe curves

    C. Box Colliders

    D. Mesh renderer components

Q5. The blue local axis arrow of an object is known as...

    A. Forward vector

    B. Right vector

    C. Up vector

    D. Pitch

Further reading

Check out the following links for more information on animations and pathfinding:

- https://docs.unity3d.com/Manual/Navigation.html
- https://www.packtpub.com/game-development/unity-2018-artificial-intelligence-cookbook-second-edition
- https://www.packtpub.com/game-development/unity-animation-essentials
- https://docs.unity3d.com/Manual/StaticObjects.html
- https://docs.unity3d.com/Manual/nav-BuildingNavMesh.html
- https://docs.unity3d.com/Manual/AnimatorWindow.html
- https://docs.unity3d.com/Manual/AnimationLayers.html

9
Continuing with Intelligent Enemies

In the previous chapter, we imported an enemy object (a fearsome chick) and created a first-person controller for the player and the environment that both the player and enemy will traverse. In this chapter, we'll build on that foundation by focusing on the theory and implementation of creating an intelligent enemy. We'll imbue our enemy chick with the ability to have multiple different behaviors and to swap between those behaviors depending on the state of the world.

In this chapter, we will discuss the following:

- How to enable the chick to see the player by using a line of sight and field of view

- How to code a **Finite State Machine** (**FSM**): This will become the brain of the chick—ensuring that behaviors are executed and transitions to different states happen at the right time

- How to create individual behavior states, and how these states fit cohesively to produce complex behavior. Each state will encompass a distinct behavior of the chick.

An FSM is one of the more popular data structures for AI programming and is also popular outside of game AI; for example, Unity's **Mecanim** animation system makes use of an FSM. The popularity of FSMs is in part due to their simplicity and ability to help break down an initial problem into several smaller, more manageable sub-problems. Instead of programming a monolithic class that maintains the chick's behavior, we can split the behavior into separate classes. This separation of states will aid maintenance and debugging issues in the future.

We'll write three separate states for the chick: patrolling, chasing, and attacking. We'll then use an FSM to run the correct behavior at the right time.

Technical requirements

In this chapter, you will start a new project that is not a direct continuation of previous projects. However, as with previous chapters, this chapter assumes that you have not only completed the previous projects but also have a good, basic knowledge of C# scripting generally, though not necessarily in Unity.

The starting project and assets can be found in the book's companion files in the Chapter09/Start folder. You can start here and follow along with this chapter if you do not have your own project already. The completed project is included in the Chapter09/End folder. These folders can be downloaded from the GitHub repo at https://github.com/PacktPublishing/Unity-2020-By-Example.

This chapter uses two assets from the Unity Asset Store, which, along with their author details, can be found at the following links:

- https://assetstore.unity.com/packages/3d/characters/animals/meshtint-free-chick-mega-toon-series-152777
- https://assetstore.unity.com/packages/3d/environments/landscapes/low-poly-simple-nature-pack-162153

Providing the enemy with sight

Let's now start developing the enemy AI by thinking about our functional requirements. The enemies in the scene will begin in patrol mode, wandering the level from place to place, searching for the player. If the player is spotted, the enemy will change from patrolling and begin chasing the player, attempting to move closer to them for an attack. If the enemy reaches within attacking range of the player, the enemy will change from chasing to attacking. If the player outruns the enemy and successfully loses them, the enemy should stop chasing and return to patrolling again, searching for the player as they were doing initially.

To achieve this behavior, we'll need some method of determining whether the chick can see the player as the chick relies on being able to see the player to decide whether it should be patrolling or chasing:

1. Create a new script called `SightLine` to represent the chick's sight:

```
public class SightLine : MonoBehaviour
{

    …
    void OnTriggerStay(Collider Other)
    {
        if (Other.CompareTag(TargetTag))
        {
            UpdateSight(Other.transform);
        }

    }

    void OnTriggerExit(Collider Other)
    {
        if (Other.CompareTag(TargetTag))
        {
            IsTargetInSightLine = false;
        }
    }
    private void UpdateSight(Transform Target)
    {
        IsTargetInSightLine =
            HasClearLineofSightToTarget(Target) &&
            TargetInFOV(Target);

        if (IsTargetInSightLine)
        {
            LastKnowSighting = Target.position;
        }

    }
}
```

The following points summarize the code sample:

The `SightLine` class should be attached to any character that requires a visual sightline. Its purpose is to calculate whether a direct line of sight is available between the player and the enemy.

The `IsTargetInSightLine` variable is a Boolean (`true`/`false`), which is updated on a per-frame basis to describe whether the enemy can see the player *right now* (for this frame). `true` means that the player is in sight of the enemy, and `false` means that the player is not visible.

The `OnTriggerStay` and `OnTriggerExit` functions are invoked when the player is within a trigger volume surrounding the enemy and when the player leaves this volume, respectively. The `OnTriggerStay` function is called in every frame that a collider intersects with this collider. As we'll see shortly, a collider can be attached to the enemy character object to represent its view. The size of the collider represents the maximum view distance of this object.

`UpdateSight` is called at every frame that an object with `TargetTag` is within this object's trigger collider (we'll configure this collider shortly). The function sets `IsTargetInSightLine` to `true` if `HasClearLineofSightToTarget` and `TargetInFOV` both return `true`. If either one of the functions returns `false`, then `IsTargetInSightLine` is also set to `false`. This means that the player is only considered seen if they are both in the specified field of view and there aren't any obstacles obstructing the view. We'll write these functions shortly.

If `IsTargetInSightLine` is set to `true` (that is, we can see the target), the `LastKnowSighting` variable is updated with the position of the target. We'll use this position in our states to move toward the player.

2. Next, add the function for checking whether there is a clear line of sight to the player:

```
public class SightLine : MonoBehaviour
{
    public Transform EyePoint;
    ...
    private bool HasClearLineofSightToTarget(Transform
        Target)
    {
        RaycastHit Info;
        Vector3 DirToTarget= (Target.position - EyePoint.
            position).normalized;
```

```
    if (Physics.Raycast(EyePoint.position,
      DirToTarget, out Info, ThisCollider.radius))
    {
        if (Info.transform.CompareTag(TargetTag))
        {
            return true;
        }
    }
    return false;
    }
}
```

The following points summarize the code sample:

The `HasClearLineOfSightToTarget` function returns `true` or `false` to indicate whether there are any obstacles with colliders, such as trees and other props, between this object's eye point and the player. The method does not consider whether the player is within the enemy's field of view. This function is combined with the `TargetInFOV` method (which we'll see very shortly) to determine whether the object can see the player—that is, it is in their field of view *and* not obstructed by any obstacles.

A **Raycast** is used to check whether there is a clear sightline to the player.

It requires a start position, direction, the `RaycastHit` object, and distance.

You can imagine a Raycast as a line extending from the start position in the direction specified for the distance specified. The first collider this line intersects with is returned in the `RaycastHit` object.

We use the position of the `EyePoint` object as the start position of the Raycast.

The direction is a **normalized** vector that points toward the player (a normalized vector has a length of `1`). We use a normalized vector as we only want the direction and don't need the distance between the two objects. It doesn't matter whether the player is 5 or 100 feet away from the player; if they're in the same direction, that is all that matters.

For the distance, we pass the radius of the Sphere Collider that we'll attach to the Toon Chick once the script is complete. The radius of the collider will represent the Toon Chick's maximum view range.

The `Physics.Raycast` function returns `true` if an object is hit, and `false` otherwise. We call the function and use the return value as an argument in an `if` statement because we only want to process the body of the `if` statement when the Raycast has hit something.

The Raycast starts at our `EyePoint` object and extends toward the player until it reaches the outer radius of our Sphere Collider and, in the process, fills `RaycastHit` with relevant information. The eagle-eyed among you may have noticed the `out` keyword in front of the `Info` object we pass into the `Physics.Raycast` function. If you're not familiar with this keyword, it means that we're passing the object as a **reference**. Therefore, any changes made to the object in the scope of the `Raycast` function will reflect in the `Info` object.

> **Important note**
> For more information on C# references, see the online documentation at `https://docs.microsoft.com/en-us/dotnet/csharp/language-reference/keywords/reference-types`.

If `Physics.Raycast` returns `true`, the `Info.Transform` tag is compared to `TargetTag`. `Info.Transform` will contain the transform of the first collider hit by the Raycast. This transform could belong to a tree, rock, another chick, or possibly the player. If it is the player, we return `true`, signifying that there is an unobstructed line of sight toward the target.

> **Tip**
> The `RaycastHit` object has several other fields worth exploring in your own projects. For the complete list, see the online documentation at `https://docs.unity3d.com/ScriptReference/RaycastHit.html`.

3. As mentioned, we need a method to check whether the player is in the field of view; let's add that now:

```
public class SightLine : MonoBehaviour
{
    public float FieldOfView = 45f;

    ...

    private bool TargetInFOV(Transform Target)
    {
        Vector3 DirToTarget = Target.position - EyePoint.
```

```
      position;
      float Angle = Vector3.Angle(EyePoint.forward,
          DirToTarget);
      if (Angle <= FieldOfView)
      {
          return true;
      }
      return false;
    }
}
```

The following points summarize the code sample:

The `FieldOfView` variable is a floating-point value that determines an angular margin on either side of the object's eye point, inside which objects (such as the player) can be seen. The higher this value, the more chance the enemy has of seeing the player.

The `TargetInFOV` function returns `true` or `false` to indicate whether the player is within the enemy's field of view. This function can tell you whether this object would see the player if there was a clear line of sight (it ignores whether the player is hidden behind a wall or another solid object, such as a tree). It takes the position of the enemy eyes, determines a vector to the player, and measures the angle between the forward vector and player. It compares this to the `FieldOfView` field and returns `true` if the angle between the object and the target is less than the variable.

> **Important note**
> Remember that these code samples are just that: a code *sample*. For the full code listing, please refer to the book's companion files in the `Chapter09/` End folder.

4. Attach the `SightLine` script to the **Toon Chick** object in the scene.

5. As the script requires a trigger collider, also attach a **Sphere Collider** component and enable the Is **Trigger** field in the **Inspector**.

6. The `SightLine` script can only see a target if it is within the radius of the collider. Set **Radius** to `10`.

See *Figure 9.1* for the **Sight Line** and **Sphere Collider** settings:

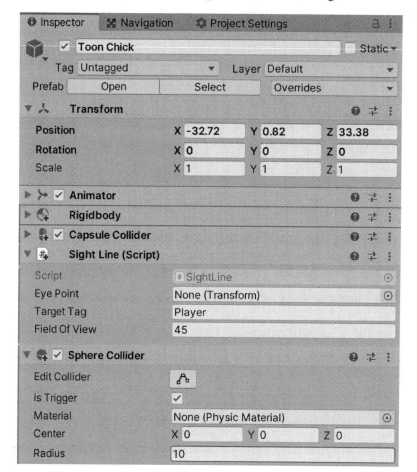

Figure 9.1 – Enabling the chick to see

7. The **Eye Point** field is, by default, set to **None**, which represents a null value. The field should refer to a specific location on the enemy character that acts as the eye position—the place from which the character can see. To create this point, add a new child object to the **Toon Chick** by right-clicking on the object and selecting **Create Empty**.

8.   Name the object `Eye Point`.

9.   Position the object to the approximate position of the character's eye area, making sure that the forward vector is facing in the same direction, as shown in *Figure 9.2*:

Figure 9.2 – Adding an Eye Point child object

10.   Drag and drop the `Eye Point` object from the **Hierarchy** to the **Eye Point** field for the **Sight Line** component in the **Inspector**. The position of this object will determine whether the enemy can see the player. Having a separate eye point instead of using the character's position allows more control over where the eyes are positioned. Also, the position of the object is based on the pivot point of the mesh and this may not be suitable for our purposes.

11. The `SightLine` script determines the player location by first finding the player object in the scene using the **Player** tag. Consequently, set the `Body` object's **Tag** property to **Player**. This process is outlined in *Chapter 2, Creating a Collection Game*:

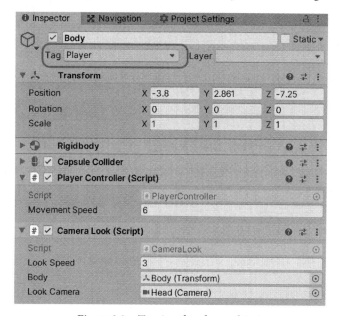

Figure 9.3 – Tagging the player object

That's it for configuring the sightline for the chick. It can now track the player in the environment—although it will be a little while before we can see this in action as we'll need to create the FSM first. Let's jump into that next.

Implementing the FSM

To create the AI for our chick character, we will be using an FSM, in addition to the line of sight code that we already have. An FSM is not a thing or feature of Unity, nor is it a tangible aspect of the C# language. Instead, an FSM is a concept, framework, or design that we can apply in code to achieve specific AI behaviors. It comes from a particular way of thinking about intelligent characters as a combination of states.

We can summarize the **non-player character** (**NPC**) for our level as existing within one of three possible states at any one time. These states are as follows:

- **Patrol**: The chick is following waypoints around the environment.
- **Chase**: The chick is running after the player.
- **Attack**: The chick has reached the player and is attacking.

Each of these modes is a state that encompasses unique behavior, with the chick only able to be in one of these states at any one time. The chick cannot, for example, be patrolling and chasing simultaneously or patrolling and attacking, because this wouldn't make sense within the logic of the game.

> **Important note**
> There are several alternative methods of AI that we could have used instead of the FSM, such as **hierarchical state machines** or **behavior trees**; however, these alternative systems are not covered here.

In addition to the states themselves, there is a rule set or group of connections between the states that determines when one state should transition to another. For example, an NPC should only move from patrolling to chasing if it can see the player and it is not already attacking. Similarly, the NPC should only move from attacking to patrolling if it cannot see the player and it is not already patrolling or chasing. The combination of the states and rules governing their connections form the FSM. Think back to the **Animator** window in *Chapter 7, Creating Artificial Intelligence*, which is also an FSM (each animation represents a state, and the arrows represent the transitions between states).

There is no right or wrong way to code an FSM per se. There are merely different ways, some of which are better or worse for particular ends. With this in mind, let's jump in by creating the data structures and classes that our FSM controller will later rely on:

1. Create a file called `FSMStateType`, which will store an enum containing the name of each state:

```
public enum FSMStateType
{
    None,
    Patrol,
    Chase,
    Attack
}
```

2. Each state will be a separate class, so we could write several different implementations that all register the state type of patrol (for example).

> **Tip**
>
> Maintaining an entry in an enum could quickly become unwieldy for larger
> projects. As an extension, you could look into removing the enum completely
> and using **reflection** to determine the states. Reflection is a relatively advanced
> topic, so the enum will fit our purposes for now if you're just starting
> your game development journey. For the more adventurous, information
> on reflection can be found at `https://docs.microsoft.com/`
> `en-us/dotnet/csharp/programming-guide/concepts/`
> `reflection`.

3. Create a class called `IFSMState` to store the **interface** for every state:

```csharp
public interface IFSMState
{
    FSMStateType StateName { get; }

    void OnEnter();
    void OnExit();
    void DoAction();
    FSMStateType ShouldTransitionToState();
}
```

The following points summarize the code sample:

Each state will have a corresponding class that implements this interface. If you're
unfamiliar with interfaces, they are a purely abstract class that is not instantiated
directly. They define a *contract* that a class must follow. If each state implements this
interface, we know they will all have a public `OnEnter`, `OnExit`, `DoAction`, and
`ShouldTransitionToState` function, as well as a `StateName` get **property**.

The `StateName` get property returns the name for this state from the enum we
created previously. This state name is used by our FSM controller class (which we'll
write shortly) to differentiate the different states.

The `OnEnter` function is called at the beginning of a state transition as we
transition into a new state. The `OnExit` function is called during a transition
between states as we exit the state to move to a new one. For example, if we are
transitioning from the patrol to chase state, `OnExit` will be called on the patrol
state, and then `OnEnter` is called on the chase state. These functions are used to
perform any setup required and revert any temporary changes. We will see clear
examples when we write the states.

The DoAction function is where the state's action occurs—that is, setting a navigation destination for patrolling and chasing or attacking the player in the attack state.

ShouldTransitionToState will be queried directly after the call to DoAction. This function will check the condition of the state and either return a different FSMStateType to signify that the FSM controller should transition to that state or return the current state name. If the state returns the current state name, no transition will be performed, and the FSM controller will stay with the current state.

4. Before we write the FSM controller, we need one more class. Create a class called EmptyAction:

```
public class EmptyAction : IFSMState
{
    public FSMStateType StateName { get { return
      FSMStateType.None; } }

    public void DoAction() { }
    public void OnEnter() { }
    public void OnExit() { }

    public FSMStateType ShouldTransitionToState()
    {
        return FSMStateType.None;
    }
}
```

5. This class, as the name suggests, is an empty state. We'll use this class shortly when we come to write the FSM controller to remove the need to check for a null state. If a required state can't be found, we'll return an empty state instead.

6. We're now ready to create the FSM controller that will run the state actions and control transitions between states. Create a new class called FSM:

```
public class FSM : MonoBehaviour
{
    public FSMStateType StartState = FSMStateType.Patrol;
    private IFSMState[] StatePool;
    private IFSMState CurrentState;
```

```
    private readonly IFSMState EmptyAction = new
      EmptyState();

    void Awake()
    {
        StatePool = GetComponents<IFSMState>();
    }

    void Start()
    {
        CurrentState = EmptyAction;
        TransitionToState(StartState);
    }
}
```

The following points summarize the code sample:

The object maintains an array of IFSMState called StatePool. This array is initialized in the Awake function by calling GetComponents. The call to GetComponents will retrieve all the scripts attached to the object that implement the IFSMState interface. This way, we can easily add new states to an object by adding them as a component.

The controller stores a reference to CurrentState. The DoAction function and a check whether a transition is required will shortly be performed using this reference.

In the Start function, CurrentState is set equal to EmptyAction, then TransitionToState is called, passing the user-specified StartState.

7. Next, add the TransitionToState and GetState function:

```
public class FSM : MonoBehaviour
{
    private void TransitionToState(FSMStateType
      StateName)
    {
        CurrentState.OnExit();
        CurrentState = GetState(StateName);
        CurrentState.OnEnter();
        Debug.Log("Transitioned to " + CurrentState.
          StateName);
```

```
        }

    IFSMState GetState(FSMStateType StateName)
    {
        foreach (var state in StatePool)
        {
            if (state.StateName == StateName)
            {
                return state;
            }
        }
        return EmptyAction;
    }
}
```

The `TransitionToState` function handles all transitions between states. The method first calls `OnExit` on `CurrentState` before retrieving the new desired state by calling `GetState` (we'll write this function shortly). Then, as `CurrentState` has been modified and we've transitioned to a new state, the `OnEnter` function is called on `CurrentState`. Lastly, a call to `Debug.Log` prints the transition to the **Console** window to help us debug the FSM, as shown in *Figure 9.4*:

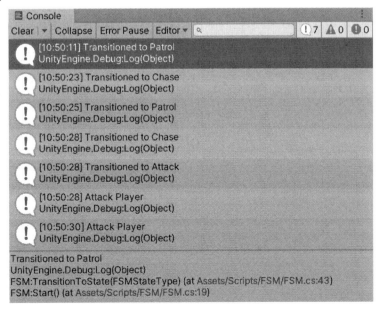

Figure 9.4 – State transitions shown in the Console window

8. The only parts left to write are the `Update` function responsible for running the action of the current state and performing transitions, and the `GetState` function:

```
public class FSM : MonoBehaviour
{
    ...
    void Update()
    {
        CurrentState.DoAction();

        FSMStateType TransitionState = CurrentState.
            ShouldTransitionToState();

        if (TransitionState != CurrentState.StateName)
        {
            TransitionToState(TransitionState);
        }
    }
}
```

The `Update` function runs every frame. It first calls the `DoAction` function on `CurrentState`. This call will perform the action associated with the state (for example, moving to a waypoint for the patrol state, or running toward the player for the chase state). Directly after the call to `DoAction`, the `Update` function calls `ShouldTransitionToState`. Each state will implement functionality to decide when and where to transition. We'll look at that in more detail as we write each state. The desired transition state is compared to the current state type. If they are not equal, the FSM attempts to transition to that state using the `TransitionToState` function we saw previously:

```
public class FSM : MonoBehaviour
{
    ...
    IFSMState GetState(FSMStateType StateName)
    {
        foreach (var state in StatePool)
        {
            if (state.StateName == StateName)
            {
```

```
                    return state;
            }
        }

        return EmptyAction;
    }
}
```

The `GetState` function loops through the array of states attached to the object (stored in `StatePool`) and checks whether the state type is equal to the desired state type and returns the state if they match. `EmptyAction` is returned if no match is found. We could have returned null here instead, but then every time we call a function or query `CurrentState`, we would first have to check whether it is a valid reference.

> **Important note**
> By ensuring that the object is never null through the use of an empty object, we are applying the **Null Object Pattern**.

9. Remove the **FollowDestination** and **Animation Controller** components from the `Toon Chick` object. We'll re-implement this functionality using our FSM.

10. Attach the FSM script to the `Toon Chick` object:

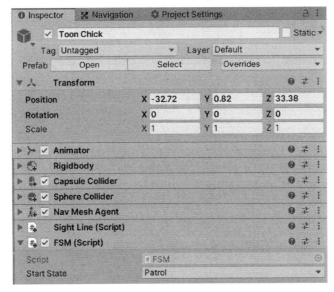

Figure 9.5 – Attaching the AI script to the NPC character

Both the **Sight Line** and **FSM** scripts are now attached to the `Toon Chick` object.

Tip

You can collapse the components by selecting the arrow to the left of their icons. As you can see from *Figure 9.5*, all the components apart from the **Transform** and **FSM** component have been collapsed.

The chick now has an FSM controller! However, if you run the game now, you'll quickly notice that the chick doesn't do anything. This lack of action is due to the absence of any states. We've created a state controller but have no states for it to control! We'll rectify this situation now by creating the first state: the patrol state.

Patrolling the environment

The first of the three states we'll implement is the patrol state. In this state, we want the chick to walk around the environment, following a predefined route. We achieved this in the previous chapter when we configured an animated `Destination` object that jumped around the environment. We'll reuse that object and the associated movement functionality for the patrol state, making a few tweaks to fit our needs. Previously, the chick followed this object without end, whereas the patrol state requires the NPC to consider whether the player can be seen on its route. If the player is spotted, the hunt should begin, and the current state should change to the chase state.

Each state will be contained in its own class:

1. Create a `PatrolState` script:

```
public class PatrolState : MonoBehaviour, IFSMState
{
    public float MovementSpeed = 1.5f;
    public float Acceleration = 2.0f;
    public float AngularSpeed = 360.0f;
    public string AnimationRunParamName = "Run";
    public FSMStateType StateName { get { return
      FSMStateType.Patrol; } }
    private NavMeshAgent ThisAgent;
    private Animator ThisAnimator;
    private void Awake()
    {
        ThisAgent = GetComponent<NavMeshAgent>();
```

```
        ThisSightLine = GetComponent<SightLine>();
        ThisAnimator = GetComponent<Animator>();
    }
    public void OnEnter()
    {
        ThisAgent.isStopped = false;
        ThisAgent.speed = MovementSpeed;
        ThisAgent.acceleration = Acceleration;
        ThisAgent.angularSpeed = AngularSpeed;
        ThisAnimator.SetBool(AnimationRunParamName,
            false);
    }

    public void OnExit()
    {
        ThisAgent.isStopped = true;
    }
}
```

The following points summarize the code sample:

The primary purpose of this state is to use the NavMeshAgent component to move the object along a series of waypoints. The class inherits from MonoBehaviour, so we can attach it to the Toon Chick and benefit from using Unity events (such as the Awake function). The class also implements the IFSMState interface. Implementing this interface and attaching it to an object that also has the FSM script attached (such as our Toon Chick) will add this state to the pool of states for an object.

> **Important note**
>
> The scripts you write must derive from MonoBehaviour (or a class that inherits from it) if you want to attach it to an object and use Awake, Start, Update, and other events that we've made use of in this book. For the full list of functions and events provided by MonoBehaviour, please see the online documentation at https://docs.unity3d.com/ScriptReference/MonoBehaviour.html.

`StateName` returns a type of `Patrol` to signify that this is a version of a patrol state. Remember, we could have several different implementations of each state (although not on the same object).

The `OnEnter` function configures the `NavMeshAgent` component's speed, acceleration, and angular speed variables. By configuring these variables on a per-state basis, the chick's movement speed can vary depending on its behavior. For example, the chick can move quickly when chasing the player and slower when patrolling. This function also sets the `Run` parameter to `false` on the animation component as the chick will be patrolling at walking speed.

The `OnExit` method stops the `NavMeshAgent` component so that the state-related movement stops.

2. You may have noticed that the class doesn't implement all of the functions of the `IFSMState` interface and won't compile as a result. We're missing two: `DoAction` and `ShouldTransitionToState`. Let's write them now:

```
public class PatrolState : MonoBehaviour, IFSMState
{
    public Transform Destination;
    private SightLine ThisSightLine;

    public void DoAction()
    {
        ThisAgent.SetDestination(Destination.position);
    }

    public FSMStateType ShouldTransitionToState()
    {
        if (ThisSightLine.IsTargetInSightLine)
        {
            return FSMStateType.Chase;
        }

        return StateName;
    }
}
```

DoAction calls the SetDestination function on NavMeshAgent. This behavior is the same as we've seen previously in the FollowDestination script.

ShouldTransitionToState uses the SightLine class to determine whether the target (that is, the player) is still within the chick's sightline. If the player lands within the sightline, then the FSMStateType.Chase is returned, informing the FSM class to transition to a chase state—the chase is on!

3. Drag and drop the PatrolState script to the Toon Chick character in the scene.

4. The patrol state is configured to track a moving object. Luckily, we have one we made earlier: a moving destination was created in the previous chapter using the **Animation** window to move an object around the scene over time, jumping from one place to another. Drag the Destination object to the **Destination** field in the **Inspector**, as shown in *Figure 9.6*:

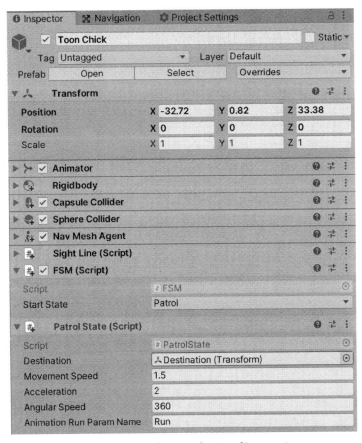

Figure 9.6 – Configuring the PatrolState script

As the `PatrolState` script implements the `IFSMState` interface, the `FSM` script will retrieve a reference to the new state when the game begins. The patrol state is the default state for the FSM, so when the game begins, the chick will transition into this state. Once in this state, it will move around the environment, following the `Destination` object, just as it did in *Chapter 7, Creating Artificial Intelligence*. While it may not seem like it to the player at the moment, we've come a long way between that chapter and now. Because of the state machine, it's easier to customize the chick's behavior in different situations. It is also easier to maintain our game's code base as each state is separated into a logical unit, with minimal overlap between states. This ease of customization will become apparent soon as we start the creation of the second state: the chase state.

Chasing the player

The chase state is the second of the three in the chick's FSM. In this state, the chick will chase down the player by running directly toward them.

This state can transition to either of the patrol or attack states. As we've seen in the *Chasing the player* section, the patrol state requests that the FSM enters the chase state if the chick establishes a direct line of sight to the player while patrolling. Conversely, as we'll see in the next section (*Attacking the player*), if an attacking NPC falls outside the reach of the player (most likely because they are running away), the NPC resorts to chasing again. From the chasing state, it's possible to move to the patrol or attack state, if the inverse conditions are met.

As with the patrol state, the chase state will exist in its own class:

1. Create a `ChaseState` script. We'll start the implementation with the `StateName`, `OnEnter`, and `OnExit` functions:

```
public class ChaseState : MonoBehaviour, IFSMState
{
    public FSMStateType StateName { get { return
    FSMStateType.Chase; } }
    public float MovementSpeed = 2.5f;
    public float Acceleration = 3.0f;
    public float AngularSpeed = 720.0f;
    public float FOV = 60.0f;
    public string AnimationRunParamName = "Run";


    private readonly float MinChaseDistance = 2.0f;
    private NavMeshAgent ThisAgent;
```

```
    private SightLine SightLine;
    private float InitialFOV = 0.0f;
    private Animator ThisAnimator;


    private void Awake()
    {
        ThisAgent = GetComponent<NavMeshAgent>();
        SightLine = GetComponent<SightLine>();
        ThisAnimator = GetComponent<Animator>();
    }


    public void OnEnter()
    {
        InitialFOV = SightLine.FieldOfView;
        SightLine.FieldOfView = FOV;

        ThisAgent.isStopped = false;
        ThisAgent.speed = MovementSpeed;
        ThisAgent.acceleration = Acceleration;
        ThisAgent.angularSpeed = AngularSpeed;

        ThisAnimator.SetBool(AnimationRunParamName,
          true);
    }

    public void OnExit()
    {
        SightLine.FieldOfView = InitialFOV;
        ThisAgent.isStopped = true;
    }
}
```

The following points summarize the code sample:

In this state, the agent's primary goal is to reduce the distance between itself and the player. To achieve this, it uses the NavMeshAgent component to find a path.

In the `OnEnter` function, `NavMeshAgent` is resumed by setting `isStopped` to `false` and the speed, acceleration, and angular speed are set to higher values than those found in `PatrolState`. These settings result in a faster-moving object.

As the object will be getting closer to the player, the `FieldOfView` field on the `SightLine` object is also increased to prevent the chick from losing the player while they're standing right in front of them. Before setting the field of view, the original value is stored in the `InitialFOV` field, then when the state exits, the field of view is reset using this value in the `OnExit` function. `SightLine` will be used in the `ShouldTransitionToState` function that we'll write shortly.

2. As the chick will be moving faster in this state, the `Run` parameter is set to `true` on the animation component in the `OnEnter` function to transition the animation state from walking to playing the run animation.

> **Important note**
>
> You can download the complete code listings from the book's GitHub repo at `https://github.com/PacktPublishing/Unity-2020-By-Example`.

3. Finish the class by writing the `DoAction` and `ShouldTransitionToState` functions:

```
public class ChaseState : MonoBehaviour, IFSMState
{
    public void DoAction()
    {
        ThisAgent.SetDestination(SightLine.
            LastKnowSighting);
    }

    public FSMStateType ShouldTransitionToState()
    {
        if (ThisAgent.remainingDistance <=
            MinChaseDistance)
        {
            return FSMStateType.Attack;
        }
        else if(!SightLine.IsTargetInSightLine)
        {
```

```
            return FSMStateType.Patrol;
        }


        return FSMStateType.Chase;
    }
}
```

The `DoAction` function looks similar to the method of the same name in the `PatrolState` class, except this time we're passing in the last known position of the player using the `SightLine` class. This way, the chick will move toward the player (or at least the last known position of the player).

The `ShouldTransitionToState` function can return one of three state types:

The `Attack` state type if the chick gets close enough to the player. `MinChaseDistance` defines the minimum distance required for this transition.

The `Patrol` state if the chick loses sight of the player.

The `Chase` state if neither of the two previously mentioned conditions is met. Returning the `Chase` state informs FSM that no transition is required.

4.   Attach the `ChaseState` script to the `Toon Chick` object:

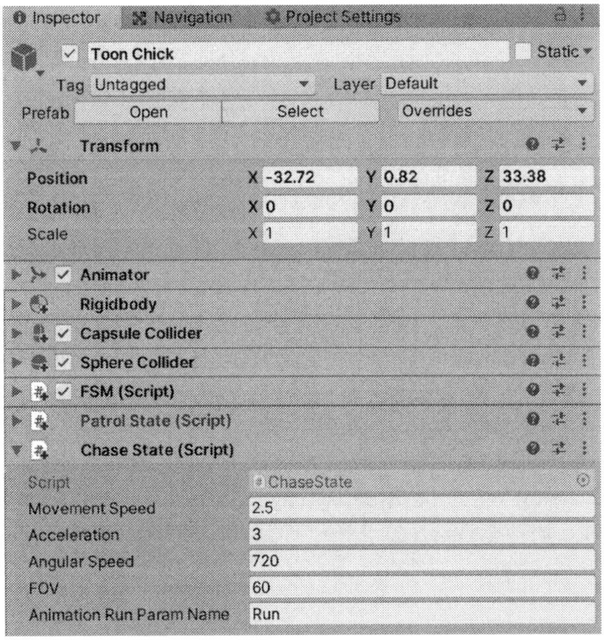

Figure 9.7 – Configuring the ChaseState script

5. Test the game to make sure that the chick patrols around the environment and chases after the player when it catches sight of them:

Figure 9.8 – The chick chasing the player

We've now got two behaviors under our belt: the patrol and chase states. Hopefully, it is starting to become apparent how easy it is to modify the chick's behavior by creating self-contained states. Next, we'll create the last state for the chick: the attack state.

Attacking the player

The third and final state for the NPC is the attack state, during which the chick will periodically attack the player (or at least pretend to attack the player, as you'll see shortly).

This state can only be reached from the chase state. During a chase, the chick will check whether they are within attacking distance. If so, the chase state will request that the FSM change from chasing to attacking. If, during an attack, the player retreats, then the chick will change from attacking to chasing.

The attack state will have a related animation, as we alluded to in *Chapter 7, Creating Artificial Intelligence*, when we created the animations for the chick; however, before we create the custom animations, we'll write the state's implementation.

Implementing the state

As with the previous two states, the attack state is contained in a separate class:

1. Create an `AttackState` class:

```
public class AttackState : MonoBehaviour, IFSMState
{
    public FSMStateType StateName { get { return
      FSMStateType.Attack;   } }
    public string AnimationAttackParamName = "Attack";
    public float EscapeDistance = 10.0f;
    public float MaxAttackDistance = 2.0f;
    public string TargetTag = "Player";
    public float DelayBetweenAttacks = 2.0f;


    private Animator ThisAnimator;
    private NavMeshAgent ThisAgent;
    private bool IsAttacking = false;
    private Transform Target;


    private void Awake()
    {
        ThisAgent = GetComponent<NavMeshAgent>();
        ThisAnimator = GetComponent<Animator>();

        Target = GameObject.
          FindGameObjectWithTag(TargetTag).transform;

    }
}
```

The `Target` variable is initialized by searching all objects for the first object with the specified `TargetTag` using `GameObject.FindGameObjectWithTag`. The `Body` object is the only object with the `Player` tag. Consequently, the `Target` field will point to that object's transform. The player becomes the target.

2. Add the `OnEnter` and `OnExit` functions:

```
public class AttackState : MonoBehaviour, IFSMState
{
    ...
    public void OnEnter()
    {
        StartCoroutine(DoAttack());
    }

    public void OnExit()
    {
        ThisAgent.isStopped = true;
        IsAttacking = false;
        StopCoroutine(DoAttack());
    }
}
```

The following points summarize the code sample:

The `OnEnter` function starts a **coroutine** by calling `StartCoroutine`. A coroutine is a function that can break at a specified point, and then execution will continue from this point during the next frame. A typical use for coroutines is building complex behavior that can run over several frames without slowing down gameplay by trying to do too much during a single frame. The delay before returning to the coroutine can also be customized, which we'll take advantage of shortly.

The `StartCoroutine` function can be passed the name of a function or `IEnumerator`. In our case, we pass an `IEnumerator` that is returned from the `DoAttack` function. We'll discuss `IEnumerator` shortly when we write the `DoAttack` function.

The `OnExit` function stops the `NavMeshAgent` and the coroutine that was started in the `OnEnter` function to prevent the chick from moving or attacking once it's exited this state.

> **Important note**
> Coroutines do not run on separate threads and can only be started from the main thread.

3. Add the DoAction and ShouldTransitionToState functions to the AttackState class:

```
public class AttackState : MonoBehaviour, IFSMState
{

    ...

    public void DoAction()
    {
        IsAttacking = Vector3.Distance(Target.position,
            transform.position) < MaxAttackDistance;

        if(!IsAttacking)
        {
            ThisAgent.isStopped = false;
            ThisAgent.SetDestination(Target.position);
        }
    }

    public FSMStateType ShouldTransitionToState()
    {
        if (Vector3.Distance(Target.position, transform.
            position) > EscapeDistance)
        {
            return FSMStateType.Chase;
        }

        return FSMStateType.Attack;
    }
}
```

The following points summarize the code sample:

The DoAction function sets the IsAttacking variable to true if the target is close. It uses the Vector3.Distance function to retrieve the distance between the target (that is, the player) and this object and compares this value to the MaxAttackDistance variable.

If the player is too far away to attack, the agent is moved toward the player using the NavMeshAgent component.

4. In `ShouldTransitionToState`, the `Chase` state is returned if the player moves far enough away from this object. Again, `Vector3.Distance` is used to calculate the distance. If that distance is greater than `EscapeDistance`, then the `Chase` state is returned, signifying to `FSM` that the chick should return to a chase state. Otherwise, the `Attack` state is returned.

5. The last update we need to make to the `AttackState` class is adding the `DoAttack` function. We'll do that now:

```
public class AttackState : MonoBehaviour, IFSMState
{
    ...
    private IEnumerator DoAttack()
    {
        while(true)
        {
            if (IsAttacking)
            {
                Debug.Log("Attack Player");
                ThisAnimator.
                    SetTrigger(AnimationAttackParamName);
                ThisAgent.isStopped = true;

                yield return new
                    WaitForSeconds(DelayBetweenAttacks);
            }

            yield return null;
        }
    }
}
```

The following points summarize the code sample:

The `DoAttack` function is executed as a coroutine. While the FSM is in the attack state, this function will run. To accomplish this, the function returns an `IEnumerator`, which is passed to `StartCoroutine` and `StopCoroutine` in the `OnEnter` and `OnExit` functions, respectively.

An `IEnumerator` is an **interface** included in the .NET framework that provides a method of enumerating over a collection. Unity uses them in coroutines to help iterate over chunks of code.

This coroutine runs on a frame-safe infinite loop for as long as the FSM is in the attack state. The `yield return null` statement will pause the coroutine until the next frame, so at every frame, the contents of the `while` loop will be processed. This practice allows prolonged behaviors to be executed efficiently over time.

If `IsAttacking` is `true`, a message is printed to the Console window for debugging purposes to inform us that an attack has taken place. Then, an animation trigger with the name held in the `AnimationAttackParamName` field is activated. We will implement this parameter in the animation system soon. After activating the animation trigger, the agent's movement is stopped by setting `ThisAgent.isStopped` to `true`. We do this as we want the chick to be stationary when attacking. It then calls `yield return`, but rather than passing `null` (which pauses execution until the next frame), we pass a new `WaitForSeconds` object. This pauses execution by the numbers of seconds specified in `DelayBetweenAttacks`, preventing the chick from attacking too frequently.

> **Important note**
> For more information on coroutines, see the online documentation at `https://docs.unity3d.com/Manual/Coroutines.html`.

The `AnimationAttackParamName` trigger is set on the animation system by calling `ThisAnimator.SetTrigger`. This call will enable a **Trigger** parameter in our animation system, which we will create shortly.

> **Important note**
> Currently, the attack is simulated, and no damage is dealt to the player. If you wish to take this project further and implement this system, you can find detailed steps on creating health and damage logic in *Chapter 3, Creating a Space Shooter*.

As with the previous states, add the `AttackState` to the **Toon Chick** object.

The patrol state has a specific animation associated with it. This animation is not connected to any other state in the object's animation system, so when our state requests the transition to that state, nothing will happen: the chick will continue to play whichever animation it is already playing. We'll fix this next.

Animating the state

In the `DoAttack` function of the `AttackState` script, a specific animation trigger parameter called `Attack` is activated. Currently, this line doesn't do anything; however, when this activation occurs, we want the chick to play an attack animation. To do this, we'll need to create the parameter and create a transition from the existing states to the attack state. We'll start by creating the parameter:

1. Select **Toon Chick** in the **Hierarchy**.

2. Open the **Animator** panel by selecting **Window | Animation | Animator** from the **Application** menu.

3. From the **Parameters** list, select the + button.

4. Select **Trigger**, as shown in *Figure 9.9*:

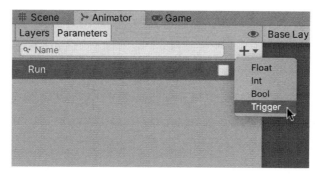

Figure 9.9 – Creating a new trigger

A trigger is a Boolean variable that, once set to `true`, is automatically set to `false` when used for a transition. For example, in our patrol state, as we attack, we activate the `Attack` trigger, which will cause the current state to transition to play the attack animation. Once this transition occurs, the `Attack` trigger is set to `false`, ready to be activated again when we next attack.

5. Name the new parameter **Attack** to match the name we gave it in the `AttackState` script.

   Now that we have the trigger parameter we require, we can create the transitions for the attack animation. We'll use the **Jump W Root** animation state to represent the chick attacking.

6. In the state panel of the **Animator** panel, right-click on **Any State** and select **Make Transition**.

7. Drag the arrow to **Jump W Root** and left-click to create the transition:

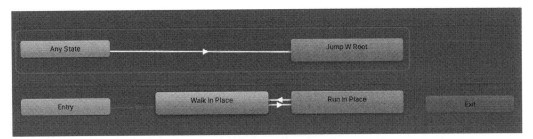

Figure 9.10 – Transitioning from Any State to the attack animation

8. Select the newly created arrow to begin editing the transition.

9. In the **Inspector**, untick **Has Exit Time** and add a new condition based on the **Attack** parameter. Conditions and their creation were outlined in detail in *Chapter 7, Creating Artificial Intelligence*:

Figure 9.11 – Transition settings from Any State to the attack state

Now that we can transition into the attack state, we need to create a transition out of the
state so that the chick isn't stuck attacking forever:

1. Right-click the **Jump W Root** state and once again select **Make Transition**.

2. Drag the arrow to the **Run In Place** state and left-click to create the transition.

3. Click the new arrow to edit the transition.

4. In the **Inspector,** make sure that **Has Exit Time** *is* ticked. We want the attack
   animation to transition to the run animation when it has completed instead of
   based on a parameter.

5. Set **Exit Time** to 1 and **Transition Duration** to 0. These settings will make sure that
   the complete animation is played, and there is no delay between transitioning to the
   running animation:

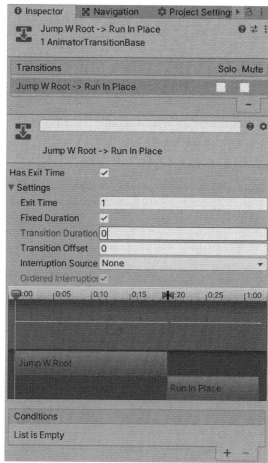

Figure 9.12 – Setting Transition Duration to 0

The **Animator** window should now look something like this:

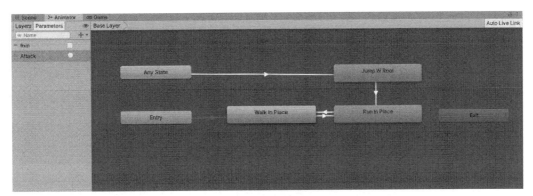

Figure 9.13 – The completed animation states

6. Test the completed level by pressing Play on the toolbar:

Figure 9.14 – The chick chasing the player

The chick should patrol around the environment until it catches sight of the player; once this happens, it will chase down the player until it is within attack range. Once in range, it will attack the player and play the attack animation (which is actually a jumping animation).

Feel free to experiment with the Destination object's animation, the chick's field of view, the movement speed in the patrol or chase state, or even the number of chicks in the game, as shown in *Figure 9.15*:

Figure 9.15 – Experimenting with the number of chicks in the game

The army of chicks each have an FSM and make their own decisions about when to transition between states.

Summary

By completing this chapter, you now have a maintainable, extendable system for creating behavior in AI agents. Continue to play around with the FSM, create new states, and combine them in different ways to create complex behavior. You could even revisit previous projects and extend existing functionality using an FSM—for example, the quest-giving NPC in *Chapter 6, Continuing the 2D Adventure*, could have a movement state and a talking-to-player state. Also, the FSM doesn't just have to be used for AI. For any system that has distinct and separate states, it's worth considering an FSM.

Although the FSM is versatile, it has a somewhat rigid structure. We can calculate what the chick will do every step of the way because we've hardcoded its behavior, which is ideal in many instances but has a few drawbacks. Firstly, there's no opportunity for emergent behavior. Any behavior we want our chick to act out needs to be explicitly programmed. The chick will never ambush the player by hiding behind a tree unless we tell it to, even if it would result in better gameplay. Secondly, as we have to program every behavior manually, this can increase the amount of code we need to write dramatically. As game AI gets ever more sophisticated, alternative methods of creating intelligent entities are being considered. One such approach, called **machine learning** (**ML**), enables entities to learn over time, adapting their behavior to fit their environment. You don't need to explicitly program behavior. Instead, the agent will teach itself how to behave over time. We'll explore this in detail in the next chapter as we implement an entity using **ml-agents**, an ML framework provided by Unity.

Test your knowledge

Q1. AI behaviors can be encoded using...

    A. An FSM

    B. GameObjects

    C. An Animator

    D. A Navigation Mesh

Q2. States can be created using a(n)...

    A. If statement

    B. Switch statement

    C. Separate classes

    D. All of the above

Q3. One alternative to a state machine is a...

    A. Mesh Renderer

    B. Behavior tree

    C. Static variable

    D. Component

Q4. Yield statements are often used to...

    A. Pause and terminate coroutines

    B. Rewind coroutines

    C. Restart coroutines

    D. Delete coroutines

Q5. Line of sight determines...

    A. Whether one object can be seen by the camera

    B. Whether one object can see nothing

    C. Whether one object can see another

    D. Whether one object can see anything

Further reading

The following resources include more information on the topics discussed in this chapter:

- `https://www.packtpub.com/game-development/unity-artificial-intelligence-programming-fourth-edition`

- `https://docs.unity3d.com/ScriptReference/RaycastHit.html`

- `https://docs.unity3d.com/ScriptReference/MonoBehaviour.html`

10
Evolving AI Using ML-Agents

Machine Learning (**ML**) has evolved drastically over the last decade. It is no longer solely the domain of scientists or companies making headlines beating world chess champions. Now, we can easily write AI that can master most human components for a wide variety of games. We can even write AI that will learn how to play a game using information only available to a human player (*MarI/O* comes to mind, an ML algorithm that taught itself to play Super Mario). I remember, many years ago, spending months writing my own evolutionary learning algorithms to do something very similar to what you will accomplish in this very chapter (and hopefully it won't take months to complete!). The best news is, we don't have to write our own ML algorithms (although this is still possible if that's the route you want to take!). Instead, we will use **ML-Agents** to create an intelligent character (or **Agent**).

ML-Agents is short for **Machine Learning Agents**. It is an open source Unity package used to train intelligent Agents using evolutionary algorithms and reinforcement learning. An Agent can be trained over time to become significantly better at a designated task.

In this chapter, we will create an Agent that will teach itself how to navigate an environment, colliding with objects we mark as safe and avoiding objects that we designate as hazards. Along the way, we'll look at how to do the following:

- Create a simple environment for our AI Agent.

- Install ML-Agents and associated Python packages.

- Write a script that will spawn objects in the scene.

- Configure the parameters for the Agent's **Artificial Neural Network (ANN)**.

- Assign rewards based on the Agent's behavior.

- Interpret the output of the learning algorithm to move the Agent around the environment.

- Use Python packages to train the Agent over time to become better at chasing down chicks and avoiding obstacles.

- Embed a model we trained so that the Agent moves around the environment performing as we would like without the need to tell the Agent what to do explicitly.

There is a lot to cover in this chapter, and some of the information can be quite complex. The goal here is not to provide an in-depth look at ML-Agents and ML in general, but to get you up and running as smoothly as possible so that you can start using ML-Agents in your own projects.

This chapter differs from the previous chapters on **Finite State Machines (FSM)** as we won't have to write the AI behavior we expect explicitly. We also won't be writing an attack or chase state. Instead, we will provide information about the Agent's environment and assign positive and negative rewards based on the Agent's behavior. The ML algorithm will use this information and adapt its behavior over time to increase the chance of obtaining a positive reward.

In an ideal world, we would be able to write one AI character that could adapt to any environment within a game and provide an engaging experience for the player. While we're a little way off from this ideal, the introduction of easy-to-use ML algorithms is a big step in the right direction, and by the end of this chapter, you'll see the possibilities offered by ML-Agents.

Technical requirements

This chapter assumes that you have not only completed the projects from the previous chapters but also have a good, basic knowledge of C# scripting generally, though not necessarily in Unity. In this chapter, you will use many of the assets from the project started in *Chapter 8, Continuing with Intelligent Enemies*, so you should read that chapter if you haven't already.

The starting project and assets can be found in the book's companion files in the `Chapter10/Start` folder. You can start here and follow along with this chapter if you do not have your own project already. The completed project is included in the `Chapter10/End` folder.

This chapter uses an asset from the Unity Asset Store, which, along with its author details, can be found at `https://assetstore.unity.com/packages/3d/characters/meshtint-free-boximon-fiery-mega-toon-series-153958`.

ML-Agents relies on a number of Python packages that require Python version 3.6.1 or higher.

Introducing ML-Agents

First released in September 2017, ML-Agents has rapidly evolved with the input from ML scientists, game developers, and the wider Unity fanbase due to its open source nature. This rapid progress can, at times, make it challenging to learn how to use it, with many tutorials quickly becoming outdated. However, with the release of version 1 of ML-Agents, these significant backward-incompatible updates should slow down as the project stabilizes. This means it is a great time to jump into the world of ML in Unity!

The ML-Agents toolkit consists of the following:

- **The ML-Agents Unity package**: This provides everything we need to implement an Agent inside the Unity environment.
- **The `mlagents` Python package**: Contains the ML algorithms that we will use to train the Agent.
- **The `mlagents_env` Python package**: Provides the functionality for Unity and the ML algorithms to talk to each other. `mlagents` relies on this.
- **The `gym_unity` Python package**: A wrapper to interface with OpenAI Gym.

> **Important Note**
>
> For our purposes, we only require `mlagents` and `mlagents_env`.
> Detailed instructions on how to install them are included in the *Installing ML-Agents* section.

We'll use the ML-Agents package to create a learning Agent in the Unity Editor. This process will be very similar to anything we do in Unity. We'll create a **GameObject** and write custom components to extend its functionality. Once we have created the Agent and are ready for training, we will then go outside the Unity Editor and run the `mlagents` Python package, which will use `mlagents_env` to talk to our Unity project and train the monster.

The learning algorithm works on a cycle with the following steps:

- **Observation**: The Agent records observations of its environment.

- **Decision**: Based on the observations, a decision is made and translated into the action vector.

- **Action**: We translate the result of the decision into an action. For our purposes, this will involve moving and rotating the Agent.

- **Reward**: Based on the action, we may assign a positive or negative reward.

Every loop through this cycle is called a **simulation step**. Multiple steps make up an **episode**. As we train our agent in the *Training the Agent* section, we'll progress through thousands of steps to achieve our goal. But that's getting ahead of ourselves. Before we start creating and training the Agent, let's take a sneak peek at the finished project so that we know where we're heading.

Setting the scene

In this chapter, we will create an Agent that will teach itself to move around the environment, avoiding rocks and eating food. We won't explicitly tell it what to do, only reward good behavior (eating the food) and punish bad behavior (eating/bumping into rocks). The Agent will then use this information to work out what to do.

We'll modify the world we created in the previous two chapters, creating a minimal version without the extra foliage and trees. For food, we'll modify the chick prefab we created in the previous chapters—the hunter will become the hunted.

As for the learning Agent, we'll use a new asset—a monster that fits the artistic style:

Figure 10.1 – The monster Agent hunting for food

In *Figure 10.1*, the monster is chasing a chick (that is, the "food"). There are several rocks randomly distributed in the environment, which the monster must learn to avoid.

We already have many of the assets we need, including the level, rock, and chick assets. We only need to import the monster asset for the learning Agent and the ML-Agents package. We'll start with the monster asset.

Importing assets

The monster asset is premade and available on the **Unity Asset Store**. We'll use the model provided in this package as our learning Agent.

The process of importing packages has been covered in detail in previous chapters and will only be outlined briefly here:

1. Navigate to `https://assetstore.unity.com/packages/3d/characters/meshtint-free-boximon-fiery-mega-toon-series-153958`.

2. Click the **Add to My Assets** button.

> **Tip**
> Many developers offer free assets on the Unity Asset Store from models such as a monster to full-blown games. It's worth exploring the store and adding any assets you think will be useful to your collection. The assets will then be available in the **Package Manager** from within Unity.

3. In Unity, open the **Package Manager** window by selecting **Window | Package Manager** from the **Application** menu.

4. Find the asset on the list. You may have to refresh the list by clicking on the refresh button at the bottom of the page.

5. Click **Import**:

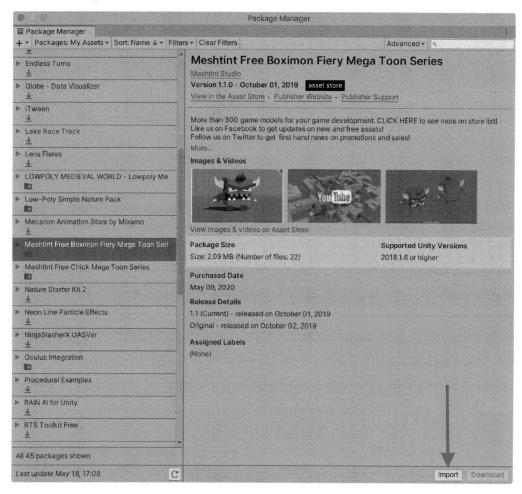

Figure 10.2 – Importing the monster assets

6.   In the window that appears, leave everything as default and once again click **Import**.

Unity will create a `Meshtint Free Boximon Fiery Mega Toon Series` folder in your `Assets` folder. This is almost everything we need to get started; there's just one thing left to install: the ML-Agents package itself. Let's do that now.

Installing ML-Agents

With the advent of ML-Agents v1.0, the process of installing ML-Agents has been improved significantly. However, there are still a few additional steps beyond installing the package through the **Package Manager**. We will cover them in detail in this section.

As outlined in the *Introducing ML-Agents* section, the ML-Agent toolkit consists of three components: the ML-Agents Unity package and three Python packages, called `mlagents`, `mlagents_env`, and `gym_unity`. If you're unfamiliar with Python, don't worry; we'll go step-by-step through how to install the packages here.

> **Important Note**
>
> As `gym_unity` is a wrapper to interface with OpenAI Gym, which we're not using, we won't be using the `gym_unity` Python package. For more information on OpenAI Gym, please see `https://gym.openai.com`.

From the components in the toolkit, we can start to understand how we'll train the Agent. We'll use the ML-Agents package to create a learning Agent in the Unity Editor. This process will be very similar to anything we do in Unity. We'll create a **GameObject** and write custom components to extend its functionality. Once we have created the Agent and are ready for training, we will then go outside the Unity Editor and run the `mlagents` package, which will use `mlagents_env` to talk to our Unity project and train the monster.

But we're getting ahead of ourselves again; before we can do any of that, we need to install the toolkit:

1.   Install Python 3.6.1 or higher from `https://www.python.org/downloads/`. The download instructions differ for each platform but are well documented online and can be installed using a traditional installation wizard.

> **Important Note**
>
> The Python installer will also install a tool called `pip`. We'll use `pip` to install the Python packages required by ML-Agents.

2. Run `pip3 install mlagents` from the command line:

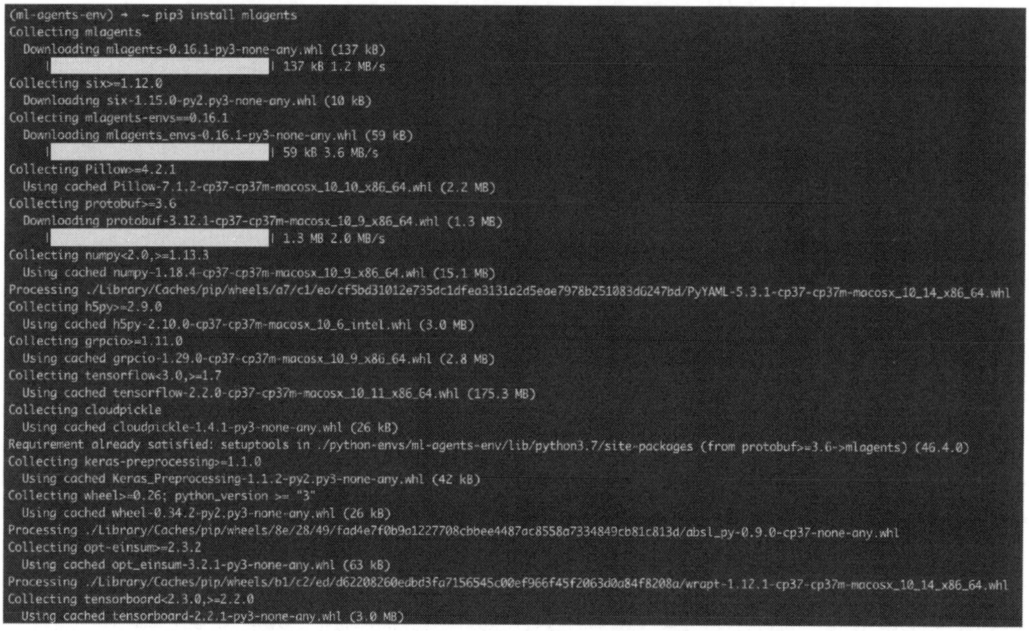

```
(ml-agents-env) → ~ pip3 install mlagents
Collecting mlagents
  Downloading mlagents-0.16.1-py3-none-any.whl (137 kB)
  |                                | 137 kB 1.2 MB/s
Collecting six>=1.12.0
  Downloading six-1.15.0-py2.py3-none-any.whl (10 kB)
Collecting mlagents-envs==0.16.1
  Downloading mlagents_envs-0.16.1-py3-none-any.whl (59 kB)
  |                                | 59 kB 3.6 MB/s
Collecting Pillow>=4.2.1
  Using cached Pillow-7.1.2-cp37-cp37m-macosx_10_10_x86_64.whl (2.2 MB)
Collecting protobuf>=3.6
  Downloading protobuf-3.12.1-cp37-cp37m-macosx_10_9_x86_64.whl (1.3 MB)
  |                                | 1.3 MB 2.0 MB/s
Collecting numpy<2.0,>=1.13.3
  Using cached numpy-1.18.4-cp37-cp37m-macosx_10_9_x86_64.whl (15.1 MB)
Processing ./Library/Caches/pip/wheels/a7/c1/ea/cf5bd31012e735dc1dfea3131a2d5eae7978b251083d6247bd/PyYAML-5.3.1-cp37-cp37m-macosx_10_14_x86_64.whl
Collecting h5py>=2.9.0
  Using cached h5py-2.10.0-cp37-cp37m-macosx_10_6_intel.whl (3.0 MB)
Collecting grpcio>=1.11.0
  Using cached grpcio-1.29.0-cp37-cp37m-macosx_10_9_x86_64.whl (2.8 MB)
Collecting tensorflow<3.0,>=1.7
  Using cached tensorflow-2.2.0-cp37-cp37m-macosx_10_11_x86_64.whl (175.3 MB)
Collecting cloudpickle
  Using cached cloudpickle-1.4.1-py3-none-any.whl (26 kB)
Requirement already satisfied: setuptools in ./python-envs/ml-agents-env/lib/python3.7/site-packages (from protobuf>=3.6->mlagents) (46.4.0)
Collecting keras-preprocessing>=1.1.0
  Using cached Keras_Preprocessing-1.1.2-py2.py3-none-any.whl (42 kB)
Collecting wheel>=0.26; python_version >= "3"
  Using cached wheel-0.34.2-py2.py3-none-any.whl (26 kB)
Processing ./Library/Caches/pip/wheels/8e/28/49/fad4e7f0b9a1227708cbbee4487ac8558a7334849cb81c813d/absl_py-0.9.0-cp37-none-any.whl
Collecting opt-einsum>=2.3.2
  Using cached opt_einsum-3.2.1-py3-none-any.whl (63 kB)
Processing ./Library/Caches/pip/wheels/b1/c2/ed/d62208260edbd3fa7156545c00ef966f45f2063d0a84f8208a/wrapt-1.12.1-cp37-cp37m-macosx_10_14_x86_64.whl
Collecting tensorboard<2.3.0,>=2.2.0
  Using cached tensorboard-2.2.1-py3-none-any.whl (3.0 MB)
```

Figure 10.3 – Installing the mlagents Python package

This command will install the `mlagents` Python package, which is the package we will use to train our Agent. As you can see from *Figure 10.3*, this will also install any dependencies that `mlagents` requires, including the `mlagents_env` package.

3. To test that the installation was successful, run `mlagents-learn --help`:

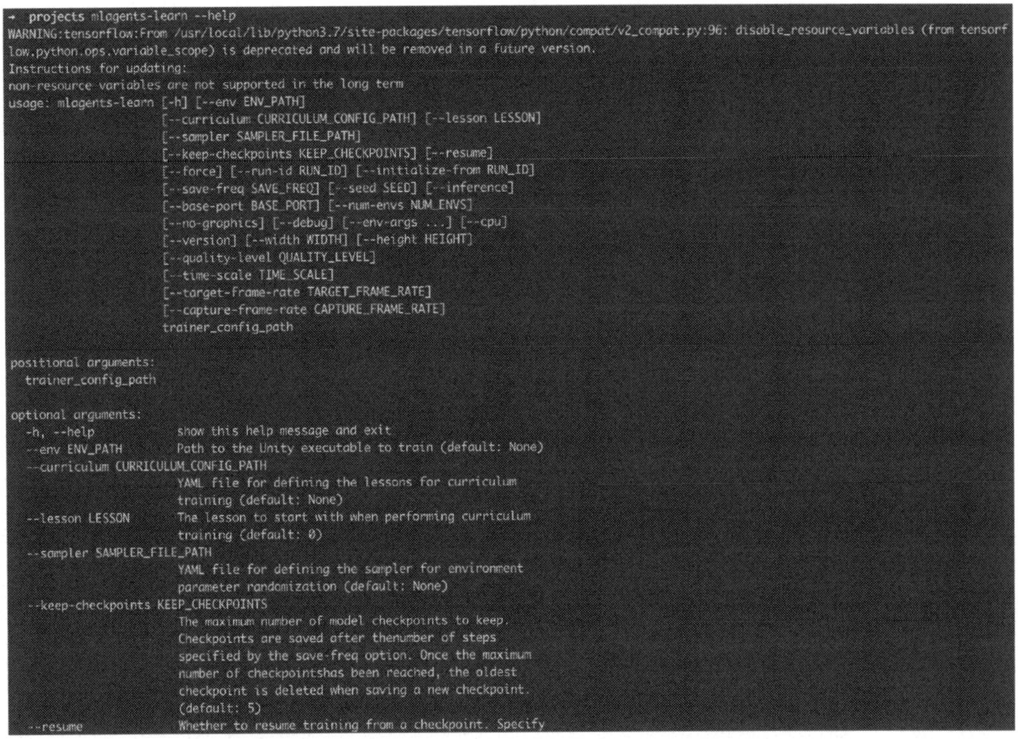
```
→ projects mlagents-learn --help
WARNING:tensorflow:From /usr/local/lib/python3.7/site-packages/tensorflow/python/compat/v2_compat.py:96: disable_resource_variables (from tensorf
low.python.ops.variable_scope) is deprecated and will be removed in a future version.
Instructions for updating:
non-resource variables are not supported in the long term
usage: mlagents-learn [-h] [--env ENV_PATH]
                      [--curriculum CURRICULUM_CONFIG_PATH] [--lesson LESSON]
                      [--sampler SAMPLER_FILE_PATH]
                      [--keep-checkpoints KEEP_CHECKPOINTS] [--resume]
                      [--force] [--run-id RUN_ID] [--initialize-from RUN_ID]
                      [--save-freq SAVE_FREQ] [--seed SEED] [--inference]
                      [--base-port BASE_PORT] [--num-envs NUM_ENVS]
                      [--no-graphics] [--debug] [--env-args ...] [--cpu]
                      [--version] [--width WIDTH] [--height HEIGHT]
                      [--quality-level QUALITY_LEVEL]
                      [--time-scale TIME_SCALE]
                      [--target-frame-rate TARGET_FRAME_RATE]
                      [--capture-frame-rate CAPTURE_FRAME_RATE]
                      trainer_config_path

positional arguments:
  trainer_config_path

optional arguments:
  -h, --help            show this help message and exit
  --env ENV_PATH        Path to the Unity executable to train (default: None)
  --curriculum CURRICULUM_CONFIG_PATH
                        YAML file for defining the lessons for curriculum
                        training (default: None)
  --lesson LESSON       The lesson to start with when performing curriculum
                        training (default: 0)
  --sampler SAMPLER_FILE_PATH
                        YAML file for defining the sampler for environment
                        parameter randomization (default: None)
  --keep-checkpoints KEEP_CHECKPOINTS
                        The maximum number of model checkpoints to keep.
                        Checkpoints are saved after thenumber of steps
                        specified by the save-freq option. Once the maximum
                        number of checkpointshas been reached, the oldest
                        checkpoint is deleted when saving a new checkpoint.
                        (default: 5)
  --resume              Whether to resume training from a checkpoint. Specify
```

Figure 10.4 – Displaying the available parameters for the mlagents-learn command

This command will print the parameters we can use with the `mlagents-learn` command. Don't worry if the number of options feels overwhelming. In reality, we'll only need the one command, and we'll go through that in detail later in the chapter.

4. In Unity, install the **ML-Agents** package using the **Package Manager**. Detailed information on the **Package Manager** can be found in *Chapter 1, Unity Fundamentals*.

> **Important Note**
>
> If ML-Agents is not in the package list, follow the instructions at `https://github.com/Unity-Technologies/ml-agents/blob/master/docs/Installation.md` to add it to the list of available packages.

And that's it for the setup; we've seen what we want to achieve and imported all the assets we need to reach that goal. Next, we will create an environment where the learning will take place.

Creating the environment

Before we dive into the world of ML, we need to create an environment to house the monster. In previous chapters, we created a level with trees, shrubs, and rocks. We'll use some of that here but will simplify it so that we can focus on training the Agent and not have to worry about level design:

1. Duplicate the Demo scene in the Assets/Scenes folder.

2. Rename the new scene ML Demo:

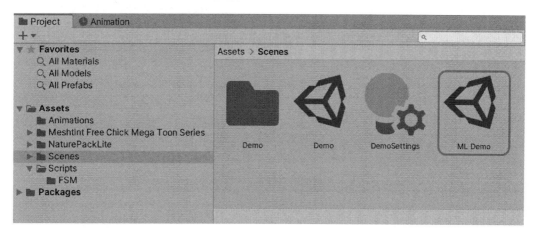

Figure 10.5 – The ML Demo scene in the Project panel

3. Open the new scene by double-clicking on it.

4. In the **Hierarchy** panel, delete Terrain_Objects, Toon_chick, Destination, and all of the ground objects apart from Ground_01. The **Hierarchy** should look the same as in *Figure 10.6*:

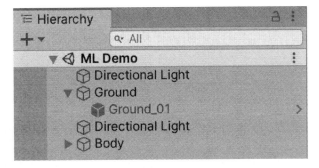

Figure 10.6 – The ML Demo scene in the Hierarchy panel

5. Select Ground_01 and set its scale to 2, 2, 2.

6. Select the **Ground** object (the parent of **Ground_01**) and assign it to the **Ignore Raycast** layer. In the popup, select **Yes, change children**:

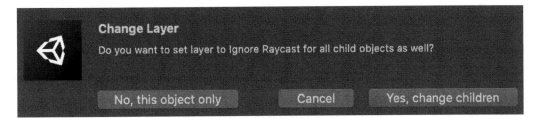

Figure 10.7 – The Change Layer options

This will also set all child objects to the same layer:

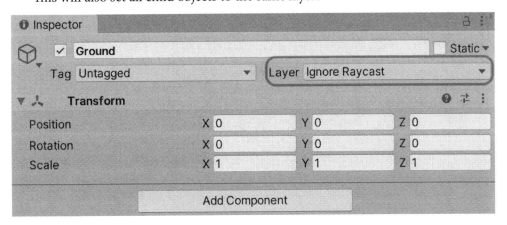

Figure 10.8 – The Ignore Raycast layer set for the Ground object and its children

7. Create four new objects and add a **Box Collider** to each of them by selecting **Component | Physics | Box Collider** from the Application menu. These will become the wall of the level to keep the Agent within bounds.

8. Adjust the scale of these objects to surround the ground object:

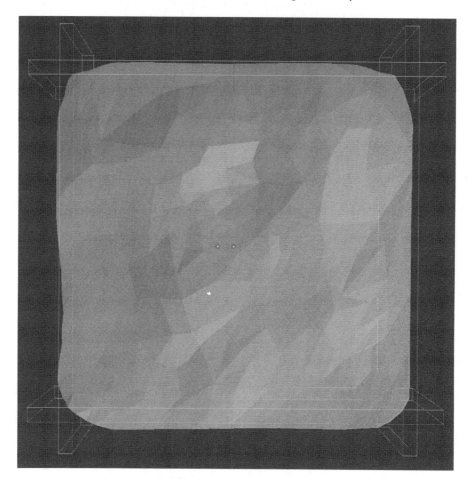

Figure 10.9 – The environment's walls

9. Create and assign the **Wall** tag to each wall object. Creating tags is explained in *Chapter 2, Creating a Collection Game*.

10. Drag the Boximon Fiery prefab to the scene. Located in the Assets/ Meshtint Free Boximon Fiery Mega Toon Series/Prefabs folder, this prefab will be the learning Agent.

11. Rename the object Agent and position it at point 0, 2, 0.

12. Add **Rigidbody** and **Box Collider** components and configure them, as shown in *Figure 10.10*:

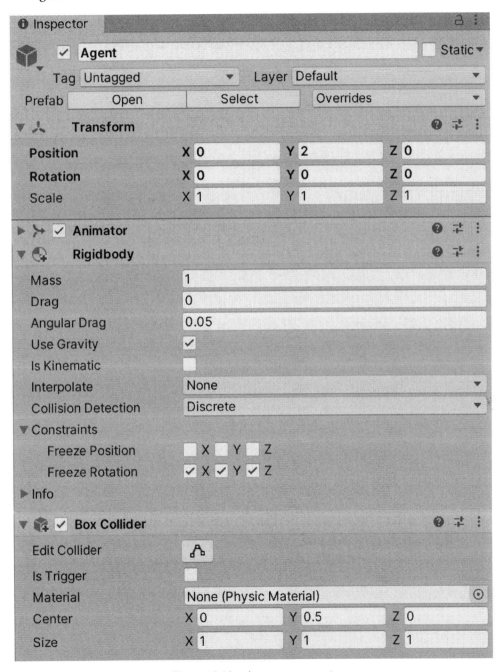

Figure 10.10 – Agent components

With the environment ready, the next step is to create the logic that will spawn the chick and rock objects before we start working on ML.

Spawning objects

The monster will interact with the environment by colliding with the level's walls, the chick, and the rock objects. When the monster collides with a chick or rock object, that object is removed from the environment, and a new object of the same type is spawned at a random location. We also need functionality to reset the environment by removing all spawned objects and re-adding them. However, before we can implement any of this, we need to create the rock and chick objects, so let's do that now.

Creating the prefabs

In this section, we'll create two prefabs: a chick and a rock. We'll base these prefabs on pre-existing assets and modify them to our needs. When we come to implement the ML algorithm, we will award the monster for eating chicks (sorry, chicks!) and penalize it for colliding with rocks:

1. Drag the `Toon Chick` prefab from the `Assets/ Meshtint Free chick Mega Toon Series/ Prefabs` folder to the scene.

2. Add **Rigidbody**, **Box Collider**, and **Capsule Collider** components. One collider will handle collisions with the environment, and the other will be much larger and will be used by our learning Agent to determine whether the chick can be seen.

3.   Configure them as shown in *Figure 10.11*:

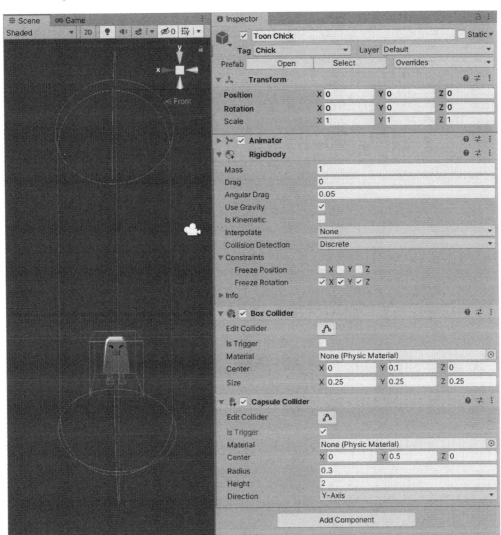

Figure 10.11 – The chick's component configuration

4.   Create a new **chick** tag and assign it to the `Toon Chick` object. We'll assign unique tags to the chick and rock prefabs to differentiate them for the ML algorithm. For instance, we can tell the Agent that there is a rock in its sightline or that it just ate a chick.

5. Drag the `Toon Chick` to the `Assets/Prefabs` folder. Create the folder if it doesn't exist.

6. A message will appear asking whether you want to create an original prefab or a variant of this prefab. Select the **Prefab Variant** option:

Figure 10.12 – Creating a Prefab Variant

Creating a **Prefab Variant** is similar to inheriting from a base class. The Prefab Variant is stored as a separate prefab but shares (or inherits) the properties of the original prefab. These properties can be overridden, or the variant extended by adding new components, differentiating it from the original. For the chick prefab, the animator and Mesh Renderer are the same as the original prefab, but we've added additional functionality in this variant with the addition of physics.

> **Important Note**
> All the data associated with the prefab is still stored with the original prefab asset. It's only the changes that are stored with the Prefab Variant. If you want to modify a property that should be applied to all the variants of the same prefab, you should modify the original prefab asset.

That's all for the chick object; next, we'll create the rock prefab:

1. Drag the `Rock_01` prefab from the `Assets/NaturePackLite/Prefabs` folder to the scene and call it **Rock**.

2. Add **Rigidbody** and **Capsule Collider** components to the object.

3. Configure the components as shown in *Figure 10.13*:

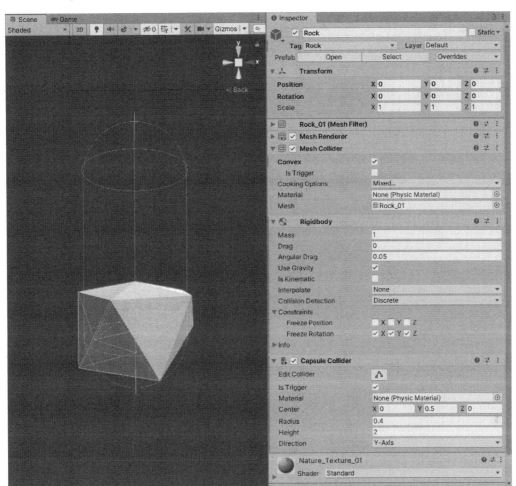

Figure 10.13 – The rock's component configuration

4. Create and assign a **Rock** tag to the object.

5. Drag the Rock_01 object to the Prefabs folder and once again select the **Prefab Variant** option as we're creating a variation of an existing prefab.

Now that we have our prefabs of both the chick and rock, we can write the code that will instantiate and position them in the environment.

Writing the spawn functionality

With the prefabs created, we could place a set number around the environment and attempt to train the Agent. However, in doing so, we would quickly realize that this will not work as we had hoped. The monster would collide with all of the objects in the scene before it learns not to, and as the objects don't re-spawn, the Agent will never learn to avoid the behavior we desire. There would not be enough data to train the Agent. As such, we must have a mechanic in place that spawns any chicks or rocks removed from the game. As we now have the rock and chick prefabs, we can create that functionality:

1. Create a new script called `ObjectSpawner`:

```csharp
public class ObjectSpawner : MonoBehaviour
{
    public int NumOfEachPrefabToSpawn = 6;
    public GameObject FoodPrefab;
    public GameObject RockPrefab;
    private IList<Transform> SpawnLocations = new
      List<Transform>();
    private int CurrentIndex = 0;

    void Awake()
    {
        foreach (Transform Child in transform)
        {
            SpawnLocations.Add(Child);
        }
        SpawnLocations.Shuffle();
    }
}
```

The following points summarize the code sample:

`NumOfEachPrefabToSpawn` defines how many of each prefab exists in the game at any one time. Once training has begun, you can tweak this number to see how it affects the speed at which the Agent learns.

A list of possible spawn locations is stored in the `SpawnLocations` variable . This list is populated in the `Awake` function by iterating over every child transform of the current **GameObject**. This list is then shuffled randomly by calling a **C# extension** that we will write shortly.

2. Add a `Reset` function to the `ObjectSpawner` script:

```
public class ObjectSpawner : MonoBehaviour
{
    public void Reset()
    {
        foreach (var SpawnedLoc in SpawnLocations)
        {
            if (SpawnedLoc.childCount > 0)
            {
                Destroy(SpawnedLoc.GetChild(0).
                    gameObject);
            }
        }

        for (int i = 0; i < NumOfEachPrefabToSpawn; ++i)
        {
            SpawnFood();
            SpawnRock();
        }
    }
}
```

The `Reset` function will be called by our Agent script (which we will write shortly). It removes any currently spawned objects by looping through all possible spawn locations and destroying any children. This works because when we spawn a prefab using the `SpawnPrefab` function, we add the prefab as a child of the spawn location, as you'll soon see.

3. To complete the `ObjectSpawner` script, add the functions responsible for spawning the prefabs:

```
public class ObjectSpawner : MonoBehaviour
{
    public void SpawnFood()
    {
        SpawnPrefab(FoodPrefab);
    }

    public void SpawnRock()
    {
        SpawnPrefab(RockPrefab);
    }

    private void SpawnPrefab(GameObject Prefab)
    {
        Instantiate(Prefab, SpawnLocations[CurrentIndex],
            false);
        CurrentIndex = (CurrentIndex + 1) %
            SpawnLocations.Count;
    }
}
```

The `SpawnRock` and `SpawnFood` functions will be called by our Agent script whenever one of those objects is removed from the game. This process ensures that there is always a set number of each object in the environment.

> **Important Note**
>
> As the `SpawnLocations` list has been shuffled, we can step through them sequentially, and the objects will still be spawned at a random location. If we didn't shuffle the list, the objects would be spawned in the order that we added locations to the `SpawnedLocations` list.

Once we've spawned an object, we increment the `CurrentIndex` by 1, and by using modulus, if we reached the end of the spawn location list, it wraps around to 0. This check ensures that we can continue to spawn objects continuously without hitting an `IndexOutOfRange` exception.

4. In the ObjectSpawner class, we call Shuffle on the SpawnLocations list.
    This function is not included with the List class by default but is an extension that
    we need to write. Create a new class called Extensions to store this function:

```
using System.Collections.Generic;

public static class Extensions
{
    public static void Shuffle<T>(this IList<T> ThisList)
    {
        var Count = ThisList.Count;
        var Last = Count - 1;
        for (var i = 0; i < Last; ++i)
        {
            var RandomIndex = UnityEngine.Random.Range(i,
              Count);
            var Temp = ThisList[i];
            ThisList[i] = ThisList[RandomIndex];
            ThisList[RandomIndex] = Temp;
        }
    }
}
```

C# extension methods provide us with the ability to add functions to existing types
without having to create a custom type. This is demonstrated perfectly with the Shuffle
function. I could have created my own list class that implements the IList interface and
add the Shuffle function that way, but instead, I can write an extension method that
adds the functionality I require.

> **Important Note**
> An extension method is static but is called on an instance of an object.

The `Shuffle` function re-orders the elements in the list in a random manner. There are many resources written on the subject of random sorting, but for our purposes, this basic algorithm is all we need.

> **Important Note**
> Extensions are part of the C# language and are not specific to Unity.

With the script complete, we can add it to our scene:

1. Back in the Unity Editor, create a new GameObject called `Object Spawner` and attach the `ObjectSpawner` script.

2. Assign the previously created prefabs to the **Food Prefab** and **Rock Prefab** fields in the **Inspector**:

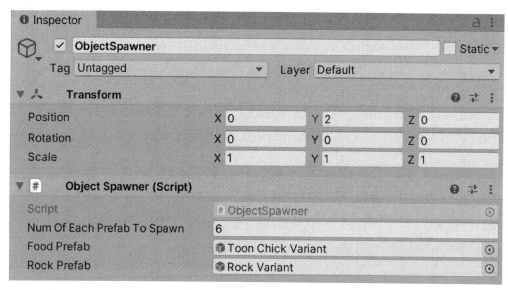

Figure 10.14 – Assigning prefabs to the Object Spawner component

3. Create several empty objects and position them around the level, as shown in *Figure 10.15*. Make sure they are child objects of ObjectSpawner:

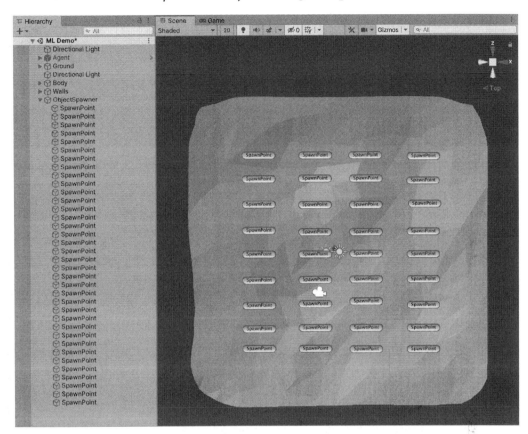

Figure 10.15 – Possible spawn locations

The ObjectSpawner script stores a list of **Transform** components. This list is populated by iterating over every child object of the ObjectSpawner parent object and storing their Transform components. Specifying every possible spawn location using GameObjects instead of spawning them at a random position provides greater control over where the objects can spawn, at the cost of the additional time required to create the spawn locations.

> **Tip**
> I've enabled the **Icon** option for the spawn points to make them visible to aid in positioning them in the environment. Instructions on how to do this can be found in *Chapter 6, Continuing the 2D Adventure*.

Having functionality to spawn objects continuously is vital for our learning Agent. The Agent will move around the environment and occasionally collide with the rocks and food we've spawned in the environment. These collisions will be random at first, but over time, as the Agent learns, they will move purposefully toward the chicks and avoid the rocks. When they do collide, the chick or rock object will be destroyed, and using the spawning functionality we wrote in this section, a new object of the same type will be added to the simulation. This consistent environment will help us control the learning process. However, we still want it to be dynamic, which is why we spawn the objects at (semi) random locations to ensure that the Agent is learning to avoid the objects and not, for example, specific parts of the map. Anyway, we're getting ahead of ourselves. We still are yet to create the learning Agent, so let's do that now.

Creating the Agent

The monster will be a learning Agent. Over time, it will get better at moving around the environment, avoiding rocks, and seeking out food. We've laid the groundwork to make this possible. It is now time to create and configure the Agent. Creating a learning Agent involves three steps:

- **Configure behavior parameters**: These parameters define what the output of the neural network will look like, among other things.

- **Configure the input into the neural network**: This is a crucial step. The input of the network can make a huge difference in how quickly our Agent will learn, and even what our Agent will learn.

- **Write a script that will handle the output of the neural network**: This step converts the output from the network into the Agent's movement.

We'll start by configuring the behavior parameters as the other two steps require this.

Configuring the Agent's behavior

Every learning Agent requires a **Behavior Parameters** component. This component defines, among other things, the size of the input and output of the learning algorithm.

We'll add one to the `Agent` object:

1. Select the `Agent` object in the **Hierarchy**.

2. Add the **Behavior Parameters** script, which is provided with the ML-Agents package. This script provides an interface to configure the neural network and to use a previously trained model (more on that later in the chapter).

3. In the **Inspector**, set **Behavior Name** to `Monster`. This will be the name of the generated Agent model. More on this in the *Training the Agent* section.

4. Under the **Vector Observation** heading, set **Space Size** to 0. The vector observation space is a collection of floating-point numbers that tell the Agent everything it needs to know about the world to make a decision. We've set this to 0 because we won't be providing any data manually. We will shortly be adding a perception component that automatically provides the data it gathers to the neural network.

5. Under the **Vector Action** heading, set **Space Type** to **Discrete** (if not set already), **Branches Size** to 2, **Branch 0 Size** to 3, and **Branch 1 Size** to 3. The vector action space is the output of the learning algorithm. We'll use this output to move the Agent around the environment. There are two types: **Discrete** and **Continuous**. **Discrete** (the one we've selected) will return an array of integers. **Branches Size** defines the number of values it returns, and the individual branch sizes define the range of the integers. For example, our learning algorithm will return two values (**Branch Size** of 2), and both values will have three possible values in the range of 0 to 2 (as we set **Branch 0 Size** and **Branch 1 Size** to 3). **Continuous** returns an array of floating-point numbers.

6. Ensure that **Use Child Sensors** is enabled. When enabled, the Agent will use any attached sensor components, which is exactly what we need, as you'll see shortly.

These settings are shown in *Figure 10.16*:

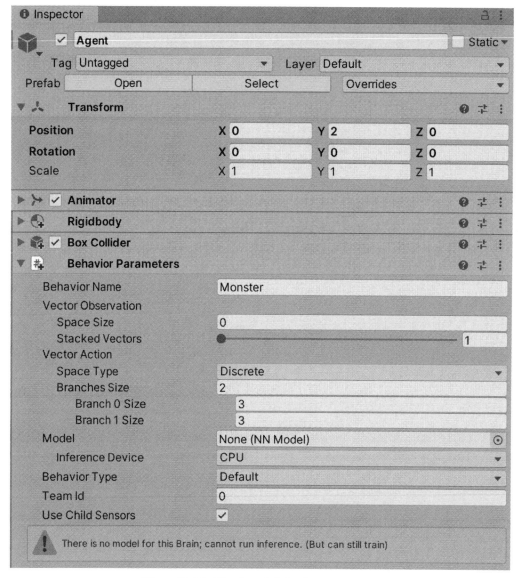

Figure 10.16 – The Agent's behavior parameters

You may have noticed the warning at the bottom of the component, stating that we cannot run inference as there is no model, but we can still train. This warning is alluding to the fact that we have not provided a model (as you can see in *Figure 10.16*, the **Model** field is set to **None**), so we will be unable to run inference. Inference is where our Agent can "infer" things about the environment using data from a pre-trained model. As we don't yet have a pre-trained model, this can be safely ignored. Later, in the *Embedding the model* section, we'll step through how to run inference.

> **Important Note**
> Unity uses a cross-platform inference library, which they have codenamed Barracuda. More information on this library can be found at `https://docs.unity3d.com/Packages/com.unity.barracuda@0.7/manual/index.html`.

The behavior type can be changed using the **Behavior Type** field. There are three choices: **Default**, **Heuristic Only**, and **Inference Only**. **Default** (which is what we've selected) will train the Agent if we connect the Python trainer or will attempt to perform inference using a pre-trained model. The **Heuristic** option will cause the Agent to use a heuristic function, which is beyond the scope of this chapter. The **Inference Only** option means the Agent will only ever perform inference use a pre-trained model. This last option would be the one to select when we want to release a game using a model that we've previously trained, and we no longer want that model to evolve.

As was alluded to earlier, the **Use Child Sensors** option is important. At the moment, by setting the observation space to 0, we have told the learning algorithm that we won't provide any input. However, without input, our Agent won't be able to make choices based on its environment. For example, it won't know that there's a chick within reach or that it's about to collide with a rock. ML-Agents provides several special sensor components that will automatically provide data on an Agent's environment. We'll configure one of those sensors next.

Defining the network's input

Defining the correct input into our Agent's neural network is crucial if we want the monster to learn from its environment. For example, we shouldn't expect the monster to evolve chick-seeking behavior if it is never told where the chicks are. We know that we want the Agent to avoid walls and rocks while eating chicks. Therefore, at a minimum, we need to tell the Agent's neural network where these objects are in relation to our Agent. To do this, we'll use a component provided with the ML-Agents package:

1. Add the `Ray Perception Sensor 3D` component to the `Agent` object. This component will use **raycasts** to observe the environment:

> **Important Note**
>
> More information on raycasts can be found in *Chapter 8, Continuing with Intelligent Enemies*.

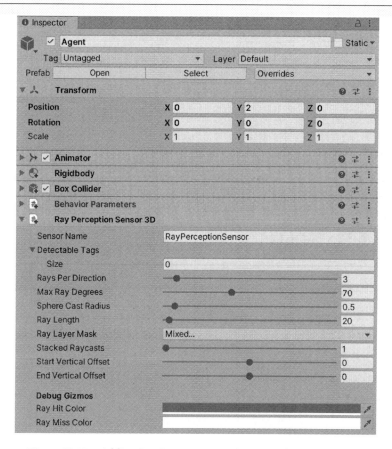

Figure 10.17 – Adding Ray Perception Sensor 3D to the Agent object

2. Set **Detectable Tags Size** to 3 and the **Rock, Chick,** and **Wall** tags as elements **0, 1,** and **2,** respectively, as shown in *Figure 10.18*:

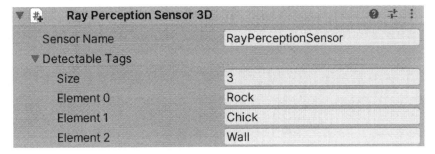

Figure 10.18 – Setting detectable tags

These tags define the objects we want to observe. Any objects with tags not on this list will be ignored.

3. Set **Rays Per Direction** to 8 and **Ray Length** to 15. Be warned that **Ray Per Direction** is not the maximum number of rays. In fact, setting 8 here will result in a total of 17 rays being cast: 8 on the left, 8 on the right, and 1 center ray.

4. Set **Start Vertical Offset** and **End Vertical Offset** to 0.5.

These settings add a vertical offset to the start and end position of the ray. By setting 0.5 here, we have raised the rays to around the monster's mouth level, as shown in *Figure 10.19*, so they collide with any objects that are on a slight hill:

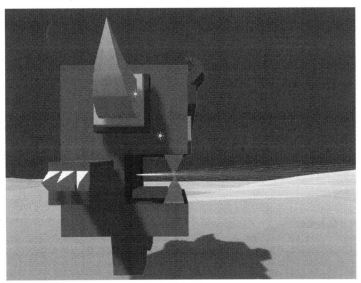

Figure 10.19 – The monster's raycasts

These settings are shown in *Figure 10.20*:

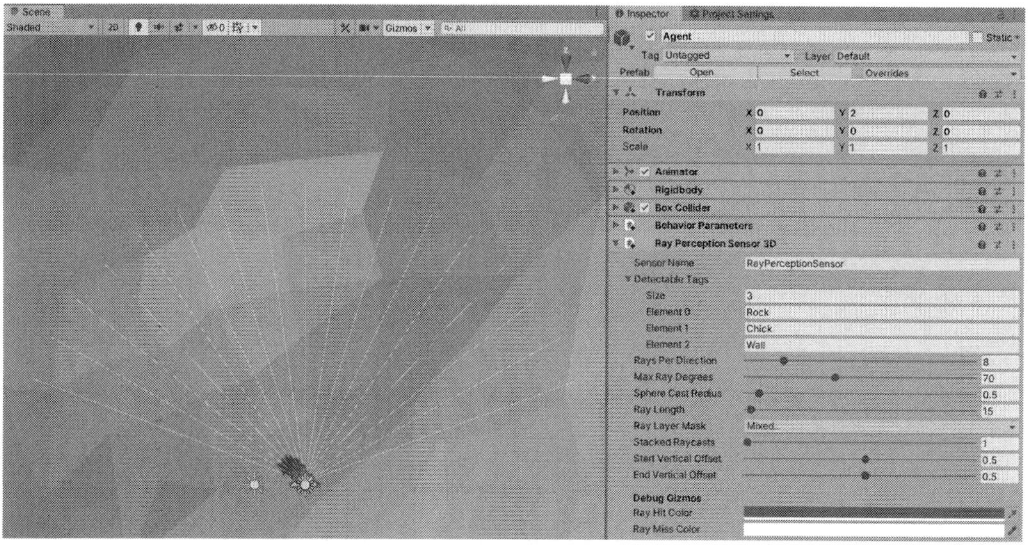

Figure 10.20 – The Ray Perception Sensor 3D settings

The learning algorithm will be informed if any of the rays hit an object and what the object type is. This information will be numerical only. For example, in our level, the Agent has 17 rays, and we're interested in 3 tags. The input into the neural network will consist of an array of 17 numbers. Each number will have a range of 4, where one number represents no object hit, and the other three will represent an object with a specific tag hit.

Now that we've configured the behavior parameters and the input component, it's time to bring it all together and write the script that will respond to the output from the neural network and assign rewards based on the monster's behavior in that step.

Writing the Agent script

Every learning Agent requires an `Agent` script. This script will receive the output from the neural network and assign rewards for good behavior (positive reward) and bad behavior (negative reward). We'll add custom behavior by creating a script that inherits from `Agent`:

1. Create a new script called `MonsterAgent`:

```
using UnityEngine;
using Unity.MLAgents;


public class MonsterAgent : Agent
```

```
    {

    }
```

Inheriting from the Agent class provides many useful helper functions. It is required for every learning Agent (although you may be able to get away with using the Agent class directly for very simple examples).

2. Next, add the variables we need, as shown:

```
public class MonsterAgent : Agent
{
    public float MoveSpeed = 1.0f;
    public float TurnSpeed = 90.0f;
    public float MaxVelocity = 10.0f;

    private Rigidbody ThisRigidbody;
    private ObjectSpawner SceneObjectSpawner;

    void Awake()
    {
        ThisRigidbody = GetComponent<Rigidbody>();
        SceneObjectSpawner =
          FindObjectOfType<ObjectSpawner>();
    }
}
```

The following points summarize the code sample:

MoveSpeed, TurnSpeed, and MaxVelocity will be used shortly to move the Agent.

We store a reference to the Rigidbody component so that we can move the object based on the output from the neural network.

A reference to the ObjectSpawner class we wrote earlier in the chapter is stored so that we can reset the spawned items at the beginning of an episode.

3. The `Agent` class provides an `OnActionReceived` function that we need to override:

```
public class MonsterAgent : Agent
{

    ...

    public override void OnActionReceived(float[]
     VectorAction)
    {
        var MovementAction = (int)VectorAction[0];
        var RotationAction = (int)VectorAction[1];

        var MovementDir = Vector3.zero;
        if (MovementAction == 1)
        {
            MovementDir = transform.forward;
        }
        else if (MovementAction == 2)
        {
            MovementDir = -transform.forward;
        }

        var RotationDir = Vector3.zero;
        if (RotationAction == 1)
        {
            RotationDir = -transform.up;
        }
        else if (RotationAction == 2)
        {
            RotationDir = transform.up;
        }

        ApplyMovement(MovementDir, RotationDir);
    }
}
```

The following points summarize the code sample:

`OnActionReceived` is called every time the Agent receives an action. The contents of `VectorAction` differ depending on whether the vector action space is **Continuous** or **Discrete**. In the *Defining the network's input* section, we defined our vector action space to be **Discrete**, have a size of 2, and each index to have a maximum value of 2.

We define the first index of the action space as MovementAction and the second index as RotationAction. This selection is entirely arbitrary. We could swap them around if we want, and the learning algorithm will adapt.

The values of MovementAction and RotationAction can be 0, 1, or 2 (as defined on the **Behavior Parameters** component). Consequently, we have three possible actions we can perform for both movement and rotation.

If MovementAction equals 1, we apply a forward force, moving the character forward. If MovementAction is 2, we add a backward force. If MovementAction is 0, no movement force is applied to the character.

It's a similar situation for RotationAction. When it is equal to 1, the character is rotated left, and if it is equal to 2, the character is rotated right. If RotationAction equals 0, no rotation is applied to this step.

4. To apply the movement and rotational force, add an ApplyMovement function:

```
public class MonsterAgent : Agent
{
    ...

    private void ApplyMovement(Vector3 MovementDir,
        Vector3 RotationDir)
    {
        ThisRigidbody.AddForce(MovementDir * MoveSpeed,
            ForceMode.VelocityChange);
        transform.Rotate(RotationDir, Time.
            fixedDeltaTime * TurnSpeed);

        if (ThisRigidbody.velocity.sqrMagnitude >
            MaxVelocity)
        {
            ThisRigidbody.velocity *= 0.95f;
        }
    }
```

There's nothing new in this function. We use the provided MovementDir and RotationDir options to move and rotate the Agent. The maximum velocity of the Agent is clamped if it is greater than MaxVelocity.

> **Important Note**
>
> One thing worth noting is that the ML algorithm updates in time with
> **FixedUpdate**, rather than **Update**, so any movement we apply using the
> `OnActionReceived` function should use `fixedDeltaTime`.

5. The training process is split into a number of episodes. Each episode ends when a
    specific condition is met, or a maximum number of simulation steps is reached. A
    simulation step is one pass through the learning algorithm. At the beginning of an
    episode, we want to reset the state of the simulation. Lucky for us, this is achieved
    easily by implementing the `OnEpisodeBegin()` function:

```
public class MonsterAgent : Agent
{
    ...
    public override void OnEpisodeBegin()
    {
        SceneObjectSpawner.Reset();
        ThisRigidbody.velocity = Vector3.zero;
        transform.position = new Vector3(0, 2, 0);
        transform.rotation = Quaternion.Euler(Vector3.
          zero);
    }
}
```

At the start of each episode, the `OnEpisodeBegin` function is invoked. We
use this function to reset the environment back to its initial state so that the
learning can begin anew. To reset the state, we call the `Reset` function on the
`ObjectSpawner` class, which destroys and re-adds the pre-determined number
of chick and rock objects. We also stop the Agent's movement and reset its position
and rotation. This function will be called automatically as we train our Agent.

The `MonsterAgent` script is almost complete. We've written the functionality
to interpret the output of the learning Agent; we move the Agent based on that
interpretation and reset the environment at the beginning of each episode. The
last piece of functionality we need is to assign a reward. You may remember, from
the *Introducing ML-Agents* section earlier in the chapter, that assigning a reward
informs the learning algorithm when the Agent has done something we approve
of, or if it is doing something we would rather it didn't. In our simulation, we
will assign a positive reward for colliding with a chick, and a negative reward for
colliding with rocks and walls.

6. Add an `OnCollisionEnter` function to the `MonsterAgent` script:

```
public class MonsterAgent : Agent
{
    ...
    void OnCollisionEnter(Collision OtherCollision)
    {
        if (OtherCollision.gameObject.
         CompareTag("chick"))
        {
            Destroy(OtherCollision.gameObject);
            SceneObjectSpawner.SpawnFood();
            AddReward(2f);
        }
        else if (OtherCollision.gameObject.
         CompareTag("Rock"))
        {
            Destroy(OtherCollision.gameObject);
            SceneObjectSpawner.SpawnRock();
            AddReward(-1f);
        }
        else if (OtherCollision.gameObject.
         CompareTag("Wall"))
        {
            AddReward(-1f);
        }
    }
}
```

The `OnCollisionEnter` function handles collisions with three objects: the chick, rock, and wall. Based on which object it collides with, it will add a positive or negative reward. The reward is a signal that the Agent has done something right (positive number) or something wrong (negative number). The size of the reward can be changed to create drastically different behaviors. For our Agent, we want to ensure that they seek out the chick objects, so we assign a reward value of 2 for every collision. The reward system can be difficult to get right, especially with complex simulations, and often requires trial and error.

As well as assigning rewards, when the Agent collides with a chick or rock object, it removes them from the simulation by calling the `Destroy` function and also requests that a replacement object is spawned in the scene using the `ObjectSpawner` class. By always replacing what we remove from the simulation, we ensure that there is a consistent number of good and bad objects in the scene.

7. Add our newly created script to the `Agent` object.

> **Important Note**
>
> You may have noticed in the **Inspector** that there is a **MaxStep** field associated with the **Monster Agent** component that we did not write. This field is provided by the `Agent` class and inherited by the `MonsterAgent` class.

8. Set **Max Step** to `5000`. This variable controls the maximum number of simulation steps that can occur before the Agent's episode ends. Once this step count is reached, if no other action has ended the episode, the episode will end, and a new one will begin (which will lead to the `OnEpisodeBegin` function that we wrote earlier being called).

9. Add the **Decision Requester** script to the `Agent` object, as shown in *Figure 10.21*:

Figure 10.21 – Adding a Decision Requester component

As discussed in the *Introducing ML-Agents* section, the learning algorithm works on a cycle with the following steps:

- **Observation**: Our monster records observations of its environment using the **Ray Sensor** component.

- **Decision**: Based on the observations, a decision is made and translated into the action vector. This data is captured in the `OnActionReceived` function in `MonsterAgentScript`.

- **Action**: We translate the decision into an action. In the case of our monster, this action involves moving and rotating.

- **Reward**: Based on the action, we may assign a reward. If the action results in the monster colliding with a chick object, we assign a positive reward.

The **Decision Requester** component performs the second stage for us. It requests a decision to be made at regular intervals. If we did not use this component, we would have to call the `Agent.RequestDecision` function manually.

Wow, we've covered a lot in this section. Give yourself a pat on the back for making it this far! You've successfully created an Agent that is capable of learning. You've defined the input into the neural network using a **Ray Perception Sensor** component. Using this component, the Agent will be able to observe its environment using several raycasts. We've also defined the output of the neural network and wrote the functionality that responds to that output. By applying either a movement or rotational force, the Agent will move around the environment, colliding with objects. With the input and output defined, we then moved on to rewarding the monster for good behavior (and telling it off for bad behavior). By assigning a reward value whenever the monster collides with an object, our training algorithm can calculate how well the monster is doing. You've now created everything the monster needs to start learning.

So far, there hasn't been much action up to this point. There has been a fair amount of setup, and that's important in a project like this. But the good news is, it's time to take our little monster for a spin. We'll use everything we've created up to this point (the environment, the spawning functionality, and the learning agent) and bring it all together to train the Agent.

Training the Agent

The chapter has been building up to this point. You will shortly be able to see your work up to now translate into something tangible—a pre-trained model that can be reused in any of your projects. We've created a suitable environment, populated it with a never-ending supply of opportunities for the monster to do right or wrong (by colliding with the chick or rock, respectively), and configured the learning algorithm's input and how we respond to its output. Now it is time to run the learning process, and this is where the Python packages we installed in the *Installing ML-Agents* section come in handy (well, *essential* really; without them, the monster won't be learning anything!). However, before we can run the learning command, we need to create a settings file. This file will store all the settings related to training the Agent and can have a small effect on how our monster learns:

1. In your file browser of choice, create a folder called `config` in the `projects` root folder.

2. Inside that folder, create a new file called `monster_config.yaml`:

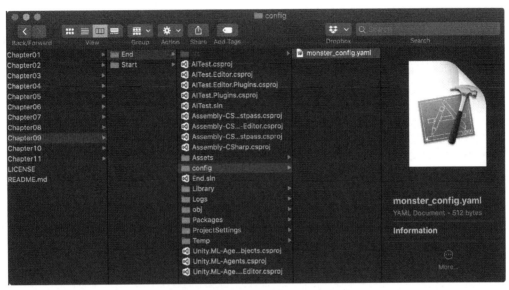

Figure 10.22 – Creating the settings file

3. Open the file in your text editor of choice and add these settings:

```yaml
default:
    trainer: ppo
    batch_size: 512
    beta: 5.0e-3
    buffer_size: 10240
    epsilon: 0.2
    hidden_units: 128
    lambd: 0.95
    learning_rate: 3.0e-4
    learning_rate_schedule: linear
    max_steps: 2.0e6
    memory_size: 128
    normalize: false
    num_epoch: 3
    num_layers: 2
    time_horizon: 64
    sequence_length: 64
    summary_freq: 10000
```

```
use_recurrent: false
vis_encode_type: simple
reward_signals:
  extrinsic:
    strength: 1.0
    gamma: 0.99
```

These settings can be quite technical in nature and are beyond the scope of this book. If you are interested in knowing what each setting is, you can find more information at `https://github.com/Unity-Technologies/ml-agents/blob/master/docs/Training-Configuration-File.md`.

> **Tip**
>
> If you would prefer not to type and add the settings manually, you can find the complete settings file in the `Chapter10/End/config` folder.

4. Save and close the file.

Now that we have the settings file, we can start training our Agent:

1. Open the **command prompt**.

2. Navigate to the `project` folder. The command for this will differ depending on the location of the project on your drive. For me, the command would be as follows:

```
cd projects/Unity-2020-By-Example/Chapter10/End
```

3. Run the command mlagents-learn config/monster_config.yaml --run-id=Monster:

```
mlagents-learn config/monster_config.yaml --run-id=Monster
```

`mlagents-learn` is the command being executed. We pass it the location of the settings file and also `run-id`. `run-id` should be unique for each type of Agent. If we wanted to train an Agent with a different type of behavior, we would pass a different `run-id` here.

When you run the command, you should receive output similar to what is shown in *Figure 10.23*:

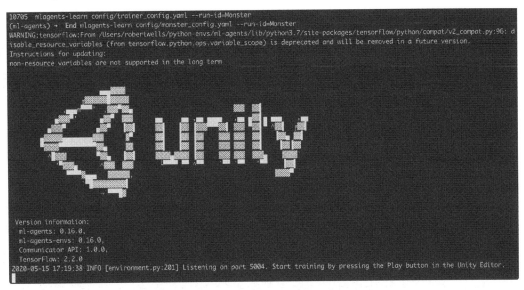

Figure 10.23 – Running the mlagents-learn Python command

4. Follow the instructions provided and press the Play button in the Unity Editor.

> **Tip**
> If you want more information on what type of parameters `mlagents-learn` accepts, you can run the `mlagents-learn –help` command.

Once the game starts, the Agent will run around the environment. And I really mean *run*, as the Agent will move much quicker than it usually would. The speed increase is normal and decreases the time required for the Agent to learn. When we embed the model and are no longer running training, the Agent will move at a more reasonable speed.

As the monster moves around the environment, the rays it casts will turn from white to red, as shown in the following screenshot. A red ray signifies that it has hit an object with a tag that we are interested in, and a white ray means no object was hit:

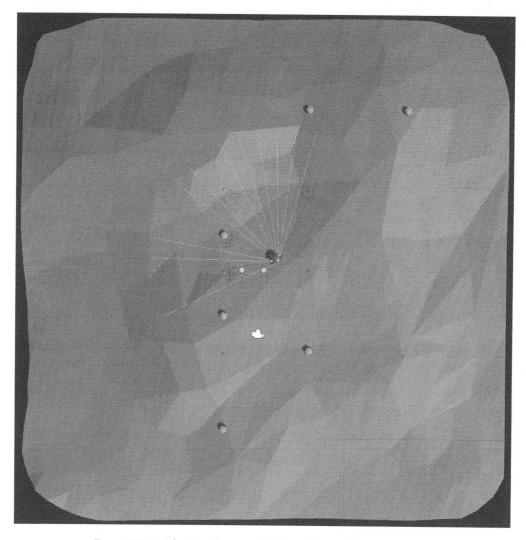

Figure 10.24 – The Agent's raycast hitting objects in the environment

The training has now begun. Leave this running for a while and observe the output in the command prompt:

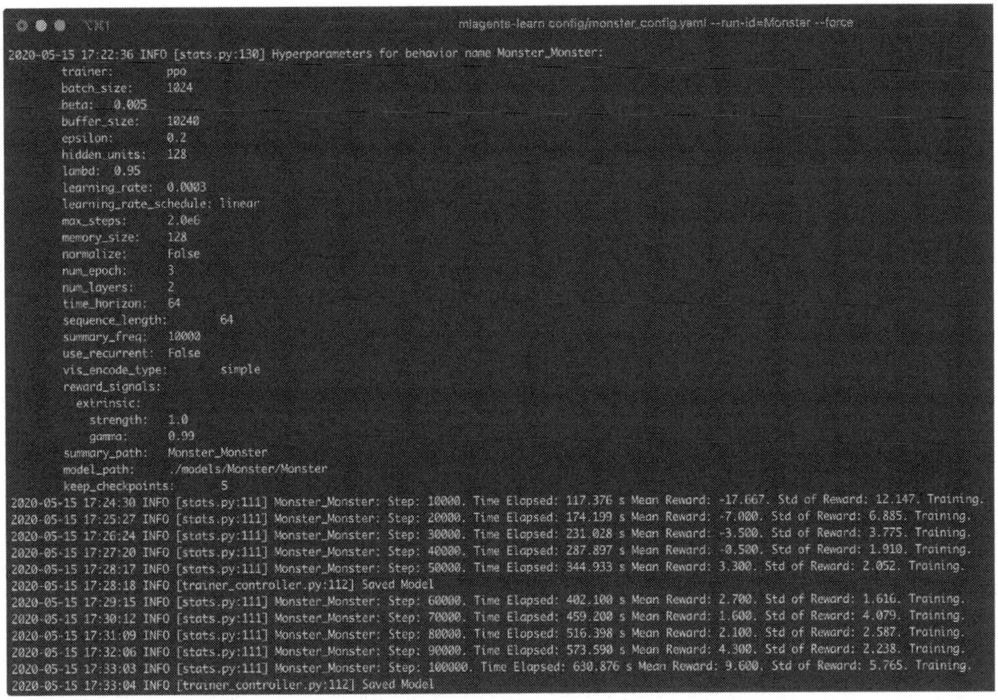

```
mlagents-learn config/monster_config.yaml --run-id=Monster --force
2020-05-15 17:22:36 INFO [stats.py:130] Hyperparameters for behavior name Monster_Monster:
        trainer:        ppo
        batch_size:     1024
        beta:   0.005
        buffer_size:    10240
        epsilon:        0.2
        hidden_units:   128
        lambd:  0.95
        learning_rate:  0.0003
        learning_rate_schedule: linear
        max_steps:      2.0e6
        memory_size:    128
        normalize:      False
        num_epoch:      3
        num_layers:     2
        time_horizon:   64
        sequence_length:        64
        summary_freq:   10000
        use_recurrent:  False
        vis_encode_type:        simple
        reward_signals:
          extrinsic:
            strength:   1.0
            gamma:      0.99
        summary_path:   Monster_Monster
        model_path:     ./models/Monster/Monster
        keep_checkpoints:       5
2020-05-15 17:24:30 INFO [stats.py:111] Monster_Monster: Step: 10000. Time Elapsed: 117.376 s Mean Reward: -17.667. Std of Reward: 12.147. Training.
2020-05-15 17:25:27 INFO [stats.py:111] Monster_Monster: Step: 20000. Time Elapsed: 174.199 s Mean Reward: -7.000. Std of Reward: 6.885. Training.
2020-05-15 17:26:24 INFO [stats.py:111] Monster_Monster: Step: 30000. Time Elapsed: 231.028 s Mean Reward: -3.500. Std of Reward: 3.775. Training.
2020-05-15 17:27:20 INFO [stats.py:111] Monster_Monster: Step: 40000. Time Elapsed: 287.897 s Mean Reward: -0.500. Std of Reward: 1.910. Training.
2020-05-15 17:28:17 INFO [stats.py:111] Monster_Monster: Step: 50000. Time Elapsed: 344.933 s Mean Reward: 3.300. Std of Reward: 2.052. Training.
2020-05-15 17:28:18 INFO [trainer_controller.py:112] Saved Model
2020-05-15 17:29:15 INFO [stats.py:111] Monster_Monster: Step: 60000. Time Elapsed: 402.100 s Mean Reward: 2.700. Std of Reward: 1.616. Training.
2020-05-15 17:30:12 INFO [stats.py:111] Monster_Monster: Step: 70000. Time Elapsed: 459.200 s Mean Reward: 1.600. Std of Reward: 4.079. Training.
2020-05-15 17:31:09 INFO [stats.py:111] Monster_Monster: Step: 80000. Time Elapsed: 516.398 s Mean Reward: 2.100. Std of Reward: 2.587. Training.
2020-05-15 17:32:06 INFO [stats.py:111] Monster_Monster: Step: 90000. Time Elapsed: 573.590 s Mean Reward: 4.300. Std of Reward: 2.238. Training.
2020-05-15 17:33:03 INFO [stats.py:111] Monster_Monster: Step: 100000. Time Elapsed: 630.876 s Mean Reward: 9.600. Std of Reward: 5.765. Training.
2020-05-15 17:33:04 INFO [trainer_controller.py:112] Saved Model
```

Figure 10.25 – Output showing the training progress

After every 10,000 steps, a summary is printed. As part of the summary, you get the **Step** count, the total time elapsed in seconds, the mean reward, and the standard deviation (**Std**) of the reward. As the training progresses, you want to make sure that the mean reward is trending upward. There may be an occasional dip between summaries, but a mean reward that is increasing over time shows that your Agent is learning. For example, in *Figure 10.25*, you can see that the monster starts with a mean reward of **-17.667**. A negative number tells us that the monster has performed more negative actions (colliding with a wall or rock) than positive actions (colliding with the chicks). You will notice that this number increases relatively quickly to reach **9.6**; the monster now performs more positive than negative actions. Our little guy is learning!

> **Tip**
> The summary frequency can be configured in the `monster_config.yaml` file by altering the `summary_freq` field.

Every 50,000 steps, you'll see the output **Saved Model**. This file is the model the monster will use to run inference in the following *Embedding the Model* section.

5. After sufficient time has passed, stop the game from running by once again pressing the Play button.

   I find that around 1 hour is enough time to provide good results (a mean reward of nearly 100). When you do this, you'll see the following output in your command console:

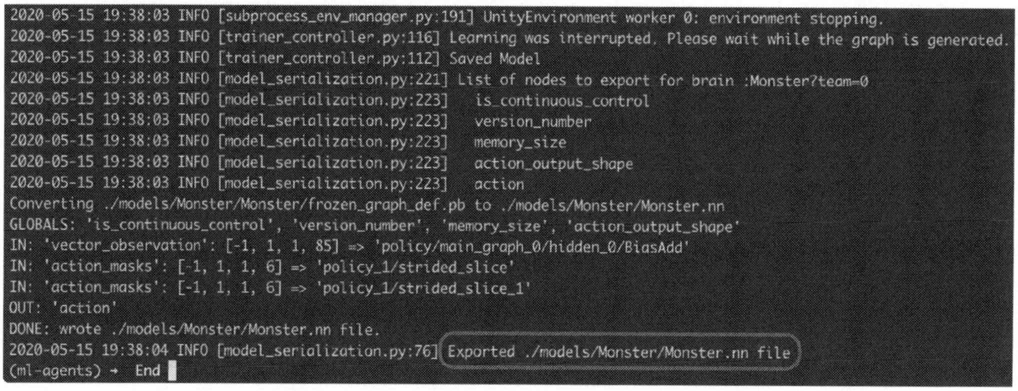

```
2020-05-15 19:38:03 INFO [subprocess_env_manager.py:191] UnityEnvironment worker 0: environment stopping.
2020-05-15 19:38:03 INFO [trainer_controller.py:116] Learning was interrupted. Please wait while the graph is generated.
2020-05-15 19:38:03 INFO [trainer_controller.py:112] Saved Model
2020-05-15 19:38:03 INFO [model_serialization.py:221] List of nodes to export for brain :Monster?team=0
2020-05-15 19:38:03 INFO [model_serialization.py:223]    is_continuous_control
2020-05-15 19:38:03 INFO [model_serialization.py:223]    version_number
2020-05-15 19:38:03 INFO [model_serialization.py:223]    memory_size
2020-05-15 19:38:03 INFO [model_serialization.py:223]    action_output_shape
2020-05-15 19:38:03 INFO [model_serialization.py:223]    action
Converting ./models/Monster/Monster/frozen_graph_def.pb to ./models/Monster/Monster.nn
GLOBALS: 'is_continuous_control', 'version_number', 'memory_size', 'action_output_shape'
IN: 'vector_observation': [-1, 1, 1, 85] => 'policy/main_graph_0/hidden_0/BiasAdd'
IN: 'action_masks': [-1, 1, 1, 6] => 'policy_1/strided_slice'
IN: 'action_masks': [-1, 1, 1, 6] => 'policy_1/strided_slice_1'
OUT: 'action'
DONE: wrote ./models/Monster/Monster.nn file.
2020-05-15 19:38:04 INFO [model_serialization.py:76] Exported ./models/Monster/Monster.nn file
(ml-agents) ➜  End
```

Figure 10.26 – The path to the trained model file

The path shown in the output is the path to the model file that represents the trained neural network for our monster. In the next section, we'll take advantage of the trained model. By embedding it in our Agent, we can take advantage of the trained network and have a functional AI that performs its role admirably without the need for hardcoding any behavior.

Embedding the model

In the last section, the neural network controlling the monster evolved to get better at navigating the environment and eating food. When we stopped the training, a .nn file was created. This file represents the trained neural network for the monster. We do not need to re-train the Agent; we can instead use this model to achieve the behavior we expect. We could even provide this model to any number of Agents (as long as they have the same configuration as our monster), and these new Agents would happily move around the environment, avoiding walls and rocks while chasing chicks. But that's getting ahead of ourselves. Let's first use the model with the original monster:

Locate the Monster.nn model exported in the previous section. As you can see from *Figure 10.26*, the path to my model is located in the <project root>/models/Monster folder.

1. Drag this file into the **Project** panel in Unity to the Assets/Models folder (create the folder if it doesn't exist). Dragging the model into Unity imports it as an asset and creates a corresponding metafile. For more information on importing assets and metafiles, refer to *Chapter 1, Unity Fundamentals*:

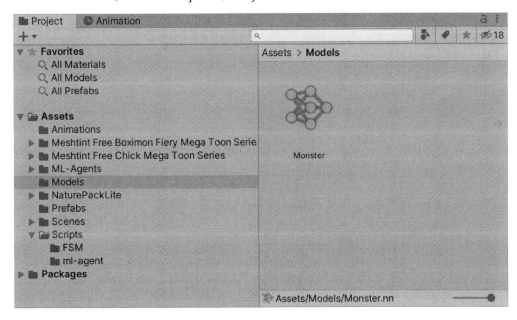

Figure 10.27 – Importing the trained model

2. Select **Agent** in the **Hierarchy**.

3. Drag the `Monster` model to the **Model** field on the **Behavior Parameters** field in the **Inspector**:

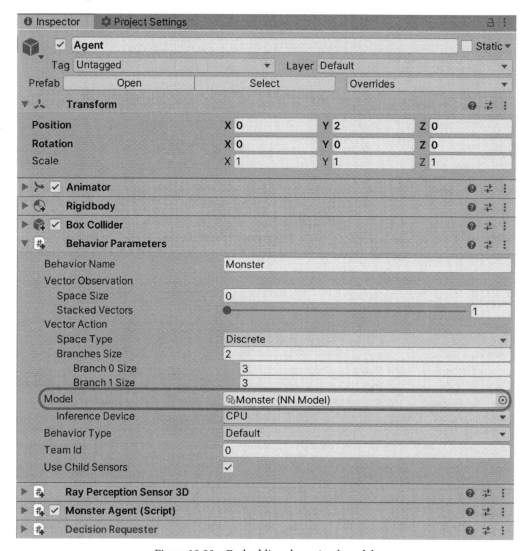

Figure 10.28 – Embedding the trained model

The model we trained has now been embedded. You'll notice that the warning shown in *Figure 10.16* is now gone. As we've selected the default behavior type, our Agent can now operate in two modes: the training mode, where we run the `mlagents-learn` command, or the inference mode, where it uses an already-trained model.

4. Press the Play button to test the model. The Agent will move around at a more suitable speed (the game is no longer sped up as we are not training the Agent). Using the neural network from the model, it will infer what action to take at any time. It will actively seek out the chicks and avoid the walls and rocks:

Figure 10.29 – The monster inferring behavior using the trained model

The Agent's ability at this point is down to how well the neural network has been trained.

> **Important Note**
>
> The monster is not being trained while running inference. If it is not performing adequately, you can redo the steps in the *Training the Agent* section.

And that's it! You've successfully trained an Agent and embedded that trained model so that it can be used by NPCs within your game. This model can be reused by any agent that has the same number of vector observations and actions. Feel free to play around with this. For example, what would happen if you duplicated the Monster object and assigned the same model to both of them? Or how about trying to introduce the monster to the FSM project completed in the previous chapter? Have the monster chase the chick, which in turn chases you. The opportunities are (almost) limitless.

Summary

By completing this chapter, you will have gained a good understanding of how to use the ML-Agents toolkit to create intelligent Agents to use in your games. We have created a monster that learns over time how to accomplish a task we set. The Agent will observe its environment using its ray sensors, and if it sees a chick, it will actively seek them out while avoiding any walls or rocks in its path. It does all of this without us ever having to write code that explicitly tells it what to do.

By adapting the input and rewards applied to the Agent, you can create drastically different AI. Want an Agent to race around a track instead? Add a reward for progressing around the track, while keeping the negative reward for hitting walls. How about making the monster shoots chicks instead of eating them? Give the little guy a gun and reward him for each projectile that hits its target. While I'm oversimplifying here – there will undoubtedly be a lot of tweaks and trial and error involved – hopefully, you can see the benefits of using ML-Agents in your own projects; and with Unity making ML so accessible to a wider audience, we will start to see even more novel uses in the future.

In this book, we have now seen two distinct methods of imbuing our game with AI characters: the FSM we started in *Chapter 7, Creating Artificial Intelligence* and ML-Agents. Both approaches have their pros and cons, and it is up to you to decide which (if any) approach is suitable for your project. In the next chapter, we will move away from AI and enter the world of **virtual reality** (**VR**). We'll look at how to set up VR, configuring input and creating a realistic environment complete with light probes.

Test your knowledge

Q1. The ML-Agents toolkit includes packages written in which language?

> A. Rust
>
> B. JavaScript
>
> C. Python
>
> D. Ruby

Q2. Each step of the learning algorithm goes through which cycle?

> A. Observation-decision-action-reward
>
> B. Decision-reward-action-observation
>
> C. Observation-action-reward-decision
>
> D. Action-observation-decision-reward

Q3. The command used to train an Agent is…

A. `ml-agents -learn`

B. `mlagents-learn`

C. `ML-Agents learn`

D. `mlagents_env-learn`

Q4. The name of the input vector into the ML algorithm is…

A. Vector Action

B. Observation List

C. Pre-Action Collection

D. Vector Observation

Q5. The name of the output from the ML algorithm is…

A. Vector Action

B. Post-Observation List

C. Vector Observation

D. Action List

Q6. The name of the function that is called at the beginning of each episode is…

A. `ResetState`

B. `OnEpisodeBegin`

C. `SimulationStepComplete`

D. `EpisodeBegin`

Q7. You can embed a generated model into a different Agent if…

A. The number of vector observations and actions are the same.

B. The name of the Agent is the same.

C. The agent has the same tag.

D. All of the above.

Further reading

The following resources include more information on the topics discussed in this chapter:

- `https://github.com/Unity-Technologies/ml-agents/blob/master/docs/Getting-Started.md`

- `https://github.com/Unity-Technologies/ml-agents/blob/master/docs/ML-Agents-Overview.md`

- `https://unity3d.com/how-to/unity-machine-learning-agents`

11
Entering Virtual Reality

In this chapter and the next, we'll create a first-person **Virtual Reality** (VR) game. The game will be targeted specifically at the *Oculus Rift S* hardware, and it's worth declaring this from the outset, as many other VR platforms exist as well. Although development methodologies do differ from device to device, the main principles of VR development within Unity are sufficiently similar that these chapters will still be helpful to any VR development on any of the hardware available today.

The lighting in a game can have a significant impact on the mood of the game. In previous chapters, we've briefly touched on how to configure basic lighting in a game. In this chapter, we'll take a deeper look into some of the techniques and tools game developers can use to create a visually appealing game.

As well as the lighting, we'll also add post-processing effects to enhance the visuals further. Post-processing effects are filters and adjustments applied to the pixels of the scene camera to stylize or improve the aesthetics of the rendered frame. By applying this knowledge in your own projects, you can create stunning-looking games with minimal effort.

Once we've looked at the lighting and post-processing effects, we'll move onto preparing the project for VR. This will involve installing the necessary packages. Luckily, as we'll soon discover, Unity provides a useful plugin management tool for this purpose.

We will build on many of the development techniques seen so far, as well as implementing new features specific to VR.

This chapter explores the following topics:

- Using **Spot Lights**, **Light Probes**, and **emissive** materials to create an atmospheric sci-fi level

- Creating your own Unity packages by exporting assets from previous projects

- Using the post-processing stack to enhance the look of each rendered frame

- Installing everything we need to get set up with VR

- Configuring VR input using touch controllers

Technical requirements

This chapter assumes that you have not only completed the projects from the previous chapters but also have a good, basic knowledge of C# scripting generally, though not necessarily in Unity.

The assets used in this project can be found in the book companion files in the `Chapter11/ Assets_To_Import` folder. The end project can be found in the `Chapter11/End` folder.

You will also require a VR device (we use the Oculus Rift S), and a computer that meets the minimum requirements for that device. The minimum requirements for Oculus devices can be found here: `https://support.oculus.com/248749509016567/`.

Preparing the project

In this game, the player will be a stationary character that can look around and shoot in any direction but cannot move around. The player will be standing in a sci-fi interior, and enemy bots will spawn into the level at random intervals. The bots will initially wander around searching for the player and, upon finding them, will run toward them, eventually attacking them. The player will be armed with plasma cannons on each hand and will have the ability to attack oncoming enemies to avoid being injured with the primary objective of seeing how long they can survive!

To create this project, we will begin by creating the core functionality for a standard first-person mode, and then migrate that to VR. To get started, do the following:

1. Create a new 3D project. See *Chapter 1, Exploring the Fundamentals of Unity*, for detailed instructions.

2. Drag the `Meshes` and `Textures` folders from the `Chapter11/Assets_To_Import` folder (included in the GitHub repo) to the **Project** panel. The `Meshes` folder includes two meshes. One mesh represents the complete sci-fi environment, and the other, a mesh for the enemy bot:

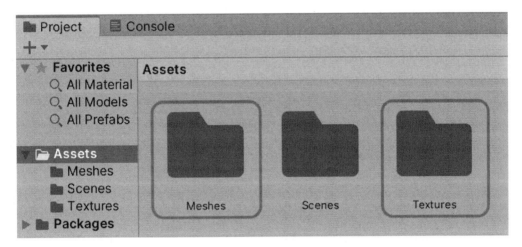

Figure 11.1 – Importing game assets

When working with different mesh assets, especially when reusing assets made by others, you'll often find they're made at different sizes and scales. To fix this, we can adjust the Scale Factor of each mesh.

3. Select the `Hallway` mesh asset from the **Project** panel.

4. In the **Inspector**, assign a new **Scale Factor** value of 2 on the **Model** tab.

5.   Click **Apply**:

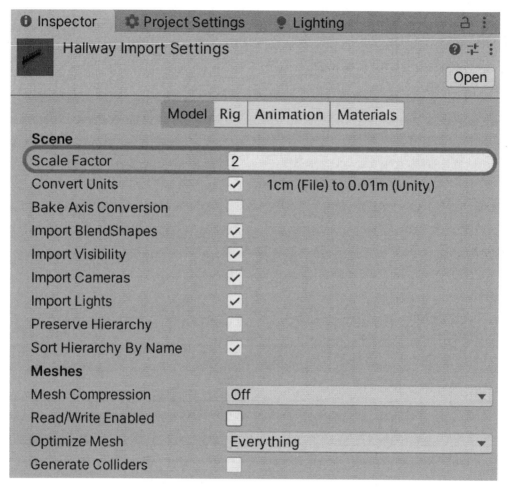

Figure 11.2 – Setting the Hallway mesh Scale Factor

Do the same for the other mesh.

6.   Select the **BlastBot** mesh asset in the **Project** panel.

7.   As the bot is slightly too big for our needs, we'll reduce the scale factor. In the **Inspector**, assign a new **Scale Factor** value of 0.4 on the **Model** tab.

8.   Click **Apply**:

Figure 11.3 – Setting the BlastBot mesh Scale Factor

With the meshes scaled correctly, we can construct the level for our game:

1.   Create a new scene.

2.   Drag the Hallway mesh from the **Project** panel to the **Scene** view.

3. Position the mesh at position 0, 0, 0. This will move the mesh's pivot point to that position:

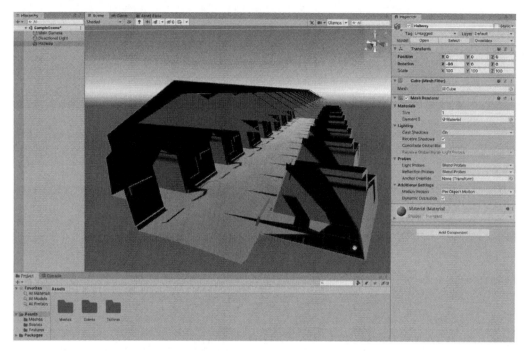

Figure 11.4 – Adding the Environment mesh to the scene

4. Mark the object as static by ticking the **Static** checkbox in the **Inspector**. By marking the object as static, we're informing Unity that this object will not move. Consequently, Unity can perform several optimizations. The one we're most interested in at the moment is the ability to **pre-bake** lighting. Unity will calculate the lighting effects and store them in a **lightmap**. This reduces the performance cost at runtime as the effect of illumination on static objects has already been calculated:

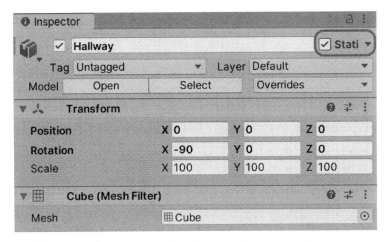

Figure 11.5 – Marking the environment as static

Now that the assets have been imported, we can improve the look and feel of the game drastically by spending some time configuring the lighting. For this reason, we'll create the lighting for the scene before we enable VR.

Creating scene lighting

Lighting is fundamental in creating a specific mood in your scene, and here we'll create an atmospheric, dystopian sci-fi interior. This kind of environment typically relies on high levels of contrast between lighting, contrasting dark colors with vibrant non-natural lighting colors, such as green, blue, and red.

In this section, we'll remove the lighting that Unity automatically adds to a new scene. We'll then add the base lighting, which, as the name suggests, will be the base of our lighting system, which we will then build on by adding **emissive** wall panels and **Light Probes**.

Removing existing lighting

When you create a new scene in Unity, it will automatically add two common objects for you: a **Camera** and a **Directional Light**. By adding these two objects, you are able to get up and running as quickly as possible. However, there are times when this default setup may need some tweaking, and this is one of those times. As we'll be creating our own lighting system, we can do away with the defaults provided by Unity:

1. Delete the **Directional Light** lighting object in the **Hierarchy** panel. This object is created by default in any new scene, but we don't need it.

2. Access the lighting window by selecting **Window | Rendering | Lighting** from the application menu:

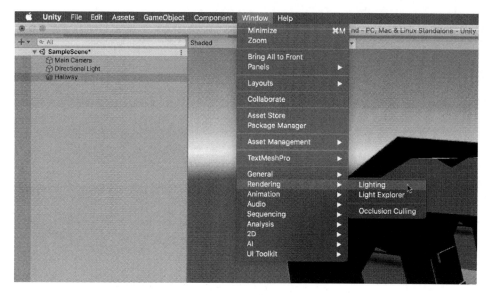

Figure 11.6 – Accessing the lighting settings

3. On the **Environment** tab, remove the daytime skybox from the **Skybox Material** field by choosing **None** via the texture selector:

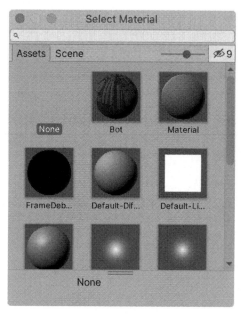

Figure 11.7 – Accessing the lighting settings

4. In the **Environment Lighting** group, set **Ambient Source** to **Color**.

5. Set **Ambient Color** to black. These settings remove all ambient lighting from the scene. This includes lighting that that pre-illuminates objects before scene lighting takes effect:

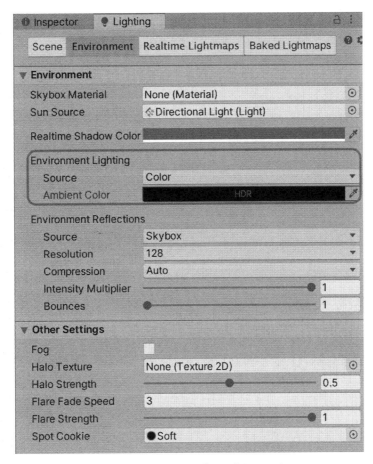

Figure 11.8 – Accessing the Lighting settings

Now with the Unity default lighting removed, we can configure our own custom lighting. By configuring lighting from the ground up and not relying on the default lighting setup, you'll gain a better understanding of how to implement lighting solutions in your own games. This information will prove valuable to ensure that your games have a distinctive look. This is arguably even more critical in a VR game, where the player enters the world like never before. We'll start our custom lighting setup with the base lighting. This lighting is the foundation on top of which our other lighting systems will provide an additive effect.

Adding base lighting

The base lighting should provide the player with the visibility they require to play the game comfortably. It should also help set the mood for the game, but we'll be adding extras such as emissive wall panels and Light Probes that will help with setting the mood. Let's start by adding a new light:

1. Choose **GameObject | Light | Spotlight** from the **Application** menu.

2. Position the newly created object close to the ceiling toward the front of the level, at position 41, 3.7, 0:

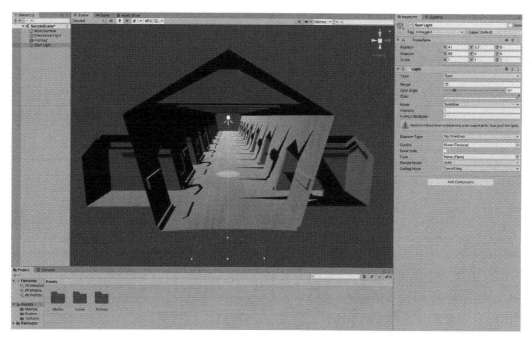

Figure 11.9 – Adding a Spotlight to the scene

3. Set **Color** to 199, 236, 199:

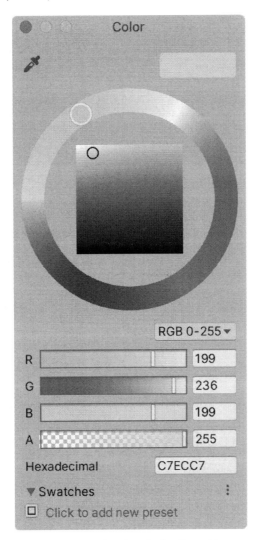

Figure 11.10 – Creating the level's ambience

4. Set **Spot Angle** to 120.

5. Set **Intensity** to 4.6:

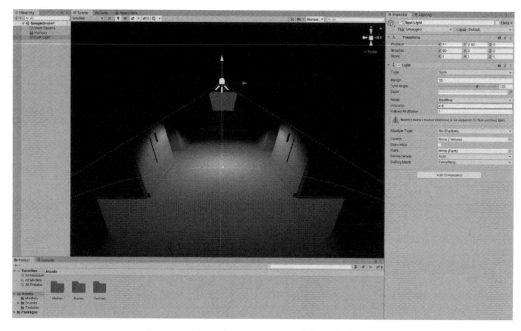

Figure 11.11 – Setting the scene's base lighting

6. Duplicate the corridor mesh itself and position it at -48, 0, 0 for a further stretch of the level. By duplicating the mesh, a significant area of the corridor will disappear into the darkness beyond the reach of the lighting:

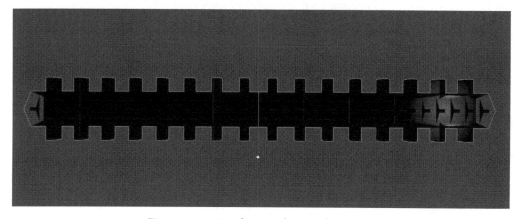

Figure 11.12 – Duplicating the corridor object

7. Duplicate the Spot Light object several times and position the duplicates along the length of the corridor.

Figure 11.13 – Duplicating scene lights

That's looking perfect so far – atmospheric but with enough visibility. For more of an atmospheric feel, we'll add wall panels that glow.

Creating emissive wall panels

Emissive lighting lets you use a material and its maps as a light source, which can be emitted from a mesh. We can add emissive lighting to wall panels in our level and they will glow, reinforcing our sci-fi theme. Start by creating a material:

1. From the **Project** Panel, right-click and choose **Create | Material** to create a new material asset:

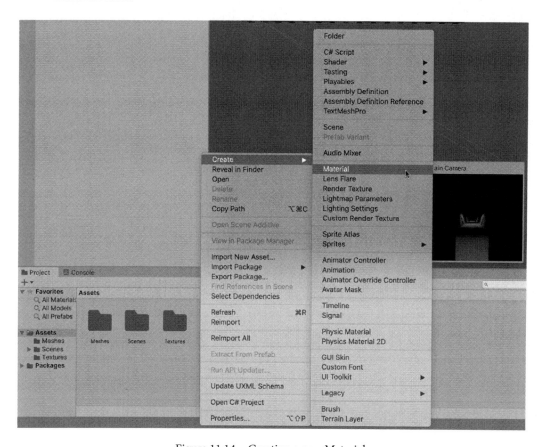

Figure 11.14 – Creating a new Material

2. Select the material and, in the **Inspector**, enable the **Emission** checkbox. Enabling **Emission** on this material means it will act as a source of light:

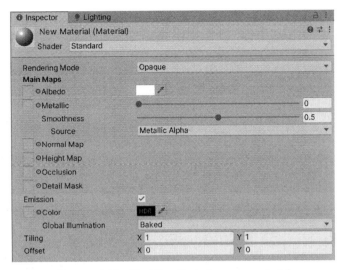

Figure 11.15 – Enabling Emission on a material

3. Click the **Emission** color swatch and, from the color selector, specify both a color
    and **Intensity** for the emission, as shown in *Figure 11.16*. This will be the color and
    intensity of the emissive light when assigned as a material to a mesh:

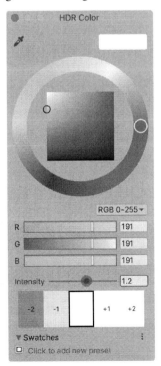

Figure 11.16 – Choosing the color emission for the material

Great! You've just created an emissive material. Now let's assign it to a mesh to illuminate the scene:

1. Create a **Quad** object by selecting **GameObject | 3D Object | Quad** from the **Application** menu.

2. Resize and position the newly spawned quad to fit inside any of the rectangular wall sockets in the environment, as shown in *Figure 11.17*:

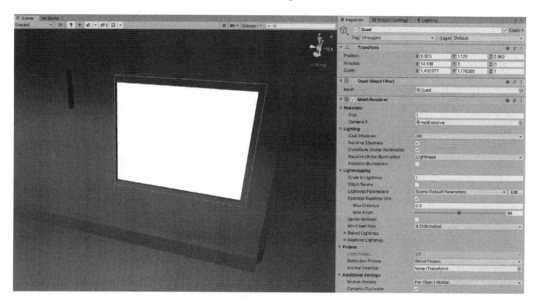

Figure 11.17 – Placing the quad in the level

3. Assign the emissive material by dragging it from the **Project** panel to **Element 0** of the **Materials** list in the **Inspector**, as shown in *Figure 11.17*.

4. Mark the quad as **Static** in the **Inspector**, and let the lighting rebuild to see the results.

> **Tip**
> If the lighting doesn't automatically rebuild, you can start the process manually by opening the lighting window (**Window | Rendering | Lighting**) and clicking on **Generate Lighting**.

5. Duplicate the quad several times, adding a duplicate into each vacant wall socket in the environment:

Figure 11.18 – Filling every recess in the corridor

6. Add a red-colored point light in each recessed alcove. The presence of an off-screen red light adds ambiance and an other-worldly feel:

Figure 11.19 – Adding red point lights

Very eerie! However, it may be a little bit dark for the player (depending on their preference). To fix this, and complete our lighting system, we'll add Light Probes to the scene.

Adding Light Probes

Light Probes are useful for adding indirect illumination to real-time (dynamic) objects, such as the player character and enemies. Light Probes refer to a connected network of empty-style objects. Each object (a node) records the average color and intensity of neighboring lights in the scene within a specified radius. These values are stored in each node and are blended onto moving objects:

1. Create a new **Light Probe Group** by choosing **GameObject | Light | Light Probe Group** from the Application menu:

Figure 11.20 – Creating a Light Probe Group

2. Move the Light Probe Group to the center of the scene, as shown in *Figure 11.21*. You will see a network of yellow spheres neatly arranged in a grid pattern. Each sphere represents a node (Probe) in the group, and it records the color and intensity of light in the surrounding areas:

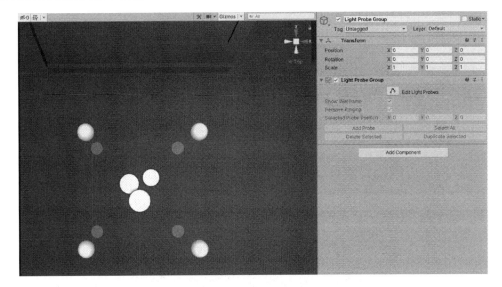

Figure 11.21 – Positioning the Light Probes

The idea is to add or duplicate more probes within the network, and to position them strategically around the level in areas where the light changes significantly, in either color or intensity, or both. The probe network should capture the distribution of light in the scene. To get started with this, do the following:

1. Select **Light Probe Group** in the **Hierarchy** panel.

2. On the **Light Probe Group** component in the **Inspector**, click the **Edit Light Probes** button. When activated, you can select, duplicate, and move around individual probes within the group:

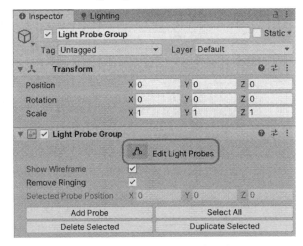

Figure 11.22 – Editing Probes within the group

3. Select a probe, click the **Duplicate Selected** button, and then move the duplicate to a new location in the scene, capturing the surrounding light.

4. Duplicate another and move that further along still.

5. Try keeping the probes regularly spaced, as shown in *Figure 11.23*:

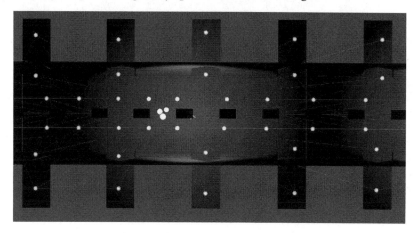

Figure 11.23 – Spacing Light Probes

Excellent, we've now completed the lighting for the environment: we've added spot and point lights, emissive lights, and Light Probes. These components are working to ensure objects are illuminated correctly. Things are looking good!

Figure 11.24 – Complete lighting

And that's it for lighting. We covered a lot in this section, including the following:

- How to remove the default scene lighting
- Using Spot Lights to add localized visibility, with some parts of the level being better illuminated than others
- Creating glowing wall panels using emissive lighting
- Adding indirect illumination using Light Probes

This is a solid foundation in Unity lighting that can be applied to any of your projects moving forward, not just VR.

With lighting complete, there's one last thing we should look at before adding VR support, and that is Unity's new post-processing stack. Becoming comfortable with implementing effects using the post-processing stack will help lend your game a unique visual appearance.

Introducing the post-processing stack

In this section, we'll add these post-processing camera effects to enhance the appeal of the scene. As mentioned in earlier chapters, post-processing effects are filters and adjustments applied to the pixels of the scene camera to stylize or improve the aesthetics of the rendered frame.

> **Important note**
> Unity 2018 and above ships with version 2 of the post-processing stack for adding volume-based post-processing effects to your project.

To use the post-processing stack, we need to perform the following steps:

1. Install the stack. We'll be using the Package Manager for this, and the process should hold few surprises at this point.
2. Create a post-processing volume. This volume will define the area in which we want the processing to occur.
3. Configure the camera by adding the required post-processing effects.
4. Enable the effects by linking the volume and the effects we added to the camera.

Unsurprisingly, we'll start by installing the post-processing stack, which provides the functionality we need to enhance our game's visuals.

Importing the post-processing stack

The post-processing stack is a Unity package that combines a set of effects into a single post-processing **pipeline**. There are numerous benefits to this, but one for you as a developer is that once you know how to apply one effect using this pipeline, you'll easily be able to add any of the other available effects.

To add the newest version of the post-processing stack, do the following:

1. Select **Window | Package Manager** from the Application menu.

2. From the **Packages** list, click **All** to filter the list and view all available or installed packages:

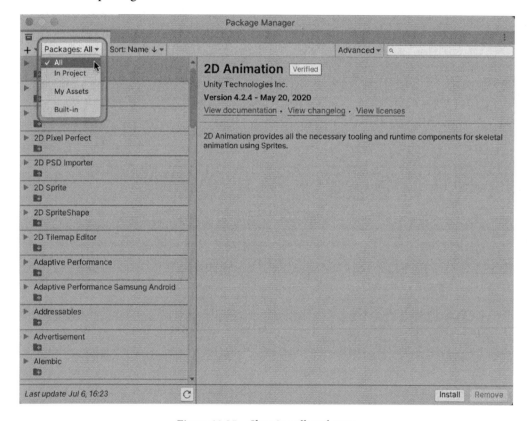

Figure 11.25 – Showing all packages

3. Select the **Post Processing** package.

4. Once selected, click the **Install** button to add the package to your project. If the package has already been added, you may have the option of updating to the latest version by clicking the **Update** button:

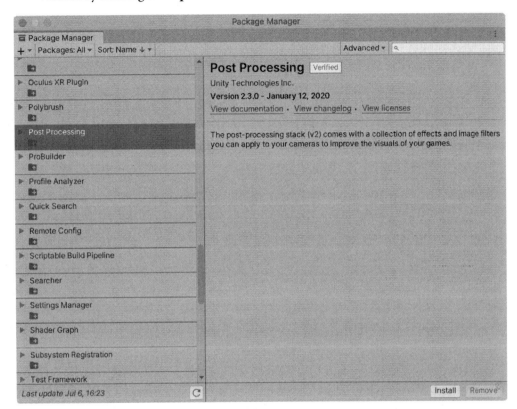

Figure 11.26 – Installing the Post Processing package

After installation, the complete post-processing functionality has been added to your project. This workflow depends on two main concepts or steps. First, we need to mark out volumes in the level that, when entered by the camera, will cause effects to be applied to it. Second, we must specify which cameras are to be affected by the volumes. We'll start by creating the volumes.

Creating a post-processing volume

Let's start by creating a single post-processing volume in the level:

1. Choose **GameObject | 3D Object | Post-Process Volume** from the Application menu. This option adds a new GameObject, complete with a trigger box and post-processing settings.

2. After creating a post-processing object, you'll need to position and resize it. The idea is to enclose the area inside which camera effects should occur. For our game, we'll enclose the complete level, as we'll make only one set of effects that should always apply. Use the **Box Collider** component fields for **Size** to resize the bounding volume, as shown in *Figure 11.27*:

Figure 11.27 – Adjusting the size of the volume to enclose the level

Now we have a volume that encompasses our tunnel. This is called a local volume as the effects are only applied in a specific area of the game.

> **Important note**
>
> The post-processing stack introduces the concept of global and local volumes, and each volume can be given a priority and a specific set of effects. You can take advantage of this in your games by creating a global volume that will apply specific effects, and then creating local volumes, as we have done with our sci-fi tunnel, that provide additional effects or override the global effects for when the player is in that area.

Next, we'll configure our camera to respond to the post-processing volume we've just created.

Configuring the camera

To test the effects, we'll need a camera. As mentioned earlier, every new scene automatically includes a camera object. However, rather than using the default static camera, we'll use the first-person controller we created in *Chapter 8, Creating Artificial Intelligence*.

> **Important note**
> We'll shortly be replacing this character controller with a VR version.

To do this, we'll need to first export the package from the previous project before *importing* the package into our new project. These steps will come in handy whenever you want to share objects and all associated data between your projects.

To export the character controller, do the following:

1. Open the project from `Chapter 10`, located in the `Chapter10/End` folder:

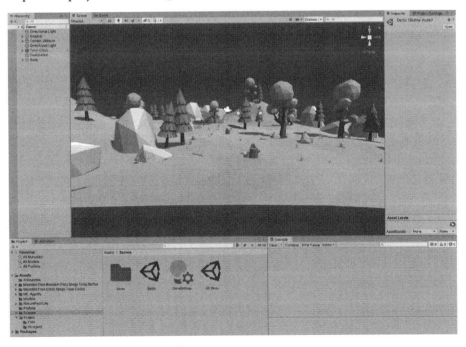

Figure 11.28 – The ML-Agents project

2. In the `Assets/Prefabs` folder, right-click on the `Player` prefab.

3. In the context menu that appears, select the **Export Package...** option:

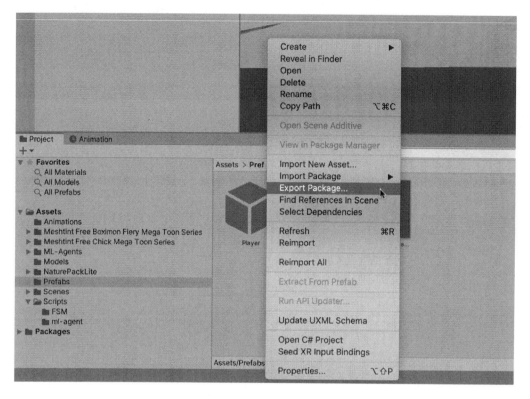

Figure 11.29 – Exporting the Player prefab

4. Untick all assets so that only the prefab and the `CameraLook` and `PlayerController` scripts are selected, as shown in *Figure 11.30*:

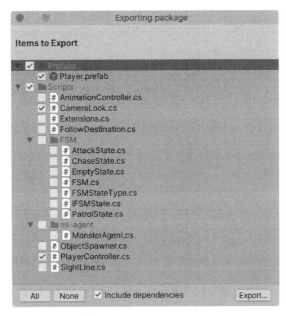

Figure 11.30 – Select only the relevant scripts

5.   Select the **Export...** button.

6.   Save the package somewhere you can easily locate it. I named the package `player_ controller`:

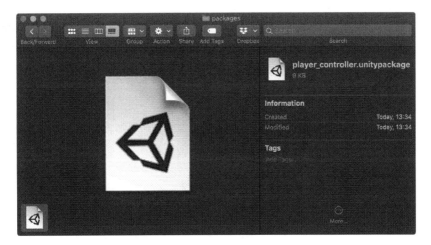

Figure 11.31 – The generated Unity package

This creates a `unitypackage` file, which contains all the data we need to use the character controller.

7.   Close the Unity project.

Now we have the Unity package, we can import it into our current project:

1. If you closed the VR project, re-open it.

2. Double-click on the recently created `player_controller` package. This will open the **Import Unity Package** window:

Figure 11.32 – The generated Unity package

3. Select **Import** to add the assets to our current project.

> **Important note**
>
> You may notice when you import the package that the assets are placed at the same location as they were when they were exported. This is something to consider when creating your folder structure if you will be exporting packages.

4. This will add the `Player` prefab to the `Assets/Prefabs` folder (the folder will be created if it didn't already exist). Drag this prefab to the scene and position it at `-3.8, 1, 0`:

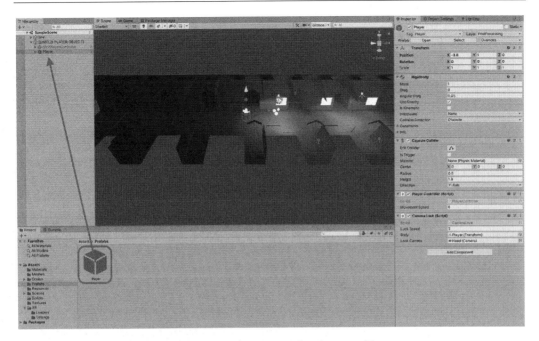

Figure 11.33 – Importing the Player prefab

With the package imported and added to our scene, we are ready to configure the camera:

1. As this asset includes its own camera, we can delete the default scene camera. Select the `Main Camera` object in the hierarchy and delete it.

2. In the hierarchy, expand the `Player` object and select the `Head` child object. This object contains the camera component.

3. Add a **Post-process Layer** component by selecting **Component | Rendering | Post-process Layer** from the application menu:

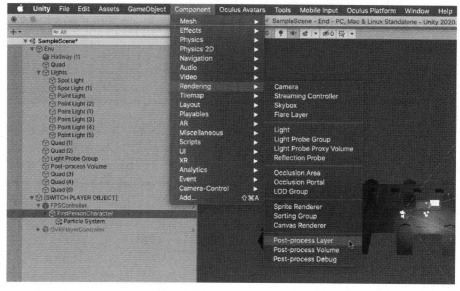

Figure 11.34 – Adding a Post-process Layer to the selected camera

4. In the **Inspector,** on the newly added **Post-process Layer** component, set the **Layer** attribute to **PostProcessing**:

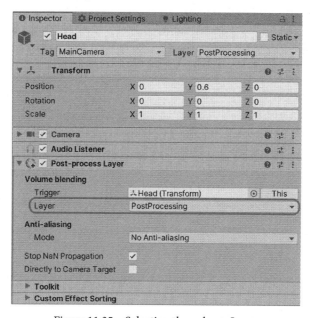

Figure 11.35 – Selecting the volume Layer

We've now added a post-process volume *to the scene* and a post-process layer *to the camera*. Next, we need to associate specific post-processing effects with the volume, which will be rendered to the camera when it enters the volume.

Enabling post-processing effects

We've laid the groundwork for using post-processing effects but have not yet selected and configured the effects we would like to apply. This will change now as we go through the last steps required to add post-processing effects to our project.

To select which effects we would like to use, we first need to associate a **Post-processing Profile** with the volume:

1. Create a profile by right-clicking inside the **Project** panel and selecting **Create | Post-processing Profile** from the context menu:

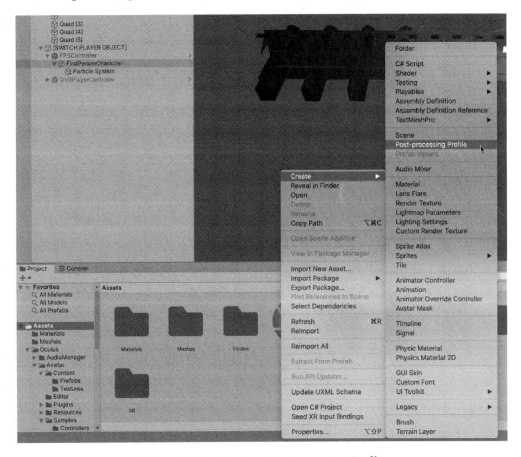

Figure 11.36 – Creating a Post-processing Profile

2. Select the newly created **Post-Processing Profile** asset.

3. From the **Inspector**, click the **Add Effect** button. You can add as many effects as desired, but each effect carries a performance implication. Consequently, you should add as few effects as needed while retaining your artistic vision.

4. Add two effects: **Bloom** and **Ambient Occlusion**. **Bloom** blurs and intensifies highlights, adding a dreamy or whimsical feel. **Ambient Occlusion** adds shadows to areas where adjacent geometry meets, such as the walls and floor or the walls and the ceiling:

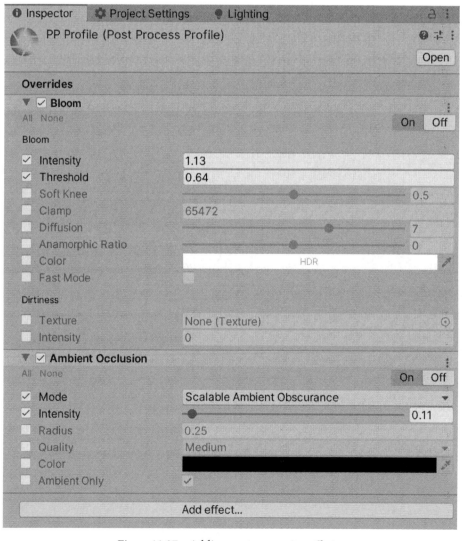

Figure 11.37 – Adding post-processing effects

5. Select **Post-process Volume** in the **Hierarchy** and drag and drop the **Post Process Profile** into the **Post-process Volume** component in the **Profile** field. This associates the profile with the volume:

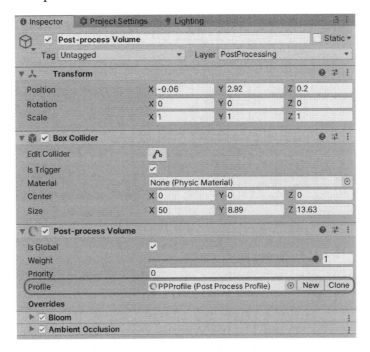

Figure 11.38 – Associating a profile with a volume

Finally, ensuring the first-person camera is inside the volume, you should immediately see the result in the **Game** tab. Excellent work. Our scene is looking great, with both lighting and post-processing combined:

Figure 11.39 – Previewing post-processing effects

We covered a lot in this section, including the following:

- Importing the post-processing package, which includes everything we need to use the processing stack.

- Creating a post-processing volume that encompasses the level and applies the effects to the camera when it is within the volume.

- Importing a player character asset from a previous project.

- Configuring the camera by adding a post-processing layer so that it works with the volume we created previously.

- And then, finally, we brought it all together and enabled post-processing in our project by creating a profile and associating it with the volume.

That's it for the lighting and post-processing effects. It's now time to prepare the project for VR!

Preparing for VR

In this chapter so far, we've been preparing the foundations for a scene, ready to add core functionality and gameplay. To recap, our game will be a first-person VR shooter, in which waves of enemy droids will spawn into the level, move toward the player, and then attack on approach. The player must dispatch all enemies and see how long they can survive the level. We still have the gameplay to implement, and whenever creating VR content, I like to make the project compatible with both VR and a standard first-person controller, both to help debugging and to aid testing without a headset.

But, before moving forward with development, let's prepare for VR development generally. This section uses the *Oculus Rift S* device, although the development workflow is similar for Oculus Go and Oculus Quest. To get started, you'll need to connect and install your Oculus Rift device. Instructions for doing this can be found online at `https://support.oculus.com/1225089714318112/`.

With the Oculus hardware connected, back in Unity, do the following:

1. Navigate to the **Project Settings** window by choosing **Edit | Project Settings** from the Application menu.

2. Select the **XR Plugin Management** tab. XR stands for extended reality and is an all-encompassing term that describes technology that blends the virtual and physical world in some way. For our purposes, it enables us to use VR, and in a later chapter, **AR (Augmented Reality)**:

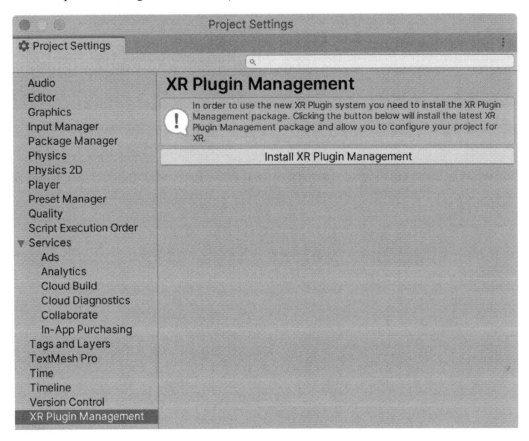

Figure 11.40 – XR Plugin Management

3. Click the **Install XR Plugin Management** button. This will install the packages required to manage the XR packages included in our project:

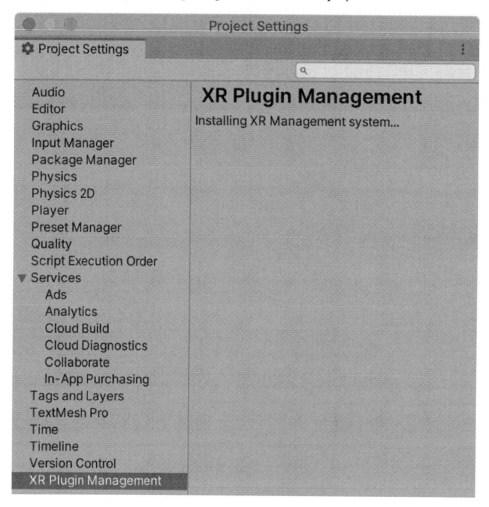

Figure 11.41 – XR Plugin Management

4. Once installed, it will display a list of supported XR providers. Near the top of the list, you'll find a checkbox for **Oculus**. Select that now and it will install the required packages to support Oculus VR:

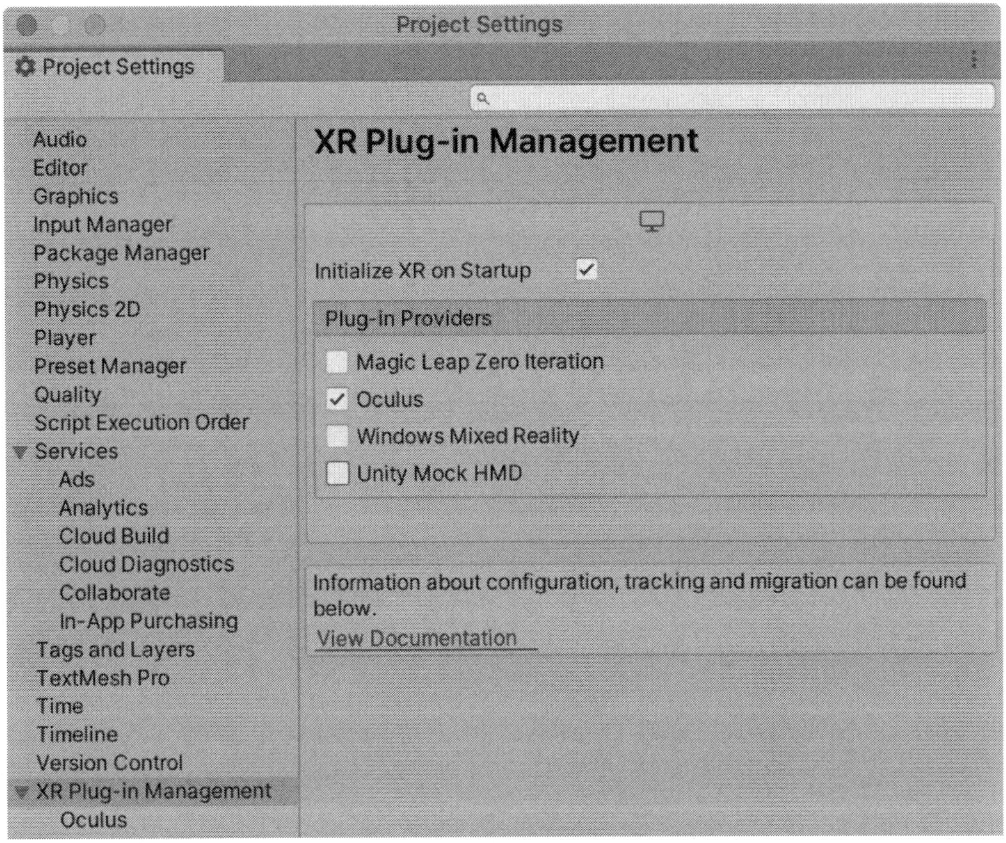

Figure 11.42 – Enabling Oculus support

Selecting the **Oculus** checkbox will automatically install the Oculus XR Plug-in Package. You can confirm this by checking in the Package Manager.

You can test whether this configuration has found your device simply by clicking play on the toolbar. The orientation of the **Head Mounted Display (HMD)** will automatically control the scene camera, so you'll be able to look around in VR. If this doesn't work, ensure the Oculus Device is connected and installed and can play VR content normally.

> **Tip**
> If you don't have a VR device, you can still test the application by selecting the Unity Mock HMD, as shown in *Figure 11.42*. For more information on how to set up testing without a device, take a look at `https://docs.unity3d.com/Packages/com.unity.xr.mock-hmd@1.0/manual/index.html`.

If all you wanted to do was look around in VR wearing the HMD, then you'd be done already! Unity makes it that easy to get up and running in VR. However, we're missing interactivity. To achieve more complex behaviors with Oculus Rift S, we'll import additional **Asset Packages** made freely available to us on the Asset Store from Oculus Technologies:

1. Navigate to the Unity Asset Store at `https://assetstore.unity.com`.

2. Search for and add the **Oculus Integration** package to your asset collection, which contains the basic libraries needed to create Oculus-compatible content quickly:

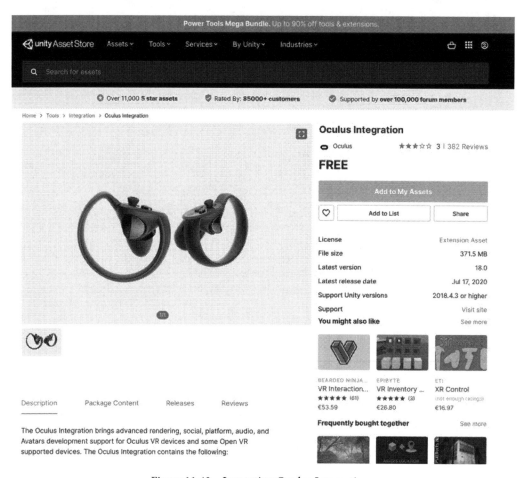

Figure 11.43 – Importing Oculus Integration

3. Back in Unity, open the **Package Manager** window and import the newly added package:

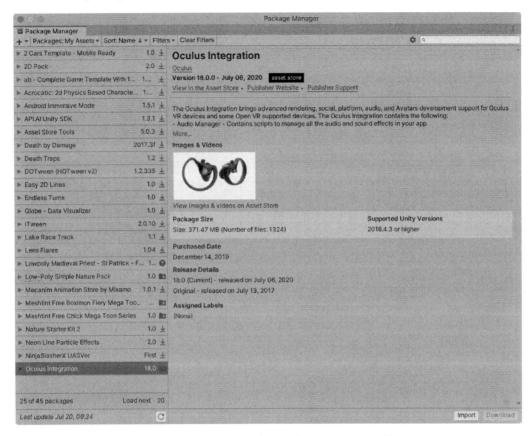

Figure 11.44 – Importing the Oculus Integration package

Once imported, you'll see a range of folders added to the **Project** panel in the Oculus folder. Many of these were previously separate asset packages but have since been integrated into one for ease of use:

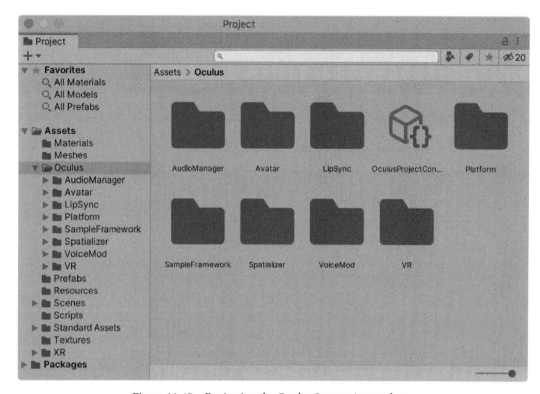

Figure 11.45 – Reviewing the Oculus Integration package

Critically important is the Oculus/VR/Prefabs folder, which contains an Oculus player character called OVRPlayerController. This controller works much like FPSController but has VR-specific functionality. Let's add this to the scene now:

1. Drag and drop the OVRPlayerController prefab into the scene

2. Position it in the hallway, at -3.71, 0.95, 0. This is where the player will stand as they face the oncoming enemies:

Figure 11.46 – Adding the OVRPlayerController prefab

After adding `OVRPlayerController`, new cameras will be added to the scene, one for the left and one for the right eye. Your post-processing effects won't work with these cameras by default. To make them work, do the following:

1. Add a **Post-process Layer** component to `CenterEyeAnchor`, which is part of the `OVRPlayerController` hierarchy of objects, as shown in *Figure 11.47*:

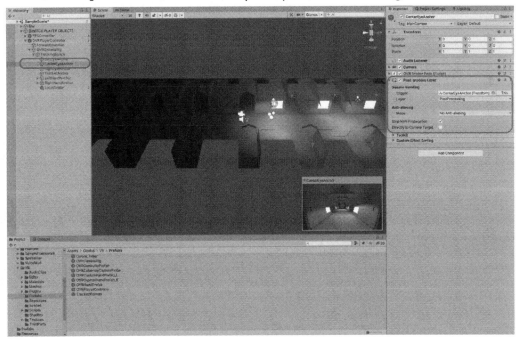

Figure 11.47 – Configuring post-processing effects for the VR camera

We'll next give the player character some hands using the **Oculus Avatar** prefab, which integrates directly into the player controller and works using input from the Oculus Touch controllers. This asset provides a mesh representation of the location and the status of the hands, as understood from player input within the tracking space (the play area).

2. Find the `LocalAvatar` prefab in the `Oculus/Avatar/Content/Prefabs` folder.

3. Drag and drop this prefab onto the `TrackingSpace` object in the **Hierarchy** panel. The `TrackingSpace` object is a child object of the `OVRPlayerController` GameObject:

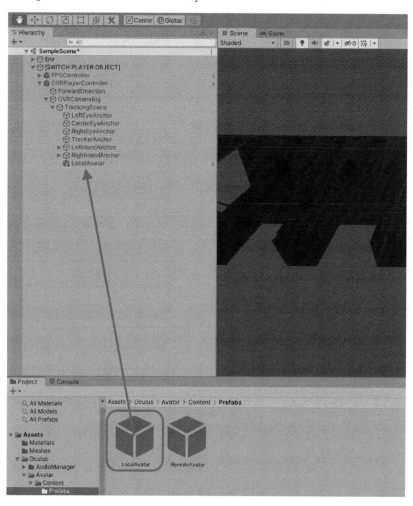

Figure 11.48 – Adding a local avatar to the OVRPlayerController tracking space

Excellent. We're now up and running with Oculus VR, ready to implement core functionality for the first-person shooter game, and we'll do precisely that in the next chapter.

Summary

Great work. So far, we've imported all project assets, configured those assets, set up the environment, and calibrated the lighting.

Using several Spot Lights to create interior lighting, as well as emissive materials applied to wall panels to make them glow, we created an atmospheric interior scene. The lighting was further enhanced by the addition of several Light Probes scattered throughout the scene. These Light Probes will come into their own as we add more dynamic objects to the project.

As well as the lighting, we implemented the post-processing stack. As we learned, these post-processing effects are filters and adjustments applied to the pixels of the scene camera and involved several steps to set up, including importing the post-processing package, creating a volume that encompasses the level, configuring the camera by adding a post-processing layer, and creating a post-processing profile and adding the desired effects to that profile.

This knowledge can be used in any of your future projects to add a certain level of visual flair or polish that can make a huge difference.

We then moved onto preparing the project for VR, which involved installing the necessary packages and setting up input using touch controllers. This preparation is essential for the next chapter, where we'll continue this project by adding enemies and a projectile system controlled using VR.

Test your knowledge

Q1. XR stands for...

    A. Extended Reality

    B. Extensible Realism

    C. X-Rated

    D. Expansive Reality

Q2. Light Probes are useful for…

    A. Adding indirect illumination to moving objects

    B. Light-mapping non-UV objects

    C. Unwrapping UV sets

    D. Adding soft shadows on static objects

Q3. Emissive lighting can…

    A. Break easily

    B. Cast light from mesh surfaces via materials

    C. Hide static objects

    D. Customize the Object Inspector

Q4. The post-processing stack version 2 includes…

    A. Terrain tools

    B. Particle systems

    C. Multiple effects in a single post-processing pipeline

Further reading

The following resources include more information on VR:

- `https://www.packtpub.com/game-development/unity-2020-virtual-reality-projects-third-edition`

- `https://support.oculus.com/1225089714318112/`

- `https://docs.unity3d.com/Packages/com.unity.xr.mock-hmd@1.0/manual/index.html`

- `https://docs.unity3d.com/Manual/LightProbes.html`

12
Completing the VR Game

This chapter continues from the previous one and completes the VR first-person shooter project by focusing on the underpinning code and functionality for creating gameplay, both in VR and using a keyboard and mouse.

Creating and destroying objects is an expensive process. An Object Pool helps to improve performance by retrieving objects from a fixed pool that was previously instantiated at a suitable time (that is, during the initial run or a loading screen). It also aids memory fragmentation by instantiating the objects together in memory in one go. Memory fragmentation occurs when the heap is broken into unnecessarily small chunks, preventing you from instantiating any new objects even if there is enough free space (just not contiguously). With this in mind, it is a good idea to become familiar with the concept, so in this chapter, we'll create an Object Pool that will store our enemy objects.

As discussed in *Chapter 9, Continuing with Intelligent Enemies*, a **Finite-state Machine (FSM)** is one of the more popular data structures for game AI programming (and beyond). The popularity of FSMs is partly due to their simplicity and ability to help break down an initial problem into several smaller, more manageable sub-problems. In this chapter, we'll reuse the core FSM functionality that we previously implemented and extend it by writing custom states.

We've used particles in previous projects to improve the overall visuals. In this chapter, we'll take it one step further, by creating particles that interact with the world around them by colliding with the enemy objects and eventually destroying them.

The Object Pool, FSM, and particle system will create the foundation of our VR gameplay experience, and by completing this chapter, you will not only gain a foundation in these topics but also complete the VR game.

In this chapter, we'll see how to do the following:

- Spawn objects using an **Object Pool**

- Implement AI using a **Finite State machine**

- Create a damage system based around particles, including configuring particle collisions with GameObjects

Technical requirements

This chapter assumes that you have not only completed the projects from the previous chapters but also have a good, basic knowledge of C# scripting generally, though not necessarily in Unity.

The starting project and assets can be found in the book's companion files in the `Chapter12/Start` folder. You can start here and follow along with this chapter if you don't have your own project already. The end project can be found in the `Chapter12/End` folder.

Spawning objects

This chapter is a continuation of the previous project, so before we add new elements to the game, let's remind ourselves of the progress so far:

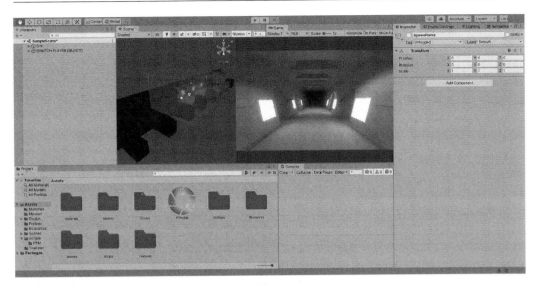

Figure 12.1 – The starting project

As you can see from *Figure 12.1*, we have an atmospheric interior hallway scene with **Spot Lights** and panels that glow. If we play the game, we'll notice that we can look around using our Oculus Rift VR headset.

In our game, we want enemy droids to spawn at regular intervals at spawn points of our choosing. Once spawned, each enemy will wander the level searching for the player, and then attack. This functionality immediately depends on a spawning system, as enemies need to be generated in the scene at a specific *location* and at a particular *interval*. The spawning behavior could be achieved using the paired `Instantiate` and `Destroy` functions for creating and removing objects. These functions are slow, however, and should be avoided as much as possible during runtime. It is more efficient to generate a batch of enemies when the level starts up, hide them away, and then recycle the enemies when needed to appear as though they've been instantiated in the scene at the moment they're needed. To do this, we'll need two elements:

- An Object Pool, which will store the collection of pre-generated objects

- A script, which will select from the pool at a specified interval and configure the spawned object

Let's create the Object Pool first.

Creating an Object Pool

As mentioned in the introduction to this chapter, an Object Pool will help improve the performance of our game. In previous chapters, we've relied on the `Destroy/Instantiate` pairing to destroy and create objects. We'll still require the `Instantiate` call in our Object Pool, however, we'll control when the objects are created. And we will no longer require any calls to `Destroy` as the enemies will be kept in memory while the scene is active.

> **Tip**
>
> If you intend to publish your game on devices with restricted memory, having an Object Pool keep the objects around for the entirety of the game may not be suitable for your needs.

We'll store the logic for the Object Pool in a new script:

1. Create a new class called `ObjectPool` in the `Scripts` folder:

```
public class ObjectPool : MonoBehaviour
{
    public GameObject ObjectPrefab = null;
    public int PoolSize = 10;

    void Start()
    {
        GeneratePool();
    }

    public void GeneratePool()
    {
        for (int i = 0; i < PoolSize; i++)
        {
            GameObject Obj = Instantiate(ObjectPrefab,
                Vector3.zero, Quaternion.identity,
                transform);
            Obj.SetActive(false);
        }
    }
}
```

The following points summarize the code sample:

The `PoolSize` defines how many instances of `ObjectPrefab` should be spawned at level startup. These will typically be instances of our enemy droids but could apply to any objects suitable for pooling. These instances will be added as child objects and hidden away in the scene until needed.

The `GeneratePool` function is called once at level startup to create the object pool, and all generated objects are children of the GameObject.

Once an object has been created, it is disabled by calling `Obj.SetActive(false)`. This call disables the object from being drawn, and it also disables any components attached to the object, including scripts. This means that script event functions such as `Update` will not be invoked, physics is not updated, and collisions do not occur with disabled objects.

2. Next, add a `Spawn` function to the class:

```
public class ObjectPool : MonoBehaviour
{
    ...
    public Transform Spawn(Transform Parent,
                Vector3 Position = new Vector3(),
                Quaternion Rotation = new
                    Quaternion(),
                Vector3 Scale = new Vector3())
    {
        if (transform.childCount <= 0) return null;

        Transform Child = transform.GetChild(0);
        Child.SetParent(Parent);
        Child.position = Position;
        Child.rotation = Rotation;
        Child.localScale = Scale;
        Child.gameObject.SetActive(true);

        return Child;
    }
}
```

The Spawn function is public, and when called, will select an object from the pool to be added to the scene as an active object. It does this by selecting the first child object, as all pooled objects are added as children. To mark the object as in use, it needs to be added to a different parent Transform, so it is no longer a child of the Object Pool. As such, the Spawn function's only required parameter is a Transform of another object.

> **Tip**
>
> The Spawn function has several optional parameters (Position, Rotation, and Scale). These parameters have been provided with default values in the function declaration. When we call the Spawn function, if we don't pass a custom value in, the fault values will be used.

3. We now have the ability to spawn objects; however, we still need some way of returning objects to the pool (or adding new objects to the pool). Create a DeSpawn function to do just that:

```
public class ObjectPool : MonoBehaviour
{
    ...
    public void DeSpawn(Transform ObjectToDespawn)
    {
        ObjectToDespawn.gameObject.SetActive(false);
        ObjectToDespawn.SetParent(transform);
        ObjectToDespawn.position = Vector3.zero;
    }
}
```

Hopefully, there is nothing too surprising in the DeSpawn function. It sets the object to false, adds the object to the pool's transform (so it can be selected for re-use), and resets its position to 0, 0, 0.

This code can be used to pool any GameObject. Although in this project, we'll use it for the enemy droids, you now have the ability to pool any object you wish! To test the Object Pool, and further enhance our game, we'll next create the functionality to spawn the enemies from the pool.

Instantiating objects using the Object Pool

Now we have the Object Pool, we can write a script that will retrieve the enemy objects from the pool and place them in the scene. We'll do this at specified intervals.

Create a new script called `SpawnTimer`:

```
public class SpawnTimer : MonoBehaviour
{
    public string SpawnPoolTag = "EnemyPool";
    public float SpawnInterval = 5f;

    private ObjectPool Pool = null;

    void Awake()
    {
        Pool = GameObject.FindWithTag(SpawnPoolTag).
          GetComponent<ObjectPool>();
    }

    void Start()
    {
        InvokeRepeating("Spawn", SpawnInterval, SpawnInterval);
    }

    public void Spawn()
    {
        Pool.Spawn(null, transform.position, transform.
          rotation, Vector3.one);
    }
}
```

The following points summarize the code sample:

> The `Awake` function searches the scene for a pool object with a specified tag, assuming this is the only such pool object, and then caches a reference to it.

> The `Start` function initiates an `InvokeRepeating` cycle to spawn objects from the pool repeatedly. We pass `null` in as the first parameter, which represents the `Transform` component. By passing `null` here, we remove the object from its parent (that is, the pool) but don't add it as a child to any other object.

To complete the spawn functionality, add the scripts to objects in the scene:

1. Create an empty object for the pool and position it outside the main level area.

2. Name the new object `EnemyPool`.

3. Attach the `ObjectPool` component to it.

4. In the **Inspector**, specify a size for the pool. I've used `20`.

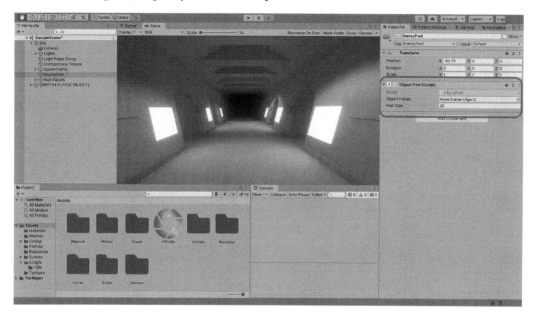

Figure 12.2 – Creating an Object Pool

5. Leave the **Object Prefab** field empty for now. We'll create the enemy object prefab in the next section.

Next, let's make a couple of spawn points:

1. Create a new **Tag** called `EnemyPool`. For step-by-step instructions on how to create tags, see *Chapter 2, Creating a Collection Game*.

2. Create an empty object in the scene.

3. Name the object `SpawnPoint`.

4. Position the new object at 8, 0.25, -4.5 to hide the spawn location in an alcove:

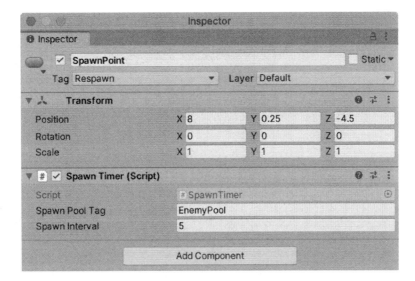

Figure 12.3 – Creating our first spawn location

5. Attach the SpawnTimer script to it.

6. Set **Spawn Pool Tag** to the recently created **EnemyPool**, as shown in *Figure 12.3*.

7. Set **Spawn Interval** to 10. This value means a new enemy will be spawned every 10 seconds:

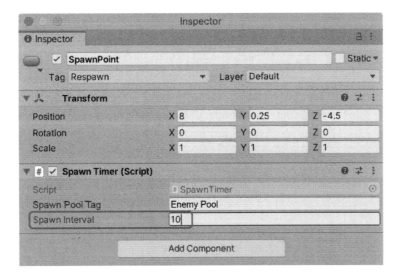

Figure 12.4 – Setting Spawn Interval

8. Tag your Object Pool with the **EnemyPool** tag, to ensure the spawner finds the pool:

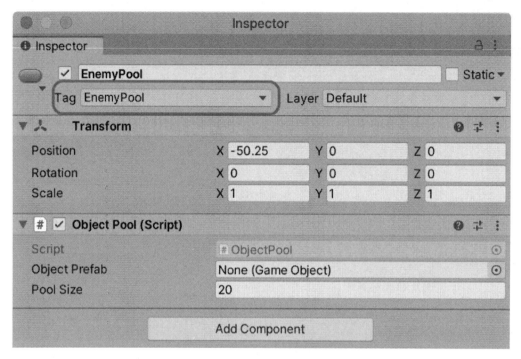

Figure 12.5 – Ensuring the Object Pool has the EnemyPool tag

9. Duplicate the **SpawnPoints** object to create an additional spawn location.

10. Position the duplicated object at 15, 0.25, 5 to hide the **SpawnPoint** in a different alcove:

Figure 12.6 – Adding an additional spawn point

Great! Now we have the Object Pool and the functionality to spawn objects from the pool; however, we still have the following problem: we have no enemy to spawn yet. So, we'll create that next.

Creating the enemy

With the Object Pool and spawning functionality in place, it's time to create the enemy prefabs that we will spawn into the scene. We'll do this in three steps:

- Creating the initial Prefab, including the visuals and physics
- Implementing navigation in our scene by generating a **NavMesh**
- Adding attack and chase behavioral states using an FSM

In *Chapter 9, Continuing with Intelligent Enemies*, we saw how to create enemy AI using an **FSM**. We'll reuse that functionality here by importing the scripts from the previous project and then extending them by writing our own custom attack and chase state classes.

We'll start by creating the enemy Prefab. By creating the **Enemy** as a Prefab, we can instantiate as many copies of it as we want during runtime.

Creating the enemy Prefab

The droid will be constructed in the scene, and a Prefab will be created from it. We'll then edit this Prefab using the Prefab Editor to add behavioral states and navigation components:

1. Drag and drop the `BlastBot` mesh from the `Assets/Meshes` folder into the scene. The enemy droid mesh will form part of a more complex object:

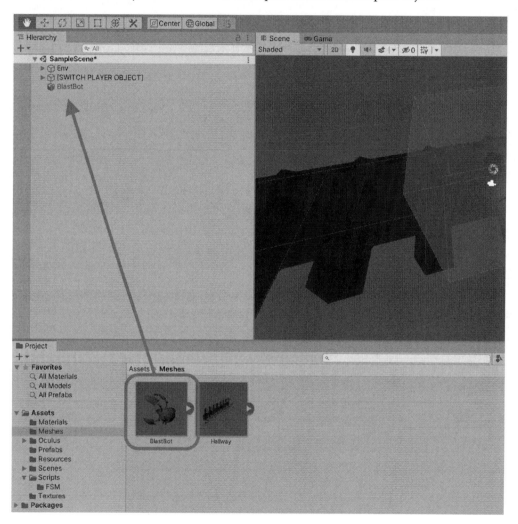

Figure 12.7 – Dragging the droid mesh to the scene

2. Create an empty object, named **Enemy**.

3. In the **Hierarchy** panel, drag **BlastBot** to the newly created **Enemy** object to make it a child object:

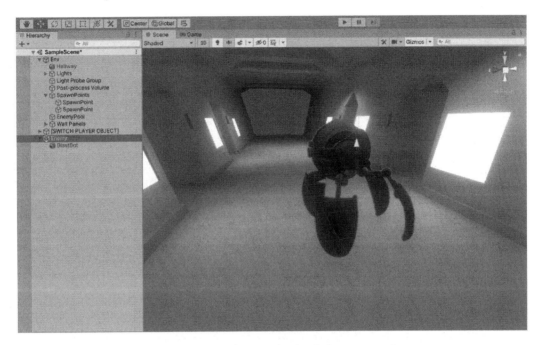

Figure 12.8 – Configuring the droid object Hierarchy

4. Ensure the empty parent has a blue forward axis representing the direction in which the enemy is looking, as shown in *Figure 12.8*.

Next, we'll configure the object's collision and physics data:

1. Add a **Rigidbody** component to the **Enemy** object.

2. Then, add a **Box Collider** component.

3. Adjust the **Center** and **Size** fields of the **Box Collider** component, so it roughly approximates the mesh, as shown in *Figure 12.9*:

Figure 12.9 – Adjusting the Box Collider

4. Ensure the **Rigidbody** is marked as **Is Kinematic**.

Let's create a Prefab from the **Enemy** object now, and we can always amend it later once we add navigation and AI:

1. Drag and drop the parent **Enemy** object from the **Hierarchy** panel to the Assets/ Prefabs folder in the **Project** panel:

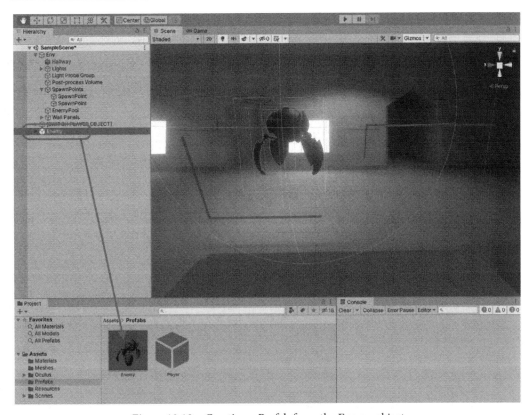

Figure 12.10 – Creating a Prefab from the Enemy object

2. As we now have the **Enemy** prefab, as shown in *Figure 12.10*, we can add the Prefab to the Object Pool. Select the **EnemyPool** object in the hierarchy.

3. Drag the newly created Prefab to the **Object Prefab** field:

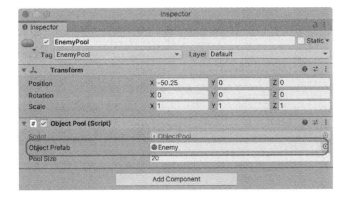

Figure 12.11 – Adding the Enemy object to the pool

The **Enemy** prefab will now be spawned 20 times by the Object Pool when the scene starts. However, the player won't see enemies as they will be instantly disabled (see the *Creating an Object Pool* section for more information). With the Prefab created, let's move on to implementing navigation so our enemy can move from its initial spawn point to where the player stands.

Implementing navigation

The droid will need to navigate around the scene intelligently, avoiding obstacles. To achieve this, a **NavMesh** can be generated for the environment:

1. First, ensure all environment meshes are marked as **Navigation Static** from the **Inspector**:

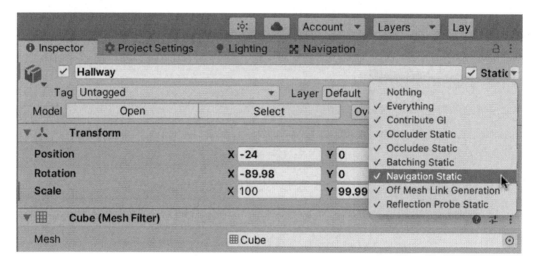

Figure 12.12 – Enabling Navigation Static for Static Environment Meshes

2. Open the **Navigation** window by choosing **Window | AI | Navigation** from the application menu:

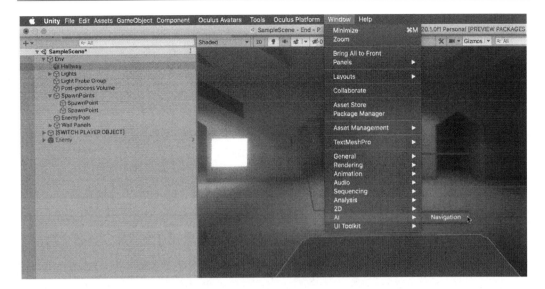

Figure 12.13 – Opening the Navigation window

3. Open the **Bake** tab.

4. Set **Agent Radius** to 0.27.

5. Set **Agent Height** to 1.46, as shown in *Figure 12.14*:

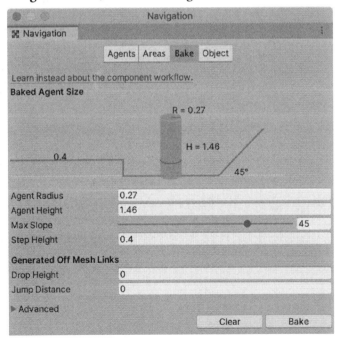

Figure 12.14: Agent size settings

Agent Radius is the average radius of an agent. This setting defines how close an agent can get to the walls in our corridor. **Agent Height** is the average height of an agent. This doesn't have a huge effect on our game, as long as the enemies can fit in the corridor.

> **Tip**
>
> For detailed information on navigation meshes, see *Chapter 8, Creating Artificial Intelligence.*

6. Click the **Bake** button to generate a mesh representing the walkable area of the floor. The blue region illustrates the complete surface area inside which an enemy droid can walk:

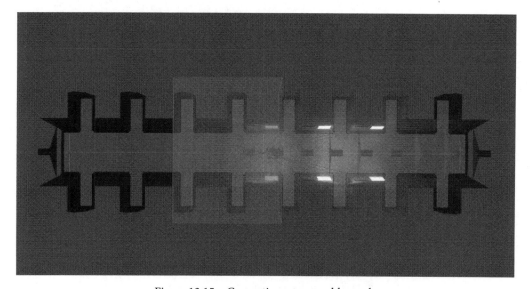

Figure 12.15 – Generating a traversable mesh

7. Now add a **Nav Mesh Agent** to the **Enemy** object.

8. Select the **Enemy** object in the **Project** panel.

9. Choose **Component | Navigation | Nav Mesh Agent** from the Application menu. The **Nav Mesh Agent** component will traverse the previously created **NavMesh**. We will control the component in our behavioral states that we write in the next section.

10. Once added, set **Agent Radius** and **Agent Height** to match the droid mesh, as shown in *Figure 12.16*:

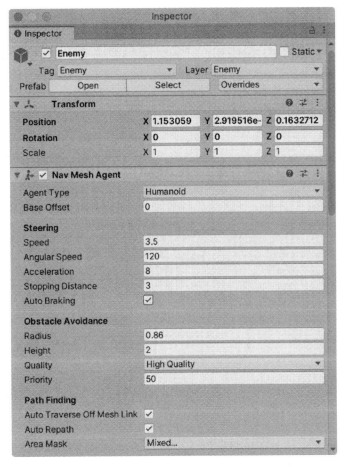

Figure 12.16 – Configuring Nav Mesh Agent

Great. We've now set up the environment to enable the enemy to move around. Next, we'll write the behavioral states that will take advantage of our navigation mesh.

Adding behavior states

In this section, we'll define the code to work with the Enemy prefab. We'll take advantage of the FSM we wrote in *Chapter 9, Continuing with Intelligent Enemies,* and extend its functionality by writing custom states. The enemy, once spawned in the level, will enter a chase state, causing it to move toward the player's location using the navigation mesh we generated in the last section. On reaching the player, the enemy will move to an attack state and cause damage to the player unless dispatched.

Start by importing the FSM from *Chapter 10*:

1. Create a folder called `FSM` in the `Assets/Scripts` folder.

2. Drag the following files to the newly created folder:

   `Chapter10/End/Assets/Scripts/FSM/FSM.cs`

   `Chapter10/End/Assets/Scripts/FSM/IFSMState.cs`

   `Chapter10/End/Assets/Scripts/FSM/FSMStateType.cs`

   `Chapter10/End/Assets/Scripts/FSM/EmptyState.cs`

> **Tip**
> If you're feeling adventurous, you could export the files as a Unity package and import them into this project instead of dragging and dropping.

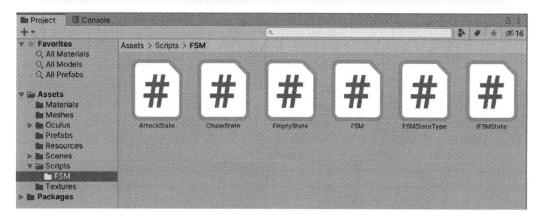

Figure 12.17 – Importing the FSM scripts

Now we have the base classes we need, we can build on them to create the states for our AI. We'll start with the attack state. In this state, the enemy will rotate to face the player and attack by shooting projectiles using a particle system:

1. Create a new file called `AttackState` in the `Assets/Scripts/FSM` folder:

```
public class AttackState : MonoBehaviour, IFSMState
{
    public FSMStateType StateName { get { return
      FSMStateType.Attack; } }
    public ParticleSystem WeaponPS = null;
    private Transform ThisPlayer = null;
```

```
public void OnEnter()
{
    WeaponPS.Play();
}

public void OnExit()
{
    WeaponPS.Stop();
}
}
```

The following points summarize the code sample:

The state inherits from IFSMState and implements the OnEnter and OnExit functions. These functions are called when we transition to a state (OnEnter) and when we leave the state (OnExit). Therefore we should perform any setup and cleanup code here.

OnEnter plays a particle system. This particle system will damage the player (as well as providing the visuals for the enemy's projectiles). The WeaponPS variable refers to a particle system component, which will be a gun for the enemy droid.

OnExit stops the particle system from playing.

2. The IFMState interface requires that we also implement a DoAction and ShouldTransitionToState function. Let's add them now:

```
public class AttackState : MonoBehaviour, IFSMState
{
    ...
    public void DoAction()
    {
        Vector3 Dir = (ThisPlayer.position - transform.
            position).normalized;
        Dir.y = 0;
        transform.rotation = Quaternion.LookRotation(Dir,
            Vector3.up);
    }

    public FSMStateType ShouldTransitionToState()
    {
```

```
            return FSMStateType.Attack;
        }
    }
```

The following points summarize the code sample:

The `DoAction` function is called every frame. In this function, we rotate the enemy to face the player.

`ShouldTransitionToState` is also called every frame. It is used to determine when the enemy should transition to a new state. Once the enemy is in the attack state, we don't want them to leave it. To prevent a state transition, we return the ID for this state.

With the attack state complete, we only need to write the chase state to complete the AI for our enemy. In the chase state, the droid will move toward the player, and once it is within a certain distance, it will then transition to the attack state to start attacking the player.

3. Create a script called `ChaseState`:

```
public class ChaseState : MonoBehaviour, IFSMState
{
    public FSMStateType StateName { get { return
      FSMStateType.Chase; } }
    public float MinChaseDistance = 2.0f;

    private Transform Player = null;
    private NavMeshAgent ThisAgent = null;

    void Awake()
    {
        Player = GameObject.FindWithTag("Player").
          GetComponent<Transform>();
        ThisAgent = GetComponent<NavMeshAgent>();
    }
}
```

The following points summarize the code sample:

As with the attack state, `ChaseState` inherits from `IFSMState`. Using a standard interface means our FSM class will interact with both of these new states without requiring any modification.

MinChaseDistance defines how close the enemy needs to get to the player before they transition to the attack state (we'll see the code that handles this case shortly).

A reference to the player's Transform is retrieved in the Awake function. This reference will be used as a target by NavMeshAgent. It will traverse the environment using the navigation mesh we generated in the previous section to reach the player.

4. Add OnEnter and OnExit functions:

```
public class ChaseState : MonoBehaviour, IFSMState
{
    ...
    public void OnEnter()
    {
        ThisAgent.isStopped = false;
    }

    public void OnExit()
    {
        ThisAgent.isStopped = true;
    }
}
```

The following points summarize the code sample:

As with AttackState, the OnEnter and OnExit functions are called when we enter and exit the state, for example, when we transition from one state to another.

When we enter the state, we set the isStopped variable to false on the NavMeshAgent component. This ensures that once a target has been set, the enemy will move toward the player.

When we leave the state, we set isStopped to true to prevent any further movement.

5. Lastly, we need to add the `DoAction` and `ShouldTransitionToState` functions:

```
public class ChaseState : MonoBehaviour, IFSMState
{
    ...
    public void DoAction()
    {
        ThisAgent.SetDestination(Player.position);
    }

    public FSMStateType ShouldTransitionToState()
    {
        float DistancetoDest = Vector3.
            Distance(transform.position, Player.position);
        if (DistancetoDest <= MinChaseDistance)
        {
            return FSMStateType.Attack;
        }

        return FSMStateType.Chase;
    }
}
```

The following points summarize the code sample:

In the `DoAction` function, we set the destination to equal the position of the player. As the player in our game cannot move, we don't necessarily need to set this every frame. However, if in future, you were to add player movement, this would be necessary.

We want the enemy to transition to the attack state when they get close to the player, so in the `ShouldTransitionToState` function, we perform a distance check between the enemy and the player. If the player is close, we return the ID for the attack state, which informs the FSM to transition to that state. See the `FSM.Update` function, which details how this works.

Next, add the scripts to the **Enemy** object:

1. Select the **Enemy** prefab in the **Project** panel.

2. Attach the `FSM` script and set **Start State** to **Chase**, as shown in *Figure 12.18*.

3. Attach the `Chase State` script.

4. Attach the `Attack State` script:

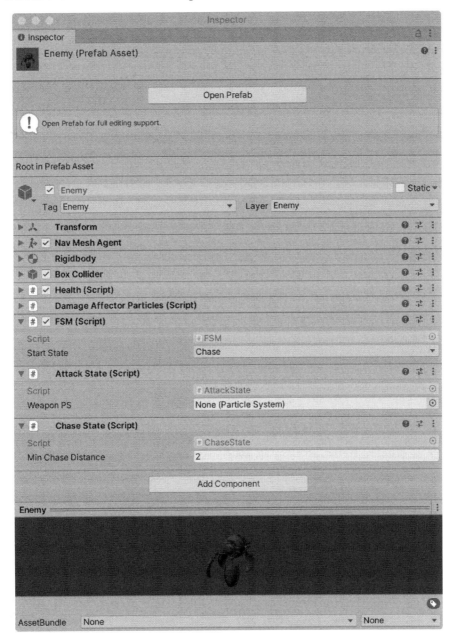

Figure 12.18 – Adding the FSM scripts to the enemy

5. Set **Min Chase Distance** to 2 .

That's it for the FSM for now. We still need to configure the **Weapon PS** field, but we can't do that yet. This field accepts a particle system that will act as the enemy's weapon; however, we haven't created the particle system yet. Let's work on that next.

Implementing a damage system

In this section, we will create the damage system for our game. Assuming that it will take more than one hit to destroy an enemy, we need to create a way to track health. We then need a way to reduce health – a weapons system. In previous chapters, we've created projectile Prefabs that would damage an enemy on collision. In this chapter, we'll do things slightly differently. By taking advantage of collidable particle effects, we'll create a visually appealing projectile system. Let's start by implementing the health system.

Adding enemy health

The enemy objects and the player must be able to take damage when hit by weapons. Therefore, both the player and the enemies require a way to track their current health. To accomplish this, we'll create one script that we can reuse for both entities:

1. In the `Assets/Scripts` folder, create a new `Health` script:

```
public class Health : MonoBehaviour
{
    public UnityEvent OnHealthChanged;
    public string SpawnPoolTag = string.Empty;

    public float HealthPoints
    {
        get { return _HealthPoints; }
        set
        {
            _HealthPoints = value;
            OnHealthChanged?.Invoke();

            if (_HealthPoints <= 0f)
            {
                Die();
            }
```

```
        }
    }

    [SerializeField] private float _HealthPoints = 100f;
    private ObjectPool Pool = null;
}
```

The following points summarize the code:

The `HealthPoints` property is used to change object health, and potentially to notify other objects and processes about the event.

The `Pool` variable allows the `Health` component to link with the Object Pool so that, if the object is dying, it can be returned to the Object Pool rather than being removed entirely from the scene.

The question mark in the `OnHealthChanged?.Invoke()` statement signifies that the event should only be invoked if it is not null, and works the same as the following:

```
if (OnHealthChanged != null)
{
    OnHealthChanged.Invoke();
}
```

2. Initialize the `Pool` variable in the `Awake` function:

```
public class Health : MonoBehaviour
{

    ...

    void Awake()
    {
        if (SpawnPoolTag.Length > 0)
        {
            Pool = GameObject.FindWithTag(SpawnPoolTag).
            GetComponent<ObjectPool>();
        }
    }
}
```

There's nothing new here. We simply find an object in the scene with the specified tag, and then retrieve the `ObjectPool` component attached to that object.

3. Add a `Die` and `Update` function:

```
public class Health : MonoBehaviour
{

    ...

    private void Die()
    {
        if (Pool != null)
        {
            Pool.DeSpawn(transform);
            HealthPoints = 100f;
        }
    }

    void Update()
    {
        if (Input.GetKeyDown(KeyCode.Space))
        {
            HealthPoints = 0;
        }
    }
}
```

The following points summarize the code sample:

The `Update` function features test code that reduces health points to 0 on a spacebar press.

When the spacebar is pressed, it calls the `Die` function. This function doesn't destroy the object but returns it to a pool and resets `HealthPoints` to 100. Setting the health to the maximum may look like a weird thing to do when the object dies, but remember it's being added to a pool, and there's a strong chance it will be re-added to the scene, and when it is, we need it to be at full health.

You can now update the **Enemy** prefab by adding the Health script:

1. Select the **Enemy** prefab in the Assets/Prefabs folder.

2. In the **Inspector**, add the Health script:

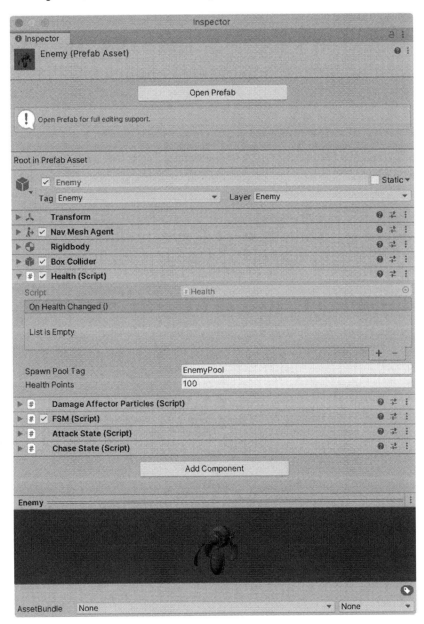

Figure 12.19 – Adding the Health script to the Enemy prefab

Excellent! Our enemy is ready. It can't attack yet, but neither can the player. In the next section, we'll create attack and damage mechanics that work for both the player and enemy at the same time.

Attacking using particles

Enemies should attack the player, and the player should attack the enemies. Both depend on the concept of attacking and taking damage. This section will use particle systems for inflicting damage, and we'll create a script to take damage. First, let's create a player weapon by generating a new particle system. In VR, this object can be made a child of the hand controllers; each hand can have one weapon. In standard first-person mode, the particle system will be a single-fire weapon:

1. Create a new particle system in the scene by choosing **GameObject | Effects | Particle System**:

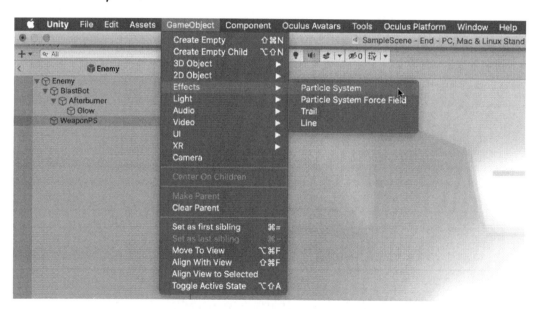

Figure 12.20 – Creating a weapon particle system

Once added to the scene, we'll need to tweak several settings to make it look like a plasma beam or a laser cannon. Expand the **Shape** and **Emission** settings from the **Object Inspector** to reveal those particle system properties.

2. Change **Start Speed** to 5 and **Start Lifetime** to 0.5 to affect the projectiles' speed and range.

3. Under the **Shape** heading, change **Shape** to **Cone** and set **Radius** to 0.04 to narrow the profile's trajectory.

4. Under the **Emission** heading, adjust **Rate over Time** to 3.5. Higher values will produce a beam, and lower values will produce bolts or balls instead:

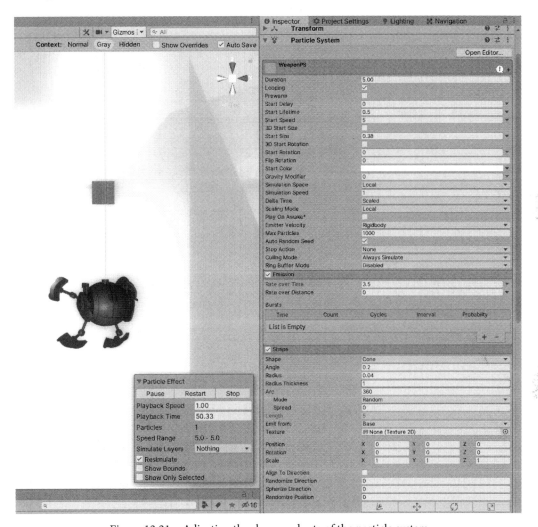

Figure 12.21 – Adjusting the shape and rate of the particle system

5. Now let's change the particle appearance using the **Renderer** section. Click the **Material** field and pick a style for the particles, as shown in *Figure 10.22*:

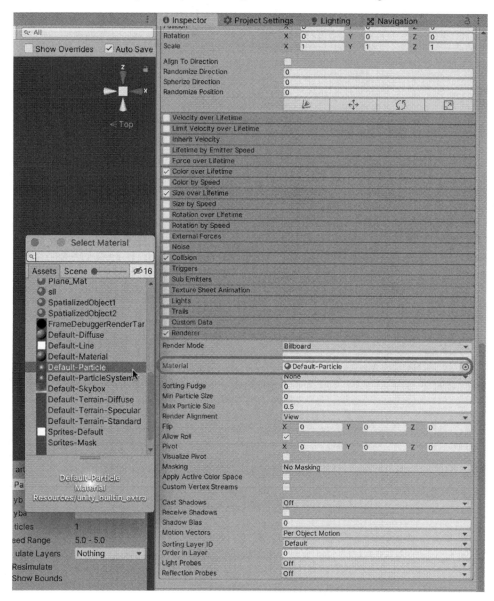

Figure 12.22 – Controlling particle appearance

Next, we'll add collision data to the particles so they can collide with other objects, such as enemies, allowing enemies to respond and take damage from a collision.

To do this, do the following:

1. Expand and enable the **Collision** group.

2. Enable the **Send Collision Messages** option.

3. Set the collision **Type** to **World**. This ensures an `OnParticleCollision` event is invoked when an object collides with the particles:

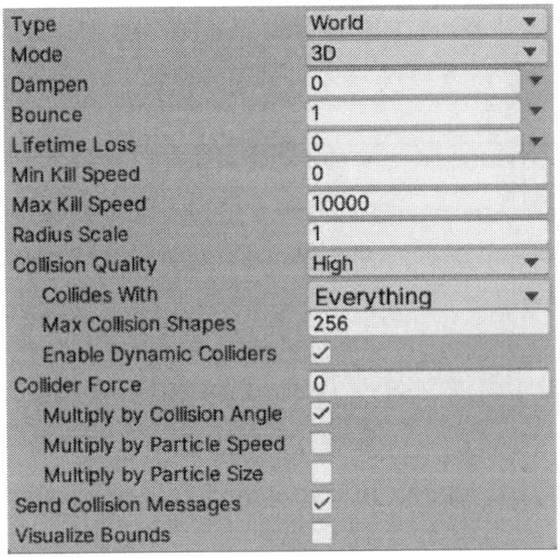

Figure 12.23 – Adding particle collisions

Now we need only two scripts: one for firing the player weapon, and another that causes an object to take damage when hit by ammo.

Create a new script called `Weapon.cs`:

```
public class Weapon : MonoBehaviour
{

    private ParticleSystem PS;

    void Awake ()
    {
        PS = GetComponent<ParticleSystem>();
    }


    void Update ()
    {
```

```
if(Input.GetButtonDown("Fire1") || OVRInput.
GetDown(OVRInput.Button.One))
    {
        PS.Play();
    }
    else if (Input.GetButtonUp("Fire1") || OVRInput.
    GetUp(OVRInput.Button.One))
    {
        PS.Stop();
    } }
}
```

The PS variable references the attached particle system to be started or stopped when a trigger is pressed. The OVRInput class is used to detect when a button is pressed on the Touch controllers. This means the code can be linked both to desktop PC input and VR controller input.

Lastly, we need to add our particle system to the player and bots:

1. Attach the Weapon script to the particle system object.

2. Create a Prefab by dragging the newly created particle system to the Assets/ Prefabs folder.

3. Drag the Prefab to **LeftHandAnchor** and **RightHandAnchor** (they are children of **OVRPlayerController**, which we created in the previous chapter):

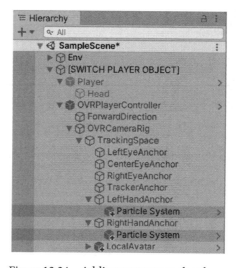

Figure 12.24 – Adding weapons to the player

4. Drag the Prefab to the **Enemy** object to enable the enemy to fire projectiles as well:

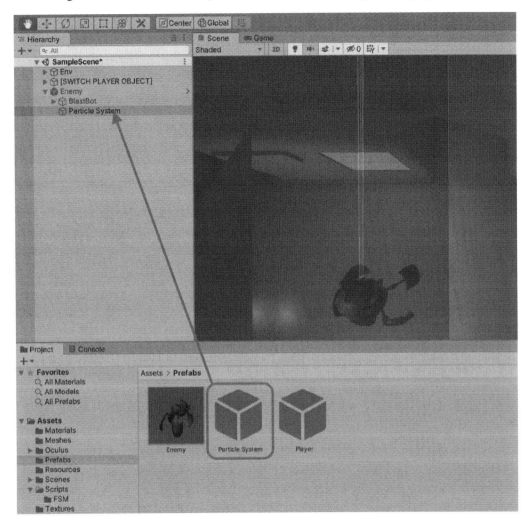

Figure 12.25 – Adding weapons to the enemy

Now both the enemy and player have the ability to attack using the same Prefab. In the future, we could create Prefab variants to differentiate a player and enemy attack, but the current setup is perfect for our modest needs. In the next and final section, we'll add the ability to take damage from our weapon system.

Damaging the enemy

We've seen several health/damage systems in the book so far. Still, this one will be slightly different, as rather than responding to a collision from a GameObject, we need to listen for collisions with our particle system.

1. Create a new script called `DamageAffectorParticles`:

```
public class DamageAffectorParticles : MonoBehaviour
{
    public string TagDamage = "Enemy";
    public float DamageAmount = 2f;
    private Health ThisHealth = null;

    void Awake()
    {
        ThisHealth = GetComponent<Health>();
    }

    void OnParticleCollision(GameObject other)
    {
        if (other.CompareTag(TagDamage))
        {
            ThisHealth.HealthPoints -= DamageAmount;
        }
    }
}
```

There's not much new here, other than we're implementing a special function called `OnParticleCollision`. As the name suggests, it is invoked whenever this object collides with a particle that has collisions enabled. This script will respond to damage from a particle system and apply it to the `Health` script we wrote previously.

2. Attach the script to the **Enemy** object.

3. Set the **Tag Damage** field to **Player** to enable the player's projectile system to damage the enemy.

4. Set **Damage Amount** to `10`:

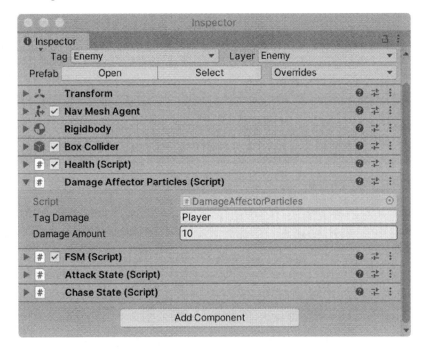

Figure 12.26 – Damage script attached to the Enemy object

5. On the **Attack State** component, drag the newly created particle system to the **Weapon PS** field:

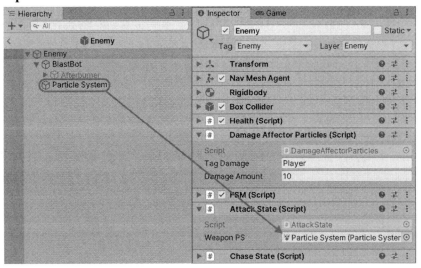

Figure 12.27 – Assigning the particle system to the Attack State

Now the player can shoot, damage, and destroy the enemies, which will continuously spawn using an Object Pool:

Figure 12.28 – Completed VR game

Congratulations! You completed the VR game. We now have a game that works with a VR headset, allows you to look around, and prevents movement. You can shoot oncoming enemies, which spawn into the level, using the Touch controllers. The damage system uses a collision-based particle system. In reaching this far, you've not only seen how to build a VR game, but also a few neat optimization tricks, including Object Pools and reusing scripts for multiple objects.

Summary

Great work! You've completed the chapter and the VR game, and in doing so have learned how to create a VR project, calibrate lighting to create a specific mood, add post-processing effects to enhance the visuals, spawn objects using an Object Pool, and create dynamic AI using the FSM we wrote in a previous chapter.

Using an Object Pool in your projects will enable you to improve performance and prevent memory fragmentation by instantiating the objects together in memory. In this chapter, we focused on spawning enemies using the pool. But any object can be spawned, including particles, reusable UI objects, and so on.

By extending the FSM we wrote in *Chapter 9: Continuing with Intelligent Enemies* with the addition of custom **Attack** and **Chase** states, you've seen how easy it will be to add dynamic AI to any future project. Separating the logic for the state machine and the states gives us the ability to add custom behavior without modifying the core state machine.

By experimenting and iteratively improving the code found in this chapter, you can create a solid foundation for any VR game. In the next chapter, we'll move away from VR but still stay in the world of **Extended Reality** by creating an **Augmented Reality** game. We'll also look at creating our first Universal Render Pipeline project, and what that means for Augmented Reality. See you there!

Test your knowledge

Q1. Particle Systems do *not* support object collisions.

> A. False
>
> B. True

Q2. FSM stands for…

> A. Finite State Machine
>
> B. Full Static Method
>
> C. Fast Linear Mode
>
> D. Fetch Sort Master

Q3. Oculus Rift is supported on Mac computers.

> A. True
>
> B. False

Q4. `OVRInput` is primarily used to…

> A. Read input from Oculus Touch controllers
>
> B. Read the orientation of the HMD
>
> C. Read the player position in the tracking space
>
> D. Reset the player position

Further reading

The following resources include more information on VR:

- `https://unity.com/unity/features/vr`
- `https://www.packtpub.com/game-development/unity-2020-virtual-reality-projects-third-edition`
- `https://docs.unity3d.com/Manual/PartSysCollisionModule.html`

13
Creating an Augmented Reality Game Using AR Foundation

This chapter starts a new **Extended Reality** (**XR**) project. In the previous two chapters, you worked on creating a virtual reality project. In this chapter, we'll start work on an **Augmented Reality** (**AR**) game where you can tap and place virtual objects in the real world using either an Android or iOS device. We'll create the game using Unity's new **Universal Render Pipeline** (**URP**).

The project creation process is similar to past projects, with a small twist. We will be using a completely new rendering pipeline. One of the reasons we will use URP for this project is that as Unity moves to URP, you will want to know how to set up AR using URP. The flow of previous projects doesn't change much in URP, but there are notable differences with AR. This chapter can also be completed without using URP; just skip the *Implementing AR in URP* section.

With most projects, there's no getting away from project setup, and AR is no exception. We will need to install various plugins and packages, and these plugins can differ depending on your target device. Fortunately, once the device-specific setup is complete, we can write code that will work for Android and iOS using **AR Foundation**, which provides a cross-platform implementation for AR.

Unity provides several premade components that we will add to the scene to enable AR. By the end of this chapter, you will have created a basic AR project without having to write a single line of code.

In this chapter, we will cover the following topics:

- Creating a new URP project
- Installing the necessary plugins and packages to get up and running with AR
- Configuring player settings to ensure the project runs on Android and iOS
- Creating our first AR scene, including importing the necessary AR objects
- Creating a turtle prefab that we will display in AR
- Testing the project on an iOS or Android device
- Implementing AR features specific to the URP

Technical requirements

This chapter assumes that you have not only completed the projects from the previous chapters but also have a good, basic knowledge of C# scripting generally, though not necessarily in Unity.

The completed project is included in the `Chapter13/End` folder.

This chapter uses an asset from the Unity Asset Store, which, along with the author details, can be found at `https://assetstore.unity.com/packages/3d/characters/creatures/rpg-monster-duo-pbr-polyart-157762`.

To run the project in this book, you require an iOS 11 or greater device, or an Android 7.0 device (or later). These are the minimum OS versions required to support AR. Due to the ever-evolving nature of AR, we recommend you follow along using Unity 2020.1, as this version has been confirmed to work with the project.

Introducing the project

Before we proceed with the implementation details, we should briefly define a couple of terms that we touched on in the introduction, that is, AR (and AR Foundation) and the Universal Render Pipeline.

We won't go into too much detail about AR as you're most likely aware of it, even if you haven't used it yourself. Using AR, we can superimpose data (in our case, it will be GameObjects) onto the world around us.

> **Tip**
>
> For a sneak peek of what our AR project will look like by the end of the chapter, see *Figure 13.34*.

Occasionally AR can be confused with virtual reality, and they both fall under the umbrella of **Extended Reality**. However, where virtual reality creates an entirely new reality for the player to be immersed in, AR is used to extend, or take advantage of, the real world inhabited by the player.

AR has received a lot of attention in the tech world in the last few years (Pokémon GO, Apple's WWDC, Microsoft's conference, and so on). Unity has taken notice, and in 2019 released AR Foundation – an easy way to create multi-platform AR apps within Unity and the first time AR has been officially supported. **AR Foundation** is a set of classes and APIs created by Unity that enables us to develop cross-platform AR games. It provides the ability to track a device's position and orientation, detect horizontal and vertical planes, and track a face or image, among other things.

> **Tip**
>
> For more information on the features provided by AR Foundation, see `https://docs.unity3d.com/Packages/com.unity.xr.arfoundation@2.2/manual/index.html`.

The URP is a complete refresh of Unity's built-in render pipeline. It contains several tools to help you easily create optimized graphics on a wide range of mobile, desktop, and game consoles. URP provides control over how Unity renders a frame by writing C# code.

> **Tip**
>
> For more information on the URP, see `https://docs.unity3d.com/Packages/com.unity.render-pipelines.universal@8.2/manual/index.html`.

We'll take advantage of some of what the URP has to offer in the next chapter, when we look at post-processing. In this chapter, you will learn how to create a URP project and configure settings specific to AR. On that note, it's time to get started developing in AR by creating a URP project.

Getting started with AR

In this section, we will create a new URP project and perform the necessary steps to prepare our project for AR. These steps include the following:

- Creating the URP project. We've created many projects in this book, but they have mostly used the 2D or 3D template. The project in the book is based on the URP template.

- Installing the plugins necessary for AR. Luckily for us, as you'll see shortly, there is a streamlined approach to adding the AR libraries.

- Once the plugins have been installed, we need to make a few changes to the player settings so we can successfully deploy to mobile devices.

- Lastly, we will import the packages required for AR. There is a common foundation package and packages specific to iOS and Android.

That's a lot of ground to cover, even before we start adding our own custom functionality. However, once you have an understanding of the process, you'll be up and running in your projects in no time.

Let's jump in by creating the project.

Creating a URP project

As touched on previously, we'll be using a different template for the AR project. As the URP has been described in detail in *Introducing the project*, we can jump right into the implementation:

1. Open **Unity Hub**.

2. Select the **Projects** tab on the left, as shown in *Figure 13.1*:

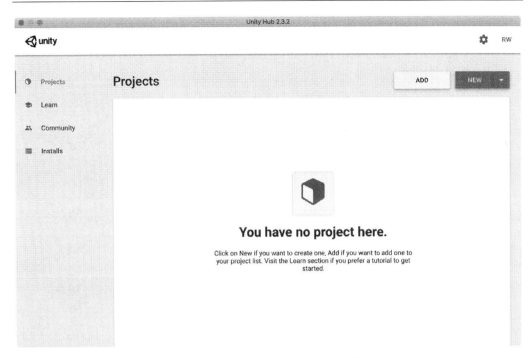

Figure 13.1 – Unity Hub Projects tab

3. Click the blue **NEW** button to open the project creation wizard.

4. This is where the flow differs from previous projects. Instead of selecting the 2D or 3D template, select the **Universal Render Pipeline** template. The template selection is shown in *Figure 13.2.*

5.   Name the project AR and set a suitable location:

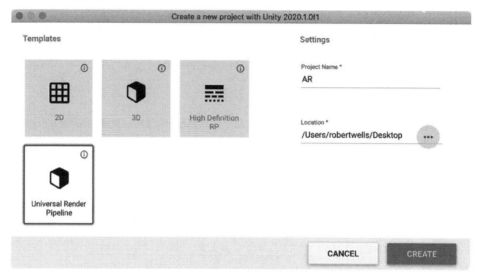

Figure 13.2 – Project creation wizard

6.   Click **CREATE** to create the project based on the URP template.

As with all previously created projects, this will create the project and open the Unity Editor. There is one noticeable difference, however. With newly created 2D or 3D projects, you're typically greeted by an empty scene (save a camera and lighting); however, with the URP template, you'll be greeted with a pretty sample scene, showing off some of the features of the URP. A sample scene is shown in *Figure 13.3*:

Figure 13.3 – Project creation wizard

Feel free to play around with the sample scene before moving onto the next step: installing the libraries required for AR.

Installing AR libraries

With the project created, we need to make a few changes to get it ready for AR. One of the necessary precursors to developing in Unity AR is installing the required plugins. Luckily, Unity provides a graphical interface to do just that:

1. Open the **Project Settings** pane by selecting **Edit | Project Settings...** from the **Application** menu.

2. Select **XR Plugin Management** from the list on the left-hand side:

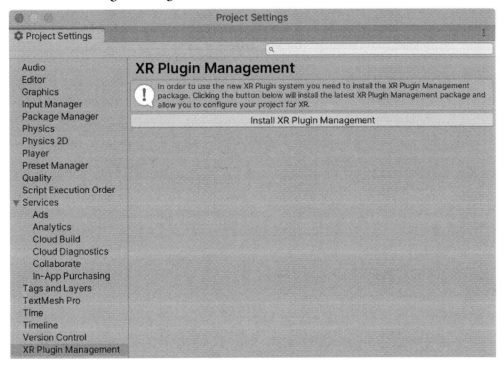

Figure 13.4 – Installing XR Plugin Management

3. Click the **Install XR Plugin Management** button. After a few moments, the screen will update to show the options in *Figure 13.5*:

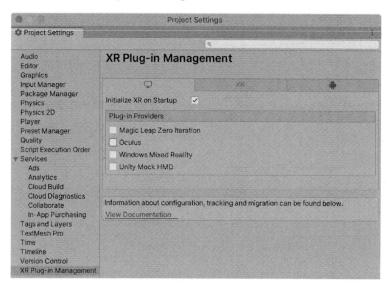

Figure 13.5 – Project Settings with XR Plugin Management installed

4. If you'll be deploying to an iOS device, select the **iOS** tab and tick the checkbox next to **ARKit** to install the AR library required for iOS devices:

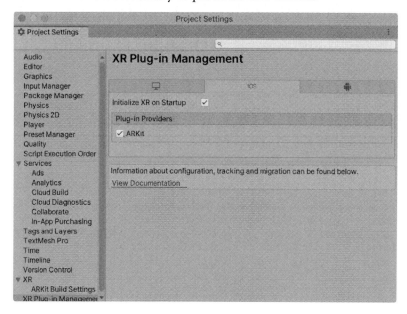

Figure 13.6 – Installing ARKit

5. If you'll be deploying to an Android device, select the **Android** tab and tick **ARCore** to install the library required for Android development:

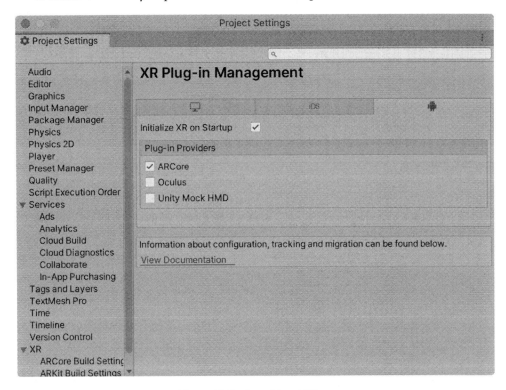

Figure 13.7 – Installing ARCore

And that's all the plugins we require (although we will install additional packages shortly).

> **Tip**
> If you don't see either the **iOS** or **Android** tab, make sure you have the necessary modules installed. You can check installed modules in Unity Hub on the **Installs** tab.

With the plugins installed, we can move on to configuring the necessary device-specific settings. Both iOS and Android require specific settings to be adjusted so that AR will run on their platforms. We'll go through each OS separately, so whichever device you have, you'll soon be able to test the AR game.

Configuring player settings

There are a couple of tweaks to the settings that need to be made to ensure that our AR game runs smoothly. The settings are device-specific; therefore, you only need to follow along with the section specific to your OS of choice. We'll start with the iOS-specific settings before moving on to Android.

Updating iOS settings

There are only a couple of small changes required for iOS:

1. Open **Project Settings**.

2. Select the **Player** tab.

3. Click the **iOS** tab.

4. Under the **Other Settings** heading, enable **Requires ARKit support**. Note that it also fills in the value for **Camera Usage Description**. It can't be blank as we'll be using the camera:

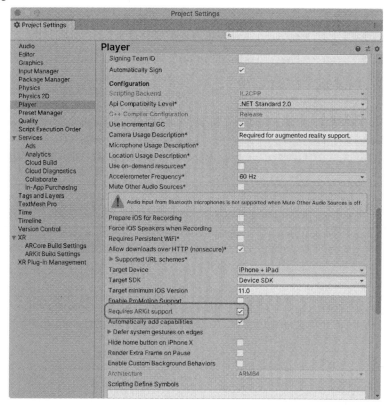

Figure 13.8 – Requires ARKit support

5.   It may provide a warning that iOS 11 or newer is required, as that is the first OS to include ARKit. Ensure that **Target minimum iOS Version** is set to 11.

> **Important note**
>
> As well as having iOS 11 as the minimum OS version, ARKit also only supports ARM64 processors. Although, it is likely that Apple will release an Apple Silicon version in the near future.

Updating Android settings

To configure the player settings for Android, do the following:

1.   Open **Project Settings**.

2.   Select the **Android** tab.

3.   Set **Minimum API Level** to Android 7.0 or later.

4.   Disable **Multithreaded Rendering** as it's not supported by ARCore:

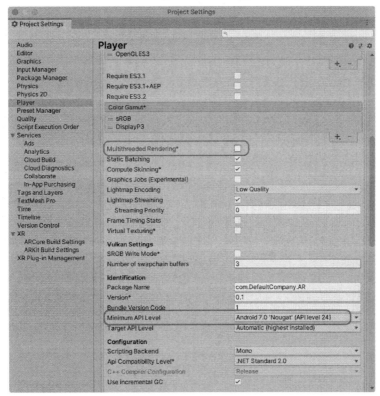

Figure 13.9 – Setting Minimum API Level

5.   Under **Graphics APIs**, remove the **Vulkan** option as it doesn't support ARCore:

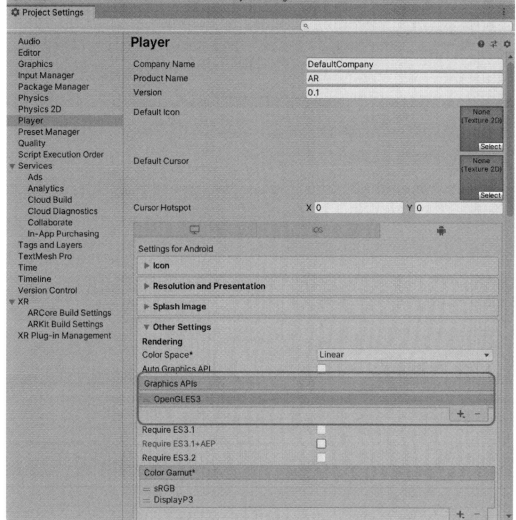

Figure 13.10 – Removing support for Vulkan

That's it for the project settings, and there's only one more step before our project setup is complete: we need to install the **AR Foundation** package.

Importing the required packages

The AR Foundation package allows us to develop multi-platform AR games. It hides the complexity of writing OS-specific code, and this project will be able to be run on iOS or Android. Sounds good to me! Let's install it now:

1. Select **Window | Package Manager** from the Application menu.

2. Change the scope to the Unity Registry by selecting **Packages | Unity Registry**:

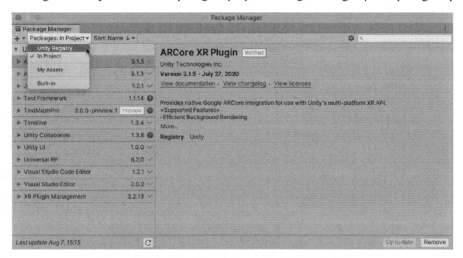

Figure 13.11 – Showing packages in the Unity Registry

3. Install the **AR Foundation** package:

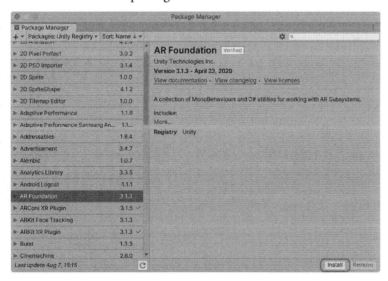

Figure 13.12 – Installing the AR Foundation package

This will install all of the necessary components to develop multi-platform AR games.

> **Tip**
> You can check whether the import was successful by right-clicking in the **Scene Hierarchy** and checking whether you have an **XR** option.

We'll be using one other package in our project. Although, it's not directly related to AR; instead, it provides a monster asset we can place in the world:

1. Navigate to `https://assetstore.unity.com/packages/3d/ characters/creatures/rpg-monster-duo-pbr-polyart-157762`.

2. Select **Add to My Assets**. This will add the package to your asset collection.

3. Back in Unity's Package Manager, once again change the package scope, this time to **My Assets**:

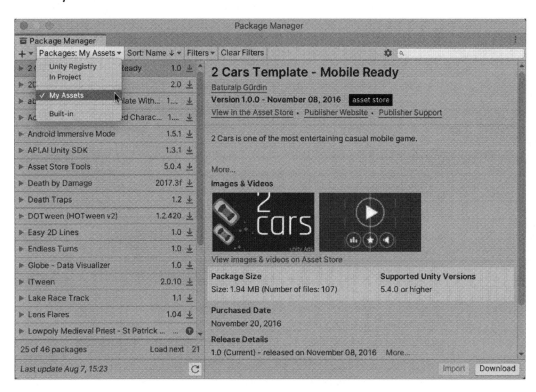

Figure 13.13 – The My Assets package scope

4. Import the **RPG Monster Duo PBR Polyart** package:

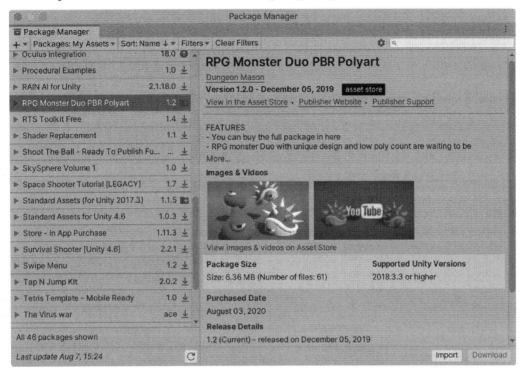

Figure 13.14 – Importing the Monster package

We now have everything we need to start developing our AR project. While the setup may seem involved, it is actually a quick way to get up and running with AR, especially considering it will work for iOS and Android. In the next section, we'll add the objects required by an AR scene.

Creating an AR scene

In this section, we'll add an **AR Session** and **AR Session Origin** object to a new scene. The **AR Session** component is necessary for any AR scene as it enables the AR experience, so let's start with that:

1. Create a new scene by selecting **File | New Scene** from the Application menu.

2. Save the new scene by pressing *Ctrl + S* or selecting **File | Save** from the Application menu and name it as ARScene. You should save the scene regularly to ensure you don't lose progress.

3. Once the scene is saved, select **GameObject | XR | AR Session** from the Application menu. You can also access this menu by right-clicking in the **Hierarchy** panel. We won't be interacting with the session object, but it provides the setup we need to work with AR:

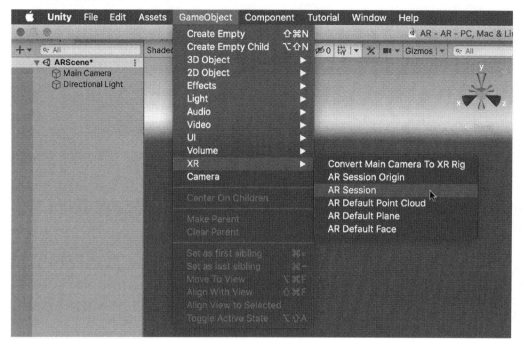

Figure 13.15 – Adding an AR Session object

An **AR Session** is an integral part of an AR scene. It controls the life cycle of the AR experience by enabling it on startup and disabling AR if the component is disabled. There is only one session per game, so even if you have multiple **AR Session** objects in a scene, they will talk to the same session. Ideally, you should not just have one **AR Session** in a scene to prevent conflicts.

> **Tip**
> If the **Attempt Update** option on the **AR Session** object is checked, the game will try to install the required AR software on the device. This option is enabled by default.

Next, we'll add the **AR Session Origin** object. This object gives us a way to query the physical world around us and change the scale of the virtual world.

4. Select **GameObject | XR | AR Session Origin** from the Application menu:

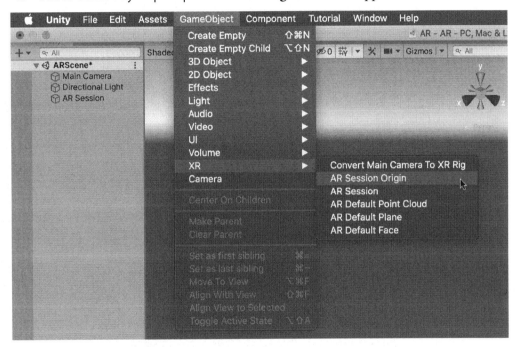

Figure 13.16 – Adding an AR Session Origin object

5. The **AR Session Origin** object includes its own camera so delete the **Main Camera** object. This is the default camera added to the scene automatically.

6. Select the **AR Camera** object in the **Hierarchy** panel (it's a child of the **AR Session Origin** object) and set its tag to **MainCamera**. It's good practice to have one camera in the scene set as the main camera:

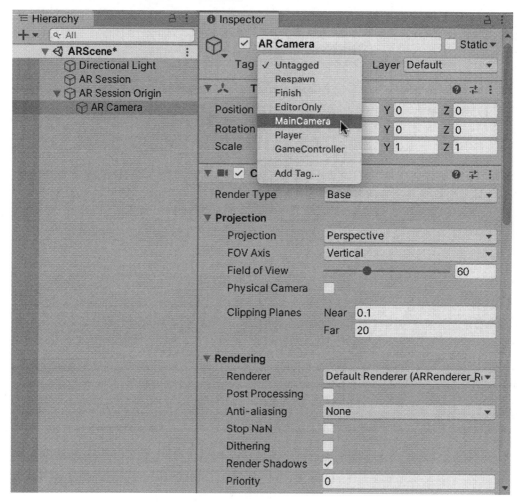

Figure 13.17 – Adding an AR Session Origin object

The **AR Session Origin** object will transform features, such as the surfaces onto which we'll be spawning the turtle, from session space into Unity space with the correct position, orientation, and scale. The session space is relative to the device's coordinate system, whereas Unity space is what we've been working in up to this point. Once the positional data has been transformed into Unity space, we can easily compare and place objects without performing any manual conversion from device space to Unity space.

> **Tip**
> You can scale AR objects by adjusting the scale of the **AR Session Origin** object. Larger values will make AR content appear smaller, and vice versa. For example, by setting the scale to 0.5, the turtle will appear twice its current size.

With those two objects created, our scene is ready for AR. Simple!

> **Tip**
> If you find the icons for AR objects in the **Scene** view distracting, you can turn them off by opening the **Gizmos** menu at the top of the **Scene** view.

In the next section, we'll create the Prefab that will be spawned in the real world (well, the AR world anyway). We'll take advantage of the Monster package we imported earlier and perform a few tweaks to update it for URP.

Placing an object in the world

In our AR game, we'll spawn an object in the world whenever we tap the screen. This section will create the object to spawn a friendly (albeit spiky) turtle:

1. Drag `TurtleShellPBR` from the `Assets/RPG Monster Duo PBR Polyart/Prefabs` folder into the **Hierarchy** (or directly to the **Scene** panel) to add the Prefab to the current scene:

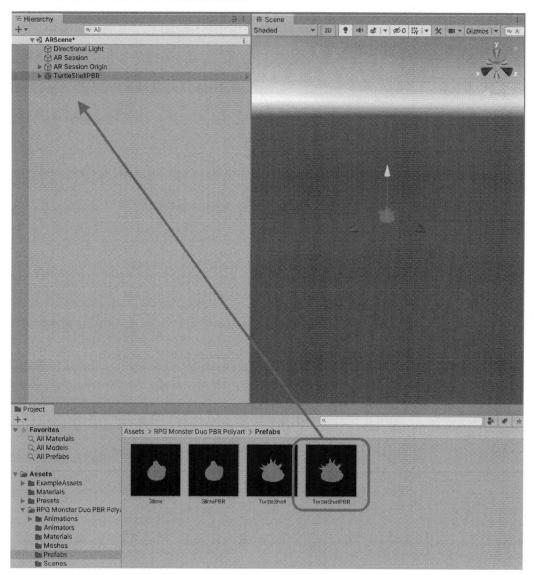

Figure 13.18 – Adding the turtle Prefab to the scene

2. Position it at point `0, 0, 0`.

3. Scale the turtle to `0.1, 0.1, 0.1` so it doesn't take over your living room.

4. Rename it `Turtle`.

You'll quickly notice that it doesn't look quite right on account of it being completely pink. This shade of pink may be familiar to you if you've ever used a broken shader (or broken one yourself – I know I have!) or have forgotten to apply a material to a mesh. In this case, the issue is down to the material not being compliant with the URP. Luckily, we can fix this easily:

1. In the **Project** panel, select the `TurtleShellPDR` material in the `Assets/ RPG Monster Duo PBR Polyart/Materials` folder. This is the material associated with the turtle mesh.

2. In the Application menu, select **Edit | Render Pipeline | Universal Render Pipeline | Update Selected Materials to UniversalRP Materials**:

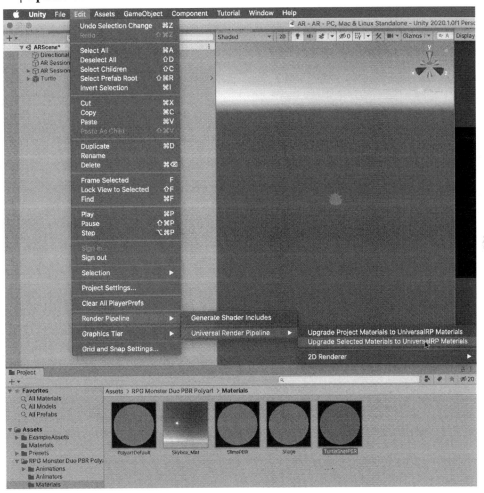

Figure 13.19 – Updating a material for use with the URP

3. In the menu that appears, select **Proceed**:

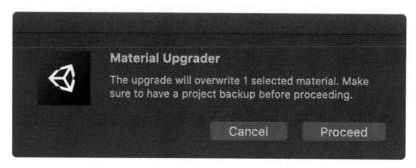

Figure 13.20 – Material Upgrader dialog

This will update the material, so it is compliant with the URP.

> **Tip**
> You can upgrade all materials in the project at the same time by selecting **Edit | Render Pipeline | Universal Render Pipeline | Update Project Materials to UniversalRP Materials** from the Application menu.

Now it looks correct, we can create a Prefab of the turtle:

1. Select the Turtle object in the **Hierarchy** panel.

2. Create a Prefab by dragging the Turtle object from the **Hierarchy** to the Assets/Prefabs folder. Create the folder if it doesn't exist:

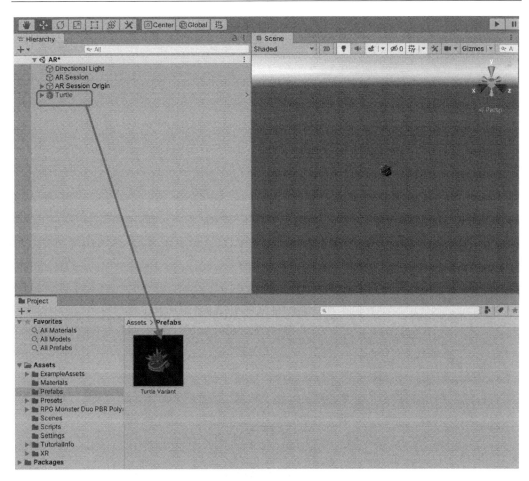

Figure 13.21 – Creating a Prefab variant of the turtle

3. If a window appears asking whether you want to create an **Original Prefab** or
    Prefab Variant, select **Prefab Variant**. We create a Prefab variant because we don't
    want to modify the original Prefab, but instead, we want to create a version that will
    work in our AR project. By creating a variant, we still have access to the unmodified
    original Prefab if we need it. For more information on Prefab variants, see *Chapter
    10, Evolving AI Using ML Agents.*

> **Tip**
> If objects appear too large or small in your AR game, rather than scaling each
> object individually, you can scale the AR world by scaling the **AR Origins**
> object.

With the turtle sitting happily in the scene and a Prefab created so we can spawn it when required, we can move on to testing our current project.

Testing on devices

Before we go any further, I think now is an excellent time to test whether we can display the turtle in AR using a real device. To do that, we will need to build and deploy the project. As you would imagine, the exact steps differ based on your chosen platform; however, before we get into platform-specific settings, we need to change a few platform-agnostic settings:

1. On the Application menu, select **File | Build Settings**.

2. In the window that appears, select **Add Open Scenes** to add our newly created scene:

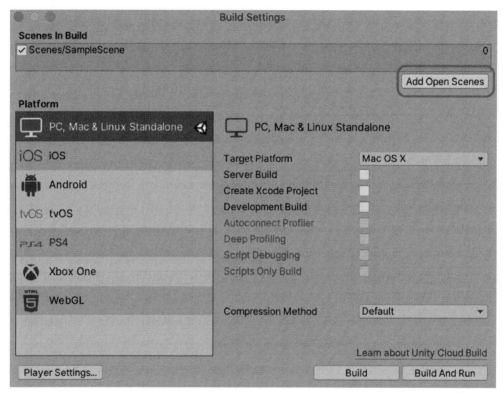

Figure 13.22 – Adding the current scene to the build list

3.   Delete **Scenes/SampleScene** from the scene list.

It's at this point the settings branch depending on your platform. We'll first look at testing on Android before moving on to iOS.

Testing on Android

To test on an Android device, do the following:

1.   Under **Platform**, select **Android**.

2.   Select **Switch Platform**:

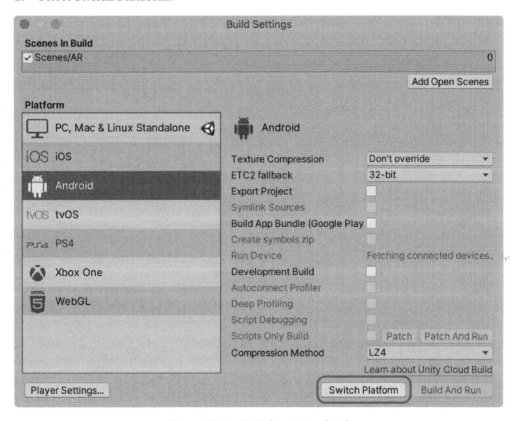

Figure 13.23 – Switching to Android

Unity will perform a number of steps, including re-importing assets, and then your project will be ready to test on your device:

1. Plug in your Android device.

2. Select the device under the **Run Device** option.

3. Click the **Build And Run** button. This will save an **APK** to your computer and deploy the app to the device specified under the **Run Device** heading:

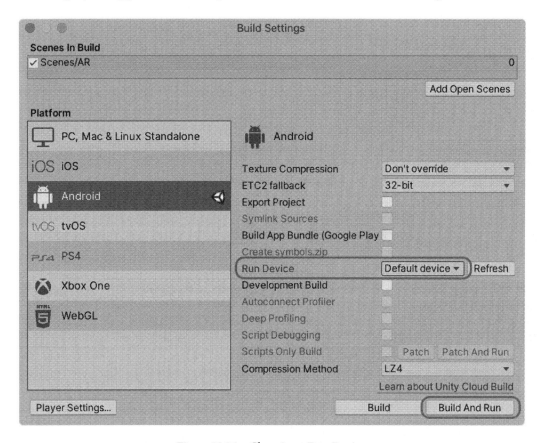

Figure 13.24 – Choosing a Run Device

Next, we'll look at testing on an iOS device.

Testing on iOS

Testing on an iOS device is slightly more involved than its Android counterpart, but will become second nature fairly quickly:

1. On the Application menu, select **File | Build Settings**.

2. Under **Platform** , select **iOS**.

3. Select **Switch Platform**:

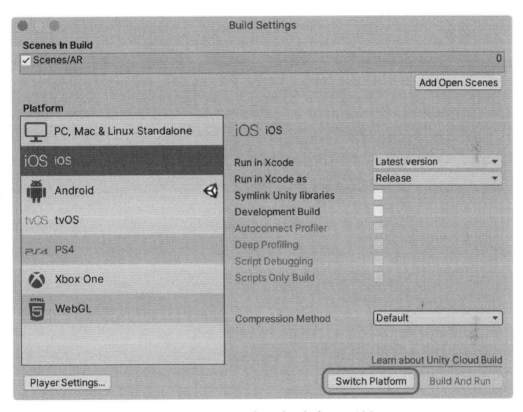

Figure 13.25 – Switching the platform to iOS

4. Wait for the platform switch to complete and then select the **Build** button and choose a location to save the build output.

5.   Once the build process completes, you'll have an **Xcode** project. Open the Xcode project by double-clicking `Unity-iPhone.xcodeproj` in the root folder of the generated project:

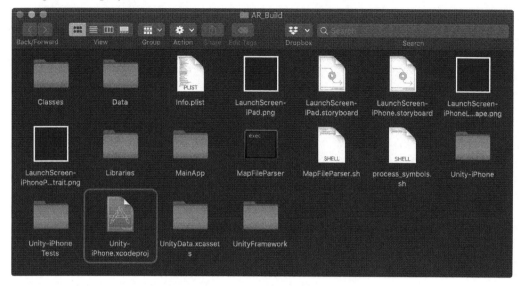

Figure 13.26 – The generated Xcode project

This will open the project in Xcode. There are a few more steps required before you can run the game on your device. In brief, you will need to do the following:

- Enroll in the Apple Developer program at `https://developer.apple.com/programs/`.

- Create an iOS development certificate.

- Add your device as a test device.

- Create a **provisioning profile**, which is required to test on a real device.

Luckily, Xcode can take care of most of this for you by enabling the **Automatically managing signing** option.

Detailed steps for configuring the Xcode project are beyond the scope of this book, however, Unity provides step-by-step instructions here: `https://learn.unity.com/tutorial/building-for-mobile#`.

> **Important note**
>
> To run the project on an iOS device, you need Xcode. Xcode is an IDE used to develop Mac and iOS apps. If you don't have Xcode installed, you can find it for free on the Mac App Store.

Whether you're using Android or iOS, once you have successfully deployed the app to a device, you may be disappointed with what you see. Running the game at this stage may greet you with a black screen, and nothing more. Lucky we tested it early! This is to do with the URP and is easy enough to fix, as you'll see in the next section. You may have been lucky, and the AR project works as expected, however, I would still recommend following the next section as it has useful information on how to implement AR using the URP.

Implementing AR in the URP

In the last section, we compiled and deployed the project to a device with disappointing results. When the game ran, we were greeted with a black screen. This is a common issue when using the URP and AR, and to resolve it, we first need to create a new rendering asset:

1. In the **Project** panel, navigate to the Settings folder.

2. Right-click and select **Create | Rendering | Universal Pipeline | Pipeline Asset (Forward Renderer)**:

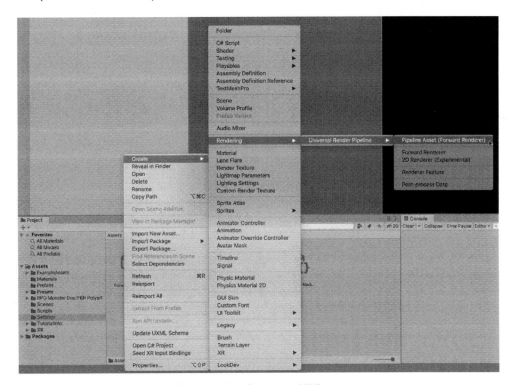

Figure 13.27 – Creating a URP asset

3.   Name the new asset `ARRenderer`.

That will create two files for us: `ARRenderer` and `ARRenderer_Renderer`. By clicking on each asset in turn, we can view the configurable options in the **Inspector**:

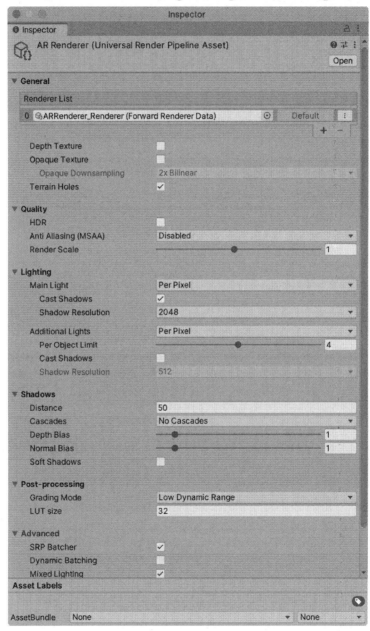

Figure 13.28 – AR Renderer settings

Many of the options are self-explanatory and it's beyond the scope of this book to explain them in depth. For more information on these settings, see `https://docs.unity3d.com/Packages/com.unity.render-pipelines.universal@7.1/manual/universalrp-asset.html`.

Next, let's take a look at the `ARRenderer_Renderer` file:

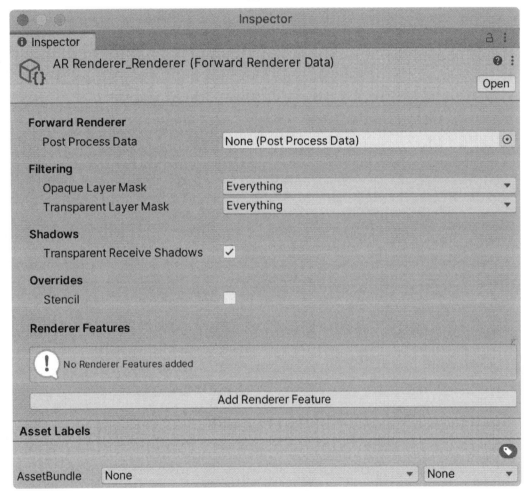

Figure 13.29 – AR Renderer

Near the bottom of the settings, you'll notice the heading **Renderer Features**. It's here that we'll add a specific feature to correctly display the AR background:

1. Select `ARRenderer_Renderer`.
2. In the **Inspector**, select the **Add Renderer Feature** button.

3.   Select **AR Background Renderer Feature** in the menu that appears:

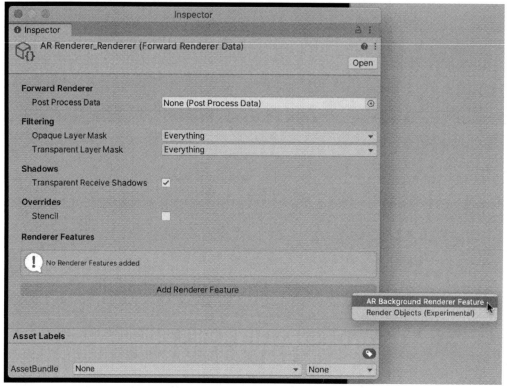

Figure 13.30 – Adding a renderer feature

This feature enables displaying the background in a URP AR application for any project using these settings.

> **Important note**
>
> If you don't see an option to add **AR Background Renderer Feature**, then please update your AR Foundation package using the Package Manager. It is only available from the AR Foundation package version 3.0.1 or above.

Now we need to configure the project to use our new custom renderer settings:

1. Open **Project Settings (Edit | Project Settings…** in the **Application** menu).

2. Click on the **Graphics** tab.

3. Under the **Scriptable Renderer Pipeline Settings heading**, select our **ARRenderer** settings:

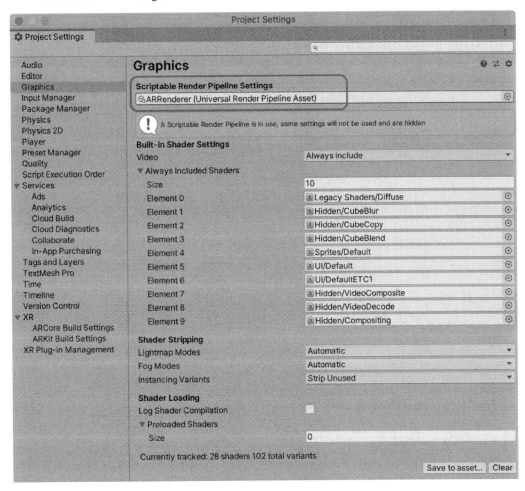

Figure 13.31 – Setting the URP settings

4.   Select the **Quality** settings tab on the left-hand side:

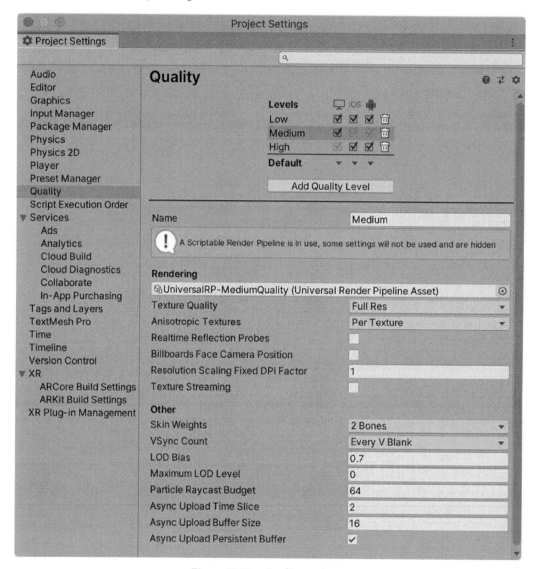

Figure 13.32 – Quality settings

It's here you can edit render settings for specific platforms.

5.   Select the **Medium** quality setting, as shown in *Figure 13.33*. This is the default quality setting for mobile devices as represented by the green checkboxes.

6. Replace the renderer with our **ARRenderer**:

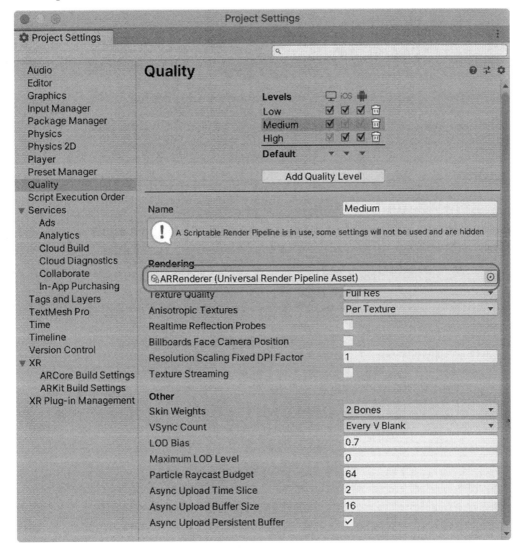

Figure 13.33 – Replacing the renderer

With that done, you should be able to successfully deploy your game to your device.

Important note

You can set different render settings on a per camera basis by selecting a camera and configuring the **Renderer** option under the **Rendering** heading.

If you build and deploy the project to your device, it should ask for your permission to use the camera and you should see the following:

Figure 13.34 – The turtle in AR

The turtle will most likely be floating in space as its initial position is determined by where your phone was in space when the game started. You may also notice that the turtle flies around the room as you move your phone. This is not ideal and something that we'll fix in the next chapter, when we look at **plane detection**.

Summary

Congratulations! You've created a cross-platform AR project without writing a single line of code. In this chapter, you've learned how to quickly create a new project, add the necessary packages, and create a new AR scene. By performing these steps, you now know how to get up and running in AR efficiently. You know which packages to install for which device, and you know how to create your first AR scene. On top of that, you've created a URP project, and updated the AR project to take advantage of this new render pipeline.

In the next chapter, we'll extend these concepts further as we look at detecting planes in the real world so we can place the turtle on flat surfaces (such as the floor or a table), and we'll also take advantage of the URP by adding postprocessing to our scene.

Test your knowledge

Q1. To develop AR games in Unity, you should install:

A. ARCore

B. ARKit

C. AR Foundation

D. All of the above

Q2. The minimum iOS version that supports ARKit is:

A. 11

B. 13

C. 9

D. 10

Q3. The AR Session component:

A. Has an AR camera

B. Controls the life cycle of an AR session

C. Isn't required in an AR scene

D. Should be added to every AR object in a scene

Q4. URP stands for:

A. Unity Render Pipeline

B. Unity's Really Pretty

C. Universal Reality Pipeline

D. Universal Render Pipeline

Q5. To run AR on devices using the URP, you should add an:

A. AR Session

B. AR Session Origin

C. AR Background Renderer Feature

D. All of the above

Further reading

For more information on AR in Unity, see the following links:

- `https://learn.unity.com/tutorial/building-for-mobile#`
- `https://learn.unity.com/tutorial/creating-urp-materials`
- `https://docs.unity3d.com/Packages/com.unity.render-pipelines.universal@7.1/manual/rendering-in-universalrp.htmlx`

14
Completing the AR Game with the Universal Render Pipeline

This chapter completes the **Augmented Reality (AR)** project we started in the previous chapter. We'll extend the project by adding custom logic to detect a horizontal or vertical surface and spawn the turtle on the detected surface by tapping the screen.

An indispensable tool for creating an AR game is the ability to detect features in the environment. A feature could be anything from a face to a specific image or QR code. In this chapter, we will leverage the tools built into **AR Foundation** to detect surfaces, which Unity calls **planes**. We'll take advantage of prebuilt components and GameObjects to visualize the planes, which makes debugging easier. We will be able to see in real time when Unity has detected a plane, the size of the detected plane, and its location in the world.

We'll then write custom logic that will extract the plane data generated by Unity and make it accessible to our scripts. We do this by ray casting from the device into the physical world.

Once we've detected a plane and extracted the plane data, we'll add a visual marker for the player. The marker will only appear on screen when the device is pointing at a valid plane. And when it's on screen, it will be placed at the correct position and rotation of the real-world surface. With that done, we'll move on to spawning the turtle that we created in the previous chapter at the marker's location.

We created this project using Unity's new **Universal Render Pipeline (URP)**, and we'll build on that in this chapter by adding post-processing effects using the URP. The URP has been designed to provide control over how Unity renders a frame without the need to write any code. We've previously touched on adding post-processing effects in *Chapter 11, Entering Virtual Reality*. However, the process differs slightly using the URP, so once you've completed this chapter, you'll be able to add these effects whether you are using Unity's built-in render pipeline or the URP.

In this chapter, we will cover the following topics:

- How to detect planes
- Visualizing planes by generating GameObjects
- Retrieving plane data including the position and rotation
- Adding a marker to visualize suitable spawn locations
- Spawning the turtle object on a horizontal or vertical surface in the real world
- Adding post-processing effects using the URP

By the end of this chapter, you will have created an AR project in which you can spawn objects onto surfaces in the real world.

Technical requirements

This chapter assumes that you have not only completed the projects from the previous chapters but also have a good, basic knowledge of C# scripting generally, though not necessarily in Unity. This project is a direct continuation of the project started in *Chapter 13, Creating an Augmented Reality Game Using AR Foundation*.

The starting project and assets can be found in the book's companion files in the `Chapter14/Start` folder. You can start here and follow along with this chapter if you don't have your own project already. The end project can be found in the `Chapter14/End` folder.

Detecting planes

An essential part of programming an AR game is adding the ability to detect features in the environment. These features can be objects, faces, images, or in our case, planes. A plane is any flat surface with a specific dimension and boundary points. Once we've detected a plane, we can use its details to spawn a turtle at the correct position and with the proper rotation.

We'll detect planes using ray casting and a custom script. However, before we write the script, we'll first add a Plane Manager to the scene.

Adding a Plane Manager

A Plane Manager will generate virtual objects that represent the planes in our environment. We'll use these virtual objects as a guide to where we can spawn the turtle. It will also provide useful debug information by drawing a boundary around any planes it detects. Using this feature, we can see in real time when Unity has detected a plane:

1. Open the `ARScene` located in the `Assets/Scene` folder.

2. As we created a prefab in the previous chapter, delete the **Turtle** object from the scene.

3. Right-click in the **Hierarchy** panel and select **XR | AR Default Plane**. This object will be generated by our Plane Manager whenever it detects a plane:

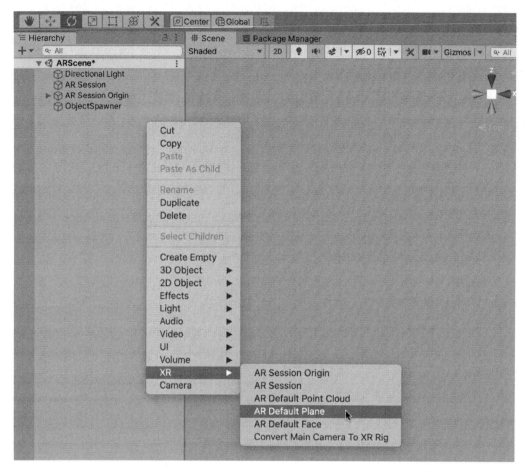

Figure 14.1 – Adding an AR Default Plane object

4. Drag the **AR Default Plane** to the `Assets/Prefabs` folder to create a prefab:

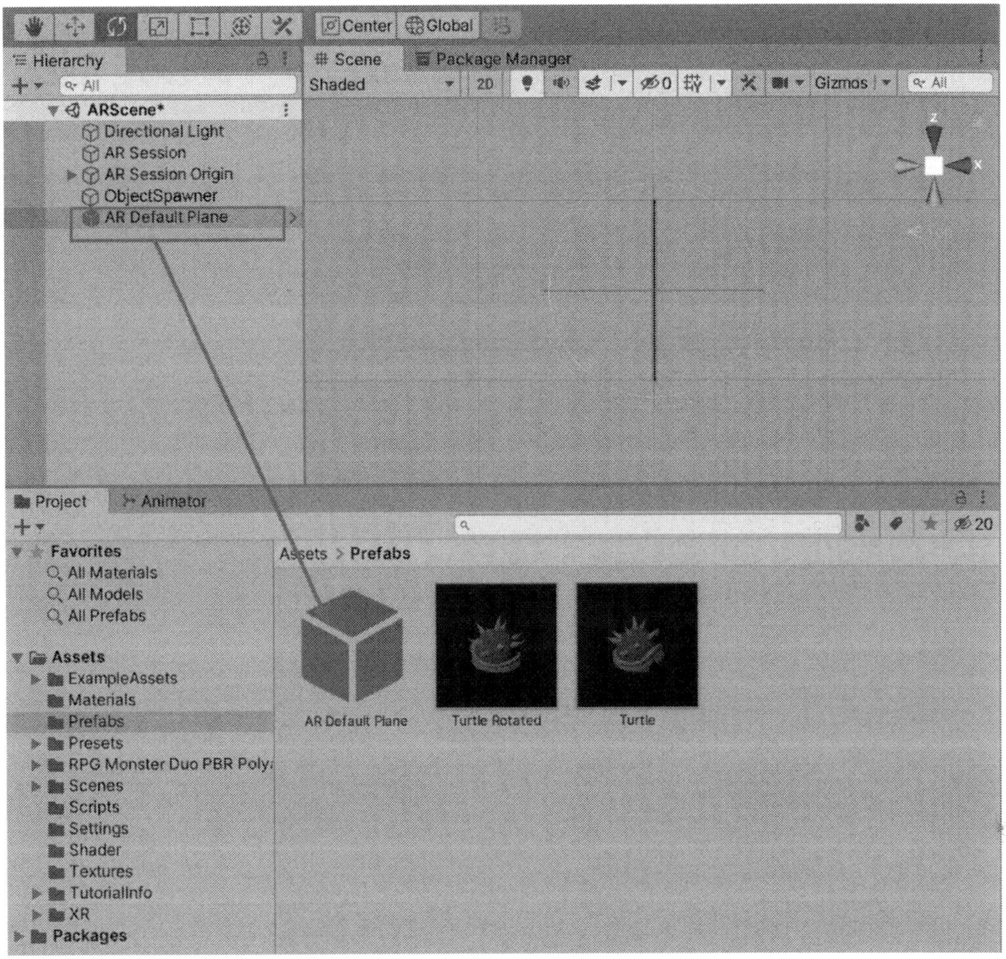

Figure 14.2 – Creating an AR Plane prefab

5. As we'll only need its prefab, delete the **AR Default Plane** object from the scene.

Suppose you select the **AR Default Plane** object and view its data in the **Inspector**. In that case, you'll notice it comes with several components already attached, including the **AR Plane** and **AR Plane Mesh Visualizer** scripts. The **AR Plane** represents the plane and includes useful data on it, including the boundary, center point, and alignment. The **AR Plane Mesh Visualizer** generates a mesh for each plane. It is this component that will be used to create and update the visuals for each plane. We will see this in action shortly:

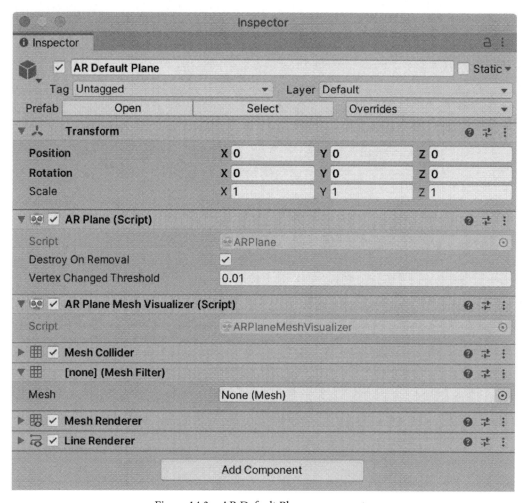

Figure 14.3 – AR Default Plane components

Next, we'll assign the prefab to a Plane Manager, so it is generated during runtime:

1. Add an **AR Plane Manager** to the scene by selecting the **AR Session Origin** object in the **Hierarchy** panel and adding the **AR Plane Manager** component:

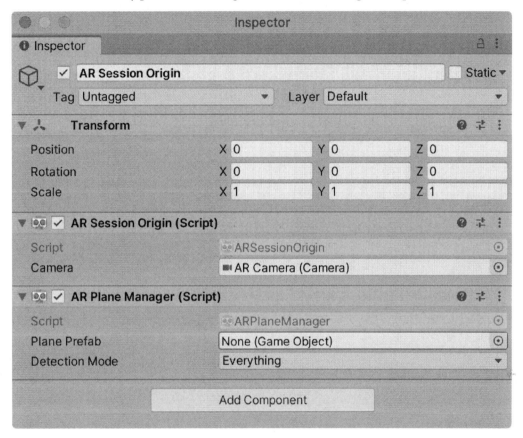

Figure 14.4 – Adding an AR Plane Manager

2. Assign the plane we created previously to the **Plane Prefab** field by dragging the **AR Default Plane** from the `Assets/Prefabs` folder to the field:

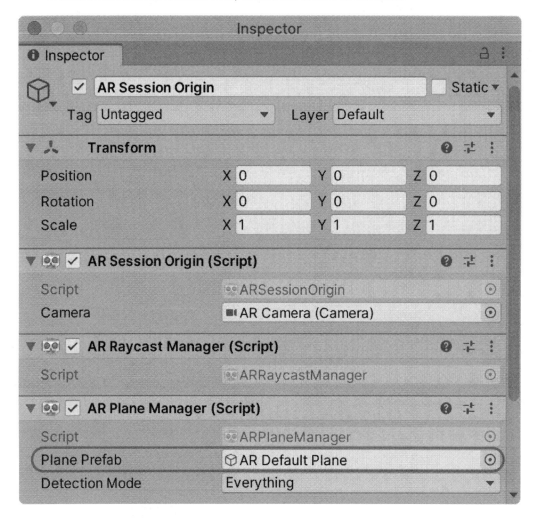

Figure 14.5 – Assigning a Plane to the Plane Prefab

The **AR Plane Manager** will generate GameObjects for each detected plane. The GameObject it generates is defined by this field.

3. Build and run the game on your device using the instructions from *Chapter 13, Creating an Augmented Reality Game Using AR Foundation:*

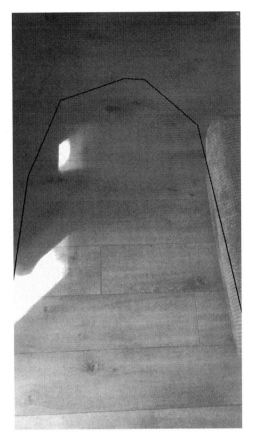

Figure 14.6 – Drawing surface boundaries

You'll notice blank lines are generated as you move around your environment. These lines represent the boundaries of planes detected by Unity. Each boundary is one AR Plane GameObject that has been spawned into the environment by the AR Plane Manager. As you move the device around your environment, the bounds should expand.

> **Important Note**
> The boundary points of a plane are always convex.

Without writing a single line of code, we can now detect planes in the environment and visualize them using Unity GameObjects. Great! Next, we need to retrieve the data associated with the detected plane, which will eventually be used to spawn the turtle.

Retrieving plane data

In the last chapter, we spawned a turtle in the world based on the device's position when the game started. Ideally, we would have control over where the turtle is placed. Instead of having it spawned when the game starts based on the phone's position, we can generate the object dynamically at a location we specify. To do this, we need to retrieve the plane data associated with the surface that is on the player's screen. To do this, we'll write a custom script:

1. Right-click in the `Assets/Scripts` folder.

2. In the context menu that appears, select **Create | C# Script**:

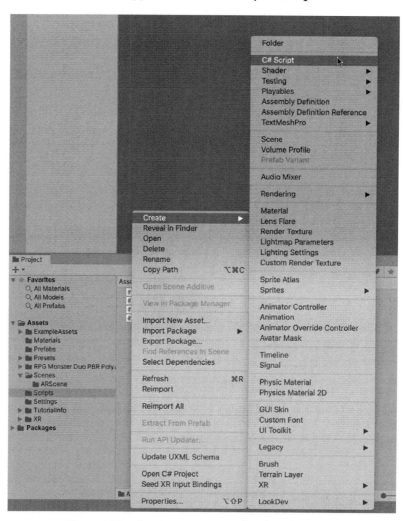

Figure 14.7 – Creating a new script for plane detection

3. Name the script `FindPlane` and add the following code:

```
using UnityEngine.XR.ARFoundation;
using UnityEngine.Events;

public class PlaneData
{
    public Vector3 Position { get; set; }
    public Quaternion Rotation { get; set; }
}

public class FindPlane : MonoBehaviour
{
    public UnityAction<PlaneData> OnValidPlaneFound;
    public UnityAction OnValidPlaneNotFound;

    private ARRaycastManager RaycastManager;
    private readonly Vector3 ViewportCenter = new
        Vector3(0.5f, 0.5f);
}
```

The following points summarize the preceding code snippet:

We create two classes: `PlaneData` and `FindPlane`.

`PlaneData` is the structure we'll use to store the `Position` and `Rotation` of the plane. We'll use this shortly.

To start the `FindPlane` class, we've added four member variables.

`OnValidPlaneFound` is a `UnityAction` that is invoked whenever a plane has been found. We can write classes that subscribe to this event and then whenever a plane is found, we will receive a `PlaneData` object. Subscribing to actions will be explained in detail when we come to spawn objects.

`OnValidPlandNotFound` will be raised on every frame in which a plane hasn't been found.

The `RaycastManager` of type `ARRaycastManager` is used in a very similar way to how we've used raycasts in previous chapters; however, instead of casting rays in the virtual world, the `ARRaycastManager` can detect features in the real world, including planes. This is perfect for our needs. This class is part of the `ARFoundation` package that we imported in the previous chapter.

`ViewpointCenter` is used to find the center of the screen. It's from this point that the ray will originate.

4. Add the following `Awake` and `Update` functions:

```
public class FindPlane : MonoBehaviour
{
    void Awake()
    {
        RaycastManager = GetComponent<ARRaycastManager>();
    }

    void Update()
    {
        IList<ARRaycastHit> hits = GetPlaneHits();
        UpdateSubscribers(hits);
    }
}
```

The `Awake` function initializes the `RaycastManager` and the `Update` function is where the action happens. It calls `GetPlaneHits`, which returns a collection of `ARRaycastHit`. This collection is then passed to `UpdateSubscribers`.

> **Tip**
>
> The Awake function is called during initialization and before other event functions such as `Start` and `OnEnable`. The `Update` function is called every frame before the `LateUpdate` event and any **Coroutine** updates. For more information on the order of events, see `https://docs.unity3d.com/Manual/ExecutionOrder.html`.

5. Add the `GetPlaneHits` function now:

```
public class FindPlane : MonoBehaviour
{
    ...

    private List<ARRaycastHit> GetPlaneHits()
    {
        Vector3 screenCenter = Camera.main.
            ViewportToScreenPoint(ViewportCenter);
        List<ARRaycastHit> hits = new
```

```
        List<ARRaycastHit>();
    RaycastManager.Raycast(screenCenter,
    hits, UnityEngine.XR.ARSubsystems.
        TrackableType. PlaneWithinPolygon);
    return hits;
}
```

The following points summarize the preceding code snippet:

- The center of the screen is found by obtaining a reference to the main camera using `Camera.main` and then calling `ViewportToScreenPoint`. This function converts viewport coordinates into screen space. Viewport space is normalized between 0, 0 (top-right of viewport) to 1, 1 (bottom-left). Therefore, by passing 0.5, 0.5, we return the center of the viewport.

> **Tip**
> `Camera.main` will return a reference to the first enabled camera that has the `MainCamera` tag.

We then create a new `List` of `ARRaycastHit`. This collection will store the results of the raycast. An `ARRaycastHit` contains useful data about the raycast, including the hit point's position, which will be very useful.

We pass this list as a reference to `RaycastManager.Raycast`. This function performs the raycast and fills the hits collection with any raycast hits. If there were no hits, the collection would be empty. The third parameter of `RaycastManager.Raycast` is `TrackableType`, which lets Unity know the type of objects we are interested in. Passing the `PlaneWithinPolygon` mask here means the ray needs to intersect within a polygon generated by the Plane Manager we added in the *Adding a plane manager* section. This will become clear when we come to draw a placement marker later in this chapter, as the placement marker will only be drawn within the bounds of a plane.

We could pass a different value as the `TrackableType`, such as `Face` or `FeaturePoint`, to detect different objects. For all `TrackableType` varieties, see `https://docs.unity3d.com/Packages/com.unity.xr.arsubsystems@2.1/api/UnityEngine.XR.ARSubsystems.TrackableType.html`.

The collection of `hits` is then returned from the function.

6. Lastly, add the `UpdateSubscribers` function. This function will update any subscribers with the data contained in `hits`:

```
public class FindPlane : MonoBehaviour
{
    ...

    private void UpdateSubscribers(IList<ARRaycastHit>
      hits)
    {
        bool validPositionFound = hits.Count > 0;
        if (validPositionFound)
        {
            PlaneData Plane = new PlaneData
            {
                Position = hits[0].pose.position,
                Rotation = hits[0].pose.rotation
            };
            OnValidPlaneFound?.Invoke(Plane);
        }
        else
        {
            OnValidPlaneNotFound?.Invoke();
        }
    }
}
```

The following points summarize the preceding code snippet:

If the hits collection size is greater than 0, we know that the `RaycastManager` has found a valid plane, so we set `validPositionFound` to `true`.

If `validPositionFound` is true, we create a new `PlaneData` using the position and rotation of the `pose` in the first `ARRaycastHit` contained in the hits collection. When the collection of `ARRaycastHit` is populated by the `RaycastManager.Raycast` function, it is sorted so that the first element will contain information on the hit point closest to the raycast's origin, which in this case is the player's device. Once the `PlaneData` has been created, we pass it to the `OnValidPlaneFound` action. This will alert all subscribers that we've found a plane.

If validPositionFound is false, we invoke OnValidPlaneNotFound. This alerts all subscribers that a plane was not found in this frame.

> **Tip**
>
> The ?. after the OnValidPlaneFound and OnValidPlaneNotFound is called a **null-conditional operator**. If the Unity actions are null, the attempt to call Invoke will evaluate to null, rather than cause a runtime **NullReferenceException**. For our purposes, it is similar to writing the following:
>
> if(OnValidPlaneFound != null) OnValidPlaneFound.
> Invoke(Plane);
>
> For more information on this operator, see https://docs.
> microsoft.com/en-us/dotnet/csharp/language-
> reference/operators/member-access-operators#null-
> conditional-operators--and-.

Now we have the code that detects plans and alerts subscribers, let's add it to the scene:

1. Back in Unity, select the **AR Session Origin** object in the **Hierarchy** panel.

2. Add an **AR Raycast Manager** component, as shown in Figure 14.8, by selecting **Component | UnityEngine.XR.ARFoundation | AR Raycast** Manager from the Application menu. The script we just wrote will rely on this to perform the raycasts.

3. Add our **FindPlane** component:

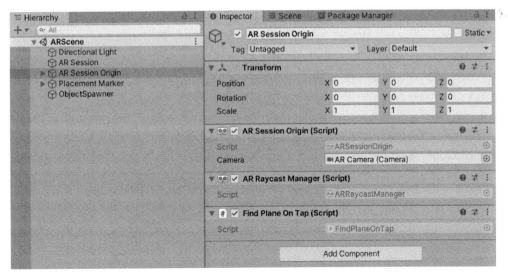

Figure 14.8 – Adding the FindPlane component

This section has covered an important topic in AR. Feature detection is used in many AR projects, and by reaching this point, you have learned how to not only detect surfaces in the real world, but also how to extract useful information about the detection – information that we will be using shortly to spawn objects. We have also added and configured a `Plane Manager`. This manager object will help us interact with the AR environment and provides useful debugging information by drawing the boundaries of any planes it discovers. Creating the manager involved adding a new Plane Manager object to the scene and assigning it a newly created plane prefab. This prefab included a component used to visualize the plane and an `AR Plane` component that stores useful data about the surface, including its size. With the `Plane Manager` correctly configured, we then wrote a custom script that uses an `ARRaycastManager` to detect surfaces in the real world.

Now we have a reliable method of detecting a plane. When we run our game, `FindPlane` will attempt to detect a plane at each frame. At the moment, even if a frame is found, nothing happens with that information. We've created two actions, `OnValidPlaneFound` and `OnValidPlaneNotFound`, but we haven't written any class that subscribes to those events. That is about change as we write the functionality to place a visual marker whenever a plane is detected.

Adding a placement marker

In this section, we'll design a visual cue that the player can use to determine when and where they can place an object. The marker will use the logic we created in the *Detecting planes* section to determine when a valid plane was found. There are two steps to adding the marker to our scene. First, we'll design the marker in Unity, and then we'll add the logic for placing the marker on valid surfaces in the real world.

Designing the marker

To add a placement marker to the game, we first need to design it. In our project, the marker will be a simple circle platform. We'll use many of Unity's built-in tools to create the marker, and the only external resource we will require is a simple circle texture. Start by creating a new GameObject in our scene:

1. Right-click in the **Hierarchy** and select **Create Empty** to create a new GameObject.

2. Name the new object `Placement Marker`:

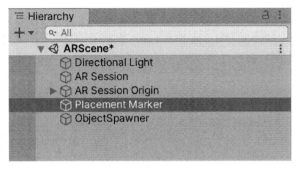

Figure 14.9 – Placement Marker in Hierarchy

3. Right-click on the **Placement Marker** object and select **3D Object | Quad** to create the visuals for the marker.

4. Select the newly created **Quad** and set its scale to `0.1, 0.1, 0.1`.

5. Rotate the Quad `90` degrees on the *x* axis:

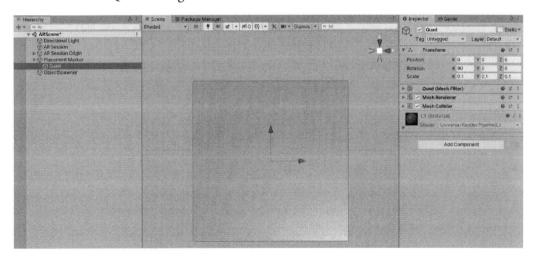

Figure 14.10 – Placement Marker child component

With the object created, we can modify its appearance by creating a custom **Material**:

1. Right-click in the `Assets/Materials` folder in the **Project** panel.

2. Select **Create | Material**.

3. Name the new material `Marker Material`:

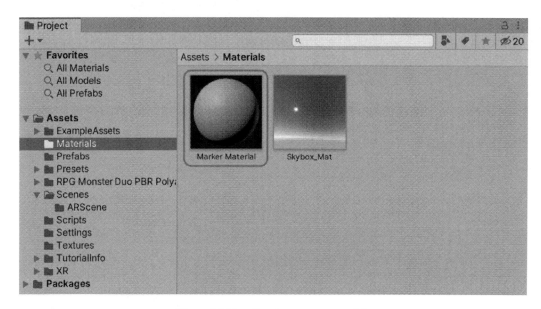

Figure 14.11 – Creating a new material

4. Drag the circle image from the `Chapter13/Start` folder to the `Assets/Textures` folder in Unity. Create the `Textures` folder if it doesn't already exist.

Now we can update the material with the new texture. With the **Marker Material** selected, do the following in the **Inspector**:

1. Change the **Surface Type** to **Transparent** to take advantage of the transparency contained in our texture.

2. Select the little circle to the left of **Base Map**, as shown in *Figure 14.12*:

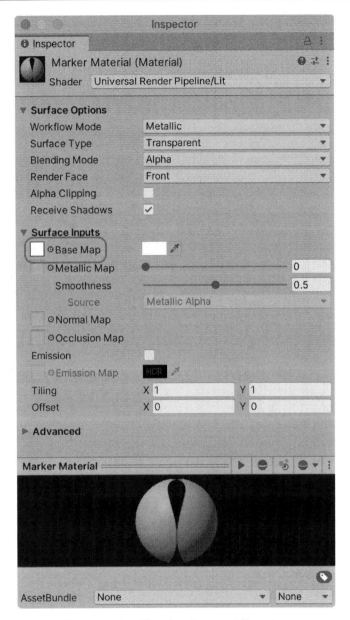

Figure 14.12 – Changing the material's texture

The eagle-eyed among you may have noticed that the shader type in *Figure 14.12* is **Universal Render Pipeline/Lit**. As we've set up our project to use the URP, all materials we create in the project will default to using the URP as their shader. This saves us time as we won't need to update them as we had to do with the turtle's material.

3. In the window that appears, select the **circle** texture. If you don't have this option, make sure you've imported the circle texture from the `Chapter13/Start` folder:

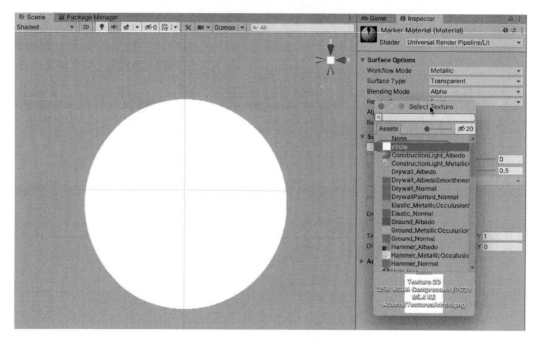

Figure 14.13 – Updating the materials image

While we've kept the marker purposefully minimalist, feel free to experiment with different images to change the marker's appearance to suit you. You only need to import a different image and assign it to the material.

With the material complete, let's assign it to the Quad object:

1. Select the **Quad** object in the **Hierarchy**.

2. In the **Inspector**, on the **Mesh Renderer** component, click on the circle next to the currently assigned material, as shown in *Figure 14.14.*

3.   In the window that appears, select the newly created **Marker Material**:

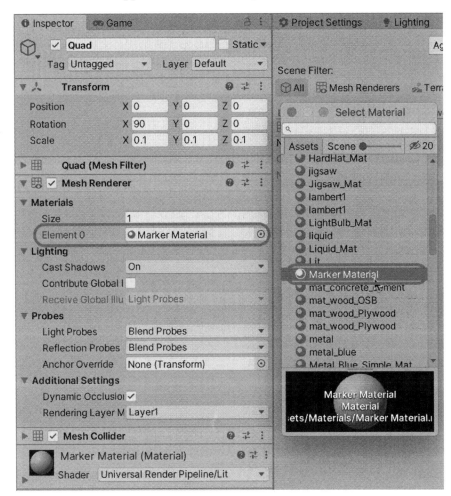

Figure 14.14 – Assigning the material to the Quad

You'll notice the appearance of the marker will change to a circle, as shown in *Figure 14.13*.

> **Tip**
> You can also assign the material by dragging it from the **Project** panel to the **Quad** object in the **Hierarchy**.

That's it for the marker's visuals. Feel free to experiment with different textures for the **Marker Material** to make it fit with your style, before moving onto the next section where we place the marker in the world.

Placing the marker

With that set up, we can write the class that will display the object on the plane. We already have the mechanism to identify valid planes in the environment and extract the position and rotation. We'll take advantage of this code by subscribing to the OnValidPlaneFound and OnValidPlaneNotFound events on FindPlane. To do this, we need to create a new script:

1. Create a new class called MoveObjectToPlane. This class will move the placement marker to a plane found by FindPlane:

```
public class MoveObjectToPlane : MonoBehaviour
{
    private FindPlane PlaneFinder;

    void Awake()
    {
        PlaneFinder = FindObjectOfType<FindPlane>();
    }

    void Start()
    {
        DisableObject();

        PlaneFinder.OnValidPlaneFound += UpdateTransform;
        PlaneFinder.OnValidPlaneNotFound +=
            DisableObject;
    }
}
```

The following points summarize the preceding code snippet:

In the class, we store a reference to FindPlane.

We disable the object when the scene starts by calling DisableObject. The marker will be re-enabled when a valid plane has been found.

In the Start function, we subscribe to the OnValidPlaneFound and OnValidPlaneNotFound events by passing a reference to the UpdateTransform and DisableObject functions, respectively. Using += means that we don't overwrite any existing data, so if any other classes have subscribed, we won't remove their subscriptions.

Whenever FindPlane calls the OnValidPlaneFound event, it will call this object's UpdateTransform function, passing in a PlaneData object. We'll write this function shortly, but it will be responsible for moving the placement marker to the plane.

Whenever FindPlane calls the OnValidPlaneNotFound event, it will call this object's DisableObject function. This function will disable the object, so if no plane is found, the placement marker will not be shown.

2. Add an OnDestroy function:

```
public class MoveObjectToPlane : MonoBehaviour
{
    ...
    void OnDestroy()
    {
        PlaneFinder.OnValidPlaneFound -= UpdateTransform;
        PlaneFinder.OnValidPlaneNotFound -=
            DisableObject;
    }}
```

In the OnDestroy function, we remove the references to this object's function to ensure they are not called on a dead object. OnDestroy is called whenever this component or the object it belongs to is in the process of being removed from the scene (or the scene itself has been destroyed).

3. Finally, we need to add the functions that are called when the two events are raised; that is, UpdateTransform and DisableObject:

```
public class MoveObjectToPlane : MonoBehaviour
{
    ...
    private void UpdateTransform(PlaneData Plane)
    {
        gameObject.SetActive(true);
        transform.SetPositionAndRotation(Plane.Position,
            Plane.Rotation);
    }

    private void DisableObject()
    {
```

```
            gameObject.SetActive(false);
    }
}
```

Both functions are relatively simple, as follows:

UpdateTransform enables the GameObject in case it was disabled previously. It also sets the position and rotation equal to that of the plane.

DisableObject disables the GameObject (somewhat unsurprisingly). We do this to prevent the marker from appearing on screen when there is no valid plane.

That's it for the code. Now, we can add the new script to the **Placement Marker**:

1. Select the **Placement Marker** object in the **Hierarchy**.

2. In the **Inspector**, add the MoveObjectToPlane script:

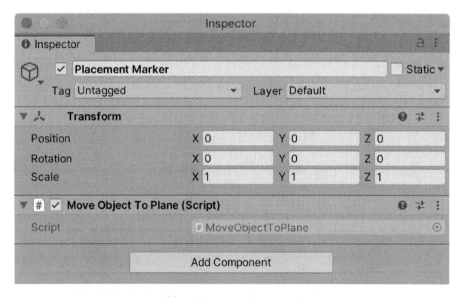

Figure 14.15 – Adding the Move Object To Plane component

As you can see from *Figure 14.16*, if you run the game now, the marker will stick to any surface found in the center of the screen:

Figure 14.16 – The placement marker in action

The black lines define the different planes. You can see the planes' boundaries expand as you move around the environment.

> **Important Note**
>
> You'll notice that the marker disappears if you move the view outside of a plane (defined by the black borders in *Figure 14.16*). In the FindPlane class, we pass the TrackableType of PlaneWithinPolygon to the Raycast function. Try experimenting with different flags to see what effect it has on the placement marker. The different TrackableType varieties can be found at https://docs.unity3d.com/2019.1/Documentation/ ScriptReference/Experimental.XR.TrackableType. html.

As you move the device around, you'll notice that the marker also disappears when there isn't a valid surface. We now have a visual indicator of when there is a suitable surface for placing objects.

In this section, you've created your first URP material and assigned it a custom texture. The material was then assigned to a Quad in the scene to represent a placement marker. We then took advantage of the plane detection code we wrote in the *Retrieving plane data* section to position the marker onto a detected surface using the `OnValidPlaneFound` and `OnValidPlaneNotFound` actions.

Now that the player has this visual indication of when a suitable surface is in view, we can write the code that will spawn objects at the marker's location.

Placing objects in the world

We've done most of the groundwork for placing the objects in the world. We already have a method for detecting a plane and providing a visual indicator for the player, so they know what a suitable surface is and, more importantly, what isn't. Now we need to spawn an object when a player taps on the screen *and* there is a valid plane. To do this, we need to create a new script, as follows:

1. Create a new script called `PlaceObjectOnPlane`:

```
public class PlaceObjectOnPlane : MonoBehaviour
{
    public GameObject ObjectToPlace;
    private FindPlane PlaneFinder;
    private PlaneData Plane = null;

    void Awake()
    {
        PlaneFinder = FindObjectOfType<FindPlane>();
    }

    void LateUpdate()
    {
        if (ShouldPlaceObject())
        {
            Instantiate(ObjectToPlace, Plane.Position,
                Plane.Rotation);
        }
    }
}
```

The following points summarize the preceding code snippet:

Similarly to the script we wrote in *Placing the marker*, we store a reference to the `FindPlane` component in the scene. We'll use this to subscribe to the `OnValidPlaneFound` and `OnValidPlaneNotFound` events.

In the `LateUpdate` function, we check if we are able to place an object, and if so, we create it with the position and rotation specified in the `Plane` member variable. This variable is set whenever a valid plane has been found. We use `LateUpdate` instead of the `Update` function because `LateUpdate` is called after `Update` so we can be certain that the `FindPlane.Update` function will have already checked for a plane this frame. If it has found a plane, we can use it on the same frame to generate an object.

2. Add the `ShouldPlaceObject` function. This function returns `true` if we should spawn an object in this frame:

```
public class PlaceObjectOnPlane : MonoBehaviour
{
    ...

    private bool ShouldPlaceObject()
    {
        if (Plane != null && Input.touchCount > 0)
        {
            if (Input.GetTouch(0).phase == TouchPhase.
                Began)
            {
                return true;
            }
        }

        return false;
    }
}
```

To spawn an object, we need to meet the following criteria:

`Plane` should not be null.

The player should have just tapped on the screen (note that the touch phase of the event is `TouchPhase.Began`).

> **Tip**
> There are several different touch states, including Began, Moved, Stationary, Ended, and Canceled. Most of them are self-explanatory, although Ended and Canceled are worth differentiating. A touch is considered ended when the user lifts their finger from the screen, and it's considered canceled when the system cancels tracking of the touch. A touch can be canceled for several reasons; for example, if a user uses applies more touches than the system can handle, previous touches will be canceled. For more information on the different touch phases, see `https://docs.unity3d.com/ScriptReference/TouchPhase.html`.

At the moment, this function will never return true as `Plane` will always be null. We'll change this now.

3. Add the `OnEnable` and `OnDisable` functions, as follows:

```
public class PlaceObjectOnPlane : MonoBehaviour
{
    ...
    void OnEnable()
    {
        PlaneFinder.OnValidPlaneFound += StorePlaneData;
        PlaneFinder.OnValidPlaneNotFound +=
            RemovePlaneData;
    }

    void OnDisable()
    {
        PlaneFinder.OnValidPlaneFound -= StorePlaneData;
        PlaneFinder.OnValidPlaneNotFound -=
            RemovePlaneData;
    }
}
```

Here, we subscribe to the events in `OnEnable` and unsubscribe to them in `OnDisable`. This code has been described in detail in the *Placing the marker* section, so I won't go into detail here. The `StorePlaneData` function is called whenever a plane is found, and `RemovePlaneData` is called every frame when there is no valid plane.

4. Add the `StorePlaneData` and `RemovePlaneData` functions:

```
public class PlaceObjectOnPlane : MonoBehaviour
{

    ...

    private void StorePlaneData(PlaneData Plane)
    {
        this.Plane = Plane;
    }

    private void RemovePlaneData()
    {
        Plane = null;
    }
}
```

`StorePlaneData` is called whenever a plane is found. It stores the plane data to be used by the `Update` function to spawn an object. `RemovePlaneData` sets `Plane` to `null` when there is no valid plane in the device's viewport. By setting it to `null` here, `ShouldPlaceObject` will return `false` until a valid plane is found again and prevent the user from spawning an object in the meantime.

Now we need to add the new script to the scene, back in Unity:

1. Create a new object called `ObjectSpawner`.

2. Add the `PlaceObjectOnPlane` script to the new object:

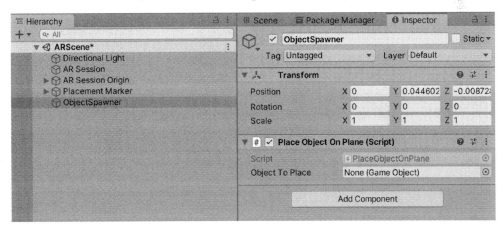

Figure 14.17 – Creating the object spawner

3. Assign the `Turtle` prefab we created in the previous chapter to the **Object To Place** field:

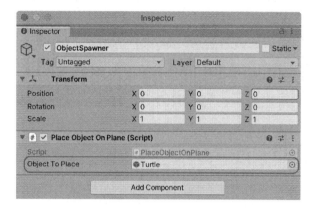

Figure 14.18 – Adding the Turtle prefab

Run the game now and you will be able to tap the screen to place objects in the world:

Figure 14.19 – Placing turtles in the world

As you can see from *Figure 14.19*, you can place the turtle on different levels and also vertical planes, and it will appear with the correct rotation.

That's it for the main functionality for the AR project. While the interaction is rudimentary, it provides everything you need to create complex AR experiences. Before we wrap up, I would like to briefly run through how we can add post-processing effects in the URP. These post-processing effects will modify the visual appearance of the turtle we place in the world. Although we covered post-processing in previous chapters, its implementation is slightly different in the world of the URP, as you will see shortly.

Post-processing in the URP

To refresh your memory, the URP is a **Scriptable Render Pipeline** developed in-house by Unity. It has been designed to introduce workflows that provide control over how Unity renders a frame without the need to write any code. So far, we've learned how to update materials and enable background drawing for AR using the URP. In this section, we'll take it a step further and add post-processing effects using the URP. To accomplish this, we first need to modify the camera:

1. Select the **AR Camera** in the **Hierarchy** (remember that it's a child object of **AR Session Origin**).

2. In the **Inspector**, under the **Rendering** heading, tick the **Post Processing** box:

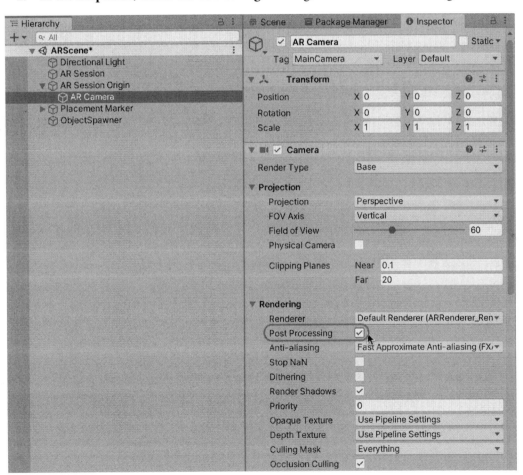

Figure 14.20 – Enabling Post Processing

If you remember from *Chapter 11, Entering Virtual Reality*, we will need both Volume and Post Processing profiles to enable Post Processing. However, we'll create both in a slightly different way:

1. Add a **Volume** component to the **AR Camera** object by selecting **Component | Miscellaneous | Volume** from the Application menu. This defines the area in which we want the processing to occur:

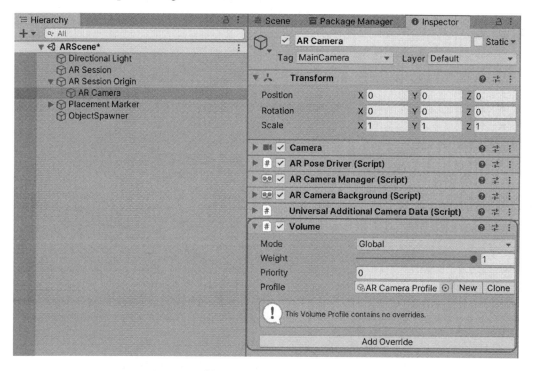

Figure 14.21 – Adding a Volume component to the camera

2. In the **Volume** component's settings, ensure **Mode** is set to **Global**, as shown in *Figure 14.21*. This means the effects will be applied to the whole scene.

3. Click on the **New** button to the right of the **Profile** field to create a new Volume Profile:

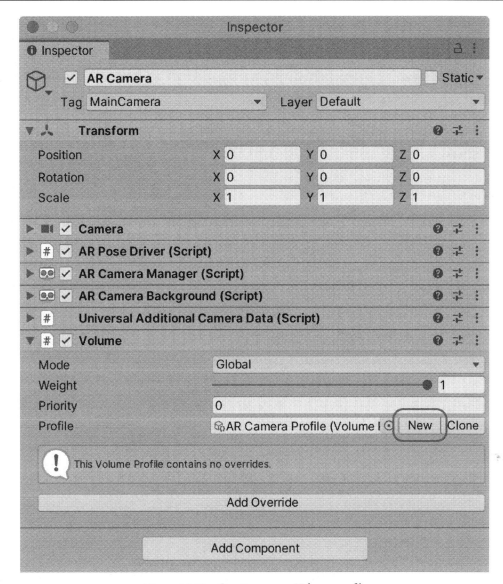

Figure 14.22 – Creating a new Volume profile

Now you are free to add custom post-processing effects. By default, no post-processing effects are enabled. Previously, we enabled the effects by selecting the profile in the **Project** panel; however, we can enable them directly from the **Volume** component:

4. On the **Volume** component, select **Add Override | Post-processing | Bloom**.

5. Enable the **Threshold** override and set its value to 1.

6.   Enable the **Intensity** override and also set its value to 1:

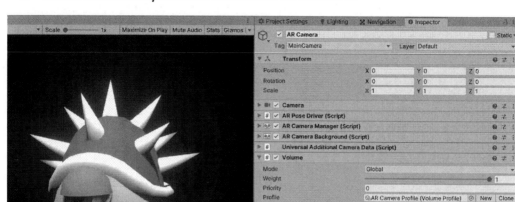

Figure 14.23 – Adding Bloom post-processing

> **Tip**
>
> If you drag the **Turtle** prefab to the scene, as shown in *Figure 14.23*, you can see
> the effect that different settings have on the scene.

Next, we'll configure the **Chromatic Aberration** post-processing effect:

1.   In the Volume component's settings, select **Add Override | Post-processing |
     Chromatic Abberation**.

2. Enable the **Intensity** option and set the value to 0.7:

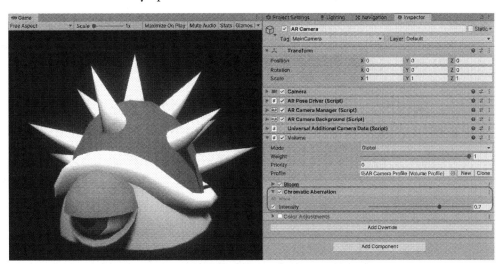

Figure 14.24 – Adding Chromatic Abberation

Lastly, we'll configure the **Color Adjustments** post-processing effect:

1. In the Volume component's settings, select **Add Override | Post-processing | Color Adjustments**.

2. Enable the **Hue Shift** option and set the value to 30.

3. Enable the **Saturation** option and set the value to 70 to create a techno turtle:

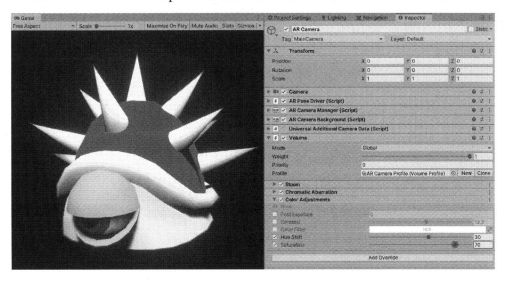

Figure 14.25 – Adding color adjustments

And that's it for the modifications we'll make to the turtle's visuals in this section. You can see the contrast between the original turtle and the post-processing turtle in *Figure 14.26*:

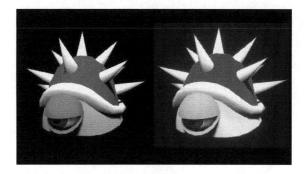

Figure 14.26 – Before (left) and after (right) post-processing effects were applied

Feel free to play around with the different overrides to see what effects you can produce. For more information on what each effect does, see the online documentation at `https://docs.unity3d.com/Manual/PostProcessingOverview.html`.

If you run the game on your device, you can spawn the techno turtle into the world yourself:

Figure 14.27 – Techno turtle in action

You will have noticed that your environment has changed appearance as the post-processing effects are applied to everything on screen, not just the turtle.

And that's it for the AR game: you can detect horizontal and vertical planes and spawn the techno turtle in your environment. And you learned how to do all of this in a URP project! In doing so, you've created a solid foundation for an AR game that can be extended in multiple ways. For example, how about creating a table-top fighting game? You will need to create the NPCs in Unity and then use the scripts we wrote here to place them in the real world. The possibilities are (almost) endless!

Summary

Congratulations! By reaching this point, you have completed the AR project and six other projects: first-person 3D games, 2D adventure games, space shooters, AI, machine learning, and virtual reality.

In this project alone, you've learned the foundations of AR development. You now know how to detect planes (and other features) in a real-world environment, extract information from the detected planes, and use it to spawn virtual objects. You've taken advantage of the tools offered by AR Foundation to create an AR game that can be played on Android or iOS. The game is easy to debug, as you can see in real time when Unity has detected a plane, the size of the detected plane, and its location in the world.

You then extended Unity's offerings by writing custom scripts to extract the plane data generated by Unity and make it accessible to any script that subscribes to updates. You designed a placement marker and object spawn script that uses this information to place objects in the environment.

Not only that, but you've also done it using Unity's URP. So on top of the AR knowledge, you now know how to convert materials to use the URP, along with how to implement AR and post-processing effects in the URP. Not bad!

Now is an excellent time to reflect on what you've learned in this book. Take the time to think about what you've read up to this point. Did any chapters stand out to you in particular? Maybe you were excited by working on AI? Or creating a project in virtual reality? I recommend you focus on those projects first. Play around with them, extend things, break things, and then work on fixing them. But whatever you do, have fun!

Test your knowledge

Q1. You can use the ... flag to select which objects to detect in the real world.

    A. `PlaneFlag`

    B. `RaycastHitType`

    C. `TrackableType`

    D. `FeatureFlag`

Q2. You can disable the detection of vertical planes using the ... component.

    A. Plane Manager

    B. Plane Detector

    C. AR Session

    D. AR Session Origin

Q3. `RaycastManager` is used to cast rays in AR.

    A. True

    B. False

Q4. A touch is defined as `Canceled` when which of the following happens?

    A. The user removes their finger from the screen.

    B. The system cancels the touch.

    C. The user double taps the screen.

    D. The tap response is used to spawn an object.

Q5. The **URP** is which of the following?

    A. A Unity quality setting

    B. A post-processing effect

    C. An animation system

    D. A Scriptable Render Pipeline

Further reading

For more information on the topics covered in this chapter, see the following links:

- https://docs.unity3d.com/ScriptReference/Events. UnityAction.html
- https://docs.unity3d.com/Packages/com.unity. xr.arfoundation@2.2/manual/index.html
- https://docs.unity3d.com/Packages/com.unity. xr.arfoundation@2.1/api/UnityEngine.XR.ARFoundation. ARRaycastManager.html
- https://docs.unity3d.com/Packages/com.unity. xr.arfoundation@1.0/api/UnityEngine.XR.ARFoundation. ARRaycastHit.html
- https://www.packtpub.com/game-development/unity-2018- augmented-reality-projects

Other Books You May Enjoy

If you enjoyed this book, you may be interested in these other books by Packt:

Hands-On Unity 2020 Game Development

Nicolas Alejandro Borromeo

ISBN: 978-1-83864-200-6

- Write scripts for customizing various aspects of a game, such as physics, gameplay, and UI

- Program rich shaders and effects using Unity's new Shader Graph and Universal Render Pipeline

- Implement postprocessing to increase graphics quality with full-screen effects

- Create rich particle systems for your Unity games from scratch using VFX Graph and Shuriken

- Add animations to your game using the Animator, Cinemachine, and Timeline

- Implement game artificial intelligence (AI) to control character behavior

- Detect and fix optimization issues using profilers and batching

Unity Certified Programmer: Exam Guide

Philip Walker

ISBN: 978-1-83882-842-4

- Discover techniques for writing modular, readable, and reusable scripts in Unity

- Implement and configure objects, physics, controls, and movements for your game projects

- Understand 2D and 3D animation and write scripts that interact with Unity's Rendering API

- Explore Unity APIs for adding lighting, materials, and texture to your apps

- Write Unity scripts for building interfaces for menu systems, UI navigation, application settings, and much more

- Delve into SOLID principles for writing clean and maintainable Unity applications

Leave a review - let other readers know what you think

Please share your thoughts on this book with others by leaving a review on the site that you bought it from. If you purchased the book from Amazon, please leave us an honest review on this book's Amazon page. This is vital so that other potential readers can see and use your unbiased opinion to make purchasing decisions, we can understand what our customers think about our products, and our authors can see your feedback on the title that they have worked with Packt to create. It will only take a few minutes of your time, but is valuable to other potential customers, our authors, and Packt. Thank you!

Index

Made in the USA
Las Vegas, NV
10 May 2021

22795030R00372